D1442610

BOOKS BY JOSEPH BLOTNER

The Political Novel
The Fiction of J. D. Salinger (with Frederick L. Gwynn)
Faulkner in the University (with Frederick L. Gwynn)
William Faulkner's Library: A Catalogue
The Modern American Political Novel: 1900–1960
Faulkner: A Biography
Selected Letters of William Faulkner

SELECTED LETTERS *of* WILLIAM FAULKNER

SELECTED LETTERS *of* WILLIAM FAULKNER

edited by

Joseph Blotner

Random House  *New York*

Published in the United States by Random House, Inc., New York,
and simultaneously in Canada by Random House
of Canada Limited, Toronto.

A limited edition of this book has been privately printed.

Library of Congress Cataloging in Publication Data

Faulkner, William, 1897–1962.
Selected letters of William Faulkner.

Includes bibliographical references and index.
1. Faulkner, William, 1897–1962—Correspondence.
I. Blotner, Joseph Leo, 1923–
PS3511.A86Z546 1976 813'.5'2 [B] 76-14163
ISBN 0-394-49485-7

Manufactured in the United States of America

2 4 6 8 9 7 5 3

FIRST TRADE EDITION

Acknowledgments

I am grateful to the recipients of the letters in this volume and to all who gave me access to them: individuals, libraries and corporations. I want especially to thank Jill Summers and to acknowledge the assistance I received from Anne Freudenberg and Joan St. C. Crane, of the University of Virginia Library, who provided materials which helped to solve specific problems. It gives me particular pleasure to express my gratitude to the Horace H. Rackham School of Graduate Studies of the University of Michigan for the Faculty Research Fellowship and supporting research grant which allowed me to complete this book.

To Jill

Contents

Introduction

Ten years ago, on the advice of my friend Lawrance Thompson, who was then working on his biography of Robert Frost and his edition of Frost's letters, I suggested a collection of Faulkner letters to Mrs. William Faulkner and her daughter Jill. Their immediate reaction was that William Faulkner would not have wanted such a volume. His personal letters were never remotely intended for publication. He had made his desire for privacy clear in many ways. "I'm old-fashioned and probably a little mad too," he had written to Malcolm Cowley. "I dont like having my private life and affairs available to just any and everyone who has the price of the vehicle it's printed in, or a friend who bought it and will lend it to him." And, "It is my ambition to be, as a private individual, abolished and voided from history, leaving it markless, no refuse save the printed books; I wish I had had enough sense to see ahead thirty years ago and, like some of the Elizabethans, not signed them. It is my aim, and every effort bent, that the sum and history of my life, which in the same sentence is my obit and epitaph too, shall be them both: He made the books and he died." But he had signed the books, and fame had found him out. He had wanted recognition as a young writer, but the full measure of it to which the work entitled him was slow in coming, and when it did come he sometimes regarded it with irony and contempt. Yet he did not shirk what he felt to be the responsibilities that came with that fame, and so he raised his voice, upon a surprisingly varied number of rostrums, both for his craft and for his country. He remained withal, of course, a very private man.

It fell to his daughter and literary executrix, Jill Faulkner Summers, finally to confront this paradox of the towering achievement and the creator who in his private life wanted something like anonymity. When I wrote *Faulkner: A Biography,* she allowed me to quote as I wished from his writings, including his letters. Although I quoted liberally, there remained much more from his correspondence that I would have included had not the study been already very lengthy. So a book of selected Faulkner letters was a logical next step. All who admire William Faulkner as artist and man will be grateful once more to Mrs. Summers for making possible this further insight into the mind and life out of which came the art that willy-nilly carried the man himself along to be a part of the inevitable intensive scrutiny.

These are selected letters rather than complete letters, a collection meant to be representative rather than inclusive. Numerous Faulkner letters are unavailable in sequestered collections. I have excluded some which treat material covered in other letters or which constitute substantially the same type of letter already represented. I have also omitted those published in *William Faulkner: Essays, Speeches and Public Letters,* edited by James B. Meriwether. The main purpose of this collection is to provide a deeper understanding of the artist, to reveal as much as possible what one can see in the letters about his art—its sources, intentions and process of creation—and beyond that to reveal attitudes basic to that art: aesthetic, philosophical, social and political. The letters also reveal different facets of the man: his relationship with family and friends and those whom he knew primarily in his capacity as a writer—fellow writers, publishers, editors, agents, directors, producers and readers.

There are omissions in these letters which are indicated by ellipses. (Faulkner himself used this device sparingly, and it will be clear to the reader at which points the ellipses appeared in the original.) Some of the omissions are of inconsequential day-to-day material which has no bearing on Faulkner the artist, on his work, or on any revealing facet of his personality. Other omissions are of repetitive material sometimes almost identical with that in other letters. Maurice Coindreau recorded Faulkner's remark about the composition of *The Sound and the Fury*: "Ecrit alors que l'auteur se debattait dans des difficultes d'ordre intime." Characteristically, this reticent artist did not reveal what those difficulties of an intimate nature were with which he was struggling. Among the letters printed here some intimate passages have been omitted. Many of these, however, are treated in *Faulkner: A Biography,* where there was space to set them forth in relation to the situations which elicited them. Some of these omissions are of the sort to be found in the published letters of James Joyce—material much less intense and sparser in quantity, however, than in the case of the great Irish writer. In any event, one hopes that the reader will not begrudge the artist this shred of privacy at this stage in the history of the Faulkner corpus. One day, very possibly, he may stand as utterly revealed as do some other twentieth-century writers, but that day seems far off. One reason is that the editor and biographer must take what he can get. Some who knew William Faulkner refused to supply any information. Others who were willing to help sometimes supplied only excerpts rather than complete letters from him. This was their privilege, and one can only be grateful to them for providing as they did glimpses into William Faulkner's mind and life as they related to his art. I hope that the reader who admires the work and respects the man will concur.

One should not conclude without a few words about William Faulkner as a letter-writer. He often said he was not "a literary man." By this he meant that he was not in what he called "the establishment of literature," as is, for instance, Malcolm Cowley. He was not a literary critic, historian or scholar. And though he wrote some literary criticism, principally as a young writer, I believe he also meant to differentiate himself from literary men such as André Gide and Thomas Mann, who not only composed fiction but discussed it formally and at length. His judgment of himself is borne out in these letters. There is relatively little of the purely literary here in content or in tone. There is nothing like the self-consciousness one finds in the correspondence between authors whose letters sound as though they were written with an eye to future publication.

This is not surprising. Apart from his basic temperament, Faulkner's indifference—sometimes his aversion—to correspondence was intensified by his work as postmaster at the University of Mississippi for the better part of three years, a time of trial for both himself and his patrons. His feelings were still fresh when he wrote his first novel, *Soldiers' Pay*: "There was a general movement into the post office. The mail was in and the window had opened and even those who expected no mail, who had received no mail in months must needs answer one of the most enduring compulsions of the American nation." Thirty years later, having mislaid a letter, he spent half an hour searching for it. A friend asked if it would not be easier to write a new one. "It's bad enough to have to write letters," Faulkner replied. "It's inexcusable to lose one that's already written. To have to rewrite one is intolerable!" In a different mood, he advised his wife that the fewer pieces of paper one signed, the less vulnerable one was.

For all these reservations, his letters make good and surprisingly varied reading. Some have a quaintly old-fashioned ring to them, as when he begins by telling his correspondent: "Yours at hand." There are actually a few which sound a bit like literary exercises, such as the one he wrote in 1925 to his Aunt 'Bama about an Italian village. But for him letter-writing was not—as it sometimes was with Hemingway—an exercise after composition, like the hot-walking of a horse after a race. There are letters Faulkner wrote for amusement, such as the one he sent from Paris to his mother about vacationing relatives. In some letters he savors a story, as when he wrote his wife about a comedy of medical errors in which he played a part. Still another—this to his stepson from Hollywood during World War II—has him remarking, like a social historian or anthropologist, what may be the passing of both an age and a culture. He could write tender letters to his family when he was away from home. Most often, however, he wrote business letters (and here one thinks of Joyce again), letters bearing on his craft and the problems of making a living from it. He would write his publisher asking for advances on royalties and would usually tell him what he could expect to receive ultimately for the advances. It was this practice that gives us remarkable previews, sometimes years before their composition, of novels such as *Absalom, Absalom!*, the whole *Snopes* trilogy, and even his last novel, *The Reivers.* We see books as they grow and develop, from the careful construction of *The Hamlet* to the long ordeal of *A Fable.* Precise aesthetic concerns come through as well, from the punctuation of *The Sound and the Fury* to the initial and final titles of *The Wild Palms.*

William Faulkner could be a hurried letter-writer but he was not a careless one. His handwritten letters, especially the early ones, are usually clear and often graceful. As time went on, he used the typewriter more and more. With it he would often cancel a phrase or a line and start over again for greater clarity and sometimes for style. It was not usually his high style, his "rhetorical" style. But these letters were always distinctive, by turns melancholy, angry or amusing. They sound in his own authentic voice, and in reading them we are privileged to know somewhat better one of America's foremost artists.

JOSEPH BLOTNER

Editorial Notes

Alterations have been kept to a minimum. Idiosyncratic punctuation, abbreviation, capitalization and the like have for the most part been retained, with changes made only for clarity. The designation [*sic*] is used in the rare instances where confusion might otherwise result. Faulkner's frequent misspellings of proper nouns have been remedied, while the variant spelling of his own name—a characteristic of his family—has been left unchanged. Obvious typographical errors have been corrected silently, and paragraphing has been regularized.

When Faulkner signed a letter, he almost always did so in script. The symbol [t] designates the few cases where he typed his name, either as the sole signature or together with his handwritten one [s]. Dates are often difficult to assign and are based on varying degrees of evidence. Footnotes are supplied wherever they seem necessary. In such instances of need where they do not appear, the necessary information was not available to provide them.

MS. and TS. designate manuscript and typescript letters, both ribbon and carbon copies. The following abbreviations are used for repositories:

ACLT Academic Center Library, University of Texas at Austin
FCVA William Faulkner Collections, University of Virginia Library.
Materials from other collections there are designated "Virginia."
JFSA Jill Faulkner Summers Archive.
NYPL New York Public Library, Astor, Lenox and Tilden Foundations.
RH Random House, Inc.

Letters at university libraries other than those above are designated by the name of the university.

A chronology and genealogy have been included at the back of the volume, with the purpose of providing a contextual reference to Faulkner's life and family relationships.

SELECTED LETTERS *of* WILLIAM FAULKNER

On 9 July 1918, William Faulkner arrived at the Royal Air Force–Canada Recruits' Depot in Toronto with the rank of Private II to begin training as a Cadet for Pilot. After preliminary basic training, he was posted on 26 July to Cadet Wing, at Long Branch, to undergo further training and to study specific Air Force subjects. Next he would go to the School of Aeronautics in Toronto. He wrote home on stationery with the RAF crest. Fragments of one letter survive.

To Mrs. Murry C. Falkner — MS. JFSA
Friday [probably 6 Sept. 1918] — [Long Branch]

I got the paper, also the bath towel and the cigs and sox. It's great, seeing the old Commercial Appeal again. Still cold and I am wearing all my sweaters and my shirts. I have to wear them all under my shirt, so I look like this.[1] Some one remarked today that this life certainly agreed with me, I have gained so much. . . .

. . . .

Lieutenant Todd is not here; being an officer, he doesn't have to go to ground school. He is at the S. of A, where we go in two weeks, I hope.

. . . .

[1] Faulkner had done a caricature-like drawing of himself.

From the time of his return to Oxford, Faulkner would occasionally visit friends in Memphis, among them Estelle Lake. Mrs. Donelson Lake made a copy of his thank-you note to Estelle.

To Estelle Lake — MS. MRS. DONELSON LAKE
[received 2 Sept. 1919] — [Oxford]

Dear Miss Lake

May I thank you again for the trouble you went to for me and my eccentricities? I am sending you a drawing[1] which, when I have become famous, will doubtless be quite valuable.

Please give my regards to your Aunt.

Sincerely
W. Faulkner

[1] The drawing illustrated a poem and apparently does not survive.

Faulkner's closest friend was Oxford lawyer Phil Stone. His older brother, W. E. "Jack" Stone IV, lived with his wife and children in Charleston, Mississippi, where Faulkner would sometimes stay as their guest. He addressed one thank-you note to Jack's wife, Myrtle.

To Mrs. W. E. Stone IV — MS. MRS. THOMAS LEATHERBURY
Tuesday [postmarked 5 Sept. 1922] — [Oxford]

Dear Miss Myrt—

I want you to be sure and know how much I appreciate yours and Mr. Jack's kindness to me during my vacation. It's been so nice, being able to pick up and go to Charleston at any time, as I have done.

My hired man's vacation begins today, so I have really gone to work at last. I had a delightful trip home last night, reaching Oxford at eleven exactly.

Please give my regards to Mr. Jack, and my love to little Myrt and young Jack.

Sincerely,
Bill F.

Faulkner had been writing poetry since eighth grade. In the years after his return from Canada, he published a number of individual poems and amassed enough work to think of publication in book form.

To The Four Seas Company, Boston, Mass. TS. FCVA
20 June 1923 University, Miss.

Sir:—

I am sending you today under separate cover a manuscript entitled 'Orpheus, and Other Poems.'

Enclosed find postage for its return if the manuscript be not accepted.

Respectfully,
[t] William Faulkner
[s] William Faulkner

Four months passed and Faulkner received no word. In early November, he wrote again.

To The Four Seas Company TS. FCVA
University, Miss.

Sir:—

Some time ago I sent you a book of verse in Mss. entitled 'Orpheus, and Other Poems.' Will you be kind enough to inform me if such a Mss was received; and if so, what disposition has been made of it? I am under the impression that I enclosed postage for its return.

Respectfully,
William Faulkner

Four Seas responded promptly, enclosing a copy of their letter of 26 June 1923 which had failed to reach him. They had liked his poems—though there were "echoes of Housman and one or two other poets perhaps"—but could not afford to publish them entirely at their own expense. If he could pay the manufacturing cost of the first edition, they would pay a royalty on each copy sold which would return his investment when the edition sold out. Should the book be a success, they would issue subsequent editions at their own expense.

To The Four Seas Company — TS. FCVA
23 November 1923 — University, Miss.

Dear Sir:—

Your letter of 13 November enclosing a copy of your previous one has been received. As I have no money I cannot very well guarantee the initial cost of publishing this mss.; besides, on re-reading some of the things, I see that they aren't particularly significant. And one may obtain no end of poor verse at a dollar and twenty-five cents per volume. So I will ask you to please return the mss.

Thank you for your kind letter.

Sincerely,
William Faulkner

A little more than half a year later, Faulkner's friend Phil Stone encouraged him to try again. When Four Seas made essentially the same offer to publish the new manuscript, entitled The Marble Faun, *Faulkner decided to pursue the matter with Stone's help.*

To The Four Seas Company — TS. FCVA
19 July 1924 — Oxford, Miss.

Sir:—

In reference to contracts for the publication of The Marble Faun, by William Faulkner, enclosed in a letter regarding this Mss. to Mr Phil Stone, of Oxford.

I believe I shall be able to supply the guarantee of $400.00, but before the matter is definitely settled, I wish to get the following information:

In clause ten of the contract it is stated '—provided that he shall pay the manufacturing cost of such plates—' Could this be changed to read 'the actual value of the melted plates?' Or, if this may not be done, can you give me an approximation of the manufacturing cost of the plates?

Could you include in this contract some definite date before or upon which the book will be offered for sale?

Yours sincerely,
William Faulkner

Four Seas agreed to Faulkner's request and stated that if the contracts were signed within the next week or two they would consent to publish the book not later than 1 November 1924. Although Faulkner at first balked at their idea of publicity photographs, Stone saw to it that they were made.

To The Four Seas Company | TS. FCVA
9 September 1924 | Oxford, Miss.

Dear Sir:—

As you requested, I am to-day sending you, under separate cover, two photographs. You will also find enclosed a short biographical sketch.[1] I hope these will be satisfactory.

Sincerely yours,
William Faulkner

[1] The sketch read as follows:

Born in Mississippi in 1897. Great-grandson of Col. W. C. Faulkner, C.S.A., author of "The White Rose of Memphis," "Rapid Ramblings in Europe," etc. Boyhood and youth were spent in Mississippi, since then has been (1) undergraduate (2) house painter (3) tramp, day laborer, dishwasher in various New England cities (4) Clerk in Lord and Taylor's book shop in New York City (5) bank- and postal clerk. Served during the war in the British Royal Air Force. A member of Sigma Alpha Epsilon Fraternity. Present temporary address, Oxford, Miss. "The Marble Faun" was written in the spring of 1919.

The Marble Faun *was not ready for publication in November and Faulkner chafed at the delay, for he had meanwhile determined to go to New Orleans to take passage for Europe. He planned to support himself by writing articles while he continued with his more serious work in the hope that he might begin to make his reputation abroad, as Robert Frost and Ernest Hemingway had done.*

To The Four Seas Company | TELEGRAM ACLT
16 December 1924 | Oxford, Miss.

IF YOU HAVE NOT SHIPPED MY TEN FREE COPIES MARBLE FAUN AND IF CAN BE SHIPPED FOR GODS SAKE SHIP THEM AT ONCE AS THIS IS HOLDING UP MY SAILING EVERY DAY. WILLIAM FAULKNER

In early January of 1925, Faulkner left Oxford for New Orleans but on his arrival took a room in the Vieux Carre instead of sailing. He met novelist and short-story writer Sherwood Anderson and got on well with him. Together they composed tall tales and wrote about the characters they created. On 7 July of that year, Faulkner sailed from New Orleans with architect William Spratling, whose apartment he had shared, and on 2 August they debarked at Genoa, preparing to travel through Italy and Switzerland to France. Faulkner's first post card was sent to his two-year-old nephew.

To James M. Falkner
[postmarked 5 Aug. 1925]

POST CARD JFSA
[Rapallo/Genoa]
[picture: "Rapallo/vista da Montallegro"]

Brother Will says 'Hello, Jimmy.' Love to your mother and daddy. Starting out tomorrow to walk to Paris. I have a knapsack—le sport baggage, they call it.

Brother Will

To Mrs. M. C. Falkner
Thursday Aug 6

MS. JFSA
[Pavia]

Italian locomotives look like this.[1]

There is a place just behind the cab where they can carry a scuttle or so of coal. Heaven knows where the water tank is. Maybe they do without it. Anyway, they go about 60 miles per hour. The conductor leans out and plays a few bars on his horn, the engineer retaliates, and the train rushes off. An Italian train has 2 speeds—0 and 60 m.p.h. The engines go either way—they never bother to turn them around, and the engineer and fireman stand up all the time. That's because they will be wherever they are going in 20 minutes.

I left Genoa for Milan—where Prof Mossaglia came from—when I looked out and saw Pavia. A bridge, where the German army got to in 1917, and a cathedral. It is a lovely place—quite old, little narrow streets, all cobbled, and only about two automobiles in town. It is so quiet and provincial—you pass an old wall and a door, and carved over the door is a date—1149 or something. All roofs are tile, and the women do their washing in the river. You see them kneeling, soaping the garments, then slapping them with wooden paddles. I am at le Pesce-d'Oro (the golden fish) built about 1400. The floors all are stone, and the father, mother, and 3 boys under 14 in evening clothes run the hotel. The older son is head waiter and two daughters are maids. You must make formal application for use of the bath, but it costs 10 lire (about 40¢) per day. Breakfast—coffee, bread, butter, 2.50 lire (10¢) dinner, 16 L. (50¢) You are conducted with honor to a vine-covered court, all around are old, old walls and gates through which mailed knights once rode, and where men-at-arms scurried over cobble stones. And here I sit, with spaghetti, a bowl full of a salad of beans and pimento, tomatoes, lettuce, a bowl of peaches, apples, plums, black coffee and a bottle of wine, all for 50¢.

It is grand—so old and quiet. No automobiles, and people enjoy themselves so calmly—no running about at all. It seems to be part of the day to do as little work and have as much calm pleasure as you can. I was in a wine shop at noon today, where all the boatmen on the river go to dinner. Instead of gulping down their food and running back to work, they were there until the one o'clock whistle blew, laughing and talking about politics and music and so forth. I ate with them. People in Italy all think I am English. Which is good, because Americans are charged two prices for everything.

I would not have missed seeing Pavia for anything. Tomorrow I am going by Milan to a little town called Spezia, on the Italian lakes, then by Switzerland to France. Paris by Aug 25.

Billy

[1] Drawing by Faulkner, with arrow to "coal car."

To Mrs. M. C. Falkner — POST CARD JFSA
[postmarked 7 Aug. 1925] — [Milano/Centro]
[picture: "MILANO—Piazza del Duomo"]

This Cathedral! Can you imagine stone lace? or frozen music? All covered with gargoyles like dogs, and mitred cardinals and mailed knights and saints pierced with arrows and beautiful naked Greek figures that have no religious significance whatever. Going to Stresa tonight.

Billy

To Mrs. M. C. Falkner — POST CARD JFSA
[postmarked 11 Aug. 1925] — [Stresa]
[picture: "Panorama di Stresa"]

I have been 2 days at a grand village on an Alp above Stresa. Awful nice—the padrone and his wife protecting me. I am writing a series of travel things. Leaving today for Monternone, Switzerland, then to France. In Paris by Aug 25 anyway.

Billy

To Mrs. M. C. Falkner — POST CARD JFSA
[postmarked 13 Aug. 1925] — [Domodossola—Milano]
[picture: "LAGO MAGGIORE"]

Full of Americans—terrible. I climbed an Alp today and found a charming place—all stones and cobbles and streets that go either up or down. You can see the lake from there, and trains, and 3 or four cities. Going there tomorrow for a couple of days. The people eat and sleep and sit on the sides of mountains, watching the world pass, and that's all. The Paris-Rome air express passes here.

Billy

There was apparently some delay in the transmission of the post card from Domodossola—Milano, for Faulkner dated his first letter from Paris on the same day.

To Mrs. M. C. Falkner — MS. JFSA
Thursday 13 [Aug.] 192[5] — care American Express Co Paris

Dear Moms—

I found Stresa full of American tourists, so I took my pack and typewriter and lit out for the mountains above Lake Maggiore. It is in the Italian Alps and I lived in a little village stuck on the side of a mountain. We talked by signs mostly, of course, but they were quite kind to me. I was there 4 days, going out with them to cut grass on the mountains, for hay, eating bread and cheese and wine at noon, coming home in the evening bringing the hay on mules while bells rang from the churches all about the mountains. The paths are cobbled with stone and all along them are stone shrines little sheds with pictures of the virgin painted in them. Always a few little bunches of sorry flowers, and an old woman or perhaps a young man or woman kneeling there, praying. Below was the lake, blue, and across it the Swiss Alps. You could see 4 or 5 towns, and trains and boats like toy ones. The day I left the whole village told me goodbye.

I met Bill again at Stresa Tuesday, and we got a train for Montreux, Switzerland. Over the Simplon Pass. There are only two ways to get out of Switzerland, you know. The Simplon and the St. Gotthard passes. All tunnels, and rushing rivers, and chalets hanging on the mountains someway. And bells everywhere. In churches, on cattle and sheep—all you hear is bells. Before we went into the Simplon tunnel (about 2 hours long) we could see the St Gotthard peak far away, capped with snow. After we got through the tunnel it was too dark to see the Jungfrau, but the next morning from Montreux we could see Mont Blanc. It was cold in Switzerland. Montreux is on Lake Geneva, where the Castle of Chillon (you remember The Prisoner of Chillon?) is, not far from Lausanne, where the peace conference was. They say it took the whole Swiss army to keep that peace conference straight. We climbed an Alp and called on a Russian princess, daughter-in-law to a member of the Czar's family, and herself a daughter of the last Doge of Venice.[1] Switzerland was expensive though, so we got a train the next day for Paris.

After a while the Alps looked like a long whale with a lot of cloud on his back and we were crossing country like a big Woodson ridge, all dotted over with rows of poplars, straight as soldiers, and villages with red tile roofs among rolling fields of grain, and hills covered with vineyards. Burgundy, famous for wine. Then straight still canals bordered with trees, and stone houses about—a lovely country in the sunset. We went through Dijon—a grand old gray city in a level plain, and on to Paris.

Reached Paris about 11 o'clock. Paris is full of American tourists too—it took us 2 hours to find a hotel. But now we have a nice one, in Montparnasse. On the left bank of the Seine, where the painters live. It is not far away from the Luxembourg gardens and the Louvre, and from the bridge across the Seine you can see both Notre Dame and the Eiffel tower. Board—3 meals—and lodging is 30 francs per day (1.50). [typewritten:] my pen is dry. I will be here for some time, I think. I am waiting to hear from my novel, as well as to write some travel things I have started. Must have my typewriter fixed soon.

Billy

[1] The last Doge of Venice abdicated in 1797.

The articles Faulkner was writing—probably the "series of travel things" mentioned in the 11 August post card from Stresa—apparently were never published, but it seems likely that he salvaged descriptive passages from them for later use in his fiction.

To Mrs. M. C. Falkner MS. JFSA
Sunday 16 Aug 1925 Paris

I've had a grand time today. Took a pacque-bot, a sort of marine trolley, that run up and down the river all day, and went down the river, past the barrier gates, on past Auteuil and Meudon, to Suresnes. The country there is hilly, with spires sticking out of the trees, and I crossed the river and walked through the Bois de Boulogne, up the avenue to the Place de l'Etoiles, where the Arch de Triomphe is. I sat there a while watching the expensive foreign cars full of American movie actresses whizzing past, then I walked down the Champs-Elysees to the Place de Concorde, and had lunch, an omelette, lettuce, cream cheese and coffee and a bottle of wine, at a restaurant where cabmen and janitors eat. Then I got the subway to the Bastille, looked about a while and then div[ed] underground again to Père Lachaise, an old cemetery. Alfred de Musset is buried there, and all the French notables and royalty, as well as many foreigners. I went particularly to see Oscar Wilde's tomb, with a bas-relief by Jacob Epstein. Then I sat down at an 'ally catty on the corner' and had a glass of beer and smoked my pipe, planning another article—I have finished two—and watching the people. The Latin peoples do their holidays so jolly, like Christmas with us, laughing and talking and wishing each other well.

I came back toward home, stopping at the Luxembourg Gardens to watch the children sailing boats on the pool. There is a man rents boats—toy ones—and even grown people sail them, while their friends look on. There will be a big man looking like a butcher and mustached like a brigand, with all his family along, holding yacht races with another gang like his, while both wives and all the children cheer. And there was an old old man, bent and rheumatic, sailing a boat too. He hobbled along around the pool, but he couldnt keep up with his boat, so other people would very kindly stop it and send it back across to him.

The cathedral of Notre Dame is grand. Like the cathedral at Milan it is all covered with cardinals mitred like Assyrian kings, and knights leaning on long swords, and saints and angels, and beautiful naked Greek figures that have no religious significance what ever, and gargoyles—creatures with heads of goats and dogs, and claws and wings on men's bodies, all staring down in a jeering sardonic mirth.

I have met one or two people—a photographer, and a real painter. He is going to have an exhibition in New York in the fall, and he sure can paint. I dont like the place I am living in. Its full of dull middle class very polite conventional people. Too much like being at a continual reception. Country folks are my sort, anyway. So I am going to move next week. I think that I can live cheaper than $1.50 per day.

My french is improving—I get along quite well now. Only I find after about 5 minutes that my opponent has been talking English to me. English spoken and American understood, you know. And—dont faint—I am growing a beard.

Billy

Faulkner wrote his mother on the day he moved to 26 rue Servandoni, which would remain his address for the remainder of his time in Paris. The street runs from the church of St. Sulpice to the Luxembourg Gardens.

To Mrs. M. C. Falkner — MS. JFSA
18 Aug 1925 — Paris

Dear Mother—

I am moving today. I have a nice room just around the corner from the Luxembourg gardens, where I can sit and write and watch the children. Everything in the gardens is for children—its beautiful the way the French love their babies. They treat children as though they were the same age as the grown-ups—they walk along the street together, a man or a woman and a child, talking and laughing together as though they were the same age.

It is quite nice here, but I am getting rather tired of cities. I think in about a week I'll be off again, to Touraine, where all the grand chateaux are, and to Brittany, on the coast. I am thinking about going to England next month. For a couple of weeks.

I spent yesterday in the Louvre, to see the Winged Victory and the Venus de Milo, the real ones, and the Mona Lisa etc. It was fine, especially the paintings of the more-or-less moderns, like Degas and Manet and Chavannes. Also went to a very very modernist exhibition the other day—futurist and vorticist. I was talking to a painter, a real one. He wont go to the exhibitions at all. He says its all right to paint the damn things, but as far as looking at them, he'd rather go to the Luxembourg gardens and watch the children sail their boats. And I agree with him.

Billy

Faulkner had begun and then put aside a novel with the working title Mosquito. *He now began another, called* Elmer, *which he would work on in various forms for some time but which would never be published.*

To Mrs. M. C. Falkner — MS. JFSA
Sunday 23 Aug 1925 — Paris
c/o American Express Co.

Dear Moms—

I am in the middle of another novel, a grand one. This is new altogether. I just thought of it day before yesterday. I have put the 'Mosquito' one aside: I dont think I am quite old enough to write it as it should be written—dont know quite enough about people.

It is cool here—no one ever wears palm-beach suits here. Wool clothes, usually a vest, and an overcoat at night. It is quite inexpensive, too. My room—a big one on a court and not far from the Luxembourg gardens, costs 11 francs a day, chocolate and a roll for breakfast, 1.50, bread and cheese which I eat in my room, or in the garden, 2, so I have about 6 or 7 francs for a good dinner and still live on 20 francs per day. A franc is 5¢.

It has rained for 3 days now, but I dont mind, so long as I can sit in my room and write. I will have this one finished by November, I think.

French people are crazy about their children. Its awful nice to see them together on the street and in the gardens. I hope to get my suitcase from the Express office tomorrow. I sent it to Paris from Geneva, and ever since I have got along on 2 wool shirts, 2 prs. socks, 2 b.v.d. Love to everyone. Be sure and write me if there is anything you'd like me to buy here.

Billy

To Mrs. M. C. Falkner — MS. JFSA
Wednesday 26 Aug. — Paris

I am settled down temporarily and am hard at work, on a novel. I think right now its awfully good—so clear in my mind that I can hardly write fast enough. I have got into a dreadful habit of sleeping late in the morning, though. It is always 8:00 when I wake, and sometimes later. I get up, dress, take a book and light out to a cafe where I sit on the street practically and have chocolate and a short crisp bread for 1½ francs, buy a roll and a half litre of wine for lunch and walk back home through the Luxembourg garden, to watch the lads laughing and playing and the just-grown people sitting and reading books and papers, while the old men who at home would sit in the court-house yard and sleep, play croquet. Always a big gallery at the croquet games, which run all day. They play for sous—about ½ cent.

I write until 2, eat my bread, then go back to the Luxembourg or take a walk (in good weather. When it rains—as it has for a week almost, —I go to picture galleries.) and at 7 I'm [all?] ready to sit on the street again and have dinner. Soup, good soup, veal, beef, pork, and a vegetable, lettuce and cheese, 7 francs. Then to one of the popular cafes for coffee while the people walk back and forth. I usually write from 9 to 12 at night. I am anxious to get this novel down on paper.

Wool clothes and a vest are certainly grateful here. Quite cool—lots of light overcoats about. Typical Paris summer weather. Lucky I didnt bother to bring many thin clothes.

The only expensive thing here is good tobacco. French tobacco not only doesn't taste, it doesn't even have an odor. So I buy imported English tobacco—10 francs (50¢) for a can the size of two Kraft cheese tins. Luckily, I'm so busy writing I dont smoke much. So a can lasts almost 10 days. Cigarettes are cheap—and terrible. Find everything in the tobacco save horse shoe nails.

While I think of it: I have written every Sunday and Wednesday since Aug 4th. They may come in irregularly, but dont worry—just remember when Sunday and Wednesday come, that I am allright, feeling fine, and sitting down at the table writing you a letter.

Love.
Billy

To Mrs. M. C. Falkner MS. JFSA
Something [30 Aug.] August (Sunday) 1925 care American Express Co., 11 rue Scribe, Paris

Dear Moms—

I wrote you, didn't I, about the old man who sails his boat in the pool in the Luxembourg gardens? He was there bright and early this morning when I came back from breakfast. It was a lovely day—(Paris weather is overcast and grey, as a rule)—the sun was out and it was crisp and cool. I saw him right away, hobbling along at top speed with his stick, sailing his boat while people watched him in a sort of jolly friendliness. (This is Sunday). There was another old man in a blue yachting cap with a toy steam yacht. He was firing it up while about 6 people stood around giving him advice. They are really beautiful boats—well made, of fine wood, and all flagged and pennoned like big ones. Think of a country where an old man, if he wants to, can spend his whole time with toy ships, and no one to call him crazy or make fun of him! In America they laugh at him if he drives a car even, if he does anything except play checkers and sleep in the courthouse yard.

Then I went on and stopped to watch two old gray haired men, a middle-aged man and a young boy play croquet. Croquet here is like baseball at home, only every one plays it. Always a big crowd watching. When my French gets better, I am going to take it up. They have another game called Longue Paume (long hand) which they play with tennis racquets but no net. The balls are dead, so you can hit them with all your might but they dont go far. Its nice to watch. Even the old ladies play it. And children everywhere. The French treat their children like they were grown people, and even 5 year old children are as polite as grown people. And here when you pay your fare on a street car the conductor says 'Thank you.' And as for buying something in a store—its like going to a reception. Like this—

Good day, sir.
Good day, madam.
What will you have, sir?
Tooth paste, if you please, madam.
Thank you, sir. (gives you the toothpaste) Here it is, sir. Thank you.
Thank you, madam (give her a 5 franc note)
Thank you, sir (takes the note: gives you the change) Thank you, sir.
Thank you, madam (you take the change) Good day, madam.
Farewell, sir.
Good day, sirs (to every one else in the shop)
Good day, sir (they reply. You go out.)

These people believe in fresh air, even if they dont bathe. (It costs 25¢ to bathe even in a hotel in Europe) In America a woman will spend the morning in her room reading or sewing in a dressing gown: here she gets dressed and sits in the park, bringing the baby with her. And the cutest babies. Think of little boys and girls Jimmy's age lisping French. Makes you feel awful uneducated.

I went out to Meudon this week, where Madame de Pompadour had a castle, where folks fought duels all over the place. And I have seen the chapel where James I of England was buried after both the French and English threw him out. Those poor Stewarts had an awful time.

Tomorrow I am going to Versailles—Marie Antoinette's hang-out,—and Fontainebleau.

Quite cool here. I am glad of my trench coat at night. Summer is almost gone. Lots of the trees are dying here, the elms about the Place d'Etoile and some of the old chestnut trees in the Luxembourg. American papers blame it on the Eiffel tower where there is a big wireless station and where they advertise automobiles by electric signs (and where Americans go and drink beer half way up) thats one thing I am looking forward to—September, when all the rich Americans will be gone. They are awful, the class that comes to Europe. Can you imagine going into a strange house and spitting on the floor? Thats the way they act.

Billy

To Mrs. M. C. Falkner — MS. JFSA
2 Sept 1925 — Paris

Dear Moms—

Got your letter yesterday. The Captain's 'washout' was funny, but it will teach him a lesson. That is, when it's got a gasoline engine in it you've got to watch it all the time. He learned his cheaper than I did, at that.[1]

I am working steadily on my novel, besides a book of poems for children

I am writing, and a few articles on the side, you might say. So much writing that I feel fairly 'wrote out.' No, I am not keeping the diary. I'll write it all someday though.

I went to the French National Exhibition today. Like a big county fair, only it was planned (houses, bridges, etc) by real sculptors and painters, I went with a sculptor, Jean Couvray, who did some of it. It was sort of nice—like reading a gorgeous fairy tale. Nothing especially good though. Too colorful and French.

Tell me about everyone—Pop and Jack and Whiz,[2] and Jimmy specially. I can always tell how you feel by your letters. You cant fool me, even if you think you can.

I have written steadily on my novel since 8:30. It is now 1:05 A.M., so I am off to bed.

Worlds of Love.
Billy

[1] Faulkner had told his family that his RAF training had culminated in a post-Armistice Day crash, thus far unsubstantiated. "The Captain" may refer to Capt. Vernon C. Omlie, from whom Faulkner would take flying lessons seven years later, but it seems unlikely that Faulkner would have taken such a patronizing tone toward a veteran pilot.

[2] "Whiz" was a nickname of athletic Dean Falkner, the youngest of the four Falkner brothers.

To Mrs. M. C. Falkner — MS. JFSA
[postmarked 6 Sept. 1925] — Paris

I have just written such a beautiful thing that I am about to bust—2000 words about the Luxembourg gardens and death. It has a thin thread of plot, about a young woman, and it is poetry though written in prose form.[1] I have worked on it for two whole days and every word is perfect. I havent slept hardly for two nights, thinking about it, comparing words, accepting and rejecting them, then changing again. But now it is perfect—a jewel. I am going to put it away for a week, then show it to someone for an opinion. So tomorrow I will wake up feeling rotten, I expect. Reaction. But its worth it, to have done a thing like this.

I have over 20,000 words on my novel, and I have written a poem so modern that I dont know myself what it means.

Cold as [time?]: even the natives admit that it is quite cool. If the rainy season comes before I finish the novel I think I'll go back to Italy. Brisk and cool, but pleasant—in my trench coat—in the garden. I have come to think of the Luxembourg as my garden now. I sit and write there, and walk around to watch the children, and the croquet games. I always carry a piece of bread to feed to the sparrows.

There is the grandest marble in the Exposition gallery: a little fat boy about 1½ old in a sweater and knitted cap, bending over to pick up his ball. He is so fat and bundled up that he can hardly bend over, or straighten up again: you want to go and help him. In French a baby up to 4 or 5 is 'Le Petit' which means 'The Little.' You say "Look at the little" which is nice, I think.

Bill S. left for New York today. I went to the station with him at 6:30 this A.M. Paris is lovely then. They wash the streets every morning, it smells so good, and no traffic except market wagons full of fresh vegetables and flowers—violets, big chrysanthemums, dahlias—good healthy hardy flowers, not hothouse ones; and the Seine is still as a pond. It is not at all a big river, like you'd think. But everything here is small and quiet and cheerful—even the bridges are all gilt and tinselled, with carved figures and paintings and electric stars on them.

I have a new vice—bus rides. You can go as far as the bus goes for 60 centimes (3½ cents) and they go everywhere. Went up on Montmartre, the highest point in this part of France—(the county Paris is in is called the Isle of France, after the time when Norman and Saxon and German and Italian nobles owned the rest of it. It certainly was an island then, the water being principally blood) to see the lights of Paris come on in the dusk. Lovely. In almost every house there is a picture of Saint Genevieve, the patron saint of Paris, staring out over Paris at dusk. There is a beautiful one by Puvis de Chavannes in the Pantheon, where the unknown soldier's grave is. There is also in the Pantheon, on a blank panel of wall, a wreath to Guynemer, the aviator, beneath an inscription. There is also a street named for him. And near the cathedrals, in the religious stores, any number of inscriptions to dead soldiers, and always at the bottom: "Pray for him." And so many many young men on the streets, bitter and gray-faced, on crutches or with empty sleeves and scarred faces. And now they must still fight, with a million young men already dead between Dunkirk and the Vosges mountains, in Morocco. Poor France, so beautiful and unhappy and so damn cheerful. We dont know how lucky we are, in America.

My beard is coming along fine. Makes me look sort of distinguished, like someone you'd care to know.[2]

Billy

[1] Cf. Temple Drake in the Luxembourg Gardens at the end of *Sanctuary*.
[2] Faulkner drew a pen-and-ink self-portrait, head only, below his signature.

Mrs. Walter B. McLean, born Alabama Leroy Falkner, was William Faulkner's paternal great-aunt, the youngest child of Col. William C. Falkner. She had always taken an interest in Faulkner and his writing.

Later he would say that before he left for Europe Aunt 'Bama had given him a twenty-dollar gold piece which he had sewn into the lining of his coat.

To Mrs. Walter B. McLean — MS. FCVA
[postmarked 10 Sept. 1925] — [Paris]

Dear Aunt Bama—

I had your letter today. I can imagine you with your charming grand-duchess air in the middle of these female cattle all saying at the same time: "But there should be mail here for me: I know there should. I wish you'd look again." And in one of those penetrating stage asides: "It's disgusting. People wouldn't stand for such service in America."

I found two beautiful towns in Italy. Pavia, a 15 cent period city where there are yet only a dozen motor cars—all narrow streets between walls, and old women carrying fagots on their backs, and an old grey red-tiled bridge crossing a stream in quiet meadows where cows ruminate in a mild wonder at the world, and sunset like organ music dying away. Imagine an inn yet called 'Pesce d'Oro' and dinner under a grape arbor that bore the very wine you drink, while a young soldier makes love to a maid servant in the dusk. The other is Sommariva, a hamlet in the mountains above Maggiore, where I lived with the peasants, going out with them in the morning to cut grass, eating bread and cheese and drinking wine from a leather bottle at noon beneath a faded shrine with a poor little bunch of flowers in it, and then coming down the mountain at sunset, hearing the bells on the mule jingle and seeing half the world turning lilac with evening. Then to eat supper outdoors at a wooden table worn smooth by generations of elbows, to get mildly drunk and talk to those kind quiet happy people by signs.

I didn't like Switzerland. Switzerland is a big country club with a membership principally American. And I am quite disgusted with my own nationality in Europe. Imagine a stranger coming in your home, spitting on your floor and flinging you a dollar. That's the way they act. I dont blame these people for charging them for the privilege.

But France, poor beautiful unhappy France. So innately kind, despite their racial lack of natural courtesy, so palpably keeping a stiff upper lip, with long long lists of names in all the churches no matter how small, and having to fight again in Maroc.

I am living a funny sort of life—for Paris. Partly financial reasons, but principally from inclination. I live just around the corner from the Luxembourg Gardens, where I spend all my time. I write there, and play with the children, help them sail their boats, etc. There is an old bent man who sails a toy boat on the pool, with the most beautiful rapt face you ever saw. When I am old enough to no longer have to make excuses for not working, I shall have a weathered derby hat like his and spend my days sailing a toy boat in the Luxembourg Gardens.

In Sommariva I wrote a sort of amusing travelogue, in Paris I wrote another one, one poem so modern I dont know myself what it means, I am writing a book of verse for children and a novel at the same time; and I have just finished the most beautiful short story in the world. So beautiful that when I finished it I went to look at myself in a mirror. And I thought, Did that ugly ratty-looking face, that mixture of childishness and unreliability and sublime vanity, imagine that? But I did. And the hand doesn't hold blood to improve on it. Boni & Liveright also have a novel of mine which should appear in the fall. And that's my history.

I will be awfully glad to see Vannye again.[1] The last time I remember seeing her was when I was 3, I suppose. I had gone to spend the night with Aunt Willie[2] (in Ripley) and I was suddenly taken with one of those spells of loneliness and nameless sorrow that children suffer, for what or because of what they do not know. And Vannye and Natalie[3] brought me home, with a kerosene lamp. I remember how Vannye's hair looked in the light—like honey. Vannye was impersonal; quite aloof: she was holding the lamp. Natalie was quick and dark. She was touching me. She must have carried me.

You didn't mention Uncle Walter directly, so I guess he is alright. Give him my love.

Thank you for the nice letter. You are a good letter writer—no, I mean a good writer of letter. A stranger could even tell the color of your eyes from your letters.

Much love.
William C Falkner

I have a beard. Like this:[4]

[1] Vance Carter Witt, daughter of Willie Medora Falkner Carter, who was Faulkner's great-aunt and Aunt 'Bama's elder sister.

[2] Willie Medora Falkner Carter.

[3] Natalie Carter Broach, elder sister of Vance Carter Witt.

[4] Pen-and-ink sketch by Faulkner.

To Mrs. M. C. Falkner — MS. JFSA
[postmarked 10 Sept. 1925] — [Paris]

The novel is going elegantly well—about 27,500 words now. Perhaps more. Still quite chilly and gray—just enough light in the sky to turn these lovely faded green and gray and red roofs into a beautiful faint lavender at sunset. After dark a glow in the sky over Paris itself—Montparnasse, where I live, is quite a distance from downtown, like Place de l'Opera and les grands boulevards.

I have got to be a croquet fiend: I waste half the day watching youths and taxi drivers and senators play croquet in the Luxembourg. Used to be I'd run out and have coffee and a piece of bread, buy my bread and cheese and wine for lunch, and go to work by 9:30. Now I never seem to get back before noon. But it's so nice to dawdle around in the gardens, helping the lads sail their boats, etc.

Went to the Hotel des Invalides today. The war museum. Full of war relics: crashed aeroplanes and guns and tanks and alarm klaxons. Napoleon's tomb is there also—a great marble slab with the single word Napoleon graven on it. Quite impressive.

I had a letter from Aunt Bama today. Vannye is to be in Paris this week, so I'll see her. Walked out to the Bois de Meudon Sunday. Fine to have dirt under my feet again. I have discovered a fine place to eat now. The Three Musketeers is the name of it, and dinner costs 5f (25¢). Breakfast costs 1f so on Sunday I have chocolate, 1f 50c. Lunch costs 2f. Tobacco per week 3f. I dont know what laundry costs, not having had any done yet. My room costs 11f. $1.00 per day is not bad for actual expenses. They keep my shoes shined for me. Landlady's a youngish energetic woman with a fat lazy husband (the women do all the work in Latin countries) who plays croquet in a new black suit stiff as armor plate every Sunday afternoon, and a black cat that when she locks it out at night gets mad and sounds exactly like an ill tempered child.

My pride and joy now is a grand knife—a good one, with a horn handle and two blades. Well, I lost it yesterday, somewhere in the Luxembourg. And do you know, I just took the afternoon off and found that knife? I sure did. The French are so courteous: whenever I asked any one about it they'd help hunt. Here, when people find things that dont belong to them, they try to find who owns it: wont have it at all themselves. And woe to you if you try to keep something someone else owns!

It is really surprising, how they live up to the golden rule in financial affairs. In a restaurant, when you are done, the waiter keeps no record, and you tell him what you have eaten and pay according to your own honesty.

I am going out now to buy a stamp from the tobacconist, and to find out what kind of a drink raspail is. It must be raspberry: if raspberries grow anywhere, they grow in France; and if they grow in France the French have made a drink out of them. And it would be just like a Frenchman to call a common raspberry a raspail. They call roast beef 'Rosbif.' Spell it that way on menus. And when you ask for just soup they put everything in it and call it 'potage millionaire americain.' And when you want horse meat in France you say so. Different from America. Also in some small inns there is '[eave?] rabbit' which is cat meat. I think that's elegant, Eave Rabbit.

They are grand people, the working classes, among whom I live myself.

To see two of them walking along a narrow cobbled street about 400 years old, smoking their pipes and gesticulating, carrying each a bottle of wine for supper—You have to ask for water, in all except the big restaurants. And coffee comes in glasses instead of cups.

Love
Billy

Beard's long enough to hold water now.

To Mrs. M. C. Falkner — MS. JFSA
Sunday 13 Sept 1925 — [Paris]

Guess what—Vannye and her daughter are in Paris. I had a letter from Aunt Bama last Wednesday telling me they would be here this month, so I sent a note around to the hotel. Saturday I had an answer from Vannye, and today I had lunch with her and her daughter. Vannye looks quite young—no gray at all. The daughter is a tall girl with (hist:) a sort of sweet dull marcelled look and bold brown eyes and her nose is too short.[1] They are very nice, of the purest Babbitt ray serene. They carry their guidebooks like you would a handkerchief. They make you think of two people in a picture show who are busy talking to each other all the time. Europe has made no impression on them whatever other than to give them a smug feeling of satisfaction for having 'done' it. Curry had gone on back to Florida to enter school.[2] Falkner Broach graduated with honors from Virginia last year and is entering Harvard this fall.[3]

I have got sort of tired of Paris. I think I'll go down into Burgundy again, and see the peasants make wine, and tramp from there down to the Mediterranean. The rainy season is due to begin here any day, then it will be cold.

I have fallen in with a gang of Chicago art students here—a girl and 3 young men. I like them—kind of loud and young and jolly, saying Paris cant compare with Chicago. And an old priest. I met him in the Luxembourg gardens. I see him occasionally and he lets me practice my french on him.

I have put the novel away, and am about to start another one—a sort of fairy tale that has been buzzing in my head.[4] This one is going to be the book of my youth, I am going to take 2 years on it, finish it by my 30th birthday.

I expect to have another letter from you today.

Billy

[1] Willie Carter was Vance Carter Witt's elder daughter.

[2] Curry was Vance Carter Witt's younger daughter.

[3] Falkner Broach was Natalie Carter Broach's elder son.

[4] The "sort of fairy tale" could have become *Mayday*, a forty-eight-page allegorical novelette Faulkner seems to have completed in the spring or summer of 1926. (See *Faulkner*, I [New York: Random House, 1974], p. 511.)

To Mrs. M. C. Falkner
17 September 1925

POST CARD JFSA
[Paris]
[picture: "PARIS. *Saint-Sulpice et la Place*"]

This is a lovely old church. I live near here and go to it Sundays. Be a good catholic soon. I am off to the country again today. Tired of cities. Vannye, bless her heart, gave me 1000 francs, in an envelope for a birthday present. She sails for New York next week. I am going to Belgium and Holland in the meantime.[1]

Billy

[1] Faulkner did not go to Belgium or Holland.

To Mrs. M. C. Falkner
[postmarked 22 Sept. 1925]

MS. JFSA
[Paris]

Well, I'm off again today. My sport baggage is all packed and as you say, I can buy the old steed a package of pipe tobacco and a glass of what the Wildcat calls vang blink and gallop off in practically every direction.[1] I think that expression is so good that I'm saving it for a story some day.

I saw Vannye several times. She took me to lunch twice, and when I saw her the last time she handed me an envelope. "For your birthday," she said when I had told her that I was off to the woods again. And when I looked in it, there was a thousand franc note. $50.00. So I taken part of it and bought her some hand-made handkerchiefs.

I'm glad to be getting away again. So much more fun not knowing where you'll be when night comes. Man here advises me to buy a map. But it isnt necessary—you are never over 2 kilometers from any village (and you never get closer than that to the one you think you want to reach. The best you can do is to keep up with them).

The Belgian Military Orchestra (all Continental bands are military and covered with epaulets and medals—for silence, probably—and swords) is in Paris and there is to be a musical combat between them and the French trombone battlers this afternoon. So I am staying over today to hear it. The bandstand is outdoors, in a grove of chestnut trees in the Luxembourg Gardens. It's lovely, the way the music sounds. And these people really love good music. The bands play Massenet and Chopin and Berlioz and Wagner, and the kids are quiet, listening, and taxi-drivers stop their cars to hear it, and even day laborers are there rubbing elbows with members of the Senate and tourists and beggars and murderers and descendants of the house of Orleans. You see often on the streets men who, had there been no Revolution, would now be dukes and princes, perhaps kings. There is still a Pretender in France, a man who should have been their king. And there really should be a king here. The other day I went to Vincennes, the first royal habitation. It is quite small—a chateau the size of the campus in a park 3 miles across. This was so small that the king moved to the Tuileries, which is on the Seine and includes the Louvre. It is smaller than the town of Oxford. Too small, so another king moved again, to Versailles this time, and built himself a regular city. But now the kings are dead, and the Republican government charges you 2 francs to look at their ruined splendor. But it would be grand to know that there *is* a king in the Tuileries, to go to the Place de la Concorde (where Louis XVI and Marie Antoinette were guillotined) and see him drive out in his carriage with footmen in scarlet and gold and powdered hair.

Went to the Moulin Rouge last night. Anyone in America will tell you it is the last word in sin and iniquity. It is a music hall, a vaudeville, where ladies come out clothed principally in lip stick. Lots of bare beef, but that is only secondary. Their songs and dances are set to real music—there was one with not a rag on except a coat of gold paint who danced a ballet of Rimsky-Korsakoff's, a Persian thing; and two others, a man stained brown like a faun and a lady who had on at least 20 beads, I'll bet money, performed a short tone poem of the Scandinavian composer Sibelius. It was beautiful. Every one goes there—often you have to stand up.

They have plays here just for Americans. The suggestive lewd, where it is indicated that the heroine has on nothing except a bath robe, say. Then at the proper time the lights are all turned off and you are led to believe that the worst has happened. Nasty things. But Americans eat it up, stand in line for hours to get tickets. The French of course dont go to them at all. After having observed Americans in Europe I believe more than ever that sex with us has become a national disease. The way we get it into our politics and religion, where it does not belong anymore than digestion belongs there. All our paintings, our novels, our music, is concerned with it, sort of leering and winking and rubbing hands on it. But Latin people keep it where it belongs, in a secondary place. Their painting and music and literature has nothing to do with sex. Far more healthy than our way.

I can tell you about paintings when I get home. I have spent afternoon after afternoon in the Louvre—(that Carnegie was a hot sport) and in the Luxembourg; I have seen Rodin's museum, and 2 private collections of Matisse and Picasso (who are yet alive and painting) as well as numberless young and struggling moderns. And Cezanne! That man dipped his brush in light like Tobe Caruthers would dip his in red lead to paint a lamp-post. . . .

I expect I shall go to Belgium and Holland. The weather is sort of rainy, but not too much so, and fairly warm. When I think of home being 100 in the shade! Here it has been an unusually cool summer. Light overcoats at night, and sleeping under a comforter.

I did this[2] from a mirror my landlady loaned me. Didnt notice until later that I was drawing on a used sheet. This [is] part of 'Elmer.' I have him a half done, and I have put him away temporarily to begin a new one. Elmer is quite a boy. He is tall and almost handsome and he wants to paint pictures. He gets everything a man could want—money, a European title, marries the girl he wants—and she gives away his paint box. So Elmer never gets to paint at all.

My beard is getting along quite well. Vannye laughed at it, because she could see right through it to the little boy I used to be. Both the french language and the French people are incomprehensible to Vannye. She cant even get what she wants to eat. So the other day I took her to lunch and got her a steak, well done, fried potatoes and sliced tomatoes and a cup of coffee. In a restaurant where they specialize in paté and snails and such, and where every dish is a work of art. They looked at Vannye and me in amazement. In France you eat things one at a time. You have meat, then potatoes, then tomatoes, then coffee. But to have them all at one time, and all fried! Vannye doesn't even drink wine. I think that was the first time they ever saw anyone drink coffee with a meal. The waitress said to me: 'What will madam drink?' I say coffee. She says 'Pardon me?' I say coffee. She says 'But—coffee?' 'Of a truth,' I say, 'but certainly. Is it not so?' 'But yes,' she says, 'it is so. But—coffee. It is perhaps the wine of Anjou to which mister refers?' 'No no one thousand,' I say. 'Madam does not admire the wine. Madam would but of the coffee. This makes himself, is it not so?' 'Yes yes,' she says, 'of the coffee makes himself here always. But—coffee.' 'Yes yes,' I say. 'Let to arrange himself for Madam the coffee.' 'Madam would that the coffee arrange himself during the march of the meal?' 'Yes yes, if one permits him.' 'Yes yes, mister. One permits him. But—coffee. It is perhaps——' So Vannye got her coffee. Coffee here is a general term which means nothing. Something black in a glass which authorizes you to sit in a cafe for an hour and watch the people pass. For breakfast you can get it, but most people take either a cup of chocolate or a glass of white wine. I prefer the chocolate. I was caught too late to drink wine before 12:00. And 1:00 o'clock is thirteen o'clock here. 10:00 P.M. is 22 o'clock.

[no signature]

[1] According to Jack Falkner, he and his elder brother very much enjoyed *The Military Wildcat*, a comic novel of a black draftee in World War I.

[2] Pen-and-ink sketch by Faulkner.

To Mrs. M. C. Falkner
22 Sept. 1925

POST CARD JFSA
[Rouen]
[picture: "ROUEN.
Église Saint-Ouen (Côte Nord)"]

[Indecipherable.] I have a good second-hand bicycle promised me next week in Paris, then I'm off for a good long trip, all about. This time I'm on my way to Amiens, and Soissons and perhaps Belgium.

Billy

To Mrs. M. C. Falkner
either the 24, 25, or 26 of Sept.
[postmarked 25 Sept. 1925]

POST CARD JFSA
[Amiens Gare/Somme]
[picture: "AMIENS—*La Cathédrale*"]

Walked from Rouen to Bucy, was there last night; came here today. Off again walking tomorrow, in the general direction of Soissons, then to Paris. Be in Paris again about Tuesday, where I have engaged to buy a bicycle. Then I think I'll go south again. But I dunno.

Billy

To Mrs. M. C. Falkner
[postmarked 28 Sept. 1925]

POST CARD JFSA
[Compiègne/Oise]
[picture: "RETHONDES.
Le Carrefour de l'Armstice inauguré
le 11 Novembre 1922"]

Walking through the war-zone. Trenches are gone, but still rolls of wire and shell cases and "duds" piled along the hedge-rows, and an occasional tank rusting in a farm yard. Trees all with tops blown out of them, and cemeteries everywhere. British, mostly.

Billy

To Mr. M. C. Falkner
29 Sept. [1925]

POST CARD JFSA
Chantilly[1]
[picture: "Chase à Courre—
La Mente et les piquers"]

A sporting place peopled principally by English. Race course, private deer and foxes, and the best-looking horses you ever saw. Every bar is full of bow-legged cockney grooms and jockeys, and swell-looking Lords and dukes spinning along in carts behind trotting horses. They go out hunting in red coats, and ride right over you if you dont dodge.

Billy

[1] The postmark indicates that Faulkner wrote this card in Chantilly but waited until his return to Paris to mail it the next day at the post office on the rue de Vaugiraud, near his lodging.

To Mr. Dean Falkner — POST CARD JFSA
[postmarked 30 Sept. 1925] — [Paris]
[picture: "Chasses à Courre/ *Le Cerf hallali sous Bois*"]

What do you think of a country like this? But you cant kill a deer like this here unless you got a red swallow-tail coat.

Billy

To Mrs. M. C. Falkner — MS. JFSA
3 Oct. 1925 — Paris

Dear Moms—

I got 3 letters yesterday, one dated Sept 21. Made good time, that one. It must have caught the boat at New York right on the dot. Bill Spratling went back to New York about the 10th of September. I had a letter from him yesterday: he has seen Liveright and my novel is to be published.[1]

Yes, my finances are all right. I will even be able to buy some clothes in London, to which town I am going tomorrow. I will tell George V howdy for you, and that you was just too busy to write. I have got sort of restless in France, in Paris, that is. When I came back from my walking trip I felt fine and peaceful, but now after only four days I am a little bit discontented. So I am going to England to walk a bit before the bad weather sets in, in November. *But when you write, address your letters to Paris,* as usual. There is a man here who admires me very much, who kind of looks after me.[2] He will forward them wherever I am. Otherwise, they may never catch up with me.

I saw so much on my trip that I shall [not] try to write it: I'll save it to tell when I get home. Grandest old, old cities like Rouen and Rennes, and Compiegne which was once a Royal city, when the king went to hunt wild boars and deer in the Forest of Compiegne. I walked through the forest, following the old hunting paths, and every so often I'd sit down and imagine I could hear horns, and dogs, and see huntsmen in green jackets galloping past, and then the king and his cavalcade in gold and purple and scarlet. Spent a whole day walking 10 miles from Compiegne to Pont Sainte Maxence, and another day from there to Senlis. Senlis is an older town than Paris, even. Once Paris had no Bishop of its own, but the Bishop of Senlis would ride over occasionally to run things for them. My expenses for the trip will amaze you: Railroad fare to Rennes $2.00, other railroad fares about $2.00. I developed a cold, and bought a throat spray for $1.00, and $1.00 of brandy to keep me warm when I was sleeping in haystacks and things, and altogether I spent $15.00 for nine days. Most of it was for eating, as I was pretty hungry with walking, averaging 25 miles a day. And I saw Bretagne, where Brest is, Normandy, capital Rouen, Picardy, capital Amiens, Artois in the war zone, a corner of Champagne, and Valois. I passed Cantigny, where American troops first entered the war. I think that was where Madden Tate[3] was wounded. Compiegne and Montdidier were 8 miles behind the front for 3 years, so they are not damaged much. But beyond that eight miles it looks as if a cyclone had passed over the whole world at about 6 feet from the ground. Stubs of trees, and along the main roads are piles of shell cases and unexploded shells and wire and bones that the farmers dig up. Poor France! And now America is going to hold their noses to the grindstone. If some of those Senators would just come over here, see what France has done to repair that country in which every single house was burned, see farmers plowing and expecting every minute to strike an unexploded shell and be blown to kingdom come, see children up to 10 and 12 crippled, jerking[?] with rickets from lack of food—when I get home I think I'll make a speech before the senate, if they'll let me. Certainly a country rich enough to afford Prohibition can help them a little. The French are polite, but not really courteous; they are not kind-hearted (Monsieur le Compte de Boisguillaume turned me out of his chateau in the rain one day in Normandy) but they are heroic. In England, in America, there would have been a revolution, as there was in Russia.

I think I'll be in England about a month.

Billy

[1] Faulkner's first novel, *Soldiers' Pay*, would be published by Boni & Liveright, Inc., on 25 Feb. 1926.

[2] The friend Faulkner referred to may have been William C. Odiorne, a photographer who belonged to the Vieux Carré group Faulkner knew in New Orleans and who did several portrait studies of Faulkner in Paris.

[3] A sixth-grade classmate of Faulkner's.

To Mrs. M. C. Falkner — MS. JFSA

7 Oct 25 — London

Left Paris at 8:30 last night, reached Dieppe under the crispest sky and the most elegant moon you ever saw. Clear and chill, but the boat was waiting, so I popped aboard. It was an English boat and I heard my native tongue (or something kind of resembling it) on all sides for the first time in quite a while. In the saloon (the dining room), was a table all laid out with joints of beef and ham and mutton, and loaves of bread and cheese and pickle and bowls of salad and fruit, and the best tea! I stayed on deck under the moon though, to see them cast off. And when they did! man, that boat stepped along. It was a regular steam ship, you know, but it had a white wave at the bow like a motor boat: we crossed from Dieppe to Newhaven in 4 hours. I dont know how far it is, but its a good thing the Mauretania didn't get in our way. When we docked everybody else got off and took an early train to London, getting here at 6 o'clock. But me, I wouldn't want to get nowhere at 6 o'clock, so I got a blanket from the steward and slept until 7, rose, passed the customs, took an accommodation train to Brighton and got an express there for London, arriving at 11:00 A.M. I thought Italian and French trains were funny, but English trains not only never bother to turn the engine around, but sometimes it is in front, sometimes behind, and this morning in our train the engine was in the middle, pulling some of it and pushing the rest. Funny.

London is awful expensive. I am leaving tomorrow. Oh yes, I arrived this morning in the usual fog. The stuff is not only greasy, but it is full of coal smoke: worse than Pittsburgh about spoiling clothes. I spent the whole day walking and riding on 'busses, looking for a hotel. And the best I could do was 7 shillings—$1.75. In Paris I paid 50¢! And dinner tonight cost $1.00. In Paris, if I paid more than 40¢ I couldn't sleep that night. And everything is in proportion, and the streets full of beggars, mostly young, able-bodied men who simply cannot get work—just no work to be had. They sell boxes of penny matches, play musical instruments, draw pictures on the pavement in colored chalk, steal—anything for a few coppers. And France moaning and groaning over her rising mortality rate! I've seen a lot: Buckingham Palace (the King never came out, though) with sentries in scarlet tunics and steel breast-plates on white horses, Westminster, the Tower, all those old coffee houses where Ben Jonson and Addison and Marlowe sat and talked, and Dickens' Bloomsbury, and Hounslow Heath where they robbed the mail coaches, and Piccadilly and St Paul's, and Trafalgar and Mayfair—everything, almost, despite the fog. The sun has looked like a half-spent orange all-day sucker.

I'm going down into Devon and Cornwall and Kent, and walk some more. But if I dont find things cheaper there, I'm going back to Paris until time to start home.

Billy

To Mrs. M. C. Falkner — MS. JFSA
[postmarked 9 Oct. 1925] — Tunbridge Wells, Kent, England

These people! The French live to make money and love, and the English live to eat. Five times a day do they eat, and nothing under heaven is allowed to interfere with it. A servant wakes you in the morning with a jug of hot water and a small pot of tea and a bit of toast, which you eat in bed. The French do neither. Wash nor eat anything at that hour. After he gets up he goes to a cafe and has a cup of coffee and a single piece of dry bread and a glass of white wine. But in England, when you have dressed you go to the coffee room (Lord knows why they call it coffee room) and you have eggs and bacon and sausage and marmalade and butter and toast and cold bread and a huge pot of tea. By this time it is 10 o'clock. At 12:30 (the saloons dont open until 11:30, and everyone, men women and children eat lunch in them) you have beef or mutton and cabbage and boiled potatoes and ale. At four o'clock everything stops. They even roll tea wagons up and down the railroad platforms with tea and muffins: I have seen the engineer in the cab with a cup. You have tea, toast, jam, cake, scones, muffins. Then at 7 o'clock for a change you have beef or mutton and cabbage and baked potatoes and ale. Then, on your way home at 11:00 or 12:00 you stop in and have a smoked herring-and-cheese sandwich and a tumbler of whiskey and water, or hot rum punch. They dont drink so much whiskey, as they are said to. The Scots, of course. Whenever you hear anyone ask for whiskey in a bar you can count on looking up and seeing a face that looks like it had been left out doors for about 5 years.

I am tramping again—en promenade, as us french fellers says. This is a funny place I have got to now. It is a watering place where the water tastes like hell and where earls and dukes that had too much fun while they were young, and old women of both sexes whose families are tired of looking at them, come to drink the water. They all have those nasty fuzzy white dogs that look like worms. The dogs are so old and blind and there are so many of them that you cant stop to look in a shop window without one of them doddering up and feebly wetting your leg and ankle.

The country is beautiful—south-eastern England: county of Kent. Hilly, with the greenest grass in the meadows full of sheep, and quiet lanes bordered by red and yellow trees and full of fallen leaves. Quietest most restful country under the sun. No wonder Joseph Conrad could write fine books here. But it is so expensive! Costs at least 3.50 a day. And in France you can live like Dives himself for 1.00 and 1.50. And the money! Its wild. 12 pence to a shilling, 20 shillings to the pound. There is one coin, a half-penny. Then a penny. Then a silver coin marked 6 pence. Then one marked shilling, and one two shillings. The next one is marked one florin, without saying how many pence or shillings it is; the one next to that is marked half-crown. I dont know what a florin is, but a half-crown is 2 s and 6 d. Their biggest one is purely imaginary—like the equator: no coin for it at all—a guinea. It is a pound and a shilling. It'll drive you crazy for a day or so. But I've got the best looking sport-jacket you ever saw. It is of hand-woven Harris tweed and has every possible color in it. The general tone is bluish-grayish-green; it is a shooting coat with natural-color leather buttons; fits me like a balloon and was cut by the swellest West-End tailor—one of those places 'By Appointment to H. M. the King, H. M. the King of Sweden, H. R. H. the Prince of Wales.' It does look like it needs a shave though. Whiz will curl up and die when he sees it.

Going to walk on into Sussex tomorrow, and I expect I'll go back to France soon, where living's cheaper. Sort of feel that I'll get to work on my novel again.

Billy

To Mrs. M. C. Falkner — MS. JFSA
15 October 1925 — Dieppe

Dear Moms—

England was too dear for me. I walked some, saw quite a bit of the loveliest, quietest country under the sun, and have spent the last two days on a Breton fishing boat—a tub of a thing that rocks and rolls in a dead calm. We made a good haul, though, including two 3 foot sharks which they killed with boat hooks. These people eat anything though: I dont doubt but what I've eaten shark without knowing it, and liked it. A french cook can take an old shoe and make it taste good. It was cold, cold! Hands raw all the time. Weather was good, though a high sea running. Fall has come here sure enough. Cold and crisp as our January almost.

I'm going back to Paris tomorrow. I have got started writing on my novel again, glory be, and I've written a queer short story, about a case of reincarnation.[1] I am expecting to hear from Liveright when I reach Paris. I waked up yesterday with such a grand feeling that something out of the ordinary has happened to me that I am firmly expecting news of some sort—either very good or very bad.[2]

Billy

[1] This story was probably "The Leg," which appeared in Faulkner's *Doctor Martino and Other Stories* (1934).

[2] On his return to Paris, Faulkner received Boni & Liveright's acceptance of *Soldiers' Pay*.

On 9 December 1925, Faulkner took the boat train from Paris for America. Back in Oxford, he worked on short stories and poems and began to spend a good deal of his time away from home, staying with friends on the University of Mississippi campus, in Memphis, and elsewhere. By the time

Soldiers' Pay *appeared on 25 February 1926, he was back in New Orleans with William Spratling in the Vieux Carre, enjoying the company of convivial friends and writing prose and verse. One of the friends he had made in New Orleans the previous year was Anita Loos, whose* Gentlemen Prefer Blondes *(1925) had become a best seller.*

To Anita Loos
Something Febry 1926

MS. MISS LOOS
New Orleans

Dear Anita—

I have just read the Blonde book, Bill's[1] copy. So I galloped out and got myself one. Please accept my envious congratulations on Dorothy—the way you did her through the intelligence of that elegant moron of a cornflower. Only you have played a rotten trick on your admiring public. How many of them, do you think, will ever know that Dorothy really has something, that the dancing man, le gigolo, was really somebody? My God, it's charming—the best hoax since Witter Bynner's Spectral School in verse—most of them will be completely unmoved—even your rather clumsy gags wont get them—and the others will only find it slight and humorous. The Andersons[2] even mentioned Ring Lardner in talking to me about it. But perhaps that was what you were after, and you have builded better than you knew: I am still rather Victorian in my prejudices regarding the intelligence of women, despite Elinor Wylie and Willa Cather and all the balance of them. But I wish I had thought of Dorothy first.

Sincerely,
[s] William Faulkner
[s] FAULKNER

[1] William Spratling. The letter was written in pencil on Spratling's stationery.
[2] Sherwood and Elizabeth Anderson.

Faulkner returned to Oxford in the spring, but with the coming of summer he accepted the invitation of Phil Stone's brother, Jack, and his wife, Myrtle, to stay with them at their summer place in Pascagoula, Mississippi, on the Gulf Coast.

He had put Elmer *aside and apparently took up* Mosquito, *the novel he had said he felt too inexperienced to write a year earlier. Now entitled* Mosquitoes, *it seems to have moved along well. When he was not working he spent time with the Stone children, with the neighboring Baird family—young Helen and her brothers—and with a few Pascagoula resi-*

dents, some of whom were regarded as disreputable by older settlers. He finished his allegorical novelette, Mayday, *and presented a copy to Helen Baird together with a booklet of sonnets. Staying in Pascagoula after many of the summer people had left, he finished* Mosquitoes *and dedicated it to Helen. In the months that followed, he worked on two rather diverse projects:* Father Abraham, *which treated the Snopes family, and* Flags in the Dust, *which traced the Sartoris family. He put aside the former to concentrate on the latter, continuing to work on it that fall in New Orleans. There he and Spratling found time before the year's end for a collaboration that amused them:* Sherwood Anderson & Other Famous Creoles, *a book of Spratling's drawings of residents of the Vieux Carre with captions by Faulkner.*

To Helen Baird — MS. FCVA[1]
[Aug. 1926] — [Pascagoula]

. . . Your book is pretty near done. Just a few more things. They are nice people[:] Jenny as ineffable as an ice cream soda, and Pete will have queer golden eyes, and Mr. Talliaferro. . . .

[1] Verso of TS. p. 269 of *Mosquitoes.*

On 1 September 1926, Faulkner completed his typescript of Mosquitoes. *He corresponded occasionally with his publisher during the novel's editing and production. The relations were cordial, as indicated in Faulkner's acknowledgment of two gifts from Liveright: Emil Ludwig's* Napoleon *(1926) and Richard Le Gallienne's* The Le Gallienne Book of American Verse *(1925).*

To Horace Liveright — TS. FCVA
11 Jan 1927 — Oxford, Miss.

Dear Mr Liveright:—

Thank you for the book, the Napoleon. It's certainly a beautiful book, binding, paper, print and all. And grand reading: I read a hundred pages before I could put it down. The world certainly owes Lytton Strachey a debt for making history readable.[1]

Enclosing a dedication for 'Mosquitoes.' Will you please put it in for me? I made the promise some time ago, and you can lie to women, you know, but you cant break promises you make 'em. That infringes on their own province. And besides, you dont dare.[2]

Thank you again for the book. That and the Le Gallienne anthology give me a good start on the library I hope to own some day. (I possess no books at all, you see.)

Regards to everyone.

William Faulkner

[1] Apparently, Faulkner felt that Ludwig had been influenced by Lytton Strachey's iconoclastic style of biographical writing.

[2] Helen Baird was by now very interested in a young lawyer named Guy C. Lyman, and in less than four months she would marry him.

When Faulkner received the galley proofs of Mosquitoes, *he found that four substantial passages had been deleted from his typescript. One was an episode with lesbian overtones. The others alluded to love-making and to perversion. Something of Faulkner's annoyance showed in another letter to Liveright.*

To Horace Liveright — TS. FCVA
18 Feb 1927 — Oxford, Miss

Dear Mr Liveright—

I'm sorry my letter about 'Mosquitoes' sounded querulous: I was not trying to complain at all. I understood why the deletions were made, and I was merely pointing out one result of it that, after all, is not very important. Regarding the punctuation: that was due to my typewriter, a Corona, vintage of 1910. I have a better one, now.

Thank you for the enclosed memoranda showing why, etc. Also for your suggestion to Mr Pell. I didn't know when the advance would be due, being practically a vestal in the field of professional lit., but I am damned tired of our [F.]99[°] winters of this sunny south.

I envy you England. England is 'ome to me, in a way.

I am working now on two things at once: a novel, and a collection of short stories of my townspeople.[1] Also, I have dug up something else for you: a mss. by one who has no literary yearnings whatever and who did this just to pass the time.[2] Some one is to see it, and it might as well be you, so I have persuaded the author to give you first shot at it. I think it is pretty fair. I'll get it on for you to see when you return from Europe.

Sincerely,
William Faulkner

[in pen:] just received a blank form from 'Who's Who in America.' So I guess maybe I am.

[1] The novel was *Flags in the Dust,* and the collection of stories would be designated in the contract as *A Rose for Emily and Other Stories.* The book would be published on 21 Sept. 1931 as *These 13* by Jonathan Cape and Harrison Smith, with the "stories of my townspeople" supplemented by others of different subject matter.

[2] Faulkner's childhood sweetheart, Estelle Oldham, had married Cornell Franklin in 1918 and gone to live in Hawaii. Later, she moved to Shanghai, where she wrote a novel called *White Beeches* that was never published.

To William Stanley Braithwaite — TS. HARVARD
[Feb. 1927] — Oxford, Miss.

Dear Mr Braithwaite—

Two years ago the Four Seas Co. published a book of verse of mine, entitled 'The Marble Faun.' I paid the manufacturing costs and I have a contract signed by Mr Brown as president, by which I am to be paid my royalties in the usual manner. In the fall of 1925 I received a statement from them to the effect that they owed me $81.00. I did not receive this money, nor have I been able to get any reply to my letters, other than an acknowledgement taken by the Postoffice department on the delivery of a registered letter.[1]

Can you give me any information about these people? Is this their customary procedure? Is there any way in which I might collect this money without resorting to legal means, which I cannot afford to do, having no income beyond that derived from more or less casual manual labor?

Please forgive me for bothering you for this information, but I dont know exactly whom to ask about such a situation. It never occurred to me that anyone would rob a poet. It's like robbing a whore or a child. I would not bother you with this were it not for the fact that you are the one national literary figure we know in the South as being tolerant of all poets, good and bad.

Respectfully,
William Faulkner

P.S. Let me take this opportunity of thanking you for including my poem 'The Lilacs' in your recent anthology.[2]

[1] *The Marble Faun* had not sold well, and most of the edition was later destroyed by a fire in the Four Seas warehouse.

[2] *Anthology of Magazine Verse for 1925*, William Stanley Braithwaite, ed.

To William Stanley Braithwaite — TS. HARVARD
25 February 1927 — Oxford, Miss

Dear Mr Braithwaite—

Thank you very much for your recent letter on the subject of my uncollectible royalties from the Four Seas Co.

I have never heard anything from them since they rendered me a royalty statement in November, '25. They do not answer letters at all. Of course, if it is just a matter of temporary financial embarrassment, I shall rest easy: I have been without money too damned often myself, to annoy anyone who is himself unable to meet an obligation. And so, since it is your opinion that these people are not delaying to take advantage of the fact that my claim will be void after two years have elapsed, I shall feel easy about getting the money some day.[1] Mr Brown should have written me to this effect himself.

It is the fact that my claim will be defunct after two years, that bothered me. Some day I shall be in Boston and I can see them in person about it, but I dont know when that will be. Meanwhile, I shant bother about it any longer.

Thank you again for your courtesy. And congratulations on the new anthology. The last two of them have revealed a very healthy thing in America, I think: the number of people more or less unknown, who are writing verse. I think I counted more than three hundred in the one for 1925.

Sincerely,
William Faulkner

[1] There appears to be no evidence that Faulkner ever received the money.

Faulkner continued to work at Flags in the Dust, *and by summer he thought he was halfway through the manuscript. From time to time there were distractions, one of which he brought to the attention of his publisher.*

To Horace Liveright — TS. FCVA
[received 22 July 1927] — [Oxford]

Dear Mr Liveright—

Lost some money last week-end gambling, and I have drawn a draft[1] on you. Turn it down, if it's no go. It will give temporary relief. Sorry to have found the necessity. If you are inclined to pay it, you can charge it off against my next advance, the mss for which I shall send in to you by Sept. 1. I'm about half done. Draft is for two hundred. Best regards to every-one.

[t] bill faulkner
[s] W Faulkner

[1] Liveright met the draft but asked Faulkner to let them know in advance if he should ever contemplate such an action in the future.

To Horace Liveright — TS. FCVA
[late July 1927] — [Oxford]

Dear Mr Liveright—

Thanks very much for the favor. I am sorry it was not possible to give you warning, but it was a case of dire necessity. Its quite a yarn. I had just purchased twenty-five gallons of whisky, brought it home and buried it in the garden. Two days later I went to Memphis, lost over three hundred dollars on a wheel, and gave a check for it. I had about one-fifty in bank, and I knew I could dispose of my whisky and raise the balance with only the minor risk of being had by the law for peddling it. So I came home in about three days, found that one of our niggers had smelled the whisky out, dug it up, sold a little and had been caught and told where the rest of it was. So I lost all of it.

I had to have the money to meet my check. I would not have turned to you were it not for the fact that, what with the flood last spring, southern people have no cash money for gambling debts. So I had to do something for temporary relief. Thank you again for honoring the draft. I shan't do that again; certainly not without asking your leave first.

The new novel is coming fine. It is much better than that other stuff. I believe that at last I have learned to control the stuff and fix it on something like rational truth. How are the reviews of Mosquitoes? I have seen one or two. Are they satisfactory, do you think? As a whole, I mean.

By the way, I have enough verse in mss. to make a book. Would you care to look at it? Rather, could you be prevailed to look at a book of poetry?[1]

[s] William Faulkner
[t] w faulkner

[1] Faulkner had been working on a collection he called *The Greening Bough.* It would be published as *A Green Bough* by Harrison Smith and Robert Haas on 20 Apr. 1933.

To Mrs. Walter B. McLean — MS. FCVA
Wednesday [late Sept. 1927] — [Oxford]

Dear Aunt Bama—

. . . .

Grandest weathers. I finished the book today.[1] Will get it off tomorrow, and next time I come up, I'll bring it to you. I dont know when that'll be, as I have a job of work I'll be doing this month. Painting signs.

Much love
William

[1] Faulkner dated the last page of the typescript of *Flags in the Dust* "29 September 1927." The fact that this date fell on a Thursday creates a discrepancy with the dating of "Wednesday" as shown above. The letter is placed here, however, because the only other possibility would be *Mosquitoes,* the last typescript page of which is dated "Pascagoula, Miss/1 Sept 1926." This date did fall on a Wednesday, but the references in the letter above to possible visits to Memphis and to imminent painting jobs suggest Oxford, and therefore *Flags in the Dust,* rather than Pascagoula and *Mosquitoes.*

To Horace Liveright — TS. FCVA
sunday,—october [16 Oct. 1927] — oxford miss

Dear Mr Liveright—

At last and certainly, as El Orens' sheik said, I have written THE book, of which those other things were but foals. I believe it is the damdest best book you'll look at this year, and any other publisher. It goes forward to you by mail Monday.

. . . .

I am enclosing a few suggestions for the printer: will you look over them and, if possible, smooth the printer's fur, cajole him, some way. He's been punctuating my stuff to death; giving me gratis quotation marks and premiums of commas that I dont need.

I dont think that even the bird who named 'Soldiers' Pay' can improve on my title.

Best regards to everyone.

William Faulkner

I also have an idea for a jacket. I will paint it and send it up for your approval soon.

To Horace Liveright | TS. FCVA
30 november [1927] | Oxford, Miss

Dear Mr Liveright—

It's too bad you dont like Flags in the Dust. Unless you are holding it against that $200.00 you advanced me in the summer, I'd like for you to fire it on back to me, as I shall try it on someone else. I still believe it is the book which will make my name for me as a writer.

I am working spasmodically on a book which will take three or four years to do; also I have started another which I shall finish by spring, I believe.[1] And so if you are not holding the mss against that super-advance, send her on back, and I'll get to work on the other one. Anyway, will you let me know as soon as possible your intentions?

Regards to everyone.

William Faulkner

[1] Probably *Father Abraham* and the "stories of my townspeople," respectively.

To Horace Liveright | TS. FCVA
[mid or late Feb. 1928][1] | Oxford, Miss.

Dear Mr Liveright—

I have gotten no further forward with another novel as yet, having put aside the one I had in mind to do some short stories. However, I want to submit the mss. which you refused, to another publisher.

Will you agree to this with the understanding that I either pay you the what-ever-it-is I owe you, or that I submit to you the next mss. I complete? I do not know just when I'll have another ready, but if I can place the one I have on hand and get an advance, I can pay you the money. I have just sent some short stories to an agent; perhaps I shall derive something from them with which to pay you. Otherwise I dont know what we'll do about it, as I have a belly full of writing, now, since you folks in the publishing business claim that a book like that last one I sent you is blah. I think now that I'll sell my typewriter and go to work—though God knows, it's sacrilege to waste that talent for idleness which I possess.

Please let me hear from you about this. Remember me to everyone, and best regards to yourself.

[s] William Faulkner
[t] W Faulkner

P.S. I mean, to pay you the money as soon as I place the rejected mss. I know a New Yorker cannot conceive of anyone being able to live day in and day out, yet without ever having as much as a hundred dollars or ten dollars, but it is not only possible in the provincial South; damn near 90% of the population does it. If I can place this mss., I will be able to pay you; at least I'll have incentive to light in and bang you out a book to suit you.—though it'll never be one as youngly glamorous as 'Soldiers' Pay' nor as trashily smart as 'Mosquitoes.'

[1] Liveright answered this letter on 27 Feb. 1928.

To Horace Liveright | TS. FCVA
[early Mar. 1928][1] | Oxford, Miss.

Dear Mr Liveright—

I have your letter of 27 February, giving me permission to try my mss. somewhere else. I shall take advantage of it immediately.

I have got going on a novel, which, if I continue as I am going now, I will finish within eight weeks.[2] Maybe it'll please you.

I want to thank you for the Isadora Duncan.[3] A beautiful book. I dont think I ever saw a more beautifully gotten up book anywhere. The text itself doesn't go so badly, but even Shakespeare himself could hardly have done that volume justice. You are certainly to be congratulated on getting the mss. and on the format of the volume.

I'll get the next mss. to you by May, I believe.

Regards to all.
William Faulkner

[1] Liveright replied to this letter on 12 Mar. 1928.
[2] It seems likely that this was *Twilight*, which would ultimately appear as *The Sound and the Fury*.
[3] Boni & Liveright published a limited presentation edition of Isadora Duncan's *My Life*. Faulkner autographed his copy on 24 Feb. 1928.

Other publishers followed Horace Liveright in rejecting Flags in the Dust. *This prompted Faulkner to do extensive revision.*

To Mrs. Walter B. McLean | MS. FCVA
Thursday [probably Spring 1928] | Oxford

Dear Aunt Bama—

I've been thinking that I'd get to Memphis again soon, and also I have been trying to get the mss. in some sort of intelligible shape to send you. But neither has come to pass, so I am sending the press clippings, and when I do get the script in order, I'll send it too. Every day or so I burn some of it up and rewrite it, and at present it is almost incoherent. So much so that I've got a little weary of it and I think I shall put it away for a while and forget about it. . . .

Love to Uncle Walter,
William

Flags in the Dust, retitled *Sartoris,* was accepted by Harcourt, Brace and Company in a contract dated 20 September 1928, with delivery of the novel specified for 7 October 1928. It was probably late September when Faulkner went to New York. There his last ties with Liveright were severed.*

To Mrs. Walter B. McLean — MS. FCVA
Wednesday [probably Oct. 1928] — New York City
c/o Ben Wasson[1]
146 MacDougal St.

Dear Aunt Bama—

Well, I'm going to be published by white folks now. Harcourt Brace & Co bought me from Liveright. Much, much nicer there. Book will be out in Feb. Also another one, the damndest book I ever read.[2] I dont believe anyone will publish it for 10 years. Harcourt swear they will, but I dont believe it.

Having a rotten time, as usual. I hate this place.

Love to Uncle Walter, and to you as ever.

William Faulkner

[1] A friend from the University of Mississippi, Wasson was acting as Faulkner's literary agent.

[2] *The Sound and the Fury.*

In his relations with literary agents, Faulkner was an irregular and unpredictable client, often submitting work directly to prospective buyers himself because of financial need. One of his new contacts was Alfred Dashiell, one of the editors of Scribner's *magazine.*

To Alfred Dashiell — TS. PRINCETON
[answered 22 Dec. 1928] — [Oxford]

My dear Mr Dashiell—

Enclosed are two stories which I hope again will conform to Scribner's present needs.

In case you recall a mss. entitled 'Once Aboard the Lugger—' which I submitted while in New York, I have merely used this same title for the rest of the episode with which the other mss. dealt, with the hope that the present half of the episode will suit you better.[1]

'Miss Zilphia Gant' may be too diffuse, still; I dont know.[2] I am quite sure that I have no feeling for short stories; that I shall never be able to write them, yet for some strange reason I continue to do so, and to try them on Scribners' with unflagging optimism.

In case you reach a decision on them before January 15, please return them to me here; if not before that date, will you please hold them and notify me here? I shall return to New York about Feb. 1, as Harcourt is publishing a novel of mine at that time.

Sincerely,
William Faulkner

[1] "Once Aboard the Lugger" was apparently excerpted from a novel of the same name. Faulkner destroyed most of the novel, but a story bearing this title was published in *Contempo*, I (1 Feb. 1932).

[2] After several rejections, this story was published by the Book Club of Texas in 1932.

To Alfred Dashiell — TS. PRINCETON
[answered 23 Feb. 1929] — Oxford, Mississippi

Dear Mr Dashiell

In December I sent you the original of this story.[1] Since I have not got it back, I am sure it has been lost. So here's the carbon.

I shall be in New York some time this month, when I do not exactly know, so will you please write to me at this address and hold the story until you hear from me?

Yours sincerely,
[t] Wm Faulkner

[1] The story, entitled "Selvage," bore Faulkner's name as well as the name "E. Oldham." It had been hers originally and he had reworked it. Rejected by Dashiell as "too febrile," it appeared in revised form as "Elly" in *Story*, IV (Feb. 1934).

To Alfred Harcourt — TS. HARCOURT BRACE JOVANOVICH
18 Feb. 1929 — Oxford, Miss.

Dear Mr Harcourt—

My copies of SARTORIS came promptly. I like the appearance of the book very much indeed. Will you let me take this opportunity to thank the office, as well as yourself? I had intended writing my thanks sooner, but I have got involved in another novel, and I have been behind in correspondence since.

About the Sound & Fury ms. That is all right. I did not believe that anyone would publish it; I had no definite plan to submit it to anyone. I told Hal about it once and he dared me to bring it to him. And so it really was to him that I submitted it, more as a curiosity than aught else. I am sorry it did not go over with you all, but I will not say I did not expect that result. Thank you for delivering it to him.[1]

Spring has come here—a false one, of course; just enough to catch fruit trees and flowers with their pants down about next month. It's nice while it lasts, though.

Sincerely,
[s] William Faulkner
[t] Wm Faulkner.

[1] Harrison Smith was leaving Harcourt, Brace to become a partner in the firm of Jonathan Cape and Harrison Smith, which would publish *The Sound and the Fury* on 7 Oct. 1929.

To Mr. Chase
[received 13 Apr. 1929]

TS. HARCOURT BRACE JOVANOVICH
Oxford, Miss.

Dear Mr Chase—

I have your letter, with many thanks. (Apr. 8th.)

I would like to see the duplicate reviews of Sartoris very much, if you will send them to me. I have not seen but one review here. I live in a complete dearth of print save in its most innocent form. The magazine store here carries nothing that has not either a woman in her underclothes or someone shooting someone else with a pistol on the cover; that includes newspapers, too.

I'm sure I must have acknowledged your kindness in sending out those copies for me. I'll thank you again, anyway.

I dont have any ideas about selling Sartoris at present. There is a druggist here who handles the book, but anything without pictures, selling for more than 50 cents is indeed a drug here; the man handles them mostly out of friendship for me. So I hope you can see fit to permit him as easy an arrangement as possible—customary, I mean. The name is

Gathright-Reed Drug Co., Oxford, Miss.

Mr Reed[1] is a good fellow. If you could permit him a consignment basis, he will sell a copy now and then for three or four years, as people here learn that I am a "book-author." I'd not like to deprive them of their Tanlac and Pinkham's Compound by tying Mr Reed's capital up in books, you know.

Please give my kindest regards to Mr Harcourt. I am working on another novel, which I hope to finish this summer.

Sincerely,
William Faulkner

[1] W. M. ("Mac") Reed was a long-time friend of Faulkner's and one of his earliest literary partisans.

On 20 June 1929, Faulkner married Estelle Oldham Franklin. While they were honeymooning in Pascagoula, Mississippi, he received the proofs of The Sound and the Fury, *which Wasson had partially edited.*

To Ben Wasson
[early summer, 1929]

MS. FCVA
c/o F. H. Lewis
Pascagoula, Miss.

Dear Ben—

Thank you for the letter.

I received the proof. It seemed pretty tough to me, so I corrected it as written, adding a few more italics where the original seemed obscure on second reading. Your reason for the change, i.e., that with italics only 2 different dates were indicated I do not think sound for 2 reasons. First, I do not see that the use of breaks clarifies it any more; second, there are more than 4 dates involved. The ones I recall off-hand are: Damuddy dies. Benjy is 3. (2) His name is changed. He is 5. (3) Caddy's wedding. He is 14. (4) He tries to rape a young girl and is castrated. 15. (5) Quentin's death. (6) His father's death. (7) A visit to the cemetery at 18. (7) [*sic*] The day of the anecdote, he is 33. These are just a few I recall. So your reason explodes itself.

But the main reason is, a break indicates an objective change in tempo, while the objective picture here should be a continuous whole, since the thought transference is subjective; i.e., in Ben's mind and not in the reader's eye. I think italics are necessary to establish for the reader Benjy's confusion; that unbroken-surfaced confusion of an idiot which is outwardly a dynamic and logical coherence. To gain this, by using breaks it will be necessary to write an induction for each transference. I wish publishing was advanced enough to use colored ink for such, as I argued with you and Hal in the speak-easy that day. But the form in which you now have it is pretty tough. It presents a most dull and poorly articulated picture to my eye. If something must be done, it were better to re-write this whole section objectively, like the 4th section. I think it is rotten, as is. But if you wont have it so, I'll just have to save the idea until publishing grows up to it. Anyway, change all the italics. You overlooked one of them. Also, the parts written in italics will all have to be punctuated again. You'd better see to that, since you're all for coherence. And dont make any more additions to the script, bud. I know you mean well, but so do I. I effaced the 2 or 3 you made.

We have a very pleasant place on the beach here. I swim and fish and row a little. Estelle sends love.

I hope you will think better of this. Your reason above disproves itself. I purposely used italics for both actual scenes and remembered scenes for the reason, not to indicate the different dates of happenings, but merely to permit the reader to anticipate a thought-transference, letting the recollection postulate its own date. Surely you see this.

Bill

The following fragment comes from one of the letters Faulkner subsequently sent to Wasson in the process of revision.

To Ben Wasson — MS. [?] SHELBY FOOTE
[early summer, 1929] — [Oxford]

Italics here indicate a speech by one person within a speech by another, so as not to use quotes within quotes, my use of italics has been too without definite plan, I suppose i.e., they do not always indicate a thought transference as in this case, but the only other manner of doing this paragraph seems clumsy still to me, since it breaks the questions interminably of Mrs Compson's drivelling talk if set like the below:

'. . . You must think, Mother said.
'Hold still now, Versh said. He put etc.
'Some day I'll be gone etc., Mother said.
'Now stop, Versh said.
'Come here and kiss . . . Mother said.

. . . .

Galley 6

Set first three lines of new scene in italics. Transference indicated then. I should have done this, but missed it. Sorry.

. . . .

Excuse recent letter. Didnt mean to be stubborn and inconsiderate. Believe I am right, tho. And I was not blaming you with it. I just went to you with it because I think you are more interested in the book than anyone there, and I know that us both think alike about it, as we already argued this very point last fall. Excuse it anyway. Estelle sends regards.

Love to all.
Bill

To Mrs. Walter B. McLean — MS. FCVA
Sunday [probably Oct. 1929] — [Oxford]

Dear Aunt Bama—

We're so glad you are coming down. Let me know when to expect you. I work all night now in a power-house,[1] and my wife is quarantined with a scarlet fever patient at her father's home, so our apartment will be at your disposal and you can stay as long as you like. I am free all day, however, and it'll be fine. Let me know when you will come and what time you will arrive. I live at Miss Elma Meek's house on University Avenue. Anybody will tell you where it is, and if you will let me know when and what hour, I will be awake. We are expecting you and Uncle Walter.

William

[1] Faulkner would later say that it was during his hours at this powerhouse that he composed *As I Lay Dying*.

After completing the typescript of As I Lay Dying *on 12 January 1930, Faulkner was free to turn to short stories as a source of immediate income. He would keep a list of submissions to various magazines. His practice was to submit first to the highest paying magazines, such as* The Saturday Evening Post. *The story referred to in the following letter may be "Red Leaves," which was published by the* Post *on 25 October 1930. If so, Faulkner probably revised it somewhat after the rejection by* Scribner's *and resubmitted it to the* Post.

To *Scribner's* — MS. PRINCETON
[early 1930] — Oxford, Miss

Dear sir (or madam)—

Having just seen the Jan. 1930 copy of Scribner's, I thought that I had written a good letter. I dont think you could possibly get [greater?] contributors or subscribers [being?] 2 [creations?] both named Gladys Rock.[1]

So here is another story. Few people know that Miss. Indians owned slaves; that's why I suggest that you all buy it. Not because it is a good story; you can find lots of good stories. It's because I need the money. The other times I wrote one of these Indian stories, it got bought again by Blackwood's in England, for 125 guineas.[2] And that's why magazines get published, is it not? To get bought and re-bought.

William Faulkner

[1] Apparently Faulkner had written a letter to the editor which had not been published. In an interview appearing in the Memphis *Press-Scimitar* on 10 July 1931, Marshall J. Smith quoted Faulkner as saying, "I was born in 1826 of a negro slave and an alligator—both named Gladys Rock. I have two brothers. One is Dr. Walter E. Traprock and the other is Eaglerock—an airplane." Smith added, "Traprock is a mythical character invented by the humorist, Dr. George Chappel." (See *Lion in the Garden* [New York: Random House, 1968], pp. 7, 9.)

[2] There appears to be no evidence that Faulkner ever made such a sale.

Although Faulkner submitted to interviews from time to time, he resented what he took to be invasions of his privacy. This feeling extended to requests from magazines for information and pictures from contributors, and it manifested itself in different ways. When Forum *purchased "A Rose for Emily," Faulkner supplied the following information about himself, a mixture of fact and fiction.*

To the editor | *Forum*
[early 1930] | [Oxford]

Born male and single at early age in Mississippi. Quit school after five years in seventh grade. Got job in Grandfather's bank and learned medicinal value of his liquor. Grandfather thought janitor did it. Hard on janitor. War came. Liked British uniform. Got commission R.F.C., pilot. Crashed. Cost British gov't £2000. Was still pilot. Crashed. Cost British gov't £2000. Quit. Cost British gov't $84.30. King said, 'Well done.' Returned to Mississippi. Family got job: postmaster. Resigned by mutual agreement on part of two inspectors; accused of throwing all incoming mail into garbage can. How disposed of outgoing mail never proved. Inspectors foiled. Had $700. Went to Europe. Met man named Sherwood Anderson. Said, 'Why not write novels? Maybe won't have to work.' Did. *Soldiers' Pay*. Did. *Mosquitoes*. Did. *Sound and Fury*. Did. *Sanctuary*, out next year. Now flying again. Age 32. Own and operate own typewriter.[1]

[no signature]

[1] The letter appeared in the same number with "A Rose for Emily," *Forum,* LXXXIII (Apr. 1930), lvi.

When The American Mercury *bought "Honor" for publication in July 1930, Faulkner refused to supply anything at all.*

To Ben Wasson | TS. FCVA
[spring 1930] | [Oxford]

Dear Ben—

It's fine about the good price for the story. You can just send the check on to me here, as I am not likely to move for a month, anyway. And get it on to me as soon as you can, please; the first of the month only ten days away now.

Sorry, I haven't got a picture. I dont intend to have one that I know of, either. About the biography. Dont tell the bastards anything. It cant matter to them. Tell them I was born of an alligator and a nigger slave at the Geneva peace conference two years ago. Or whatever you want to tell them.

[t] bill.

Faulkner's tone was more businesslike when he returned portions of the proof of As I Lay Dying *to Edith R. Greenburg, his copy editor at Jonathan Cape and Harrison Smith.*

To Edith R. Greenburg | MS. EDITH R. GREENBURG
[summer 1930] | [Oxford]

Dear Miss Greenburg—

Enclosed are the sheets which contained major errors. The proof was quite clean, I thought; I found few errors that could be called major ones.

I will return the rest of the proof by parcel post.

Yours sincerely,
William Faulkner

When Faulkner sent "That Evening Sun Go Down" to The American Mercury, *editor H. L. Mencken found it "a capital story" but wrote Faulkner on 7 November 1930, that two changes would be necessary if he were to publish it: Nancy's pregnancy must be treated less explicitly and her husband's name, Jesus, must be changed. Faulkner drafted an explanatory note on the back of Mencken's letter, which he returned to him.*

To H. L. Mencken
[fall 1930]

MS. NYPL
[Oxford]

I did not delete the section, the dialogue about the pregnancy altogether, because it seems to me that it establishes Judah [Jesus] as a potential factor of the tragedy as soon as possible. Otherwise, to me, the story would be a little obscure for too long a time. However, if you think best, it might be taken out completely. I am glad you like the story; I think it's pretty good myself.

I did remove the 'vine' business. I reckon that's what would outrage Boston.[1]

[no signature]

[1] His wife obviously pregnant, and by another man, Jesus tells the Compson children that Nancy has a watermelon under her dress. When Nancy retorts, "It never came off of your vine," Jesus replies, "I can cut down the vine it did come off of." (*Collected Stories* [New York: Random House, 1948], p. 292.)

Faulkner returned the altered typescript of "That Evening Sun Go Down" with an undated note which Mencken dated "1931."

To H. L. Mencken
[1931]

TS. NYPL
[Oxford]

Here is the story, corrected according to your letter. Will you please have them hold the check until you hear further from me? I expect to be in New York in November.[1] I'll be obliged to you.

[no signature]

[1] This note may have been written as late as Oct. 1931, when Faulkner agreed to attend the Southern Writers' Conference in Charlottesville, Va.

To Alfred Dashiell
25 Feb., 1931

TS. PRINCETON
Oxford, Miss.

Dear Mr Dashiell:

Thank you for your letter. 400 suits me fine for the story. About the title: Why not call it simply 'Horses'?

HORSES.

That's all that's necessary. If this doesn't suit you, I'll try to think of some more titles by the time I get the galley.[1]

[t] faulkner
[s] William Faulkner

[1] The story appeared in *Scribner's* for June 1931 under the title "Spotted Horses" and was later rewritten for *The Hamlet* (1940).

It was in response to a query about this story that Faulkner wrote one of his rare letters to a reader.

To Mr. Thompson — TS. FCVA
[summer 1931] — [Oxford]

Dear Mr Thompson—

As you say, I am availing myself of my prerogative of using these people when and where I see fit. So far, I have not bothered much about chronology, which, if I am ever collected, I shall have to do.

'Spotted Horses' occurred about 1900, at Varner's Store, a village in the county of which Jefferson is market town. Suratt must have been about 25. In Sartoris, 1919, he is 45 say.[1]

[no signature]

[1] In *The Hamlet* Suratt would be changed to Ratliff.

Although Ben Wasson was still acting as his agent, Faulkner continued to send stories out himself in the face of financial pressure. On 5 June 1931, he sent three stories to Wasson without, however, telling him where he had already submitted the stories. He supplied the missing information in a subsequent letter.

To Ben Wasson — TS. FCVA
[June 1931] — [Oxford]

I'm sorry about crossing you up with the stories, my boy. I very carefully made a list of all the places where I had submitted them. I must have left it out when I put them in the envelope. I'm awful sorry.

Too bad about the rheumatism. I had it in my right shoulder for a while, myself. But last winter I laid my skull bare in a wreck, and after I was patched up I never had rheumatism again. You might try that.

I may get up there in the fall. I hope so. I need a change. I'm stale. Written out.

DR MARTINO	DEATH DRAG	IDYLL IN DESERT
Sat. Eve. Post	Mercury	Forum
Woman's Home C	Sat. EVE. Post	Sat. Eve. Post
	Scribner	Scribner
	Collier's	Liberty
		Harper
		Woman's Home C
		(this one seems to be about wore out)

Bill

In September 1931, Prof. James Southall Wilson invited Faulkner to attend a meeting of a group of Southern authors including Ellen Glasgow, James Branch Cabell, Paul Green, Allen Tate, Sherwood Anderson and others. It was to be held on 23–24 October at the University of Virginia in Charlottesville.

To James Southall Wilson
24 September, 1931

MS. VIRGINIA
Oxford, Miss.

Dear Mr Wilson—

Thank you for your invitation. I would like very much to avail myself of it, what with your letter's pleasing assurance that loopholes will be supplied to them who have peculiarities about social gambits. You have seen a country wagon come into town, with a hound dog under the wagon. It stops on the Square and the folks get out, but that hound never gets very far from that wagon. He might be cajoled or scared out for a short distance, but first thing you know he has scuttled back under the wagon; maybe he growls at you a little. Well, that's me.

So I shall be very glad to avail myself of the invitation and I will be there on the twenty-third, without something comes up in the meantime over which I have no control. So if you can take this as an acceptance without it outraging your plans, please do so, and thank you again. If the unforeseen does happen and I cannot come, of course I will let you know.

Yours sincerely,
Wm Faulkner

To Estelle Faulkner MS. JFSA
Thursday [22 Oct. 1931]

Monticello Hotel
Charlottesville, Va.

The mountains were grand, yesterday. Still are, since I can see the Blue Ridge from both of my windows. I can see all Charlottesville, and the University too. The fall coloring is splendid here—yellow hickory and red gum and sumach and laurel, with the blue-green pines. It's just grand. For some reason, all yesterday on the train I was thinking about Cho-Cho,[1] about taking her to New York with me soon. You know: having her at my mercy to talk history to; to tell her how Jackson won this battle here and that battle there.

The people here are mighty nice to me. When I arrived last night I found waiting for me guest cards to a country club and to the faculty club. I wired Mrs Sherwood Anderson (who lives in Marion, Va.) from the train at Bristol yesterday, but got no answer. Maybe she is still mad at me.[2] I'll find out within the next day or so.

I am going out to the University to lunch today, and this afternoon I expect Hal Smith in. There is a formal to-do tomorrow a.m. which I will tell you about later. . . .

Billy

[1] Victoria Franklin, Estelle Faulkner's daughter by her first marriage.

[2] After their intimacy during the first half of 1925, the friendship between Faulkner and the Andersons had cooled, due in part to Anderson's resentment of Faulkner and Spratling's *Sherwood Anderson & Other Famous Creoles* (1926).

At the conclusion of the conference, Faulkner went to New York, where the reception of Sanctuary *made him a celebrity sought after by publishers and editors.*

To Estelle Faulkner MS. JFSA
[postmarked 4 Nov. 1931]

Hotel Century
111 West 46th Street
New York City

I have the assurance of a movie agent that I can go to California, to Hollywood and make 500.00 or 750.00 a week in the movies. I think that the trip would do *you* a lot of good.[1] We could live like counts at least on that, and you could dance and go about. If you feel it possible for you to do this, let me know and I will talk to him. Hal Smith will not want me to do it, but if all that money is out there, I might as well hack a little on the side and put the novel off. We could go out just after Xmas.

I have been meeting people and being called on all day. And I have taken in about 300.00 since I got here. It's just like I was some strange and valuable beast, and I believe that I can make 1000.00 more in a month. So I want to stay a month longer, or until the middle of December. . . .

[no signature]

[1] On 11 Jan., Estelle Faulkner gave birth to a daughter, Alabama, who died five days later. It had been a difficult pregnancy and a premature birth, and Estelle's health was still precarious.

To Estelle Faulkner MS. JFSA
[postmarked 13 Nov. 1931] [Tudor City, New York City]

I am writing a movie for Tallulah Bankhead. How's that for high? The contract is to be signed today, for about $10,000.00. Like this: yesterday I wrote the outline, the synopsis, for which I am to get $500.00. Next I will elaborate the outline and put the action in, and I get $2500.00. Then I write the dialogue and get the rest of it. And then likely we will go out to the Coast, to Hollywood. I will let you know as soon as I can.

I have created quite a sensation. I have had luncheons in my honor by magazine editors every day for a week now, besides evening parties, or people who want to see what I look like. In fact, I have learned with astonishment that I am now the most important figure in American letters. That is, I have the best future. Even Sinclair Lewis and Dreiser make engagements to see me, and Mencken is coming all the way up from Baltimore to see me on Wednesday. I'm glad I'm level-headed, not very vain. But I dont think it has gone to my head. Anyway, I am writing. Working on the novel, and on a short story which I think Cosmopolitan will pay me $1500.00 for.[1] As well as the Bankhead play.[2] That's why these letters are so short—I spend most of the time writing, you see. But I think of you all the time. Tell Cho-Cho I sat next to Jack Oakie in a restaurant yesterday, and that I am going to see Nancy Carroll next week.[3]

Billy

I met Pauline Lord at a dinner party last week.[3] She gave me a white rose. She said, 'I'm famous, too.' The play from Sanctuary is about finished.[4] Rehearsals start next week, I hear. P.S. *In my workroom there is a big envelope addressed to Harrison Smith, containing some poems. Will you please get it and send it to me at 320 East 42 st.*

[1] He continued to work at the novel, *Light in August,* but *Cosmopolitan* did not buy the short story.

[2] The play, as such, was not completed, but it is possible that it served as a basis for two unproduced properties he would work on at MGM, called *Night Bird* and *The College Widow.*

[3] Popular actor and actresses of the time.

[4] This dramatic version of *Sanctuary* apparently does not survive.

To Alfred Dashiell — MS. PRINCETON
Wednesday [probably 16 Dec. 1931] — Oxford, Miss

Dear Alf—

Have you a mss. of mine named 'Smoke'? I sent it to you on 16 October, this year. I may have asked you to hold it, as I planned to be in New York soon. If you have it and dont want it, will you return it to Ben Wasson, at 33 W. 42, the American Play Co? and notify me. Anyway, let me know if you have it or not; otherwise I have lost it.

Home again now, where it is quiet. The novel is going fine.

My respects to Mrs Dashiell, and I wish you both, and Crichton[1] too a merry Xmas.

Bill Faulkner

[1] Kyle S. Crichton was one of Dashiell's editorial associates, who had also dealt with Faulkner.

To Harrison Smith — MS. FCVA
[probably early Jan. 1932] — [Oxford]

Dear Hal—

This is a fair sized book[1] now, and the stuff does not seem so bad, on rereading. I wish you would let the blank pages remain in, as they supply some demarcation between separate and distinct moods and methods—provided such terms can be used in respect to 2nd class poetry, which this is. But worse has been published. The blank pages can be just one side of the page and not a whole blank leaf. Let me know what you think about it, also a name. I reckon "Poems" will do.

Also, I will need money soon[er] than I thot. Can I have that (or part of) advance on the novel now? It is coming in good shape; I am doing

about 1000 or 1500 words every day, sometimes more. Did 3000 Thursday.
Give Claire and Pat my kindest regards.[2]

Bill

Happy New Year to you and Louise and Harter.[3] Tell Louise I will write her as soon as I catch up.

[1] A *Green Bough* would be published on 20 Apr. 1933.
[2] Smith's wife and daughter.
[3] Louise Bonino and Evelyn Harter, who worked for Smith.

By the end of the Southern Writers' Conference, Faulkner had been drinking heavily. He had traveled to New York with Milton Abernethy, Paul Green and Hal Smith. Shortly afterwards, Smith paid for the trip south for Faulkner and Abernethy, intending to keep Faulkner as far as he could for as long as he could from the blandishments of other publishers willing to offer him contracts in the aftermath of Sanctuary*'s success. Abernethy and Faulkner traveled by boat to Jacksonville, Florida, returning by way of Chapel Hill, North Carolina, where Abernethy and Anthony Buttitta published a magazine called* Contempo*. Before the two resumed their journey, Faulkner had promised that they might use some of his work in the next issue of the magazine. In early January 1932, Buttitta visited Oxford, and when he left he had with him one story and ten poems he had selected from among the material Faulkner offered him. When Smith read that Abernethy would like to print a limited edition of the verse he had been given, he wrote to Faulkner, who responded immediately to the matter of the material in* Contempo *but appeared not to have taken in another concern Smith voiced.*

To Harrison Smith — MS. FCVA
[mid-Jan. 1932] — [Oxford]

Got your letter. Wired Abernethy at once: he answers that the paper has already gone to press. I'm sorry. I didn't realize at the time what I had got into. Goddamn the paper and goddamn me for getting mixed up with it and goddamn you for sending me off . . . in the shape I was in. I dont think it will happen again. But if I should do so, for God's sake find Ben and turn me on to him next time, for your sake and mine too.

Bill

He has one bum short story and some verse.[1] I don't know if any of the verse is in the batch you have or not.

[1] The story was "Once Aboard the Lugger." The poems were "April," "Vision in Spring," "My Epitaph," "Spring," "Twilight," "I Will Not Weep for Youth," "Knew I Love Once," "To a Virgin," "Winter Is Gone," and "A Child Looks from His Window."

A letter Faulkner wrote the same day to Ben Wasson revealed more information about his promise to Abernethy and Buttitta. In Chapel Hill, he had left with them a section of Light in August. *Characteristically, he had gotten himself into a scrape attempting to extricate himself from another one.*

To Ben Wasson — TS. FCVA

[mid-Jan. 1932] — [Oxford]

Dear Ben—

When I wrote Abernethy to send me back the novel section, I promised him and Buttitta something to replace it with. Before Xmas I had a letter from Buttitta, who was in New Orleans, that he wanted to stop over and see me between trains. I told him all right. I thought it would be a good time to give him some stuff. It was the promise to him I was keeping, as I was sure that it was Buttitta who got the other stuff from Abernethy. You know that state I seem to get into when people come to see me and I begin to visualise a kind of jail corridor of literary talk. I dont know what in hell it is, except I seem to lose all perspective and do things, like a coon in a tree. As long as they dont bother the hand full of leaves in front of his face, they can cut the whole tree down and haul it off.

I gave Buttitta a bum short story, and then I gave him a batch of verse and told him to take what he wanted. Still running, you see. Trying to stay there and run at the same time. When he said he had what he wanted, I was just thinking Thank God that's over, I suppose. I didn't look at what he chose at all. Some of it may be ones which Hal is going to publish. I dont know. I also remember now (still trying to run and still trying to be host) his talking about a complete F. issue of his paper. I was just saying Yes. Yes., not thinking at all. And when he was gone, I was still just breathing free, thinking I was rid of the whole thing at last.

Yesterday I had a howl from Hal. . . . I gather from Hal that A's plan is to print some kind of a 100,000 unlimited limited edition, which Hal says will be bad for any limited editions of me properly printed and sold for money. I realised then that that was not my promise to Buttitta and Abernethy at all. That I thought they would print the stuff in current issues, without any fuss about it. I wired Buttitta to go ahead with the story, but to send the verse back to me and let me take out what I had already sold to Smith. Abernethy answered that Buttitta is in New York and that the paper has gone to press. . . .

Anyway, I am all worried about it again. What do you think? Should we try to stop the paper, until I can straighten them out? I want Buttitta to have something of mine, since I promised and he seems to want it. But I didn't intend to have them actually get out what amounts to a deluxe edition of W.F. Can they be held up? Or is Hal just jealous? If it is best to hold them up, and it can be done, go ahead and do it. I'll pay the costs, of course. If you can get in touch with Buttitta in New York (Harry Hansen[1] might know where he is) he is reasonable. He wont lie, anyway. Or if I had better go to Chapel Hill myself, I'll do that. Anyway, I want to get completely rid of it. I have already wasted ten novel chapters of energy and worry over that goddamn paper. I am writing Hal today. Goddamn me for ever getting mixed up with them, but goddamn him most for sending me off in the shape I was in . . . instead of getting in touch with you and turning me over to you, if he couldn't bother himself. In a way, it serves him right.

This is the situation, I think. I dont know if it is as serious as Hal says. But anyway, my country innocence has been taken advantage of. Which is no one's fault except mine, of course. I think I am madder at that than I am at the financial part of it. So you do what is best, or possible. And I solemnly swear that after this I'll never promise anyone anything without first asking your permission.

Bill.

Do you see any money for me soon? I want to take some insurance. Can get a good rate if within next two weeks.

[1] Literary editor of the New York *World*.

On 15 January 1932, Smith replied to Faulkner's letter, reassuring him about the issue of Contempo *but cautioning him against limited editions in general and the one Abernethy proposed in particular. That one must be stopped, he said, and he had written Abernethy telling him so. Recently he had learned from a newspaper that Casanova Booksellers in Milwaukee were publishing* Salmagundi, *by William Faulkner, in two limited editions. What was it, Smith asked, and did Faulkner want Smith to write to Casanova about it?*

To Harrison Smith — TS. FCVA
[mid-Jan. 1932] — [Oxford]

Dear Hal—

The SALMAGUNDI business is this. For about a year I had been receiving book lists and telegrams and letters of praise from Casanova Book Shop, Milwaukee. Last winter, right after Xmas, I had a letter from the man asking permission to reprint some things which were published in a New Orleans magazine in '24. He may have said in book form. I dont know. I realise now how inexperienced or how careless I was. I even forget the sum he named. I told him, all right. At that time (SANCTUARY not yet out) I was not selling short stories even. Later on I had another letter from him, that the project was going forward and that we include in it two stories out of magazines. I said No at once, to stick to the original, which were poems and stories written and published in the small New Orleans magazine before I had written SOLDIERS' PAY. So as far as I know, and as my permission went, that is what the thing is to contain. He later wrote me to sign some of them. I refused to do this. So if he has not included anything except the Double Dealer, New Orleans, stuff, he has my permission, my word. But if he is including anything else, he has overshot himself, though I kept no witnessed duplicate of the letters I wrote him. Carelessness. But never again. I will never make any agreements about my stuff hereafter without letting you know. But at that time, like the Contempo business, I didn't realise that I had a commercial value, since it was stuff which I had been starving to write for several years.[1] But I have learned my lesson now, and these two instances are all my mistakes. I learned a whole lot during my visit in New York. And what Contempo has is pretty poor stuff generally. Though there may be a few of the poems included which are in your lot. They worried me and worried me until I gave Buttitta a batch of verse and told him to take what he wanted. I didn't look at what he chose, having a certain faith in the infallibility of his poetic judgment. i.e, I believed that he would pick the bum ones without my help.

Bill.

[1] Advance copies of *Salmagundi* arrived in Milwaukee on 30 Apr. 1932. The volume included one poem by Ernest Hemingway entitled "Ultimately" and six by Faulkner—"New Orleans," "The Faun," "Dying Gladiator," "Portrait," "The Lilacs" and "L'Apres-Midi d'un Faune"—with two Faulkner essays: "On Criticism" and "Verse Old and Nascent: A Pilgrimage." *Contempo* had appeared on 1 Feb.

To Ben Wasson | MS. FCVA
[received 26 Jan. 1932] | [Oxford]

Dear Ben—

Good news about the money. I cant send you Light in August because none of it is typed yet. I had not intended typing at all until I finished it. It is going too well to break the thread and cast back, unless absolutely necessary. But I may strike a stale spell. Then I will type some.

I will be better off here until this novel is finished. Maybe I can try the movies later on. . . .

Bill

Although no novel is named, it is possible that Faulkner sent the following note to Wasson when he began typing Light in August.

To Ben Wasson? | MS. FCVA
[early 1932?] | [Oxford?]

I have lost a page from the novel mss. Page No 12. For God's sake see if I left it in the office. It is a complicated chapter and I cant reconstruct it. Send it right away if you find it.

Bill

Through the winter of 1931–32, Faulkner continued to work on Light in August *and the collection of poems that would become* A Green Bough, *drawing upon Smith as necessary.*

To Harrison Smith | MS. FCVA
[winter 1932] | [Oxford]

Dear Hal—

$250.00 will stave me off for the time. Send it on. Sorry to bother you at all right now, when you are cluttered up yourself with overhead instead of revenue. But it's either this, or put the novel aside and go whoring again with short stories. When it's convenient, send me another slug. . . .

Bill.

I wont bother you about the 'Poems' contract. Give me the best you can, tho. I am going cold-blooded Yankee now; I am not young enough anymore to hell around and earn money at other things as I could once. I have got to make it by writing or quit writing. If you can give me 15% I'll promise not to bother you about any advance on it. Is it to be a strictly limited edition, or will it be reprinted in case it sells? I have forgotten.

To Ben Wasson — TS. FCVA

[winter 1932] — [Oxford]

Dear Ben—

The contract for 'Light in August' is all right. The clause which has to do with further options and which was filled in for two succeeding books, is stricken out.

After I signed that one, I signed a contract for the poems. The same clause is in the body of this contract. The blank space for the number of succeeding mss. is not filled in, but the clause itself is not stricken out. Will this hold me to another mss.?

I also find, damn my soul, that in signing with Cape & Smith for my previous books, that this same clause, filled in for two mss., was in each one of them. I thought I was just signing for the present one each time, not having read the contract. I think that this accounts for Hal's request for mss. to submit to Cape. He wrote me that he had cleared the poems all right, and that he needed mss. to clear Light in August.[1]

Hence the 'Light in August' is clear, but the later contract, for the poems, includes that clause without any number filled in. Let me know if this will bind me to one more mss. after 'Light in August.' If so, I will send the contract back to Hal and ask him to strike it out.

The novel is about finished. Shall I write Hal now and tell him I intend to try to serialize it in a magazine?

About Harold.[2] I wont go behind Hal's back. When I get ready to swap horses, I will tell him. So suppose you dont say anything about it to him until I get this other straight and give you the word.

Estelle sends love to everyone.

bill.

[1] After the dissolution of the Anglo-American firm of Jonathan Cape and Harrison Smith, the new firm of Harrison Smith and Robert Haas, Inc., became Faulkner's American publisher. Chatto & Windus, not Cape, remained Faulkner's English publisher.

[2] Harold Guinzburg, of Viking Press, was one of the publishers who had approached Faulkner during his visit to New York in the fall of 1931.

To Ben Wasson | TS. FCVA
[probably late winter 1932] | [Oxford]

Dear Ben—

I have not finished typing yet. That's why you have not heard from me. I am still making changes, and for that reason I do not send you what I have typed. I see that I shall not know until I have typed it all, whether what I have done already will stand as it is. I should finish it in about two weeks more. I will not want to take less than $5000.00 for it, and not a word to be changed. This may sound not only hard, but a little swell-headed. But I can get along somehow if it is not serialised. But I will take five thousand and no editing.[1]

I will write again soon. Love to all. I liked Corey's takeoff fine. I enjoyed it a lot. I want to write him, but I have been and am busy as I can be getting this thing typed. Explain to him and tell him how much we both liked it. When I get caught up, I think I will write some John Riddell in the style of Faulkner. Love to Sullivan.[2]

bill.

[1] The novel was not serialized.

[2] Corey Ford and Frank Sullivan were among the friends Faulkner had made in New York, and he had briefly worked in the apartment they shared. In the March issue of *Vanity Fair*, Ford had published "Popeye the Pooh," a good-natured burlesque of Faulkner's *Sanctuary*.

To Paul Romaine[1] | TS. CARL PETERSEN[2]
Something March. Wednesday, anyway | Oxford, Miss.
[probably 16 Mar. 1932]

Dear Mr Romaine—

Thank you for the check. Excuse my not writing sooner, but I have been sick. Certainly I'll sign a few for you. I hate to be stingy, but the damned autograph is like cotton down here: the more you make, the less it is worth, the less you get for it. And I have got to live on either it or cotton, and I cant make anything farming. Let it be a mighty few, and I'll do better for you later on in something else. I will appreciate my complimentary copies.

The word from Hemingway is splendid.[3] This is the second time he has said something about me that I wish I had thought to say first.

This is an out-of-way town and hard to reach, but I'll be glad to see you if you should straggle off into these wilds. I dont move much, but you had better give me some warning when you make the New Orleans trip.

Excuse the tardiness of this reply.

Yours sincerely,
W Faulkner

[1] Proprietor of Casanova Booksellers, Milwaukee, Wisc., and publisher of *Salmagundi*.

[2] Carl Petersen, *Each in Its Ordered Place: A Faulkner Collector's Notebook* (Ann Arbor, 1975), pp. 183–84.

[3] When Ernest Hemingway wrote Romaine giving him permission to reprint "Ultimately" in *Salmagundi*, he had asked him to wish Faulkner the best of luck, adding that Faulkner was going well and sounded like "a good skate." Parke-Bernet Sale No. 2350, May 4, 1965. Collections of Manuscripts, Ernest Thompson Seton et al., p. 24.

To Ben Wasson — MS. FCVA
[spring 1932] — [Oxford]

Dear Ben—

The mss. goes to you today by express. If you can get $5000.00 with no changes, take it. If not, and the movie offer is still open, that should tide me along.[1] If you cant get $5000.00, I reckon I'll just turn it over to Hal. He wrote that he agreed to wait until October to publish it. You might remind him of that when you let him have the mss. I would like to hear from you about it as soon as possible, as I want to have it all cleared up when I go to California. I hope you will like it. I believe it will stand up. I will depend on you to protect Hal's equity in the matter, and also my own. I *dont* want it published in a book until fall. As you say, I have enough momentum to coast a while now; particularly as the next novel will take about 2 years in the writing.[2]

Bill.

Regards to Sullivan, and to all of them. Spring here; beans and peas and dogwood and wistaria next week.

[1] On 18 Dec. 1931, Samuel Marx, of Metro-Goldwyn-Mayer Studios, had wired Leland Hayward, of the American Play Company (the firm for which Wasson worked), inquiring about Faulkner's availability and price.

[2] Faulkner was meditating the first Snopes novel, which he would at first call *The Peasants* and which would be published as *The Hamlet* in 1940.

To Ben Wasson | MS. FCVA
[spring 1932] | [Oxford]

Dear Ben—

You wrote me some time ago that you intended coming home. I am today sending to Harper's a mss.[1] with return postage, because I want to hear from the story as soon as I can, in order to try it on someone else, and I dont want to chance having the story lie idle in your office in case you are not there. So if you are not coming home soon, and you wish to, take this letter to Harper's and take charge of the story there. I just dont want the story to lie idle in case you are not in town, you see. If Harper's do not want it, try elsewhere. It has been only to Scribner's, and I need money. Dont try it on Mencken save as a last resort; he only pays me $150.00 for stories.

Bill

[1] It is possible that Faulkner may have submitted a revised version of a portion of *Elmer* called "A Portrait of Elmer" or a war story entitled "With Caution and Dispatch," though it seems more likely that he offered them for sale at a later date.

In November of 1931, Prof. Maurice Edgar Coindreau of Princeton University had obtained from Faulkner and Harrison Smith authorization to translate into French As I Lay Dying *and any of the short stories collected in* These 13. *Coindreau had published a short article on Faulkner in the* Nouvelle Revue Française *for June 1931, and translations of "Dry September" and "A Rose for Emily" in the* N.R.F. *for January 1932 and the Winter issue of* Commerce, *respectively.*

To Prof. Maurice E. Coindreau | TS. PROF. COINDREAU
14 April, 1932 | Oxford, Miss.

Dear Mr Coindreau:

Please accept these belated thanks for sending me La Nouvelle Revue in which was Septembre Ardent. I thought the translation excellent there, but the one of A Rose for Emily, in Commerce lost nothing at all, even of that which a writer perhaps alone feels in his story but never quite gets into the actual words. But principally I wish to thank you for your critique among the Lettres Etrangeres in a recent number of La Nouvelle Revue, which I received from a friend in Paris. I see now that I have a quite decided strain of puritanism (in its proper sense, of course; not our American one) regarding sex. I was not aware of it. But now, on casting back and rereading now and then or here and there of my own work, I can see it plainly. I have found it quite interesting.

Thank you again for your thoughtfulness in sending me the Revue.

Sincerely,
William Faulkner

To Ben Wasson — TS. FCVA
[late Apr. 1932] — [Oxford]

Dear Ben—

I have Hayward's contract, but I cant leave here until I have got my royalty check from Cape. . . .

The statement says it is due May first.[1] Would it do any good if you were to see Cape and ask him if he can get it to me as soon as possible? If I can get it by the fourth, I will leave here the fifth. Otherwise I will have to wait upon it, and I dont want to jeopardise the movie money. I have written Hayward that Business prevents me reaching Cal. May first. This letter is confidential, of course. If you think you can do any good by asking Cape to send me the check on the first, I can get away right afterward.

Bill.

[1] In a letter fifteen months later, Faulkner would write Harrison Smith that the royalty statement had shown $4,000 due him but that he had received not a cent of it when receivership was followed by liquidation in early May 1932.

To Estelle Faulkner — MS. JFSA
Thursday [postmarked 2 June 1932] — Metro-Goldwyn-Mayer Studios
Culver City, Cal.

Sweetheart—

Here is $100.00. I got my second pay check yesterday, as they pay one week late here. That is, I will get the last one a week after I stop working. Write me if you need more. Otherwise, I will go ahead applying it on debts.

I have written one scenario, and I am now writing on one for Wallace Beery and Robt. Montgomery, in collaboration with an actor-author named Ralph Graves.[1] I am a sort of doctor, to repair the flaws in it. I ran into Laurence Stallings, whom I knew before in N.Y. He is a Georgian, author of 'What Price Glory' and he has given me some good advice about keeping my balance with these people. Also, a man named Conselman has helped me a lot.[2] He is with Fox.

. . . .

Billy.

[1] Neither was produced.
[2] Screenwriter James Conselman.

Faulkner's stay in Hollywood was prolonged when Howard Hawks bought his short story "Turn About" and hired him to work on the screenplay. Faulkner remained on the payroll and continued to work on the script when he was called home following the death of his father on 6 August 1932.

To Ben Wasson — MS. FCVA
[received 25 Sept. 1932] — [Oxford]

Dear Ben—

I dont know when I will go back to Cal. I finished a script of Turn About for Hawks, here at home. I had to leave Cal. before I finished it because of my father's death. I finished it here with the understanding that I would return to Cal. to make the final changes when Hawks said the word. I have not heard from him yet, though through last week I was still being paid. The option on Turn About was taken up. I got the $2250.00

About Light in August. Marx asked me about it before I left. I told him I didn't think they could use it. It would make a good Mickey Mouse picture, though Popeye is the part for Mickey Mouse. The frog could play Clarence Snopes. I hope to hell Paramount takes Sanctuary.[1] Dad left mother solvent for only about 1 year. Then it is me.

Estelle is pretty well. She sends love. Any chance to sell the short stories which you have of mine? I will write some more when I get settled down some more. Haven't done a lick since I reached home.

Regards to everyone.

Bill.

[1] Paramount Pictures Corp. did buy *Sanctuary* and made it into *The Story of Temple Drake*, released 12 May 1933.

To Ben Wasson TS. FCVA
[probably late Sept. 1932] [Oxford]

Dear Ben—

My contract with M.G.M. via Joyce & Selznick was up about July 1. It was $3000.00 and their commission was paid to the [m?], as you know. Later, Selznick approached me with an offer from M.G.M. of $250.00 a week. I refused this. He approached me with a contract to let them handle all my subsequent business with movies. I refused to sign it.

Later, they handled the sale of TURN ABOUT with Hawks, who asked me to make a script of it. [marginal note in pen: This is wrong: Turn About was handled and I signed the contract before Selznick approached me with a contract to handle all subsequent business, which I refused to sign]I agreed and did some work on it before pay was mentioned; I would have made this script for nothing, being interested in the story. Then I agreed with Marx in person to take $250.00 a week as long as I worked on the story: no signed contract at all. Today I received a statement from Joyce & Selznick asking for their ten percent of this TURN ABOUT weekly pay. Do I owe it to them? and is there any danger of them coming down here and taking a tithe of my pigs and chickens and cotton? Advise me at once.

I was too busy and too mad all the time I was in California to write you. But now I am home again, eating watermelon on the back porch and watching it rain. I have just finished reading the galley of LIGHT IN AUGUST. I dont see anything wrong with it. I want it to stand as it is. This one is a novel: not an anecdote; that's why it seems topheavy, perhaps.

Let me hear about Selznick. I think he owes me 10%. I certainly made a better contract with those Jews than he seemed able to: I get $250.00 a week for staying in Oxford: he got that for only a six months' contract in California. I think I'll send him a bill today.

Bill.

To Harrison Smith MS. FCVA
[probably late Oct. 1932] [Oxford]

Dear Hal—

Here I am home again, thank God. The book looks fine,[1] and thank you for sending the mss of 'Sound & Fury.' It's fine that you are planning to come down. I will write you later and give you the word. I made enough jack in Hollywood to do a lot of repairs on the house, so all the floors will be out of it next month, and we will be living with kinfolks. So you wouldn't have much fun then. I'll write you as soon as we open the house again and I have a keg ready to broach. Then we will look for you.

About the poems. O.K. about anything that Contempo published, that is included in the mss. as I sent it to you. You are not going to add to it, are you? Some of the Contempo stuff was pretty bad. I chose the best ms and built a volume just like a novel. You have that, you know. What about a title? I like 'Poems' myself. Or 'A Green Bough.'[2]

We will look for you as soon as we open the house again. Estelle sends love.

Bill

[1] *Light in August* had been published on 6 Oct. 1932.
[2] A *Green Bough* would appear on 20 Apr. 1933.

To Ben Wasson TS. FCVA
[possibly Nov. 1932] [Oxford]

Dear Ben:

What status on my balance on SANCTUARY? Has Paramount gone busted too?[1] Morty[2] wrote me about three weeks ago that a rider had gone through for the check, and it would be sent me in a few days. My address has been the Postoffice steps ever since.

I have been sick this week, but am better now. Estelle is well, and we are planning to come up to New York for New Year's. If you are going to come home Xmas, lets all go back together.

Bill.

[1] Faulkner had signed the contract in Los Angeles on 17 Oct. 1932.
[2] Morton Goldman was Ben Wasson's assistant at the American Play Company.

Before Faulkner left California, Howard Hawks had told him to let him know when he wanted to work again. When Faulkner did, he received a prompt response.

To Ben Wasson TS. FCVA
[probably Nov. 1932] [Oxford]

Dear Ben—

I am going to get loose from Joyce & Selznick. After that first contract of 6 weeks last spring, they have done nothing about me except collect ten percent of what I made. They wouldn't even try to keep up with where

I was. And when that contract was up July 1, they made no effort to get me a decent contract or offer. I didn't even know what they were doing until I had talked to Marx and he offered me $250.00 a week for a year and I said No, then I had a letter from Selznick saying 'Have you fixed up at $250.00 a week for six months. When will you sign?' I went to see them in person, told them I would not take that, and they dropped the matter. Then Hayward sold Hawks TURN ABOUT, I saw Hawks and I myself arranged with Marx to have $250.00 a week, without any signed contract at all, to work on TURN ABOUT alone and no interference from any Jew in California, with the privilege of returning to Oxford to do the work—thus accomplishing an arrangement which my so-called agents either could not or would not attempt. Yet I paid them ten percent of this. And when I left California, they didn't even try to find out where I was. They wouldn't even keep my living address; the only communication I ever had with them would be when they would send me bills, one of which was for money I had already paid them.

And now I have another offer from M.G.M. through Hawks, a good offer, handled through Hawks' brother, who is also an agent. If I accept it, I will have to accept the brother too. I firmly expect Joyce and Selznick to try to get ten percent of this also. I am not trying to go behind your back in this matter. But Joyce & S. have been of no benefit to me—I'm too small potatoes for them to bother with, I imagine, except to bleed at ten percent. So I want to get loose from them, and as long as it is Hawks who gets me the jack, I am going to let his brother handle any business that requires an agent out there. Let me hear from you. And about the Sanctuary check. I do need it, provided I can count on getting it soon.

bill.

On 8 December 1932, Bennett Cerf wrote Faulkner proposing a special Random House edition of The Sound and the Fury. *It would be limited to 550 copies and Faulkner would be paid $500 to sign the sheets and provide an introduction of ten to twelve printed pages.*

To Bennett Cerf — TS. RH
16 December [1932] — Oxford, Miss.

Dear Bennett:

Excuse delay in answering. I have been thinking about the matter. It sounds very attractive, as I too have a soft spot for the book, and no one can beat you all for making fine volumes. But I dont think five hundred is enough. Why not wait until better times, when you can pay me a thousand or fifteen hundred? I imagine this sounds outrageous right at present. But maybe times will mend soon, and the book will wait.

We are hoping to come East this winter sometime, but I dont know for certain. I'm trying to squeeze every nickel now to fix my house up. It hasn't been touched with either hammer or paint brush in about fifty years now.

Give our regards to Harold and Alice, and Don and George,[1] and my best to your father, and our wishes for a merry Christmas to yourself.

Bill. Faulkner

[1] Harold and Alice Guinzburg, Donald S. Klopfer of Random House, and George Oppenheimer of Viking Press.

To Bennett Cerf — TS. RH

[Christmas 1932] — [Oxford]

Dear Bennett—

The Red Badge is a beautiful book.[1] I thank you a lot for it. It's the only good war story I know.

We wont get to New York. Estelle has been sick, and so we cant make it, besides needing the money for other things. I would be proud to have you do THE SOUND AND THE FURY, and I hope that some day we can agree. But I dont need five hundred bad enough today to take that, when I believe that later we can both get more out of it.

Rotten weather here, as usual. However, I have a keg of good moonshine and four pounds of English tobacco, so what the hell, as the poet says.

Best wishes for New Year, and thank you again for the book.

The Viking Press sent me a galley of GOD'S LITTLE ACRE.[2] I read it with a good deal of interest, but I still think the guy is pulling George Oppenheimer's leg. I believe that Alex. Woollcott and Lon Chaney's ghost wrote it.

Bill.

[1] In July 1931, Random House published a limited edition of Stephen Crane's *The Red Badge of Courage* printed by Grabhorn Press. The special edition of *The Sound and the Fury* which Cerf had proposed was to have been printed by Grabhorn Press, and Cerf presumably wanted Faulkner to see a sample of their work. Faulkner inscribed his copy "Xmas 1932."

[2] By Erskine Caldwell.

To Harrison Smith | TS. FCVA
[answer to Smith's letter of 23 Dec. 1932, probably early Jan. 1933] | [Oxford]

Dear Hal—

I have been busy as hell, writing a movie script and taking care of the sick.[1] Estelle and the children have been sick in rotation since the middle of November, and the day after Xmas Estelle succeeded in falling down stairs (no one would have been surprised if it had been me now, on Dec. 26) and she has been in bed ever since. She is getting up today, though, I think. But our trip East will be off. We have decided to save the money and put heat in the house, anyway. So I wont see you unless you can still arrange to come down here later on.

I imagine Claire is having a grand time in Taxco. I know the place. I am about done with the movie, I hope, and next year I shall work on the Snopes book.

Best wishes to you all for New Year. Will you send Louise a flower or something for a wedding gift from me?[2]

Bill.

P.S. Have four gallons of charred corn and four pounds of English tobacco. Ha ha.

[1] Faulkner was working for Hawks on *War Story*, based on *War Birds: Diary of an Unknown Aviator* (1926) by Elliott White Springs, based in turn upon a diary by John McGavock Grider.

[2] Louise Bonino.

To Ben Wasson | TS. FCVA
12 Feb. 1933 | Oxford, Miss.

Dear Ben:

I received the Scribner's.[1] Thank you. But what has happened to the check? You recall, when I saw you in Memphis, you asked me if I had received it and I said no, and you evinced both surprise and annoyance. If the matter is not finished to the paying off point yet, let me know and I wont worry you anymore about it.

I have enough money now to finish my house. Going to add another bedroom and bath, and put in heat and paint it. You said something in Memphis about following through all my stories which you handle, into movies, etc. I would like you to do this, myself. But apparently I can do better for myself through Howard Hawks than agents can, and I must approach Hawks through his brother, who is also an agent. I dont think I should have to pay two agents when I do my own shopping for prices.

Still, I would like to have you to protect me from myself, but how to do it? I am under no written contract with anyone. This arrangement is like that of a field hand; either of us (me or M.G.M.) to call it off without notice, they to pay me by the week, and to pay a bonus on each original story.

....

Bill.

[1] "There Was a Queen" was published in *Scribner's*, XCIII (Jan. 1933), 10–16.

To Ben Wasson MS. FCVA
[received 27 June 1933] [Oxford]

Well, bud, we've got us a gal baby named Jill. Born Saturday and both well.[1]

About Bennett and "Sound & F." All right. Let me know about it, if he will use the colored ink. I like that. I will need time to lay it out again. How many different colors shall I be limited to? Just what does he want in the introduction? I'm ready to start right away. $750.00 is right, is it?[2]

What about the Cape & Smith business? Is all that lost?[3]

Working spasmodically at a novel.

Bill.

[1] Jill Faulkner was born on 24 June.

[2] Faulkner marked the Benjy section of his own copy of the novel with three colors to indicate time shifts and sent the book to Cerf, who sent it on to Grabhorn Press. The project fell through, and Faulkner's book was never returned to him.

[3] The royalties owed to Faulkner were lost when Cape & Smith went into receivership.

To Ben Wasson TS. FCVA
[summer 1933] [Oxford]

Dear Ben:

I have the Harper proof and the letter.[1] But I dont know how to go about explaining it. To me the answer seems obvious:

The writer is trying to explain a story and some characters by writing it down; that's what a story is. If it doesn't come off to the reader, the only alternatives I know are, to delete that part which needs explanation, which as Mr Hartman says, seems to do nothing toward carrying forward with the story; or explain it by a footnote, like this: the agnostic progresses far enough into heaven to find one whom his intelligence, if not his logic, could accept as Christ, and who even offers him an actual sight and meeting with his dead son in exchange for the surrender of his logic, agnosticism. But he naturally and humanly prefers the sorrow with which he has lived so long that it not only does not hurt anymore, but is perhaps even a pleasure, to the uncertainty of change, even when it means that he may gain his son again.

That is what I intended to tell, and hoped that I had. I thought I had chosen the best method, touching the whole thing pretty lightly by careful deliberation in understatement. It is a tour de force in esoteria; it cant be anything else. I have mulled over it for two days now, without yet seeing just how I can operate on it and insert a gland. I'll hold the proof, and you get in touch with Hartman and if he can tell us just what he would like to have inserted, I'll invent some way to do it.

Bill.

[1] "Beyond" was published in *Harper's*, CLXVII (Sept. 1933), 394–403.

To Harrison Smith TS. FCVA
[received 20 July 1933] [Oxford]

Dear Hal:

Thank you for the check. I will hold it until I hear from you in ref. to the enclosed proposition of what about stepping up the royalty percent.? What about fifteen on the first printing, and 20% from then on?[1]

About clause VIII. I think you know that I will give you first look at any novel I do, as witness Light in August, with guys waiting with contracts in their hands and the advance and percentage left blank, outside my hotel door when the waiter fetched the morning coffee. Also one reliable reference to $10,000.00. But in this contract the option is not to you, but to a company. Vide the J. Cape affair, excusing which I would not be needing two thousand dollars now, not having got a cent of the four thousand odd which their royalty statement showed for April of last year. That's why I dont like option clauses; though if you insist, etc.

We are all well. I have turned out three short stories since I quit the movies, so I have not forgot how to write during my sojourn downriver.[2]

Bill

[1] The check and the contract were probably for the first of the Snopes novels.

[2] These stories may have been "Lo!" "Elly" and one which Faulkner had tried as a screenplay under the title "Manservant" and later revised as "Love."

To Samuel Marx TS. INDIANA
19 July, 1933 Oxford, Miss.

Dear Sam:

The contract forms received.

All save the one for HONOR seem to be correct. Perhaps the HONOR one is correct too, though I have a question to ask about it. (P.S) Also WAR STORY

I wrote the story HONOR previous to my association with the studio. Howard Hawks sent me a treatment by Behn,[1] as I recall, to look over. I read it and returned it, though I did not change it or do any work on it at all, being at the time engaged on the WAR STORY. The two original stories in WAR STORY I did work on and adapt myself, and for this work I was paid in weekly salary.

It was my understanding in conversation with Howard re. my last connection with the studio that the studio would pay me bonuses for all previous original material which they used, regardless of whether I did the adaptations or not. Is this correct? That is, will the studio pay me for the rights to use HONOR, AD ASTRA, and ALL THE DEAD PILOTS?

I know you all are too busy to write idle letters, but I would like to know how Tod is coming with LOUISIANA LOU.[2] I was getting pretty steamed up over it when I got the air. He's a fine fellow. Give him my best when you see him, and Howard Hawks too. I'm going to write Howard a note some day.

Remember me to everyone.

Bill Faulkner

[1] Harry Behn.

[2] Tod Browning was directing *Louisiana Lou.*

To Ben Wasson TS. FCVA
[summer 1933] [Oxford]

Dear Ben—

Here is another story.

I have your letter about the Miss. river book. I think I would like to write a book like that, but I believe it would take some time; first, to write something as outside of my line as nonfiction; and second, to get done with what I have on hand now to start it. I am hot with a novel now, and until I get that underway, a short story now and then is about all I had better undertake. I'd like to talk about it with the guy later on. Maybe I could promise something definite, which I cant do now, as I am about to contract with Hal for the novel, setting it for the fall of 1934. If he doesn't farm the idea out in the meantime, we'll talk about it in the fall. We are going to christen Jill about October, and you are expected down then.

The house not elaborate, but heat in and two new rooms, and paper and paint which it has not had in 25 years, and lights which it has never had. I didn't know your sister was here. I will see her.

Bill.

To Ben Wasson — TS. FCVA

[mid-Aug. 1933] — [Oxford]

Dear Ben:

The enclosed explains itself.[1] I have worked on it a good deal, like on a poem almost, and I think that it is all right now. See what Bennett thinks and let me know.[2]

We are fine. Jill getting fatter and fatter. Estelle has never been so well.

Bill.

[in pen:] I never received but the one check for the stories. The first check which you mentioned in your letter was lost in the mail or never mailed or never issued. What part of the $750.00 do I now get, and when?

[1] This was Faulkner's introduction to the projected Random House special edition of *The Sound and the Fury*.

[2] Wasson sent the introduction to Cerf on 24 Aug. 1933.

To Bennett Cerf — MS. RH

24 Aug 1933 — Oxford

Dear Bennett—

I mislaid your letter r.e. 'The Sound and the Fury' and just found it. Please excuse me for not acknowledging it. I sent the introduction to Ben; you already have it now, I am sure. I will send you at once the color-marked copy. As I have only the one copy of the book, please ask the printer to take good care of it and return it to me.

We are getting along fine. I hope to see you this fall.

Bill

To Morton Goldman[1] MS. FCVA
[probably summer 1933] [Oxford]

I suppose 'Lo' is another dud. But maybe this one will sell. I'd hate to see it gutted, but I hope the Post will take it. Or maybe Cosmopolitan: they ought to pay well. Think I will try the 'Mississippi' article for Vanity Fair if its still open, or something for 'Esquire.' Just what did they want, if you remember?

F.

[1] When Ben Wasson left there to join the Shulberg, Seldman Agency in Hollywood, Goldman became Faulkner's agent, particularly for short-story sales.

To Harrison Smith TS. RH
something October [1933] Oxford, Miss.

Dear Hal:

I dont think the novel will be ready for spring. I have been at the Snopes book, but I have another bee now, and a good title, I think: REQUIEM FOR A NUN. It will be about a nigger woman. It will be a little on the esoteric side, like AS I LAY DYING.

About a collection of short stories. It has been almost 16 months since I have written anything original or even thought in such terms. I dont know what I have in short stories. I will take a day off soon and go through them and see if we can get a book we wont be ashamed of. I'll let you know.

I shall have to peg away at the novel slowly, since I am broke again, with two families to support now, since my father died, and so I shall have to write a short story every so often or go back to Hollywood, which I dont want to do. They are flirting with me again, but if I can make a nickel from time to time with short stories, I will give them the go-by.

Remember me to the children.

Bill

To Morton Goldman TS. FCVA
[autumn 1933] [Oxford]

Dear Morty:

I was glad to get your letter, as I had failed to get your address.

I am now working at a story which the POST should like.

I want to send BLACK MUSIC to MINOTAURE, PARIS. I dont know the address, but perhaps you can find it. I doubt if they will pay at all, but I had a very nice letter asking for something, and as I like BLACK MUSIC and I dont believe anyone in America will want it, please send it to them. You could explain to them that it is to be included by Smith....

Please attend to BLACK MUSIC. Hal shouldnt mind.

Yours,
Faulkner

To Morton Goldman — TS. FCVA
[autumn 1933] — [Oxford]

Dear Morty:

I am mailing today to the Saturday Evening Post a story, BEAR HUNT.[1] I sent it direct so as to save time, with a letter asking them to send any communication (which infers a check, I hope) to you at this address.

Get in touch with them; they keep on protesting how they love me; make them pay $1000.00 if you can. And for God's sake, get the money to me as soon as possible. Of course, if they dont want it, get what you can and where you can, and quick. Tax time is coming here, and I dont want to draw on Smith unless I have to.

Best regards.
Faulkner

[1] "A Bear Hunt" was published in *The Saturday Evening Post,* CCVI, (10 Feb. 1934), 8–9, 74, 76.

To Morton Goldman — TS. FCVA
[Dec. 1933] — [Oxford]

Dear Morty:

I have your letter, with the office address. I will use it from now on.

$900.00 is all right for the Post story, and $200.00 better than I expected from the Mercury.[1] Needless to say, I shall be glad to have the checks, what with Xmas and tax time too close for comfort.

I will write Smith myself regarding the stories you mentioned. I doubt if he would want BEARHUNT, and I dont think I would want it in the collection, either.[2] I have just sent him a long unpublished short story to include, so the others should be all right with him; they will have to be, in fact. You could see him too, if you like, giving yourself three or four days to let him get my letter.

I will take this opportunity to wish you a merry Xmas too, and when or if you hear from Ben, tell him to write to me, goddamn him.

Faulkner

[1] "Pennsylvania Station" would appear in *The American Mercury*, XXXI, (Feb. 1934), 166–74.
[2] *Doctor Martino and Other Stories* would be published by Harrison Smith and Robert Haas in Apr. 1934.

To Morton Goldman — TS. FCVA
[probably winter 1933–34] — [Oxford]

Dear Morty:

The CHRISTMAS TREE story which you mention was a continuation of that one by the same title which you now have: the same characters who got married at the dance, with the dice and the forged license, etc. I wrote it first years ago, and I have mislaid it. I rewrote it from memory, the first part, in the short story which you now have, and I had forgot the characters' names: hence the difference.[1]

It may have been with Ben, though if it were, I imagine you would have found it when the company folded up. However, I can rewrite it, as I rewrote the part which you have. But I had rather have some promise of a sale. If you could show some editor the part which you have and tell him what the rest will be—it should run about 20,000 words, maybe less—I will try to rewrite it all. If you can interest someone and he wishes, I will send a kind of synopsis of the rest; I probably could take a word limit also. You might see what can be done, as I had rather not undertake it right now unless I knew it would sell at once.

Let me know as soon as you sell any thing. I am living on credit now and trying to write a novel at the same time.

Faulkner

[1] "Christmas Tree" was revised and published as "Two Dollar Wife" in *College Life*, XVIII (Jan. 1936), 8–10, 85, 86, 88, 90.

To Morton Goldman — TS. FCVA
[probably winter 1933–34] — [Oxford]

Dear Morty:

Enclosed. I would like for Dashiell at Scribner's to see this, but they wont pay much. I dont know what to say about it, since we may get $1000. from the Post. Suppose you ask him if he would like to see it and make an offer; then see what the Post will pay, and wire me.

I suppose XMAS TREE is still hanging fire.

Faulkner

To Harrison Smith TS. FCVA
[received 31 Jan. 1934] [Oxford]

Dear Hal:

This is answer to two letters; excuse delay.

I dont read French easily enough to do justice to Malraux' book, and I doubt if I could write an introduction to anything, anyway.[1] I'll look at the translation if you like, though.

About the novel. I still think that SNOPES will take about two years of steady work. I could finish the other one in good time, if only the Snopes stuff would lie quiet, which it wont do. However, I will have my taxes and insurance paid and off my mind by March first. Then I intend to settle down to the novel and finish it. As it is now, and trying to not have to draw on you, I have written one short story each month, trying to sell to the Post. The last one hung fire with them; unless someone else takes it before Feb. 1, I shall have to draw upon you as per the agreement. I will not need over $1000.00 and perhaps only $500.00, as I am now writing another short story. As I explained to you before, I have my own taxes and my mother's, and the possibility that Estelle's people will call on me before Feb. 1, and also my mother's and Dean's support, and occasional demands from my other two brothers which I can never anticipate. Then in March I have $700.00 insurance and income tax of about $1500.00. So I seem right now to rush from pillar to post and return. Perhaps the best thing as regards the novel would be for me to draw from you to the full amount of our agreement and get all this off my mind and concentrate on the novel. If I did this, I believe I might promise it for late fall printing—provided I could stop worrying about what I would use for money next year, with royalties already spent. Anyway, I will settle upon the one which I can finish soonest, and I will try to give you a definite promise by March first.

Bill

[1] Smith & Haas would publish a translation of *Man's Fate* in 1934 and one of *The Royal Way* the following year.

To Harrison Smith TS. FCVA
[probably Feb. 1934] [Oxford]

Dear Hal:

I believe that I have a head start on the novel. I have put both the Snopes and the Nun one aside. The one I am writing now will be called DARK HOUSE[1] or something of that nature. It is the more or less violent breakup of a household or family from 1860 to about 1910. It is not as heavy as it sounds. The story is an anecdote which occurred during and right after the civil war; the climax is another anecdote which happened about 1910 and which explains the story. Roughly, the theme is a man who outraged the land, and the land then turned and destroyed the man's family. Quentin Compson, of the Sound & Fury, tells it, or ties it together; he is the protagonist so that it is not complete apocrypha. I use him because it is just before he is to commit suicide because of his sister, and I use his bitterness which he has projected on the South in the form of hatred of it and its people to get more out of the story itself than a historical novel would be. To keep the hoop skirts and plug hats out, you might say. I believe I can promise it for fall.

Now hold your hat. I have two short stories out which should sell, but have not yet. I will have to draw some more money; I want $1500.00. I have a $600.00 odd insurance due March 4, and income due the 15th. If I can have this by March 1, I will send back whatever part I wont need after arranging to pay the income tax in quarterly installments, if necessary. I have heard of writers who got themselves, or their publishers, into this fix, but I never thought I would do it too. But I am, and you are too. But anyway, I'm still sober and still writing. On the wagon since November now.

Bill

[1] *Dark House* would become *Absalom, Absalom!*.

To Morton Goldman — TS. FCVA

[probably late winter or early spring 1934] — [Oxford]

Dear Morty:

Maybe this one will hit Cosmo.[1] If so, please get the money as soon as possible. Ask them to please let us have it quick. I always need money bad, but this time I am desperate, as I had believed the Post would take the other surely.

I am going to work on something else right away, though I dont know what yet. I have a plan, a series to be called

A Child's Garden of Motion Picture Scripts[2]

They will be burlesque of the sure-fire movies and plays, or say a burlesque of how the movies would treat standard plays and classic plays and novels, written in a modified form of a movie script.

Anyway, I will send you something else right away. And in God's name get me the money as fast as you can.

Faulkner

[1] Probably "Mule in the Yard," published in *Scribner's*, XCVI (Aug. 1934), 65–70.

[2] There is no evidence that Faulkner completed any of these.

To Morton Goldman | TS. FCVA
[probably late spring 1934] | [Oxford]

Dear Morty:

I'll leave this to your judgment: The Post paid $900. for the other one, a sketch; maybe they will pay $1500. for this.[1] If they will, I will promise to let them see three or four more as good or better than this one during the year. Tell them that with $1500. I can pay my N.R.A. income tax.

[t] faulkner

[in ink:] Dont tell them though that I said to take what you can get for it.

[1] The first story was probably "A Bear Hunt," *The Saturday Evening Post,* CCVI (10 Feb. 1934), 8–9, 74, 76; the second was "Ambuscade," which appeared in the *Post,* CCVII (29 Sept. 1934), 12–13, 80, 81.

To Morton Goldman | TS. FCVA
[probably late spring 1934] | [Oxford]

Dear Morty:

The enclosed letters and copies explain themselves.[1]

What do you think of this? Let the Post keep this second story until I finish the third and send it to *you* before you talk price, because I think the third story will be the most novel (damn the word) of all.[2] Then tell them they can have the two for four thousand and I will let them have the subsequent three for five thousand more. That will be ten thousand for the series of six, and I believe they have paid more than that for serieses.[3]

I will write the third one and send it to you soon.

Faulkner

[1] Probably correspondence with *The Saturday Evening Post.*

[2] The "second story" was "Retreat," published by *The Saturday Evening Post,* CCVII (13 Oct. 1934), 16–17, 82, 84, 85, 87, 89; the "third story" would be "Raid," which would also be published by the *Post,* CCVII (3 Nov. 1934), 18–19, 72, 73, 75, 77, 78.

[3] The series of stories here envisioned would constitute, after publication and revision, most of *The Unvanquished* (1938).

To Morton Goldman | TS. FCVA
[probably late spring or early summer 1934] | [Oxford]

Dear Morty:

I have been stewing for about three weeks now on the Post stories. I have been trying to cook up three more with a single thread of continuity, like the other three, with the scene during Reconstruction time. I cannot get started, I seem to have more material than I can compress. I have just now decided that the trouble is this:

The Reconstruction stories do not come next. In order to write them, I shall have to postulate a background with the characters which they embrace. Therefore, there must be one or two stories still between the War-Silver-Mule business and the Reconstruction; I am just starting one which will be a direct continuation of the return home with the mules, which should be included in the series of three which are done; perhaps it will bring to an end that phase, and I can get into the Reconstruction ones which for some reason will not start themselves. Please pass this on to the Post; I will send in this fourth story as soon as possible.

[t] Bill. F.

When the Post *did not offer as much for the series of stories as Faulkner wanted, he put the idea aside for the time and accepted a short-term offer from Howard Hawks to work at Universal Studios on the adaptation of a novel by Blaise Cendrars called* Sutter's Gold *(1926).*

To Mrs. William Faulkner
[postmarked 7 July 1934]

MS. JFSA
Hollywood Roosevelt Hotel
Hollywood, California

I made a synopsis of the play, and yesterday Howard and I talked, and we decided that I shall spend another week here in order to get as much of the script on paper as possible, have a talk for final corrections, then come home and make what we hope will be the final draft. So unless something unforeseen comes up, I now plan to start home about next Monday.

Weather good and cool here, fine sleeping. Starr now lives down on the beach, in a canyon.[1] I am moving down to stay with him today. It is a good place to hide out and work; he is alone now and I will have the house to myself all day long. I can put on bathing suit right in the house and walk 2 blocks to the beach.

I [tried?] some very good ale at a German Hof-brau restaurant, a lady [string?] band there, and the proprietor's daughter, about 3 or 4, like a Dresden doll, with a toy violin helping them. I enjoy it—heavy, good German food and sentimental Bavarian music under a vine trellis.

. . . .

Billy.

. . . .

[1] Hubert Starr had graduated from the University of Mississippi law school some time before.

To Mrs. William Faulkner
[postmarked 12 July 1934]

MS. JFSA
Paramount Productions, Inc.
Hollywood, California

. . . .

Finished another synopsis today, and am waiting now to hear about making a movie of the recent play, Mary of Scotland. Will get to work on that right away, as it is the next job. Will let you know soon as I can when to expect me. . . .

Billy.

To Mrs. William Faulkner
Friday [20 July 1934]

TS. JFSA
Santa Monica, Calif.

Dear love:

. . . .

The situation is now this. I made a draft of 'Sutter's Gold,' then Hawks came in with the second story, the crisis affair of which I wrote you. I made a treatment of that, finished it, took it to Hawks (this was about Tuesday of last week) whereupon he told me of the plan about Mary of Scotland. We discussed it that afternoon while he was waiting to hear from the studio if they had permission to do it or not. No word came; Hawks drove me back to Santa Monica, told me he would send me word tomorrow (Wednesday). Dead silence until Friday, when I telephoned him myself (no phone here; you walk down to the beach to find one) and he said nothing about MARY at all, but that he was making corrections on SUTTER and would send that to me tomorrow (Saturday). Dead silence again until Tuesday. The corrections came, I tried to telephone Howard, could not get him, telephoned his brother, my agent, told him Howard had told me (as I wrote you) that I could get away about this coming weekend. He told me that Howard had talked to him, and that he was at the moment arranging to get my money for the second or Sullavan[1] story, and that I would hear from him (Hawks 2) tomorrow, which would have been last Wednesday. I have not heard yet, though today I finished the final treatment of SUTTER, and have just telephoned to Hawks' home, telling him so and that I will wait here for word. I will have to see him, get an o.k. on the script, keep after his agent brother and get my pay for this and for the second treatment. Right now I believe that I will be in Memphis at eleven o'clock Tuesday morning. Surely they can clean things up for me by then, and Monday I will get a few presents for us and ours and take the plane Monday night. . . .

. . . I am getting nervous and a little jumpy to get home, at the fingernail chewing stage. I wasted a whole week doing nothing at all; that's what frets me about this business.

Billy

[in pen:] Saw Hawks this p.m. Told him I plan to leave here Monday. Seems to be all right. Should be in Memphis Tuesday on the 11:00. Will write you.

Done a little on the novel[2] from time to time.

[1] Actress Margaret Sullavan.
[2] *Absalom, Absalom!*.

To Morton Goldman — TS. FCVA
29 July [1934] — Oxford

Dear Morty:

Your letter to hand. I will give you the dope and you can answer Lorimer as seems best.[1]

I could not get enough out of them for the series. So at the end of June I went out to California and got lined up with a moom pitcher script. I am working on it now, and I cannot say just when I will finish it. Maybe in a month; if I do, I may write the other stories or I may go back to the novel; it all depends on how much or badly I need money at the time. That is, I would like to keep the Post hot for a while longer, so if, when I finish the script, I need more cash I can write the other stories. But I would not like to promise to do so, since I have had to put off the novel too much already.

So you use your own judgment about what to tell them. If they insist on a definite deadline, we had better not accept it. If they will leave the matter open for a few months longer, I will let you know as soon as I can whether or not I can write the other three, and when.

I saw Ben. He looks fine and seems to be happy as a cockroach.

Faulkner

[1] Graeme Lorimer, of *The Saturday Evening Post.*

To Harrison Smith — TS. FCVA
Thursday [Aug. 1934] — Oxford, Miss.

Dear Hal:

I wrote you in the spring that in August I would let you know definitely about the novel. The only definite news I can tell you is, that I still do not know when it will be ready. I believe that the book is not quite ripe yet; that I have not gone my nine months, you might say. I do have to put it aside and make a nickel every so often, but I think there must be more than that. I have a mass of stuff, but only one chapter that suits me; I am considering putting it aside and going back to REQUIEM FOR A NUN, which will be a short one, like AS I LAY DYING, while the present one will probably be longer than LIGHT IN AUGUST. I have a title for it which I like, by the way: ABSALOM, ABSALOM; the story is of a man who wanted a son through pride, and got too many of them and they destroyed him. . . .

Bill

To Morton Goldman — TS. FCVA

[Aug. 1934] — [Oxford]

Dear Morty:

Enclosed the letters you asked me to return.

About the Post: as I recall the business, I wrote them that I was going ahead with a series before the question of price came up. When price came up, they offered promptly to send the stories back to us if we did not want to take what they would pay. All I answered then was, to take what they would pay; my later correspondence consisted of manuscripts. So perhaps the thing for us to do now is to recopy their letter to us and say, if they dont like the way in which the stories are submitted, to send them back to us and get a refund of the money. As far as I am concerned, while I have to write trash, I dont care who buys it, as long as they pay the best price I can get; doubtless the Post feels the same way about it; anytime that I sacrifice a high price to a lower one it will not be to refrain from antagonising the Post; it will be to write something better than a pulp series like this.

I have caught up with the movie now; I have a good story out of California I want to write. I may do that first; otherwise I will get another one in the series; you should have it within four weeks. You can tell the Post this, if you think best; say I am starting the fourth one and you will submit it as soon as you get it.[1]

Hot as hell here; I have to work in front of a fan; I write with one hand and hold the paper down with the other.

[no signature]

[1] The fourth story would be "The Unvanquished," to be revised as "Riposte in Tertio," *The Saturday Evening Post*, CCIX (14 Nov. 1936), 12–13, 121, 122, 124, 126, 128, 130.

To Morton Goldman — MS. FCVA

[Sept. 1934] — [Oxford]

Dear Morty—

The enclosed is O.K. with me. I mailed to the Post Monday the 4th story in series: will start on 5th at once.[1]

F.

[1] The fifth story would be "Vendée," *The Saturday Evening Post,* CCIX (5 Dec. 1936), 16–17, 86, 87, 90, 92, 93, 94.

To Morton Goldman — TS. FCVA

[probably 18 Oct. 1934] — [Oxford]

Dear Morty:

Yours received. Post mss. was altered to their wishes and returned Friday, last week;[1] also I wrote sixth story, DRUSILLA,[2] sent that in Monday following; I mean, two weeks ago now, October 4th it will be.

Did you get wire about air story, COURAGE?[3] I am writing a novel out of it, so please return it.

Enclosed is a letter. I have no photographs and am too busy to fool with this, but if you can dig up a picture and some mss. for him, it is all right with me. I like to help all these earnest magazines, but I have too goddamn many demands on me requiring and necessitating orthodox prostitution to have time to give it away save as it can be taken from me while I sleep, you might say. But fix him up if you can.

faulkner.

Dont forget the story, THIS KIND OF COURAGE.[4] Send it back to me.

[1] "Vendée."

[2] "Drusilla," revised and renamed "Skirmish at Sartoris," would appear in *Scribner's,* XCVII (Apr. 1935), 193–200.

[3] The novel was *Pylon* (1935).

[4] Morton Goldman had sent the story to Alfred Dashiell at *Scribner's* on 10 May 1934.

To Morton Goldman — TS. FCVA

[early or mid-Dec. 1934] — [Oxford]

Dear Morty:

Excuse not writing. I have worked forced draft on the novel and finished it yesterday.[1]

I will try to get around to rewriting DRUSILLA as soon as I finish typing. Is Ben in New York? Ask him.

What became of Gloria Stuart's two books on Sutter and California gold which he was to return. Ask him to wire me collect about them, as she is raising hell. Damn it, she should not have trusted me with a book you cant buy in the drug store. He will know.

[t] faulkner

[1] The last two chapters of *Pylon* were received in New York by Faulkner's publishers on 15 Dec. 1934.

To Morton Goldman — TS. FCVA
[Dec. 1934] — [Oxford]

Dear Morty:

Here is the rewritten Drusilla story.

I have sent in the novel manuscript, to Smith. I think I will send a copy of it to Howard Hawks, in California. I have not done it yet, though I am writing him today. I will let you know what he says about it.

I shall take a holiday until after Jan. 1, then I will be sending you some more stuff.

Faulkner

To Harrison Smith — TS. FCVA
[late Dec. 1934[1]] — [Oxford]

Dear Hal:

. . . .

I mailed you the last two chapters on December 18.[2] I haven't got an acknowledgement yet, so maybe we had better check on them, since I sent the mss. to you in sections. From first to last they run in this order:

Dedication of an Airport	*rec'd* 11/5
An Evening in New Valois	*rec'd* 11/23
Night in the Vieux Carre	*rec'd* 11/30
Tomorrow	*rec'd* 12/5
And Tomorrow	*rec'd* 12/10
Lovesong of J. A. Prufrock	*rec'd* 12/15
The Scavengers	*rec'd* 12/15

And perhaps I had better mention this, too. "New Valois" is a thinly disguised (that is, someone will read the story and believe it to be) New Orleans. The "Feinman Airport" is the Shushan Airport of that place, named for a politician. But there all actual resemblance stops. Shushan Airport has a lot of capital S's about it, and an air meet was held there.[3]

But the incidents in Pylon are all fiction and Feinman is fiction so far as I know; the only more or less deliberate copying of fact, or the nearest to it, is the character "Matt Ord," who is Jimmy Weddell. That is, Jimmy Weddell held the land plane speed record at one time in a ship built by himself, Weddell-Williams Co, near New Orleans.

But as I said, the story and incidents and the characters as they perform in the story are all fictional. But someone may read it and see into it what I didn't. Someone may or may not see a chance for a suit. You might decide whether there would be grounds for a suit, whether a suit would help sell the book, or whether to alter the location, etc., so there would be no grounds.

Bill

[1] Smith replied to this letter on 28 Dec. 1934.
[2] Someone's dating is in error, for the last two chapters were marked as received in New York on 15 Dec., according to the notations (printed here in italics) which were made in New York.
[3] Faulkner attended a portion of the dedication ceremonies and meet held at Shushan Airport in mid-Feb. 1934.

To Morton Goldman — TS. FCVA
[late Dec. 1934 or early Jan. 1935] — [Oxford]

Dear Morty:

Enclosed is the best short story in the year 1935.[1] Have you sold the Drusilla story yet?[2] I can use money right now to beat hell.

faulkner

[1] "Lo!" appeared in *Story*, V (Nov. 1934), 5–21, and would be reprinted in *The Best Short Stories 1935 and The Yearbook of the American Short Story*, Edward J. O'Brien, ed. (Boston, New York, 1935).
[2] "Skirmish at Sartoris."

To Morton Goldman — TS. FCVA
23 January, 1935 — Oxford, Miss.

Dear Morty:

I am glad the story sold somewhere.[1] I know you got the best price it could have brought.

Here is a suggestion I want to make in regard to GOLDEN LAND. Hal Smith has been down here with me for a week; he thinks, and I agree with him, that I should have some other outlet for stories with the good-paying magazines besides the Post. As it is, I sell either to Scribners and Harpers for pittances, or to the Post. He says that he has a line, a contact, with the Cosmopolitan; a string that he can pull. I want to try it and see what comes of it. So suppose you recall Golden Land and give it to Smith and let him try his idea, as a test case. As you say, with its flavor of perversion, possibly the only magazine which will consider it and which will or can pay well, will be Cosmopolitan. Of course, you will have your commission on this story, since it is yours to agent. But I want to see if I can establish a wellpaying alternative to the Post. Possibly it will help me get a better price from them.[2]

I am going to dope out another series for the Post and work on it right away. I will keep you posted. Let me hear.

[t] Faulkner.

[1] "Skirmish at Sartoris."

[2] "Golden Land" appeared in *The American Mercury*, XXXV (May 1935), 1–14.

To Harrison Smith — TS. FCVA

[probably early Feb. 1935] — [Oxford]

I wrote Goldman last week. He says the Golden Land story is out, but that he will turn it over to you as soon as he can get hold of it. That was what you wanted me to write him about, wasn't it? He has no claim on the novel, nor on anything else save what I send him. If you like—or when I write him again—I will tell him to let you handle the novel business for the time being.

I am looking forward to the pipe and the check; for at least twenty minutes after it comes I should be solvent. The weather is fine now; temperature around forty, and I have done a good deal of quail shooting. The season will be over on the twentieth; then I will settle down to work proper. I hope to hell you can gouge somebody for a thousand for GOLDEN LAND. That will give me two months to work at the novel before I have to boil the pot again.

We are all well. All the ladies express bright pleasure and appreciation of the suave metropolitan breath which you brought into our snowbound and bucolic midst.

When and if the notion occurs to you to try to send some liquor, send me a bottle of good brandy. Pack it in excelsior and put a fictitious return address on it and send it by express.

Bill

To Morton Goldman
18 Feb., 1935

TS. FCVA
Oxford, Miss.

Dear Morty:

Enclosed letter from Centaur Press. NO. Absolutely NOT. There is no copyright; I made about six of the books by hand. I dont know if they can be stopped or not, but stop them if you can. Get Smith to help you if necessary. Let me hear.[1]

Copy of yours to my brother. I have not seen him since, but I will see him soon. He is working on another story. He will follow your advice in regard to present one.[2]

About Mississippi River book. I dont believe I can do it. I am a novelist, you see: people first, where second. To do a book like that would mean a sort of holiday, extra curricular work, you might say. And when I take a holiday, I damned sure wont spend it writing.

I have nothing in mind at present for Mercury. I am trying to bugger up an air story for Cosmopolitan. You might tell them I will try to get something in soon. I must either hang something on them or on the Post; it all depends on which one I can invent first.

Vanity Fair I think it was wrote me for a lynching article. Tell them I never saw a lynching and so couldn't describe one.

Faulkner

[1] Nothing came of this effort to publish *The Marionettes*, an experimental one-act play Faulkner had composed in late 1920.

[2] John Falkner's stories would be published as *Chooky* (1950). Writing as John Faulkner, he published his first novel, *Men Working*, in 1941.

To Morton Goldman
9 March, 1935

TS. FCVA
Oxford, Miss.

Dear Morty:

Under my contracts with Smith, he has the handling of the novels with regard to the movies and the stage. I hope you will forgive me for not straightening this out with you before, and hence confusing or embarrassing you.[1]

The only understanding that Ben and I ever had was the verbal one that the American Play[2] would handle short stories and magazine stuff and that all novels etc. would be handled by myself. I was going along under that same idea, though you and I never discussed it. But as I submitted COURAGE to you as a short story, you may have, under the rules governing author and agent, an equity in it.[3] You will have to let me know about that.

I should have made this clear to you before. I took it for granted that when you approached Smith about it, he would tell you the status of the contract between us. But that still does not excuse my negligence about correspondence.

I will try to get the story for Cosmopolitan soon. I am at work on another novel now, but as soon as I can cook up a yarn I will put the novel aside and write it.

I am sorry about the other business.

Faulkner

[in ink:] Returned Mercury galley today.[4]

[1] Goldman and Harrison Smith had discussed the sale of *Pylon* as a motion-picture property.

[2] The American Play Co., where Wasson had been employed.

[3] After it had been offered for magazine sale, Faulkner had withdrawn the short story "This Kind of Courage" in order to use it as a basis for *Pylon*.

[4] The galley proofs of "Golden Land."

To Morton Goldman — TS. FCVA
[probably Mar. 1935] — [Oxford]

Dear Morty:

Here is another one.[1] I dont know who to suggest to try it on, since I made such a bust about the Post with FOOL ABOUT A HORSE, and Cosmo with THE BROOCH. The Post might take it, since they took one last year about the same hunting camp.[2]

Thank you for your letter. I contracted with Smith and took an advance on the novel I am now working on. However, I do believe I can make more money through someone else. That is, I am not exactly satisfied. This in absolute confidence, of course. I am coming East in the fall and get myself straightened out. So in the meantime, just let the matter ride as it is until you hear from me. You might listen to what you hear, but dont let any suggestion come from us. I would rather come up there, tell Smith what I intend to do, try to get an offer from someone else and then see if Smith wants to come up to it or not. But I cannot and will not go on like this. I believe I have got enough fair literature in me yet to deserve reasonable freedom from bourgeoise material petty impediments and compulsion, without having to quit writing and go to the moving pictures every two years. The trouble about the movies is not so much the time I waste there but the time it takes me to recover and settle down again; I am 37 now and of course not as supple and impervious as I once was.

So just let the matter ride until you hear from me about it.

[t] Faulkner

[1] "Lion" would appear in *Harper's*, CLXXII (Dec. 1935), 67–77.

[2] "A Bear Hunt."

To Morton Goldman — TS. FCVA

[probably Apr. 1935] — [Oxford]

Dear Morty:

Much obliged for getting offer 250.00 from Mercury.[1] But that wont help me enough. I need a thousand. I will just have to knock out something for Post. I wish to hell I could find some man who would gamble on my future on a note, no contract. Damn these fool laws about usury anyhow.

Golden Book reprinted SMOKE. They promised me $25.00. I dont recall even getting it. Will you look into it for me?

F.

Thank you for kindness in getting offer. $1000.00 is least that would help me. What I really need is $10,000.00. With that I could pay my debts and insurance for two years and really write. I mean, write. The man who said that the pinch of necessity, butchers and grocers bills and insurance hanging over his head, is good for an artist is a damned fool.

[1] For "That Will Be Fine," which appeared in *The American Mercury*, XXXV (July 1935), 264–76.

To Morton Goldman — TS. FCVA

[probably Apr. 1935] — [Oxford]

Good God yes, let them have the story and do anything they want with it, just so I get the money soon as possible.[1] I couldn't wire you because I have no money to pay telegram with. Haven't had one cent since last story sold, wherever that was. and now I have to get a blasted check like this that the bank here wont or cant cash. I have indorsed it. Can you cash it there? It's for reprint of That Evening Sun.

Did you see Golden Book about the $25.00 they promised me for SMOKE?

I am writing two stories a week now. I dont know how long I can keep it up. This makes six or seven. Did you receive one named MOONLIGHT?[2]

[no signature]

[1] "That Will Be Fine."

[2] "Moonlight" would remain unpublished.

To Morton Goldman | TS. FCVA
[probably late July 1935] | [Oxford]

Dear Morty:

The checks have arrived; thank you a lot for getting them out to me; also the pipe, for which thank you too.

The checks relieved the pressure somewhat, but, since none of the recent stories seem to be Post stuff, big check stuff, I can see another squall in the near future. On Sept. first I am going to need at least two thousand dollars. The only way I can think of to get it or part of it, apart from writing, is to try to sell some of my manuscript. It's all written in long hand; besides the short stories, I have SOUND & FURY, AS I LAY DYING, SANCTUARY, LIGHT IN AUGUST, PYLON. Will there be any market for it? Will you inquire around, without committing yourself, and see? I hate like hell to sell it, but if I dont get some money somehow soon, I will be in danger of having some one put me in bankruptcy and I will then lose my house and insurance and all. So just ask around and see what the reaction is. Meanwhile, I finished last week another chapter of the novel[1] which I owe Smith, and now I shall try some more short stories, still with hopes of the Post; two for them would do the business. I am trying to get the novel done as soon as possible, so that when I come East I can make a better contract than I have. Keep this under your hat, of course.

Faulkner

[in ink:] Had letter from Dashiell at Scribner's. Send 'The Brooch' to me and I will rewrite it. Also send him 'Fool About a Horse' if he has not seen it. Will rewrite that too if necessary.

[1] *Absalom, Absalom!*.

To Mrs. William Faulkner | MS. JFSA
Friday [27 Sept. 1935] | Harrison Smith and Robert Haas, Inc.
17 East 49th St, New York City

I arrived Wed. a.m. to everybody's surprise. I saw Perlman at once, but the Mercury's owner, Spivak, will not take the novel, as it is too long. Goldman is now trying Scribners and Harpers. If that will not work, I have told Hal that I am coming down on him for money. He is noncommittal; I dont know just what he will do about it. I will wait until I hear from the 2 magazines, then I will put it to the test.

My headache is gone now, and I feel better. I feel good and ready and 'hard-boiled' now, enough to cope with Shylock himself. I have not seen anybody in town except Cerf and Don Klopfer. Sullivan, Ford, Parker, etc.

all in California, and I am saving H. Guinzburg until I have the round with Hal.[1] Kiss all the children for me, Sister, Mac,[2] and Little Missie.

Billy.

[1] Bennett Cerf, Frank Sullivan, Corey Ford, Dorothy Parker and Harold Guinzburg of Viking Press.
[2] Faulkner's stepson, Malcolm A. Franklin.

To Mrs. William Faulkner — MS. JFSA

[5 Oct. 1935]

Murray Hill Hotel
Park Avenue, New York

Had your letter yesterday, and I am mighty happy that you feel better and things are going well at home. I have settled the business. There are strings to it, of course, and I have agreed to go to California for 8 weeks in March if Hal can get me a contract and so pay back the money which they loaned me. I took only the bare minimum, so it is not such a staggering sum. It will pay all bills, taxes, insurance, etc. and I included in it a sum for winter clothes for you and the children. We will shop carefully and pay cash, and it will do.

I will leave here about the end of next week, as I have an appointment with Lorrimer, Sat. Eve. Post.[1] Thursday. Saw Harold and Alice G. yesterday.[2] Marc and Madeleine Connelly are divorced and Mad. is now Mrs Playwright Sherwood. Sullivan is in Saratoga and everybody else in Hollywood, where I have heard that Ben now actually has a job.[3] Harold and A. send you their regards. I have seen 2 shows, dined out once, and I have a typewriter in my room and I am working on a story for Scribners. . . .

Bill.

. . . .

Address me at Hal's office, not here, as I may leave this hotel and go up to Hal's place in Connecticut.

[1] Graeme Lorimer.
[2] Harold and Alice Guinzburg.
[3] Ben Wasson.

To Morton Goldman — TS. FCVA

4 December [1935] — Oxford.

Dear Morty:

Excuse delay, as I am working like hell now. The novel is pretty good and I think another month will see it done. Needless to say, I have written no short stories nor contemplated such nor do so until after the novel.

Tell Bennett I will agree about the Elmer story as he wants it.[1]

About movies. I dont care how I get a contract, just so I do. I had rather it came through you, as you are handling my short stories and I have no other agent arrangement but that. My feeling about the movie contract is, as you know, that I dont particularly want to go at all but I am doing so as a part of my agreement with Smith: so let them find the way to farm me out, if that's what they want.

I am writing Hal today, telling him that you wrote me you can get a nibble from movies, and suggesting to him that he get in touch with you and, if you get the best offer, we take that; if he gets the best offer, we take his. I will tell him that I have written you to this effect, and if you dont hear from him soon, you might get in touch with him yourself and tell him you are going to do a little fishing for me. I dont see why this is not ethical. The only agreement I made was, to take a contract if Smith and Haas got me one for February. I then talked, in Mr Haas' presence, with Ober, who I gather is their Pacific coast representative, who was leaving for Los Angeles that week and would include my business in the trip.[2] I understand that he returned and told Hal what I had already told him: that they were not going to contract for Shakespeare himself 3 months ahead, but that he (Ober) left strings out for later.

Faulkner

[1] Goldman had sent Cerf "A Portrait of Elmer," which Cerf had thought of for publication in a limited edition, but the story remained unpublished.

[2] Harold Ober, who would succeed Goldman as Faulkner's agent.

On 10 December 1935, Faulkner flew to California to work for Howard Hawks at Twentieth Century–Fox on a war film called Wooden Crosses, *later renamed* Zero Hour. *On 7 January 1936, he had done his part of the script and ten days later returned to Mississippi, where, on 31 January, he completed the manuscript of* Absalom, Absalom!. *Before he finished the revision and typing on the novel, he returned to California to begin work at the same studio on 26 February 1936, under Nunnally Johnson and then David Hempstead, on a film called* Banjo on My Knee.

To Mrs. William Faulkner — MS. JFSA
Monday, 5:30 P.M. [2 Mar. 1936] — Twentieth Century–Fox
Beverly Hills, Cal.

Getting along fine, am well and busy at new picture, though I go and see the making of the other one every day.[1] It is coming along fine. I wish I was at home, still in the kitchen with my family around me and my hand full of Old Maid cards. Bless the fat pink pretty. In haste, but with much love.

[no signature]

[1] Presumably *Zero Hour.*

To Mrs. William Faulkner — TS. JFSA
Sunday [9 Mar. 1936] — Beverly Hills Hotel

. . . .

About meeting in New Orleans. That is a good plan. But I may not know until the last day, when the present script is approved, just when I will be through with it and can leave. I am arranging to be offered a long contract, as I told you, and I will be able to ask and get more money when this script is finished than I will now. So that (unless I get the price before hand that I am holding out for) may take another week or even two after I am finished with this script. So I cant say just exactly when for you to go down to start your 2 weeks. I will try to let you know tho, soon as I can.

[no signature]

To Morton Goldman — TS. FCVA
[probably late Mar. 1936] — [Beverly Hills]

Dear Morty:

Writing Hal at once to let Palmer[1] have mss. I sent it in last week. I will also have a shot at the book.

I have signed a six months contract out here, beginning Aug 1. I am going to try to make some money without having to borrow it. I intend to get you a short story from time to time, but nothing in the wind now.

Bill

[1] Probably Paul Palmer, then editor of *The American Mercury.*

To Morton Goldman — TS. FCVA
[probably June 1936] — [Oxford]

Dear Morty: enclosed is another of the best short story in 1935,[1] though I dont expect to get anything for this one either. Since last summer I seem to have got out of the habit of writing trash but I will still try to cook up something for Cosmopolitan. Maybe I can get hold of one of the magazines and take a story that they will buy and change locale and names, etc. That's probably hard work too and requires skill, but I seem to be so out of touch with the Kotex Age here that I cant seem to think of anything myself.

Faulkner

[1] "That Will Be Fine," which had appeared in *The American Mercury*, XXXV (July 1935), 264–76, was reprinted in *The Best Short Stories 1936 and the Yearbook of the American Short Story*, Edward J. O'Brien, ed. (Boston, 1936).

To Morton Goldman — TS. FCVA
Sept. 4, 1936 — Twentieth Century–Fox
Beverly Hills, Cal.

Dear Morty,

Excuse me for not answering your letter sooner. As you see, I am in California again up to my neck in moving pictures, where I shall be for about a year.[1]

I am going to undertake to sell this book[2] myself to the pictures, first. I am going to ask one hundred thousand dollars for it or nothing, as I do not need to sell it now since I have a job. I am going to try it first and if I don't have any luck I will write you later.

Bill

[1] Faulkner had returned, bringing Estelle and Jill with him, to begin work on 1 Aug. 1936.

[2] *Absalom, Absalom!*. He did not succeed.

To Harrison Smith — TS. FCVA
Sept. 4, 1936 — Twentieth Century–Fox
Beverly Hills, Cal.

Dear Hal,

I am going to try to sell the manuscript to the movies myself, and see what luck I have. Please send me a copy of it, or clean galleys or something, as soon as you can. Also, when the printer is done with it, I would like to have that galley which I proof-read and returned to you a few days ago. Will you please be sure and return it to me?

I am getting along pretty well and gradually getting out of debt. I have hope of paying you some of the money which I owe you and Mr. Haas by the first of January.

Be sure and send me this galley which I corrected. I am going to write Louise to remind you to do it.

Bill

To Louise Bonino
November 5, 1936

TS. FCVA
Twentieth Century-Fox
Beverly Hills, Cal.

Dear Louise,

If I am to receive a few books as usual, will you please send them to me here and not to Oxford? I received the special edition. I was very much pleased with its appearance.

I am getting along pretty well, but I still don't like it. My regards to Evelyn, Hal, Mr. Haas, Bennett and Don.

Bill

To Morton Goldman
Dec 28 [1936]

MS. FCVA
Twentieth Century-Fox
Beverly Hills, Cal.

Dear Morty—

Have no stuff now, but am going to write some more short stories soon, also another novel in my bean. See Ben now and then. Hope you had good Xmas & have good year in 37. Hope to hell I do too.

Bill

To Bennett Cerf
December 28, 1936

TS. FCVA
Twentieth Century-Fox
Beverly Hills, Cal.

Dear Bennett,

Thank you for Captain Liddell Hart's book.[1] You sent me two copies so I am sending one of them on to my brother who was a soldier and is quite interested in Captain Liddell Hart's war stuff, so we both thank you.

I have a series of six stories about a white boy and a negro boy during the civil war. Three of them were published in the SATURDAY EVENING POST about two years ago, in three successive numbers. They were titled 'Ambuscade,' 'Retreat,' and 'Raid.' I do not remember the exact dates. The fourth one was published by SCRIBNERS about the same time, titled 'Skirmish at Sartoris.' The fifth and sixth were published in the POST in November of this year, titled 'The Unvanquished,' and 'Vendee.' They should average between five thousand and seventy-five hundred words apiece. What do you think about getting them out as a book? Hal may be familiar with the stories. I cannot find my carbon copies without making a trip back to Mississippi. If you could get these back numbers from the POST it would be simpler. Let me hear from you about it.

Thank you again for the book, and my regards to Mr. Haas, Hal, and Don.

Bill Faulkner

[1] Basil Henry Liddell Hart's *The War in Outline, 1914–1918.*

To Mrs. Claude Selby[1] — MS. MRS. WILLIAM F. FIELDEN
Thursday [early Jan. 1937] — Twentieth Century–Fox
Beverly Hills, Cal.

My dear Sister—

The box came yesterday. Jill's miniature faces me on my desk as I write this. It is the picture of an angel, a cherub (or rather, a seraph) yet it looks exactly like her. I am so pleased and proud that I am almost bursting, bless yours and Claude's hearts. Everything came, and we are all pleased and happy. The best thing, to me, is the fact that Jill likes the Stevenson poems. We have read it from cover to cover 5 times now, and I will wager that she could repeat some of the verse. I am quite pleased over that.

We had a nice Xmas and are all well and we love you and Claude very much. Give Mac happy new years from

Billy

[1] Faulkner's stepdaughter, Victoria Franklin, had married Claude Selby, and she and her husband had sent a parcel of Christmas gifts. The poems were those of Robert Louis Stevenson.

To Morton Goldman — TS. FCVA
Jan. 21, 1937 — [Beverly Hills]

Dear Morty:

Good news about the story.[1] Send check to me, care Hawks-Volck Corp., 9441 Wilshire Blvd., Beverly Hills, Cal.

About contract for new book. If Bennett wants to give me an advance, I will take whatever necessary to pay to Mr Haas and Hal the balance I owe them on that loan of October, 1935, which I have been unable yet to pay back. I will write Bennett (or Mr Haas) myself and discuss this. What further arrangements i.e. the monthly parched corn and tobacco business, I will discuss later, and I will keep you informed.

I have had letters from Palmer about short stories. Perhaps I may get at some soon, also a novel in my mind. I see Ben now and then. He is all right.

Bill

[1] Probably "Monk," which would appear in *Scribner's*, CI (May 1937), 16–24.

To Prof. Maurice Edgar Coindreau — TS. PROF. COINDREAU
26 February, 1937 — Beverly Hills, Cal.

Dear Mr Coindreau:

This is mainly to ask your pardon for not answering your letter about 'Sound & Fury.' I probably stowed the letter away unopened, since I do not recall receiving one which I knew to be from you. I would not have been so discourteous otherwise.

Write me in care of the address below and I will give you any information you wish and I can about the book. After reading 'As I Lay Dying' in your translation, I am happy that you are considering undertaking S&F. I want to see this translation, indeed, because I feel that it will probably be a damned poor book, but it may be a damned good one (in French, I mean, of course) but in either case, particularly in the latter, it will be Coindreau and not Faulkner, just as the Rubaiyat which English speaking people know is a little more Fitzgerald than Khayyam. Have you any such feeling about it? Anyway, I wish you luck with it and I will be glad to draw up a chronology and genealogy and explanation, etc. if you need it, or anything else.

I will probably be in the East some time in this autumn. If I am, I hope we can have a meeting.

Sincerely,
William Faulkner

To Mrs. William Faulkner — MS. JFSA
Monday [postmarked 28 June 1937] — Twentieth Century-Fox
Beverly Hills, Cal.

Dear Estelle—

. . . I am still in the house. Thought I might just as well stay there until I hear from contract and make one moving do.[1] Have given two dinners. Mammy[2] and me—one to the Davenports', one last week when Coindreau, my French translator came out from Princeton and spent 3 days.[3] Had just men then, played poker—Davenport, Ben, Coindreau & two painters. I should hear from contract in 2 weeks now.

I want to hear about birthday party.

Much love.
Pappy

[1] The house was located at 129 North Le Doux, Beverly Hills.

[2] Narcissus McEwen, the Faulkners' cook and Jill's nurse, had stayed on to work for Faulkner when Estelle and Jill returned to Mississippi from their stay in California.

[3] Maurice Coindreau had translated *As I Lay Dying* and was working on *The Sound and the Fury*.

To Mrs. William Faulkner MS. JFSA
Wednesday [postmarked 21 July 1937] Twentieth Century–Fox
Beverly Hills, Cal.

Contract not taken up and renewed. Mammy and I will be home sometime between Aug 22–Sept 1, if we live and nothing happens. . . .

Billy

To Morton Goldman TS. FCVA
July 24 [1937] [Beverly Hills]

Dear Morty:

Random House is going to collect the Civil War stories we sold the Post into a book. They needed one more story to finish them, which I have just completed, named "An Odor of Verbena." The Post might buy it, though it is pretty long. Since I have not heard from you lately and it is just possible your address has been changed, I am sending the story direct to the Post, asking them to communicate with you, as they doubtless have your correct address.[1]

I want you to do this: tell them you have heard from me, that the stories are to be collected, and if they want this last one, ask them if they could print it as soon as possible so the book itself can appear; naturally I'll hold the book back until after whoever buys the story prints it. If Post dont want it, try someone else.

I will be through here Aug 15. I will go to Oxford. About Oct 1 I am coming to New York. . . .

Bill F

[1] The *Post* did not buy the story, which first appeared in print as the last chapter of *The Unvanquished* (1938).

To Mrs. William Faulkner — MS. JFSA
Wednesday [postmarked 28 July 1937] — [Beverly Hills]

Nothing has happened yet. As far as I know, I will be through at studio Aug 15 and will start home sometime during that week, though according to my contract they can give me an assignment and hold me overtime until I finish it. I will let you know of course as soon as I know myself. It's hot here and I dont feel very good, but I think it's mostly being tired of movies, worn out with them. Love to the children. Bless Pappy's girl, I want to see her damn bad.

[no signature]

In mid-October, Faulkner went to New York, where he worked at Random House to transform the series of short stories into the novel The Unvanquished, *which would appear on 15 February 1938. His visit lengthened into November when he suffered a mishap in his hotel bathroom: a third-degree burn on his back from a steam pipe leading to an overhead radiator. After medical treatment, he returned home in the company of his friend Eric James Devine, and by 10 November he was recuperating.*

To Robert K. Haas — TS. RH
19 Nov. [1937] — Oxford

Dear Bob:

I am feeling a little better, though it will take my back some time to heal, and it is still damned painful. However, that is that, and curse my own folly.

I have the contracts and check. First, will you consider 15% first printing, 20% second, 25% thereafter? I have a feeling that I should be stepped up from the last few contracts. Or am I wrong?

Secondly, now that I have got myself mentally together, I would like to do this. I wish to keep a balance with the firm, without any skulduggery to show on the books. Would not the best way to do this be to send this check back to you and have you send me one of mine which you hold in the same amount? if you agree, send to: John Falkner, Junior, Oxford, the first of the checks and I will return yours to you for credit on the books. If you think there is no point in making this exchange, I will endorse the cashier's check which you will send and return it to you for credit on the firm's books, and cash your check here. I am inclined to think the first plan best: that I return your check for cancellation so that your books will show me to have a thousand odd balance on which to draw, and cash one of my cashier's checks for present use.

Best regards to everyone. If and when you send any of my six checks, send them to my cousin, as above; any other mail can come direct to me.[1]

Sincerely,
Bill

[1] John Falkner, Jr., had previously handled some of Faulkner's legal work.

To Robert K. Haas — TS. RH
29 November [1937] — Oxford

Dear Bob:

Enclosed the signed agreement, also your check returned for credit.

I have got into the novel.[1] It has not begun to move very fast yet, but I imagine it will soon and that I will be able to send it in by May first, though I cant give my word as to this, not having any great degree of peace in which to write.

Thank you for sending check. Did Devine speak to you about a pair of dingy pigskin gloves which I left on the smoking table in your office one day? If you still have them, will you send them to me? I've only had them eight years and they are just exactly ripe now.

Bill

[1] The title, *If I Forget Thee, Jerusalem,* would be changed to *The Wild Palms*.

To Robert K. Haas — TS. RH
Dec. 21 [1937] — Oxford

Dear Bob:

This is a belated moment to ask if the signed agreement reached you. I suppose it did though?

The novel is coming pretty well; I found less trouble than I anticipated in getting back into the habit of writing, though I find that at forty I dont write quite as fast as I used to. It should be done by May first, though.

Meanwhile, will you please send me the next three of my checks, leaving one in your possession? No, send all four of them to me, registered. I had a talk with Bennett before I left, and also with my lawyer here, and I realise that it will be almost impossible to conceal this business from the questions of a lawyer in court without committing perjury. So I think I shall endorse one of them back to you and so reestablish my advance credit on the novel at $2000.00, with the others I will pay my income tax in full, also other debts, and keep about $1000.00 in cash to live on, and when that's gone, we'll all just have to sweat it out.

This letter can be an acknowledgement in full for all private funds of mine you held, or send your receipt and I will sign it.

Best regards, and best wishes of the season.

[s] William Faulkner
[t] William Faulkner

To Eric J. Devine
Dec. 28 [1937]

TS. ERIC J. DEVINE
[Oxford]

Dear Jim:

. . . .

Novel going pretty well. I have about a third of it done, should come in under the wire May first with my tail up and my eyes flashing; under blankets even.

Beautiful balmy spring weather now, overcast and muggy, some rain. My pointer works well and I shoot quail almost every day. My back has about broken me of sleeping, so I write at night. I will have to have some grafting, as one spot is not going to cover. But I am putting that off until after quail shooting is over, as it will lay me up for about a month: no stooping, lifting, etc.

Give my best to Hal.

Bill

To Morton Goldman
19 February, 1938

TS. FCVA
Oxford, Mississippi

Dear Morty:

The agreements on 'The Unvanquished' sale have come and I have signed and returned them. So I imagine it will go through, so now you and I can try to get together about your commission. I take your letter of Feb. 8 to mean that you understand yourself to be due 10% of the sale price of all these stories which comprise the book which MGM bought. According to your resume of any discussion on the subject of material handled by you, this was understood (that is, you had agent's rights in all resales of the same material) between us, but that I myself would handle all novels, etc.

I understood this to mean that you were to sell and resell any material I sent to you as often and to what market you could, and take your commission, until I should recall such material from circulation, my only reason for recalling it naturally being either to rewrite it or collect it into a volume, in the first case, that of rewriting it to make it more salable to a market other than my publisher, upon returning it to you it would have become a new material. In the second case, that of collection for book publication, it would cease to be a matter between you and me and become one between the publisher and myself under the contract I had with him. I understood it to mean that only stories which you had actually sold would come under either of these categories; when I recalled COURAGE to make PYLON out of it, because of the fact that I might not have left it with you long enough for you to have sold it and so been recompensed, I (as I thought) voluntarily offered to share any money derived from it outside of book sales; didn't I even send you the novel mss. first to try it on studios?

On the premise of the above being my understanding of the relations between us, I consider that I owe you a commission on 'An Odor of Verbena,' which like 'COURAGE' you tried to sell and failed through no fault of your own, because you have already taken your commission on the other six when you handled them singly, and the present sale of them as a unit was made not by you, though you could have attempted this (and may have) at any time after they began to be printed singly and after they were all printed complete, which was in October, 1936, but by the publisher himself on a contract I made with him on the day he accepted them in their rewritten state as an approximate novel. So my contention is, since you had the offering of 'An Odor of Verbena' and derived no compensation because of the fact that I wished to call it in unaltered, I owe you a commission on this under the Pylon terms. And since I have had a stroke of good luck and nobody knows it better than I and so I would like to share it with those who were associated with it, I figure your commission on the gross of the sale instead of my net after the publisher has taken his share. That would be 10% of one seventh of $25,000.00, which is $357.14.

Let me hear from you at once.

Yours,
Bill

I'm in fair shape now. Will finish a novel this spring, and for a year or so now I can write in leisure, when and what I want to write, as I have always someday fondly dreamed, etc.

[in ink:] Will send your check as soon as the studio check comes through. It may blow up yet; I wont believe it until I have the money.

To Morton Goldman — TS. FCVA
28 February, 1938 — Oxford, Miss.

Dear Morty:

I have your letter about commission, and your offer to compromise at 5%. I figure the commission as follows:

The price paid Random House and me was $25,000.00. Under contract as co-owner, Random House gets 20%. I received $20,000.00. Five percent, is $1,000.00.

I wish we had settled such a contingency as this before hand, had had an understanding about it. It was my fault we didn't, as you brought up the matter of a contract between us and I declined, believing as I did that agents' equities in mss. did not extend to collections in volumes, etc. But that was my fault, and I am grateful for your offer to compromise, even though I do feel I have been screwed about 600.00 worth. But then, you probably feel you have been screwed 1,000.00, which is worse, I reckon.

Yours,
[no signature]

To Robert K. Haas — TS. RH
April 1, 1938 — [Oxford]

Dear Bob:

I do not think I can possibly have the novel in your hands by June, though I do have two months yet, and I once wrote an entire book in six weeks.[1]

I have had a bad experience with my back, which has never healed. At the end of February I had the place skin-grafted. The grafts did not take. I became disgusted, I said to hell with it, let it all rot off and be damned. I was a little mad, I think, nerves frayed from three months' pretty constant pain and inability to sleep. So I got it infected and had to have the wound scraped and constantly treated for the past two weeks, from which I am just recovering—bromides, etc. I have just got back at the book today, though I still feel pretty bad. I would guess that I have the mss. somewhere between a third and a half done, nearer the third than the half. So for your sake [*in ink:* of your plans] I will say I shant have the mss. in by June. I'll get on with it, of course, steadily now, I believe, but probably slowly.

Regards to everyone.

Bill

[1] Faulkner frequently said that he wrote *As I Lay Dying* in six weeks.

To Random House — TELEGRAM RH
17 June 1938 — Oxford, Miss.

NOVEL FINISHED. SOME REWRITING DUE TO BACK COMPLICATIONS. SENDING IT ON IN A FEW DAYS. WILLIAM FAULKNER

To Robert K. Haas TS. RH
8 July, 1938 Oxford

Dear Bob:

I was glad to read your letter. I have lived for the last six months in such a peculiar state of family complications and back complications that I still am not able to tell if the novel is all right or absolute drivel. To me, it was written just as if I had sat on the one side of a wall and the paper was on the other and my hand with the pen thrust through the wall and writing not only on invisible paper but in pitch darkness too, so that I could not even know if the pen still wrote on paper or not.

About objectionable words. There are more than just one. Do you want them all out? Might just as well be consistent. It could be done as I have done it before, substitute a dot for each deleted letter, like this:

"Women, ...," the tall convict said.

This should whitewash it sufficiently, shouldn't it? It is only what people see that shocks them, not what they think or hear, and they will recognise these words or not and no harm done in either case. But these words are exactly the ones which my characters would have used and no other, and there are a few people whom I hope will read the book, among whom the preservation of my integrity as a faithful (even though not always successful) portrayer of living men and women is dear enough for me to wish not to betray it, even in trifles.

Or why not let me swap you the objectionable words for the title? you to do as you see fit about the words, and let the title stand? The movies could change it as they did Sanctuary, and I think it is a good title. It invented itself as a title for the chapter in which Charlotte died and where Wilbourne said 'Between grief and nothing I will take grief' and which is the theme of the whole book, the convict story being just counterpoint to sharpen it, just as 'The Unvanquished' was the title of the story of Granny's struggle between her morality and her children's needs, which was the theme of that book and which we extended to cover the whole book successfully. Dont you think this title might do the same?

Thank you very much about the money, and bless you for the kindness of it. I am all right for a while. . . . I invested most of the movie money in business. . . . But I still have some of it left, though not enough to buy my own freedom yet and not enough to buy an aeroplane, which I had intended to buy when Unvanquished sold. But I still have $1000.00 of those checks of last winter hidden, and I am thinking about going to England for a month perhaps about September. But I will see you in the fall, anyway.

Back is pretty good now. It still cracks open when I exercise too violently; seems to be a drawn muscle somewhere. A good masseur could fix me up I imagine, if I had one.

Thank Bennett for sending the Roosevelt speeches.[1] I should have written him but I failed to as usual. I should get a royalty statement this month, shouldn't I? I would like to know what Unvanquished did.

Bill

[1] *The Public Papers and Addresses of Franklin D. Roosevelt*, 5 vols. (New York, 1938).

To Mrs. William Faulkner — MS. JFSA
Sunday [postmarked 10 Oct. 1938] — Hotel Algonquin

Jillykin's Scots plaids should come today. I know they are too big, but you will know how to fix them. She will have room to grow in them now. Tell Buddy[1] I saw good football game Sat. at West Point, Army vs. Columbia. C-20, Army 18, a regular last minute hair raiser, Army 18, Columbia 13, 12 minutes to play, ball on Columbia's 20 yard line, Army loses on downs and failed field goal, Columbia makes steady drive of 80 yards, 9 plays. 5 first downs on 4 20 yd. passes, wins. Rest of novel galley proofs will be finished tomorrow. I think I can leave here Wednesday. . . .

Pappy

[1] Malcolm A. Franklin.

To Robert K. Haas — TS. RH
[received 15 Dec. 1938] — [Oxford]

Dear Bob:

I am working at the Snopes book. It will be in three books, whether big enough to be three separate volumes I dont know yet, though I think it will. The first one I think will run about 80,000 words. I am half through with it. Three chapters have been printed in mags. as short stories, though not in my collections yet.

The title is THE PEASANTS. Has to do with Flem Snopes' beginning in the country, as he gradually consumes a small village until there is nothing left in it for him to eat. His last coup gains him a foothold in Jefferson, to which he moves with his wife, leaving his successor kinsmen to carry on in the country.

The second volume is RUS IN URBE. He begins to trade on his wife's infidelity, modest blackmail of her lover, rises from half owner of back street restaurant through various grades of city employment, filling each post he vacates with another Snopes from the country, until he is secure in the presidency of a bank, where he can even stop blackmailing his wife's lover.

The third volume is ILIUM FALLING. This is the gradual eating-up of Jefferson by Snopes, who corrupt the local government with crooked politics, buy up all the colonial homes and tear them down and chop up the lots into subdivisions.

This is the plot, if any. Flem gets his wife because she is got with child by a sweetheart who clears out for Texas; for a price he protects her good name. No, before this, his youngest brother tries to keep his father from setting fire to his landlord's barn, believes he has caused the father to be shot, and runs away from home,[1] goes west, has a son which the other Snopes know nothing about.

Flem moves to town with his wife whose child pretty soon sees what a sorry lot Snopes are. She goes to New York (has money from her actual father) and is overseas in the War with ambulance corps, where she meets the son of the boy who ran away from home, finds him a kinsman, finds how his father has tried to eradicate the Snopes from him. After the war she brings together this Snopes and the daughter of a collateral Snopes who also looks with horror on Snopeses. She and her remote cousin marry, have a son who is the scion of the family.

What this will tell is, that this flower and cream, this youth, whom his mother and father fondly believed would raise the family out of the muck, turns out to have all the vices of all Snopes and none of the virtues—the ruthlessness and firmness—of his banker uncle, the chief of the family. He has not enough courage and honesty to be a successful bootlegger nor enough industry to be the barber for which he is finally trained after Flem has robbed his mother of what money her father and husband left her. He is in bad shape with syphilis and all the little switch-tailed nigger whores call him by his first name in private and he likes it.

By this time Flem has eaten up Jefferson too. There is nothing else he can gain, and worse than this, nothing else he wants. He even has no respect for the people, the town, he has victimised, let alone the parasite kin who batten on him. He reaches the stage where there is just one more joke he can play on his environment, his parasite kin and all. So he leaves all his property to the worthless boy, knowing that no other Snopes has sense enough to hold onto it, and that at least this boy will get rid of it in the way that will make his kinfolks the maddest.

It ends like this. Flem is dead, all the kin have come in to the funeral, to see what they are going to get. The boy, who does not know he is the heir since his uncle will hardly speak to him on the street, needs money for something, is convinced his uncle will leave him nothing, waits till everybody is gone to the funeral and breaks into Flem's house to see what he can find. All he finds is a signed photograph to Flem's pseudo daughter, from her actual father. The boy thinks he is his aunt's lover, takes enough whiskey to brave himself up, goes to the aunt to blackmail her with the picture. She practically scares him to death, he gets drunker than ever, is sitting in a backroom some where with his friends bolstering him up, he will probably get a hundred dollars in the will, etc., so that finally he tilts his hat, struts along the street, passes two nigger girls who say 'Hi, knocker' out of the sides of their mouths, he replies, 'Hi, bitches' and goes on.

. . . .

[s] Bill
[s] William Faulkner

[1] The youngest brother's story became "Barn Burning," which would appear in *Harper's*, CLXXIX (June 1939), 86–96.

To Bennett Cerf — TS. RH
[received 19 Jan. 1939] — [Oxford]

Dear Bennett:

Excuse lateness of this. I am close to half done with the first volume of this proposed Snopes book, and I have been so busy at it that I have just got around to correspondence.[1] Your advertising approach sounds all right to me, but then Random House usually is, aint it?

This volume will be about 80,000–100,000 words I think. I'll send it in as soon as I finish it, which should be about April. Do you think you will publish it at once, or wait for the other two? You could print them as I write them, under the titles I wrote Bob about, later print them all in one volume, about 1,000 pages, call it SNOPES.

I am grateful for the checks as sent now. It may be I will have to have some money, maybe $1,000.00 at income tax time. If so, can I have this sum off the tail end of the present $150.00 a month arrangement, which would leave six 150.00 checks in place of 13?

Will you send a copy of Wild Palms to Mrs Wolfgang Rebner, 166 West 72 st.

Bill F

Copy of book to Eric Devine, 334 West 70.
" Sherwood Anderson, Marion, Virginia

[1] The book in progress was called *The Peasants*, which would later become *The Hamlet*.

To Robert K. Haas — TS. RH
[received 7 Feb. 1939] — [Oxford]

Dear Bob:

I have 215 pages on the new one. There is another chapter, about forty. The last two chapters are already written, with rewriting to tie them into it. I would get nowhere trying to tell you about it. Maybe the best thing would be to send it on in. What shall I do? The mss is in about the same condition as if I had all The Unvanquished except the last three stories, one of which needs to be written entire, the last two waiting for something to hang them onto it. It takes Flem Snopes from when he first appears in his father-in-law's country store, until he gets the wherewith to move to Jefferson on.

[no signature]

To Robert K. Haas TS. RH
[received 17 Mar. 1939] [Oxford]

Dear Bob:

By express [*in ink:* in a few days] Books 1 and 2 of the mss. There will be two more books, which will complete the first volume, THE PEASANTS. I will send them in as I finish them.

I want some advice from you, both as a friend and as one familiar with the financial prospects of a writer, the emoluments of this more or less unpredictable profession. That is, I ask the advice because a publisher would know more how to answer, and I ask it of you because of friendship.

When I first went to the movies, I believed I saw there a sort of small gold mine which I could work at will and at need more or less for the rest of my active writing life. I undertook to buy some insurance, under that expectation; I had already discovered I would be unable to carry it otherwise.

I found pretty soon that I was not a movie writer, yet I continued to carry the insurance as long as I drew money from Cal. I now believe that movies are done as far as I am concerned, unless they should buy my novels, etc. Therefore I can see a time in the near future when these premiums will be difficult to meet and perhaps even impossible, unless I should produce a book which the movies would want—which God Himself could not promise Himself to write.

I pay on three policies, 1 $650.00 premium, 1 $350.00 premium, 1 annuity $600.00 premium. I have paid them five or six years. If I should be killed flying, the $650.00 becomes void, the other two will be paid. The $650.00 is due now. I think I had better cash it in for what I can get now instead of scratching around to meet it this time and then have to let it go next year. I might possibly be able to carry the other two for a while longer then.

What would you do in this case? I have no other source to get money from than by writing, and, as you know, that is already mortgaged ahead of me. I have a big family to support, and a fair investment in property to protect. My farm will not produce enough profit above supporting itself to be counted upon for $1600.00 insurance premiums each year. I have no other source save to borrow from publishers on work I have not even written yet. I tried last month to put the novel aside and hammer out a pot-boiler story to meet this premium with, but I failed, either the novel is too hot in my mind or I failed to keep from stewing over having to make a home run in one lick, to cook up a yarn. So my feeling is, I had better let this immediate policy go, continue with the novel, either meet or renege on the other two as they fall due, and when this first volume is finished, try then to sell some short stories.

I hope you can give me your cold opinion on this as a theoretical case—whether I should borrow the money (probably from Random House but not necessarily so; if you like, keep this out of your mind when you weigh the matter) and make this payment, or let it go now and save the money.

Sorry to trouble you with this, but I want the opinion of a man familiar with the prospects and emoluments of the writing profession.

Bill

To Robert K. Haas TS. RH
[received 22 Mar. 1939] [Oxford]

Dear Bob, I think you are right. Thank you for the letter. I will follow that advice.

I mailed you the signed contracts last Saturday, the day after your wire? You have not got them?

I have a friend here, I have known him all my life, never any question of mine and thine between us when either had it.[1] His father died few years ago, estate badly involved, is being sued on $7000.00 note, which will cause whole business to be sold up. He must have money in 3 weeks. How much can Random House let me have? Of course I will sign any thing, contracts, etc. I should be able to realise something when I cancel insurance policy, can use sum you mentioned in your letter. I have all my original manuscript, most of them in handwriting. I will sell or mortgage. Can you suggest anyone I might approach? $6000.00 is what we have to raise. He has $1000.00. I dont have to tell you matter can not be compromised. I would not have mentioned this sum if any less would do. If you will name what sum you can allow, I will know then just what difference to try to raise. It will probably be hard to find anyone to buy mss. but that is best chance I see now. I would not want to sell any of it unless I was sure of getting what he must have.

[no signature]

[1] Phil Stone.

To Robert K. Haas — TS. RH
March 25, 1939 — Oxford, Mississippi

Dear Bob:—

Excuse me for being so indefinite in the return of the contracts.

Thank you very much for the check. I did not mean to hold you up at once, but since you were kind enough to send it, it will save any further correspondence.

About the status of it—the present book will be in three volumes, which I will send to you in sections as I finish them. They could be published as each complete volume is sent in, or you could hold them until all three are done. I think of the one contract as covering all three of them, although if you prefer to send me two more contracts to cover the next two volumes, I will sign them right away. Or if you prefer to send me a contract titled in blank to cover the effort succeeding these three volumes, or this present work, I will sign that;—or you might send me a note for this balance of $1200.00. This seems to be an Alphonse and Gaston tableau, as whatever you prefer will be agreeable to me.

What little preference I have is toward considering this $1200.00 as a loan to be discharged when my royalties accrue to that amount at any time. But if it is simpler for your bookkeeping to call this an advance on some subsequent contract, send whatever contract you wish along, I will get it back to you by return mail.

Along with the insurance policy, this will take care of the business.

Thanking you very much again, and best regards,

Yours,
Bill

WCF: sp[1]

[1] This letter was probably typed in Stone's office by his secretary.

To Robert K. Haas — TS. RH
Wednesday [29 Mar. 1939] — [Oxford]

Dear Bob:

I am hashing all this over to you to explain next request.

I now have your 3,000.00. I will get about 3,300.00 from *annuity* policy. Agent advises me to hold on to insurance policies a while longer, as it will not pay as much as annuity, and I would be unable to buy it again.

The 650.00 premium is due now. Also, the 1400.00 of the 3,000.00 is my subsistence for this year. Therefore, I must hold back this 1400.00 plus the 650.00 premium, plus 330.00 premium due in September. This will leave me 2400.00 or thereabout short of my 6,000.00, not to mention the additional 1200.00 needed to complete the 7200.00 due on the mortgage.

There is a banker who has intimated that he might make up the rest of the sum needed before Friday week, on my note, if I can secure the note by giving him an assignment on royalties. I could, or he will accept, an assignment on Random House for royalties to that amount when *due for payment.* I explained books are made up July and Jan. 1, payment due after that. I will explain payment is due when publisher's books are complete for term, may be 3,4,5 months, but no longer. Naturally I will not promise him any definite sum, but royalties only as they are earned. That is, once he is into it, he can only renew note if royalties are not that much. Will you allow me to do this?

Let me know what you think of the novel I am sending in, when you have time to read it.

Incidentally, I may have enough short stories to make another volume. What do you think about it?

Bill

To Robert K. Haas — TS. RH

[received 24 Apr. 1939] — [Oxford]

Dear Bob:

The enclosed pages insert into the manuscript which you have. I have tried to be especially careful with them, indicating on blank sheets among the pages just what sheets are to be lifted from the old copy. They should dovetail. But of course it will be wise to hold on to the discarded sheets and let me give them a check-over when I have finished.

The book was getting too thin, diffuse. I have tightened it up, added some more here and there to give it density, make the people stand up. As you can see, the portion you have, as corrected, constitutes but *one* book, which is BOOK ONE, Chapters 1–5. There will be two books in the first volume. That is, this is about half of it, possibly a little more. I guess about 400 pages entire. I suggest you have someone make these substitutions who will read the mss. for sense as he goes, and *renumber* the old pages to fit the new sequence, but WITHOUT COMPLETELY OBLITERATING THE OLD NUMBERS so that we can check back and forth from here if necessary. But I hope to come East in the Fall and give the complete mss. a look-over.

Bill

[in pen:] I am the best in America, by God.

To Robert K. Haas — TS. RH
Saturday [received 3 May 1939] — [Oxford]

Dear Bob:

Yours of 25 April received. Hold the script, and the sheets on which I indicated in handwriting where substitutions go. When I finish the Book Two, which will complete volume one, I will know better when I can come East. If it is along toward September, when my crops are finished,[1] I will come up and fetch the rest of the first volume, and put the first book in order. If not, there will be plenty of time then to send your batch back to me, and I will get it all straight.

Am going to try a Memphis bank re. the assignment matter next week. I will let you know at once if they will accept assignment on you for royalties when due to $3,000.00. I can make the grade on that. I cashed in one insurance policy for enough to pay premiums on the other two, pay remaining income tax installments, and leave my remainder of $2,000.00 intact. God knows what I will do after it is gone. Maybe what I need is a bankruptcy, like a soldier needs delousing.

Bill

[1] Faulkner had invested part of the proceeds from the sale of *The Unvanquished* to MGM in Greenfield Farm. See his letter to Haas of 8 July 1938.

To Random House — TS. RH
Monday [probably mid-Aug. 1939] — [Oxford]

Dear Sirs:

There are two more chapters after this. They are already printed as short stories, will need some rewriting, I dont know how much. I have had to put the mss. aside twice to write short stories to keep pot boiling, will have to hammer out another one now. Then I will get back at the mss. I should have it all done by Oct 10. I want to come to town then. I will polish mss. up while there.

I am pinched for money this year. Have no business coming up at all, but shall do so if I can. What chance of finding myself some place to stay for a month or so, cheaper than usual hotel? Not boarding house, and I wont care where it is. Do you suppose I can find a room, about 50$ a month, where I can do as I like, go and come as I like. I could then buy liquor, and cadge grub from you all.

Bill

To Saxe Commins TS. RH
[Oct. 1939] [Washington, D.C.]

Saxe—

Here is the last chapter, first volume complete in your hands, correct?
Suggested titles:

Vol. one THE HAMLET
Vol. two THE TOWN
Vol. three THE MANSION

What do you think about naming these chapters? Some already printed as short stories & already named. Not important.

Acknowledgements:

Saturday Evening Post. Last Chapter, Book Four, LIZARDS IN JAMSHYD'S COURTYARD.

Scribner's. Chap. 2, Book One. FOOL ABOUT A HORSE. Chap. 1, Book Four. SPOTTED HORSES

Harper's. Chap. 2, Book Three. THE HOUND

Possible inconsistency in chronology. I seem to remember it, but not where.

Book Four happens in 1890, approximately. Hence Civil War ended 25 years ago. Have recollection of dating War somewhere in script as 40 years ago. Please watch for it. I will catch it in galley if you have not.

[in pen:] In Washington today.[1] Will come up before I go home maybe Saturday. Will wire.

[no signature]

[1] About 10 Oct. 1939, Faulkner testified in a plagiarism trial in Washington arising out of the film *The Road to Glory*.

To Robert K. Haas TS. RH
[received 29 Nov. 1939] [Oxford]

Dear Bob:

Is this some kind of cash prize, or is it just honor? I hadn't heard about it.[1]

Unless I am summonsed back to Washington on that trial, where my expenses will be paid, I wont come East. No money at all now. Incidentally, I consider myself to really have done pretty good this year. Collected on two stories so far, $1400.00. Most of what I got from you I loaned to a friend. Statement from you showed I am something like $300.00 in red. That means I have not earned enough to have much tax to pay next year and more or less lived within modest income and got a novel written. I will finish book as soon as I can. I am going to need about $2000.00 before Jan. 1, and I am trying to write short stories and earn it. If I can put bee on Sat Eve Post twice, I will get back at novel.

Bill

[1] Faulkner was glad to learn that the first O. Henry Memorial Award for the best short story in an American magazine during the year, bestowed upon "Barn Burning," carried a prize of $300.

To Robert K. Haas — TS. RH

Monday [received 7 Dec. 1939] — [Oxford]

Dear Bob:

I have been notified that I shall be called to Washington again on that trial; I understand it will be some time this week. I wasted a month writing two stories to sell to Sat. Eve. Post, which they refused, obvious reason being that I need money, was trying too hard to write mechanical stories in which I had no faith while my mind was still on the novel; hence a bust. Last week I got at the novel again. I believe, by keeping at it until I am called to Wash. and bringing script along to work at when I can, that I will have it done by Jan. 1 as planned. This is provided I cant kick another plot story out of what I call my mind to write in meantime, though I believe I can do both by Jan. 1. By God, I have got to.

I have heard nothing from O. Henry prize yet, though I have not written anyone.

In statement received about Oct. 1, my accrued royalties appeared about $3,000.00. This was to be minus Memphis bank's note of $1700.00. After my visit in New York, when I drew money, statement by letter showed I was in red about $150.00. You sent $150.00 more by wire. I assumed at time that these two statements included all money drawn by me to date. They did *not* include the last $2,000.00 advance you gave me?

In either case, can I have $500.00? If yes, write me first and hold check until you hear from me again. If statements did *not* include last $2000.00, that advance will apply to the book which I am about to complete, will it not? So that will be clear when I send in mss, and the $500.00 can be advance on next volume, which I shall get at soon. But first, I am going to make myself some money. This is a nuisance to you, and a damned nuisance to me. I'm going to take about six months of next year and try to write stuff that will make me a bank account for a little while, for the rest of the year anyway. If I have $500.00 from Random H. and the $300.00 prize and hang something on Post for $1000.00 by first of year, I will have a breather in which to invent salable stuff without having to haunt the post office for the check to pay coal and grocery bills with.

Bill

On 31 January 1940, Caroline Barr died. "Mammy Callie" had come to work for William Faulkner's parents in 1902, shortly after their move from Ripley to Oxford. In a funeral service in the parlor at Rowan Oak, Faulkner delivered the eulogy over her body.

To Robert K. Haas — TS. RH
5 Feb. [1940] — [Oxford]

Dear Bob:

Galley being returned today.[1] Sorry I am late with it, but the old hundred-year-old matriarch who raised me died suddenly from a stroke last Saturday night, lingering until Wednesday, so I have had little of heart or time either for work. Therefore I read carefully only about half-way through galley, after that I merely answered indicated queries. But it seems to be a very clear printing, and from what of it I did read word for word, the mss. was followed to the letter. So I am sure it's all right.

The old lady was about 95. The old records were lost years ago, after she was freed, and we didnt know for certain. Yet up to Saturday night she could hear perfectly and thread needles and sew by lamplight, and would walk for several miles. She didn't suffer. She had a paralytic stroke in the kitchen just before supper, had lost consciousness within 30 minutes and never regained it, died Wednesday while my wife was sitting beside her bed. She couldn't have gone better, more happily.

Sold $1,000.00 story and am in fair condition.[2]

Bill

[1] *The Hamlet.*
[2] "A Point of Law," *Collier's*, CV (22 June 1940), 20–21, 30, 32.

Faulkner also wrote about Mammy Callie's death to May Bell Barr, her daughter.

To May Bell Barr — TS. JFSA
February 7, 1940 — Oxford, Mississippi

Dear May Bell:

Mammy's last years were, I hope pleasant and peaceful. She had her half a house in my back yard, close to my house. A young couple live in the other half of her house. They were very good to her. The man kept her in wood and such, and they were handy to hear her if she took sick or needed anything. She took her meals in my house, and spent most of her time with my little girl, seven years old.

She was stricken while sitting in the kitchen just before supper one Saturday night. We put her to bed and she went into a coma at once and never waked again, though she lived until the next Wednesday. When she died, Mrs. Falkner was with her. She was buried last Sunday in the cemetery here. I'll be glad to show you her grave if you ever come to Oxford.

William Faulkner

The Memphis Commercial Appeal *had recorded Faulkner's brief remarks at the service for Mammy Callie, and they had reached Bob Haas through an account carried by one of the wire services. Haas sent it to Faulkner.*

To Robert K. Haas — TS. RH
Wednesday [7 Feb. 1940] — Oxford

Dear Bob:

Thank you for note and clipping. This is what I said, and when I got it on paper afterward, it turned out to be pretty good prose:

'Caroline has known me all my life. It was my privilege to see her out of hers. After my father's death, to Mammy I came to represent the head of that family to which she had given a half century of fidelity and devotion. But the relationship between us never became that of master and servant. She still remained one of my earliest recollections, not only as a person, but as a fount of authority over my conduct and of security for my physical welfare, and of active and constant affection and love. She was an active and constant precept for decent behavior. From her I learned to tell the truth, to refrain from waste, to be considerate of the weak and respectful to age. I saw fidelity to a family which was not hers, devotion and love for people she had not borne.

'She was born in bondage and with a dark skin and most of her early maturity was passed in a dark and tragic time for the land of her birth. She went through vicissitudes which she had not caused; she assumed cares and griefs which were not even her cares and griefs. She was paid wages for this, but pay is still just money. And she never received very much of that, so that she never laid up anything of this world's goods. Yet she accepted that too without cavil or calculation or complaint, so that by that very failure she earned the gratitude and affection of the family she had conferred the fidelity and devotion upon, and gained the grief and regret of the aliens who loved and lost her.

'She was born and lived and served, and died and now is mourned; if there is a heaven, she has gone there.'

Bill

To Harold Ober
7 Feb., 1940

TS. FCVA
Oxford, Miss.

Dear Mr. Ober:

I dont have a copy of the story.[1] I transcribed from a rough draft.

It's fine you got a good price for it; I can certainly use the money at present. Do Collier's pay on acceptance, or on publication? I would like to know when to expect it, as, if it will not come in soon, I shall have to raise the wind somewhere by March first, when I have a note at bank.

In straightening up my desk, I found an old letter of yours mentioning a story called A RETURN.[2] I remember this title, but I cant quite place the story. Do you still have it? and could you name a character or so, then I will remember it.

Sincerely,
William Faulkner

[1] "A Point of Law."
[2] A rewritten version of "Rose of Lebanon."

To Harold Ober
[received 18 Mar. 1940]

TS. FCVA
[Oxford]

This is the good story I mentioned in my recent letter.[1] Hope some one takes it quick. If so, will you get check to me soon as possible? Govt. has put the finger on me for more tax on my 1937 income, and I was broke even before that.

[no signature]

[1] "Pantaloon in Black," which appeared in *Harper's*, CLXXXI (Oct. 1940), 503–13.

To Mrs. M. L. Stone[1] TS. JFSA
Saturday [postmarked 6 Apr. 1940] Oxford, Miss.

Dear Maggie Lea:

Thank you for sending the tax receipts. Reason for lateness in acknowledging your kindness is, I had hoped to do so in person, when returning the book, which I had hoped to return by hand because of its value. But as I see no prospect of soon being in Coffeeville, I am sending the book by insured mail today.

It is the only one I have. The other volume you mentioned I do not find here, and my recollection is that I borrowed from Mr Will only THE PLANTATION OVERSEER, though I have looked among my books to make sure.[2] Being a book man myself, I try to be very careful with all books, and with borrowed ones particularly, and with any of the nature of these documentary-historical-personal records such as I would have borrowed from Mr Will, I would have been more careful than ever because of their rarity and value. That is why I feel sure that my recollection is right, and THE PLANTATION OVERSEER is the only one he loaned to me.

Let me hear from you again about the missing one. I know how you feel about it, and I will make any effort within my power to find the book. If I had it, it should still be here in my home. I have not stopped looking for it each time I go through my library, getting books in order and such, but my recollection is that I had only the one which I am returning.

Sincerely yours,
William Faulkner

[1] The daughter of Mr. and Mrs. Will C. Bryant, from whom Faulkner bought Rowan Oak and surrounding property.

[2] The proper title was probably *The Southern Plantation Overseer, As Revealed in His Letters*, John Spencer Basset, ed. (Northampton, Mass., 1925).

To Robert K. Haas TS. RH
Thursday [18 Apr. 1940] [Oxford]

Dear Bob:

This is a joint letter to Bennett also, in regard to his letter about the broadcasting business. I could not come up and do it because I did not have railroad fare to New York at the time, and in the second place the Fed. Govt. had made demand on me for additional $450.00 1937 income tax; I was due in New Orleans on that same Tuesday to try to get it deferred. I now have until July 1 to pay it.

In addition to that 450, due then, I need about five hundred now. I can get that by a mortgage on some of my horses and mules at the bank.

If I mortgage them though, I cannot sell them. So I want to do what I did last summer at the Memphis bank—give an assignment on royalties accrued Nov. 1. Do you remember this transaction last summer? Will you send me an assignment due that date, sum of $1,000.00, leave the bank's name blank, which I can hold until needed, then go to the bank, whatever bank will accept it as collateral, insert the bank's name and have you ratify by wire if necessary? The one of last year was First National Bank of Memphis; they should do the same thing again. But if the bank's name is left in blank, I can shop around with it. I have three short stories with Ober which may sell. But I need the 500.00 at once, beside the 450.00 July 1, and I dont want to keep my stock mortgaged where I cannot sell them when the price is offered.

What I am trying to prevent is drawing any more money against royalties in advance from the firm. I have got my account with you down under five hundred, not counting THE HAMLET, and I want to keep it that way until it shows black again if possible. This alternative will come to the same thing, beside the interest, but at least it will be the bank's money and not the firm's. I have written 4 short stories this year and I would have been all right if they sold as I wrote them. But maybe a man worrying about money cant write anything worth buying, and I have been stewing all year about that damn assessment for income spent 3 years ago. I'm a lug of the first water; what I should do (or any artist) is give all my income and property to the bloody govt. and go on WPA forever after.

Bill

To Robert K. Haas — TS. RH

Sunday [28 Apr. 1940] — [Oxford]

Dear Bob:

Your letter about assignment of royalties is at hand. I will make use of it after hearing from this one.

I need $1,000.00 now, to pay debts and current bills. I want $9,000.00 more, say $400.00 per month over two years.

I had planned, after finishing THE HAMLET, to try to earn enough from short stories by July 1 to carry me through the year, allow me six months to write another novel. I wrote six short stories by March 15, trying to write the sort of pot boilers which the Post pays me $1,000.00 each for, because the best I could hope for good stories is 3 or 4 hundred, and the only mag. to buy them is Harper's etc.

So I wrote the six stories, but only one of them has sold yet. Actually I would have been better off now if I had written the good ones. Now I have not only wasted the mental effort and concentration which went into the trash, but the six months between November, when I finished THE

HAMLET, and March 15, when I finished the last story, as well as the time since March 15 which I have spent mortgaging my mares and colts one at a time to pay food and electricity and washing and such, and watching each mail train in hopes of a check.

Now I have about run out of mules to mortgage. I can raise the thousand on the assignment. By the time I have paid the income tax assessment and a note at the bank here, that will be gone. And I will still have to keep trying to write trash stories which so far are not selling even fifty percent., because I am now like the gambler who simply has to double and pyramid, the poker player who can neither call nor throw in his hand but has got to raise. I have a blood-and-thunder mystery novel which should sell[1] (they usually do) but I dont dare devote six months to writing, haven't got six months to devote to it. I have another in mind in method similar to THE UNVANQUISHED, but since the chapters which I have written and tried to sell as short stories have not sold, I haven't the time to continue with it.[2]

Will Random House consider any sort of contract like this, say even $300.00 a month in addition to first $1,000.00. We can go into matter of security in case of my death later. If not, can I have your blessing to try somewhere else for some similar arrangement?

Bill

[1] Probably *Intruder in the Dust* (1948).

[2] *Go Down, Moses* (1942).

To Robert K. Haas — TS. RH

Friday [3 May 1940] — [Oxford]

Dear Bob:

Letter received. Your promptness was kind, your response comforting, your suggestion generous.

Every so often, in spite of judgment and all else, I take these fits of sort of raging and impotent exasperation at this really quite alarming paradox which my life reveals: Beginning at the age of thirty I, an artist, a sincere one and of the first class, who should be free even of his own economic responsibilities and with no moral conscience at all, began to become the sole, principal and partial support—food, shelter, heat, clothes, medicine, kotex, school fees, toilet paper and picture shows—of my mother . . . [a] brother's widow and child, a wife of my own and two step children, my own child; I inherited my father's debts and his dependents, white and black without inheriting yet from anyone one inch of land or one stick of furniture or one cent of money; the only thing I ever got for nothing, after the first pair of long pants I received (cost: $7.50) was the $300.00

O. Henry prize last year. I bought without help from anyone the house I live in and all the furniture; I bought my farm the same way. I am 42 years old and I have already paid for four funerals and will certainly pay for one more and in all likelihood two more beside that, provided none of the people in mine or my wife's family my superior in age outlive me, before I ever come to my own.

Now and then, when pressed or worried about money, I begin to seethe and rage over this. It does no good, and I waste time when I might and should be writing. I still hope some day to break myself of it. What I need is some East Indian process to attain to the nigger attitude about debt. One of them is discussing the five dollars he must pay before sunset to his creditor, canvasses all possibilities, completes the circle back to the point of departure, where there is simply no way under heaven for him to get five dollars, says at last, 'Well, anyway, he (the creditor) cant eat me.' 'How you know he cant?' the second says. 'Maybe he wont want to,' the first says.

I suggest this change in the plan you described. Ober has six stories of mine; surely some of them will sell somewhere soon. I have three more I intend writing soon, now that some of the money pressure is off my mind, thanks to your letter.

Our arrangement has been $2,000.00 advance on new mss. I understand from your letter that I have taken $500.00 on a novel which does not exist. Let me have $1,000.00 now. I will pay current bills, etc, make the balance last as long as possible. If necessary, let me have permission to draw $500.00 more to pay the income tax assessment which I have got deferred to July 1. Maybe after that I shant need more. But if I do, then let me take up the proposition, less of course what I have already drawn beyond schedule. If, at that time, I should be still in this same fix, I will try to arrange to do on, say, $200.00 per month. On the day the plan goes into effect, I will get at a novel. I think I have a good one; I intend to get at it soon anyway. It is a sort of Huck Finn—a normal boy of about twelve or thirteen, a big, warmhearted, courageous, honest, utterly unreliable white man with the mentality of a child, an old negro family servant, opinionated, querulous, selfish, fairly unscrupulous, and in his second childhood, and a prostitute not very young anymore and with a great deal of character and generosity and common sense, and a stolen race horse which none of them actually intended to steal. The story is how they travel for a thousand miles from hand to mouth trying to get away from the police long enough to return the horse. All of them save the white man think the police are after the horse. The white man knows the police have been put on his tail by his harridan of a wife whom he has fled from. Actually, the police are trying to return the boy to his parents to get the reward. The story lasts a matter of weeks. During that time the boy grows up, becomes a man, and a good man, mostly because of the influence of the whore. He goes through in miniature all the experiences of youth which mold the man's character. They happen to be the very experiences which in his middle class parents' eyes stand for debauchery and degeneracy and actual criminality; through them he learned courage and honor and generosity and pride and pity. He has been absent only weeks, but as soon as his mother sees him again, she knows what has happened to him. She weeps, says, 'He is not my baby anymore.'[1]

May I have the $1,000.00 at once?

Bill

[1] Faulkner used some elements of this story in *Notes on a Horsethief* (1951), which was revised for inclusion in *A Fable* (1954), and other elements in *The Reivers* (1961).

To Robert K. Haas — TS. RH
Wednesday [22 May 1940] — [Oxford]

Dear Bob:

Thank you for check. Will count on the $500.00 for July 1. Also, am sure I will need something each month about then too.

Do you want to consider a collection of short stories, most of them from magazines since 33 or 34, perhaps one or two unpublished yet? Could get it together in a month.

Also, Ober has four stories about niggers. I can build onto them, write some more, make a book like THE UNVANQUISHED, could get it together in six months, perhaps.[1]

If I get at the novel I described, I might need at least a year, during which time I shall have to be underwritten at least $200.00 a month. Incidentally, I know Ober will sell those stories when he can, but I'm just one frog in his puddle. When you see him, suppose you say something like this: 'If somebody dont buy something of Faulkner soon, I dont know what Random House will do.'

Bill

[1] *Go Down, Moses* (1942).

To Harold Ober — TS. FCVA
Monday. 27 May [1940] — [Oxford]

Dear Mr Ober:

All right about Barn Burning story reprint.

I suppose you have tried the stories on Esquire and Sat Evening Post.[1] I would have thought Harpers would take Pantaloon in Black.[2] Wish somebody would buy something. I'm so busy borrowing money from Random House I dont even have time to write.

Faulkner

[1] According to an Ober office notation on Faulkner's letter, "Gold Is Not Always" and "The Fire on the Hearth" were then at *Harper's*, but none of his stories had been sent to the *Post* or *Esquire*.

[2] According to another notation, "Pantaloon in Black" was at *Red Book*, with *Harper's* the next magazine to be tried.

To Robert K. Haas — TS. RH

Monday [27 May 1940] — [Oxford]

Dear Bob:

I imagine you have the signed contract by now. The reason it was late was, at the time of returning it I was in the middle of a letter about this business in Europe, then tore it up instead. Your note of yesterday gives me to believe you are in the same frame of mind. What a hell of a time we are facing. I got my uniform out the other day. I can button it, even after twenty-two years; the wings look as brave as they ever did. I swore then when I took it off in '19, that I would never wear another, nohow, nowhere, for no one. But now I dont know. Of course I could do no good, would last about two minutes in combat. But my feeling now is better so; that what will be left after this one will certainly not be worth living for.

Maybe the watching of all this coming to a head for the last year is why I cant write, dont seem to want to write, that is. But I can still write. That is, I haven't said at 42 all that is in the cards for me to say. And that wont do any good either, but surely it is still possible to scratch the face of the supreme Obliteration and leave a decipherable scar of some sort. Surely all these machines that can destroy a thousand lives or stamp out an entire car gassed and oiled and ready to run in two seconds, can preserve, even by blind mischance and a minute fault in gears or timing, some scrap here and there, provided it ever was worth preserving.

Will you send along the $500.00. I will pay the back income tax. Incidentally, it has gone up. It is now about $1300.00. Also, as far as you can foresee, can you send me something per month, beginning July 1? If not, say so. It might as well bust now as later. I believe I am about to get at a book of some sort. I might start at it anyway. But 150.00 or 200.00 sure each month will be pretty good to count on.

Bill

To Robert K. Haas **TS. RH**
Saturday [1 June 1940] [Oxford]

Dear Bob:

I believe we both understand the arrangement. I will state it again, or as I understand it.

I have signed with you a contract for a novel, new, original material, not a collection of short stories. After receiving $500.00 more, which I must have in order to submit income tax checks for tax in arrears, before July 1, 1940, I will have received an advance of $2000.00 on this contract.

If I make a connected book-length mss. from material written as short stories, such as Ober now has, you can exercise an option to print this volume in lieu of the one described in the above paragraph, if you wish. If you do not wish to do this, the contract regarding a new, original, intact novel still stands, with the $2000.00 advance already taken on it by me, and another agreement regarding this volume of connected material shall be entered into between us.

This letter to be your option on this volume of connected material, or on a possible collection of short stories, in return for which I may draw further advances against my general royalty account, the exact total amount to be agreed upon between us later. I would like to have at least $200.00 per month for possibly 12 months, this option to take effect when I draw the first money of this further advance or loan and to exist until you have received the specified mss. or until my accrued royalties on other books have discharged the loan or advance, or I have paid the loan in cash.

William Faulkner

That's it, isn't it? Tax situation is as follows: $450.00 to Fed. on 1937. $360.00 to state on 1938, which I had expected and had saved for until friend got in trouble last summer, and the same 1938 assessment from Fed, which will arrive at any time. I can pay Fed 300.00, state 200.00 before July 1, put off next installment to Oct 1. In Nov. I will get some revenue from farm, but meantime I need money for my family and mother's family. I believe if I had $400.00 a month I could quit stewing and get to work; would do better with $400.00 per month for 6 months than $200.00 per month for twelve. But (provided you wish to undertake it at all) $200.00 each month, beginning July 1, will be pretty fine. Will be at least 200.00 more than I have now.

I really meant what I said in my first letter. If you think this is a bad risk, say so. I have learned well what a goddamn nuisance anyone becomes who, each time you see or hear him, you think, 'How much does he want now?' You and Don and Bennett have been my good friends for a long time, and I would hate to spoil it like this.

Have tried tentatively for Hollywood job. But I am afraid that's out for me. No good for them.

Bill

To Robert K. Haas — TS. RH
Friday [7 June 1940] — [Oxford]

Dear Bob:

Yours of 4 also June 5 received.

$1,000.00 more advance on a new novel would be welcome, naturally. But it would only serve temporarily, and soon I should be almost as badly off as before.

That is, I am still, helped though I was by the recent $1,000.00, in the position where I need $9,000.00 more to give me economic freedom for two years, in which to write, or $5,000.00 more for one year. Otherwise, I will have to liquidate myself, sell some of my property for what I can get for it, in order to preserve what I might. I wont hesitate to do this when I come to believe that I have no other course. At present I still believe I have something else to sell in place of it—namely, the gamble on my literary output for the said two years, provided these two years will be free of pressure.

Here is the situation; I may have itemised it before:

Local debts		$1000.00
Note at Bank, due November		650.00
Amount due on another note		725.00
Income tax, 1937, due July 1		450.00
" 1938 "		350.00
" " anticipated,		350.00
Insurance premium, Oct. 1		333.00
" loan, due Feb. 1941		2400.00
Taxes " Jan. 1		400.00
Insurance premium, March 1, 1941		650.00
Current.		
Mother's household	$100.00 per month	1200.00
My "	100.00 "	1200.00
Farm	50.00	600.00

Against this I have

35 acres of wooded parkland inside Oxford corporate limits, can sell as subdivision lots, will be worth more if I can hold for price, since town is growing.

Normal increase of stock, mules and such, from farm if I can hold them for right market instead of forced auction. That is, the farm pays itself back after harvest in fall, but needs cash for other 11 months.

1 novel, of which one publisher approves. 1 year.

5 short stories already written, two others planned, both of which might sell, one of which is a mystery story, original in that the solver is a negro, himself in jail for the murder and is about to be lynched, solves murder in self defense.[1] Of these I can make a more or less continuous narrative, somewhat after THE UNVANQUISHED. 6–12 months.

Four other short stories, unwritten, of the first class, but which I now dare not put any time on because first class stories fetch no money in America.

Likelihood of other commercial stories during that period. Certainty of them if pressure eased, in which case the liability of publisher underwriting me would be lessened to the amount of these sales.

So I must have

July 1	Income tax payment, half, at least	500.00
	Possibly, additional	200.00
	Self, mother, farm	250.00
Aug 1	" "	250.00
Sep 1	" "	250.00
"	Payment on note	200.00
Oct 1	Self, mother, farm	250.00
"	Insurance premium	333.00
"	Income installment tax, balance	300.00
	" possibly, additional	150.00
Nov 1	Self, mother, farm	250.00
"	Note at bank, interest at least	650.00
Dec 1	Self, mother, farm	250.00
31	Taxes	300.00
		4133.00

What short stories I might sell will reduce this, also what revenue from farm after harvest.

Obviously this is too high a rate of spending for my value as a writer, unless I hit moving pictures or can write at least six commercial stories a year. I am still convinced that I can do it, despite the fact that I have not so far. But as I said before, when I become convinced I cannot, I will liquidate what I am trying to hold on to. It's probably vanity as much as anything else which makes me want to hold onto it. I own a larger parcel of it than anybody else in town and nobody gave me any of it or loaned me a nickel to buy any of it with and all my relations and fellow townsmen, including the borrowers and frank spongers, all prophesied I'd never be more than a bum.

So besides the $3,000.00 advance on the new unwritten novel, I need $4,000.00 more by Jan. 1. If your judgment forbids you to get more deeply involved, let me take the collected story idea and try to sell it somewhere else for that much advance. As I said before, I dont want the personal friendship between us, and Random House's unfailing past kindnesses and such to me, to become a burden to us both. I dont want the proposition to be on the basis of an importunity through friendship, to be accepted with a bitter taste in the mouth. Let me try to sell it somewhere else, this one book if possible. But if I must sign a longer contract in order to get this sum, let me have your blessing to ask for enough in additional to buy back from Random House the contract which I recently signed. This notion springs from the fact that, years ago, before I knew you, before I ever anticipated a connection with Random House, a publisher intimated to me that I could almost write my own ticket with him.[2] This may not even hold now. But it is one thing more I can try before I decide to liquidate my property and savings.

Bill

[1] This story would become *Intruder in the Dust* (1948).
[2] Harold Guinzburg, of Viking Press.

To Robert K. Haas — TS. RH
Wednesday [12 June 1940] — [Oxford]

Dear Bob:

Yours received. Thank you for promptness. Of course I take letter in spirit it was written in, you know that. It is considerate of you to be plain; then we will know always exactly where we stand, regardless of outcome of this particular matter.

I am writing other publisher today. I will quote gist of your letter. But as I must get if possible 4000.00 by Jan 1, without doubt I will have to contract for more than one book of short stories. Also, I may have to be able to give him a clean bill of health on me as far as any other future commitments on my writing go; in which case, I will have to be released from the unnamed future novel contract with Random House. It is possible, however, that he will agree to let this new contract stand between me and Random House, provided there is no date stipulated and no specific manuscript involved. That is, in order to get the sum I need, I may have to contract for short story volume to be delivered at once, and a novel to be delivered immediately afterward. Or he may not even want the short story book; it may be I can get this money only by contracting for a novel, to be commenced and completed as soon as possible, in which case I will write the one which I described to you. But again, as I wrote you, he may not be interested at all now, in which case I will take the additional 1,000.00 you offered in your recent letter, and try to write some salable short stories, then sell my mules etc. as I can.

I will let you know as soon as I hear from him.

Bill

To Random House — TELEGRAM RH
18 June 1940 — Oxford, Miss.

RECEIVED CONTRACT OFFER FOR SHORT STORY BOOK AND A NOVEL.[1] INFERENCE IS THAT I WILL BE PUBLISHED FROM NOW ON BY NEW FIRM. WOULD LIKE TO HAVE YOUR ACKNOWLEDGEMENT BEFORE CLOSING. WILL WAIT UNTIL NOON WEDNESDAY. WILL COME NEW YORK TO SETTLE DETAILS. WILLIAM FAULKNER

[1] From Harold Guinzburg of Viking Press.

In Haas's absence, Bennett Cerf wired Faulkner asking him to wait until he received a letter to follow. Dated 19 June 1940, it was Random House's counteroffer. Cerf noted that Faulkner still had $1,000 due him in advances on the new novel and proposed to add a $2,000 advance on a book of short stories, the total payable over a year's time at $250 per month. With the $2,000 Faulkner had already received, this would total a $5,000 advance on the two books. If at the end of the year Faulkner had completed only one of the books and neeeded more money, Random House would provide an advance against Faulkner's general royalty account. Cerf also wrote that he had telephoned Guinzburg and they had agreed that if Random House's offer was as good as the Viking Press offer, Guinzburg would bow out. Cerf asked Faulkner to remember that Random House had a considerable investment in several thousand copies of his books, including about 2,500 copies of The Hamlet *still in stock, which would create a problem if he were to change publishers. They were desperately anxious that Faulkner should remain with Random House and would do everything within their power to see that he remained there.*

To Bennett Cerf — TS. RH
Thursday [20 June 1940] — [Oxford]

Dear Bennett:

Here is the situation. I did not know Bob has been occupied with the training camp business. Because of that, it is possible you have not kept up with the development of this matter between us.

About three months ago I wrote Bob, stating generally my financial predicament. I said that if I had $10,000.00, $5,000.00 available at once upon demand, the other $5,000.00 strung out in monthly payments as far as I could stretch it, I would have at least two years free of money worries and of the necessity of trying to write salable trash, five specimens of which I had in the hands of an agent had not sold, the reason being perhaps that no one under the pressure of money need could write anything anyone would buy.

Bob answered promptly, commiserated with me, stated the condition of my account, suggested that I still had a balance of advance on my next work which could be drawn against, that this remaining $1500.00 would take care of most pressing matters and that later we might work things out someway, as we had usually managed to do so.

I answered him, asked for the balance, said I would try to hold on a while longer, as some of the 5 short stories might sell.

Then I received a demand for $360.00 more state tax on my income for 1938, in addition to Federal demand for $460.00 on 1937. I will also receive in time, at any time, the same $360.00 demand on the same 1938 income from the Federal govt. In the meantime I had heard from the agent who had the short stories. He seemed quite gloomy about prospects of selling them.

I wrote Bob at once. I itemised my financial situation, which totaled a minimum sum which I must have by Jan 1, or I would have to liquidate what property I could, for what I could get for enough of it to pay these income tax demands by July 1. Against this I itemised what I had to offer: a volume based upon the unpublished short stories, and the plan of a novel. I suggested that, if Random House declined to advance this amount, that I approach a publisher from whom I had received an offer years ago, before Random House and I met.

Bob answered, stated that my books had averaged $3400.00 each, that under these conditions, in conjunction with the times, war, etc., he could go no deeper, that if I approached another publisher with an offer of the short story book he wished me luck, but asked me not to commit myself on any other book without letting him know.

On that day I wrote Guinzburg, told him the sum I wanted, described the short story book and the novel which I had to offer against it, explained that I had signed a contract and taken an advance with Random House for a novel. On the same day and mail I wrote Bob what I had done. That was on a Tuesday, I think. On Friday I received an acknowledgement of my letter to Guinzburg, advising that I would receive an answer on the following Tuesday, when Guinzburg returned to town. On that second Tuesday, I received a wire from Guinzburg, accepting my offer. But I had had no further word from Bob, so I wired Random House at once, asking acknowledgement of my intention to close with Guinzburg, stating that

I would not answer Guinzburg until Random House had had a chance to answer.

So this is the situation, Bennett. I must have that minimum sum, on my writing future if I can get it. I made the offer first to my present publishers, who declined. I made it to another publisher, who accepted, in the same good faith with which he must have believed I made him the offer. I cant play fast and loose with him this way. I cant use one publisher to blackjack another into advancing me money which that second publisher had otherwise declined to advance.

I will come to New York next week.

Yours,
Bill

Copy to Harold Guinzburg.

On 24 June 1940, Cerf acknowledged receipt of Faulkner's letter and restated Random House's position in further detail. They had printed rather heavily on The Hamlet, *assuming that they would also publish the other volumes of the trilogy. They would expect Guinzburg to buy the copies in stock at manufacturing prices and the plates for the book at a reasonable figure. There were 2,700 copies of the regular edition, which had cost Random House 40¢ each, and 101 copies of the limited edition at 66¢ each. The original cost of the plates was $1,162.00.*

By the time Cerf's letter arrived in Oxford, Faulkner was in New York. On Tuesday, 25 June, he talked with Guinzburg, who, however, was leaving town immediately and would not return until Monday. Guinzburg felt he could do nothing until he spoke to Cerf about the purchase of the stock and plates of The Hamlet. *He would see Cerf on Monday, and if he could not agree to the purchase, he would withdraw from the negotiations. Meanwhile, Faulkner would draw the additional $1,000 from Random House and return home.*

On 3 July, Harold Guinzburg wrote Faulkner that Cerf had valued the stock and plates at $1,500, which he did not find excessive, but this additional amount made the total sum involved greater than business conditions warranted and he had to withdraw his offer. He hoped Faulkner would be able to solve his financial problems and stood ready to reopen negotiations at any future time.

On 8 July, Cerf wrote Faulkner telling him of his conversation with Guinzburg and of Guinzburg's conclusion that it was impossible for Viking to advance Faulkner the $6,000 originally contemplated and spend an addi-

tional $1,500 for the stock and plates of The Hamlet *as well. Cerf's offer of 19 June 1940 still stood, he said, and he hoped that Faulkner would be able to accept it and at the same time solve his financial problems. Random House wanted to do as much for him as they could while protecting their own interests during a period of unusual difficulties confronting the whole publishing industry. Not until 28 July would Faulkner reply directly to the issues Cerf had discussed.*

In the interval, he turned to short stories in the hope of some financial relief. Harold Ober had written Faulkner on 3 July about the short story "Almost," which had been rejected by The Saturday Evening Post. *He suggested several points for clarification that would increase the chances of a sale and offered to return the typescript if Faulkner had no carbon. On 12 July, Faulkner wrote requesting the typescript.*

To Harold Ober — TS. FCVA
Thursday [18 July 1940] — Oxford, Miss.

Dear Mr Ober:

Here is the story, with the points clarified as you suggested. It's not a very neat script now, as I merely cut into it at the points in question. Might do with retyping.[1]

What do you think about trying Harper's or Esquire with PANTALOON IN BLACK? That is, I am pressed for money, and Post and Colliers have declined it, have they not? It might be strong meat for anyone except them anyway. That is, if you cant get more than 400.00 for it, at this time I am agreeable.[2]

I read Gallico's piece in the Post.[3] I doubt that twenty-four year old service machine myself, though that's not very important, and the story is a little treacly on top to my taste. But the story itself and his approach to it are all right. They are all right enough to overshadow the other. It's all right.

Faulkner

[1] No one bought "Almost," which became "Was" in *Go Down, Moses* (1942).

[2] "Pantaloon in Black" was printed in *Harper's,* CLXXXI (Oct. 1940), 503–13, and revised for incorporation in *Go Down, Moses.*

[3] Paul Gallico's story about a twenty-two-year-old British aircraft was entitled "Wings of Atonement" and appeared in *The Saturday Evening Post,* CCXIII (13 July 1940), 16–17, 40, 42, 44. The story contained John Philpot Curran's statement on liberty and vigilance which Faulkner would later quote. (See *Faulkner in the University* [New York: Vintage, 1965], p. 149.)

To Bennett Cerf — TS. RH
Wednesday [24 July 1940] — [Oxford]

Dear Bennett:

I have read THE OX BOW INCIDENT.[1] I found it dull. To my notion, it is only a short story to begin with. Hemingway could have written it (and, I think, has) in about three thousand words, and in more distinguished and arresting prose.

What has happened to writing, anyway? Hemingway and Dos Passos and I are veterans now; we should be fighting tooth and toenail to hold our places against young writers. But there are no young writers worth a damn that I know of. I think of my day. There were Lewis and Dreiser and Sherwood Anderson and so forth, and we were crowding the hell out of them. But now there doesn't seem to be enough pressure behind us to keep Dos Passos and Hemingway writing even. What's your explanation for it?

I'm getting along pretty well. Still writing short stories. Some of them are bound to sell soon. If I can sell one for top price, it will get me through to October, which will give me two months to write and sell another.

I brought DEATH OF LORD HAW HAW home with me. That's a good piece. I enjoyed it.

Bill

[1] Faulkner had brought back with him from New York two Random House books, Walter Van Tilburg Clark's *The Ox-Bow Incident* and Brett Rutledge's *The Death of Lord Haw Haw*.

To Harold Ober — TS. FCVA
[24 July 1940] — [Oxford]

Mailed today to Sat Eve Post GO DOWN, MOSES, with postage and instructions to communicate with you.[1]

Faulkner

[1] This story appeared in *Collier's*, CVII (25 Jan. 1941), 19–20, 45, 46, and was revised for inclusion in *Go Down, Moses* (1942).

To Bennett Cerf — TS. RH
Sunday [28 July 1940] — [Oxford]

Dear Bennett:

I should have written sooner. I took it for granted that Guinzburg had clarified the situation for you.

With conditions as they are now, he did not want to invest money in the plates, etc. for THE HAMLET, besides the advance which I was to have, which sum would do neither him nor me any good. You were out of town at the time I saw him; he was departing immediately after lunch, to be gone over week-end. I suggested that I go back to Bob, whom I knew to be in the office that day (Thursday), get the additional $1,000.00 from him, which would pay the additional income assessment, and return home. Whereupon he, Guinzburg, would see you the following Monday, following which he would write me what decision you and he reached. I heard from him in the following week, saying that since he did not feel justified in buying THE HAMLET material from you, he would withdraw and call the business off.

The situation is now as it was before the matter came up. I have taken the other $1,000.00 from Bob. I have not approached any other publisher, and at present I do not intend to. Harold Ober, agent, has been holding my short stories for best prices. I suggested to him that he sell them for whatever he can get. I wrote another last week, and will keep on at it.[1] If I can get another $1,000.00 for one of them, it will carry me through Oct. 1. If I can sell two of them, I can raise mortgage I had to put on my mules, and sell some of the mules. If I can get through to Nov. 15, I will begin to collect on my cotton and tenant crops, etc, though because of excessive rain in June-July, this crop will be only 40%.

One more story will complete a mss. based on short stories, some published, something like the UNVANQUISHED in composition.[2] This last story will be pretty long though, and I dont feel warranted in putting the time on it now, since I have got to write something short and quick to sell; this last story will be a novella, actually. Also, it might be best not to publish it, but to wait until I have time to write the Huck Finn novel which I described to Bob. It will be impossible to get at it though before next year at the earliest, unless lightning in some form strikes me a golden blow.

Bill

My brother has written a novel. I have not read it, am too busy to intend to. Do you want to look at it?[3]

[1] "Go Down, Moses."

[2] *Go Down, Moses.*

[3] John Faulkner's *By Their Fruits* was retitled *Men Working* and published by Harcourt, Brace in 1941.

To Harold Ober
[5 Aug. 1940]

MS. FCVA
[Oxford]

To Sat Eve Post today, short story "Tomorrow"[1]

Faulkner

[1] The story appeared in *The Saturday Evening Post,* CCXIII (23 Nov. 1940), 22–23, 32, 35, 37, 38, 39.

To Harold Ober — TS. FCVA
16 August, 1940 — Oxford, Miss.

Dear Mr Ober:

Your letter and checks received.[1]

In regard to the Saturday Evening Post check: I accept your generosity with gratitude, due to the fact that my financial situation was badly complicated this year by a demand for additional tax of $1100.00 on my 1937 income. So I accept the full amount which the story brought, under the condition that, when you succeed in upping my price with the Post, you will repay yourself this $100.00 commission which you did not collect on TOMORROW, of which there is attached herewith the carbon you requested.

My brother has written a novel. I have not read it, am too busy at present to do so. Attached is a letter from Bob Haas declining it. Will you look at it?

Thank you again for your generosity in supplying me with the additional hundred of sea-room.

William Faulkner

[1] *Harper's* had bought "Pantaloon in Black" for $400, and the *Post* had bought "Tomorrow" for $1,000.

To Robert K. Haas — TS. RH
Saturday [5 Oct. 1940] — [Oxford]

Dear Bob:

You are welcome about signing poem.[1] No, I didn't know about Lewis and Random House.[2] I didn't know about Cerf and marriage either, and I still dont know why and even if he told me why, I still wouldn't believe it. My God, what a man. To have escaped once, and then daring fate again. If Bennett dont watch out, the gods are going to look around and see him some day.

There is a C.A.A. primary flying school here, attached to the University. I am a sort of advisor without portfolio to it, and I think I shall teach a course in navigation and radio in the ground school. Am doing considerable flying on a low-wing monoplane which is a sort of a caricature of an underpowered service machine, am also trying to get a National Guard unit here, U.S. comm. for myself. I have received no call from RAF. I take it that ex-members who are aliens may volunteer for back-area service, but no call to be made upon them until things are worse than now.

I am doing no writing save pot-boilers. Ober sells just enough of them to keep my head above water, which is all right. I still have the novel in mind, may get at it when bad weather stops farming and flying and I become better adjusted mentally to the condition of this destruction-bent world. Saxon fighting Saxon, Latin against Latin, Mongol with a Slav ally fighting a Mongol who is the ally of a Saxon-Latin ally of the first Slav; nigger fighting nigger at the behest of white men; one democracy trying to blow the other democracy's fleet off the seas. Anyway, it will make nice watching when the axis people start gutting one another.

Bill

[1] Haas had asked Faulkner to sign one of his poems for William McFee, another Random House author.

[2] Haas had told Faulkner that Sinclair Lewis had joined their list.

To Harold Ober — TS. FCVA
[received 12 Nov. 1940] — [Oxford]

This strikes me as being a pretty good Who-done-it. Maybe you can up the Post with this one.

[t] faulkner

as usual, will take the quickest sale before the highest[1]

[1] The short story, "An Error in Chemistry," was sold five years later for $300. It appeared in *Ellery Queen's Mystery Magazine*, VII (June 1946), 4–9, and was reprinted in *Knight's Gambit* (1949).

To Harold Ober — TS. FCVA
[received 12 Nov. 1940] — [Oxford]

Mr Ober:

I discovered I had left out a very important point of my story AN ERROR IN CHEMISTRY, mailed to you today.

Will you please substitute the attached page, numbered 14, for the page numbered fourteen in the manuscript?

Faulkner

To Harold Ober — TS. FCVA
[received 9 Dec. 1940] — [Oxford]

Dear Mr Ober:

I thank you for getting John's book placed.[1]

About South America. My belief is, Random House has a kind of unwritten power of attorney to handle foreign rights. That is, I find myself translated and published, and my royalties come to me from Random House. Will you consult Bob Haas or Cerf? This is your authority from me to take whatever steps necessary in the matter.

Attached is a poem, brought up to date. It was in my volume A GREEN BOUGH. It is timely now.[2]

Faulkner

[1] *Men Working* (1941).
[2] The poem was a rewritten version of "The Husbandman," an Armistice Day poem which had become poem XXXI of *A Green Bough* (1933).

To Bennett Cerf et al. TS. RH
15 December, 1940 [Oxford]

Dear Bennett, Bob, Don, Louise:, Saxe et al:

This is to wish you all a merry Christmas and happy New Year and many more, happier, maybe even peaceful again if we live long enough.

Will you send me two Faulkners, complete as you have it, *not deluxe*,

2 Hamlet
2 Unvanquished } —nice ones for Xmas gifts
2 Wild Palms

We have a few duck in here so far. I spent last week in November in the big woods after deer but never shot my rifle. Saw one fawn only. We have some quail and I have two good setters. One nice thing about the woods: off there hunting, I dont fret and stew so much about Europe. But I'm only 43, I'm afraid I'm going to the damn thing yet.

Bill Faulkner

To Harold Ober TELEGRAM FCVA
16 Jan. 1941 Oxford, Miss.

WIRE ME COLLECT WHAT POSSIBILITY OF ANY SUM WHATEVER AND WHEN FROM ANY MSS OF MINE YOU HAVE. URGENTLY NEED ONE HUNDRED BY SATURDAY. WILLIAM FAULKNER

To Harold Ober TS. FCVA
18 January, 1941 Oxford, Miss.

Dear Mr Ober:

Thank you for the money. I did not intend the wire to ask for a loan, but I have used the money and I thank you for it. I thought that possibly one of the stories had received favorable comment from Harper's or some 3- or $400.00 mag., with which you could place it quickly in an emergency. I was badly bitched up last summer by a demand for $1600.00 additional on my 1937 California movie income tax. I have not got over the blow; I earned only $4000.00 last year. When I wired you I did not have $15.00 to pay electricity bill with, keep my lights burning.

Faulkner

To Robert K. Haas
Friday [21 Mar. 1941]

TS. FCVA
Oxford

Dear Bob:

I was glad to hear from you. I'm not at a book now: I am still writing short stories, to finish paying the back income tax. I have worn it down from $1600.00 to $403.00, which I hope to finish if and when Ober sells a story I sent him last week.[1]

I am flying fairly steadily, still very restless. Civilian Pilot Training is not enough. If I had money to take care of my family and dependents, I would try for England under my old commission. Perhaps I can yet. If not (and when and if I get money) I will try the U.S. air corps. I could navigate, or teach navigation, even if I could not fly service jobs because of my age.

I have the book in mind. If I ever get out of hock and settle down to being too old to fight in wars, I will get at it. I will get at it someday anyhow.

My best to everyone.

[no signature]

[1] "The Tall Men," which appeared in *The Saturday Evening Post*, CCXIII (31 May 1941), 14–15, 95, 96, 98, 99, and was reprinted in *Collected Stories of William Faulkner* (1950).

To Robert K. Haas
Thursday [1 May 1941]

TS. RH
Oxford, Miss.

Dear Bob:

Last year I mentioned a volume, collected short stories, general theme being relationship between white and negro races here. This is the plan:

Title of book: GO DOWN, MOSES

Stories:

THE FIRE AND THE HEARTH

Part One: published Collier's.

" Two: Atlantic Monthly.

" Three: Unpublished.
PANTALOON IN BLACK: Harper's
THE OLD PEOPLE: "
DELTA AUTUMN: Unpublished.
GO DOWN, MOSES: Collier's

I will rewrite them, to an extent; some additional material might invent itself in process. Book will be about the size and similar to THE UNVANQUISHED.

Do present conditions warrant such a book? That is, do you want to publish such a book, and will it do enough to ease the financial situation between us for me to get at it, or shall I hold off until I can earn enough from short stories, or collect enough of the loan I made the friend two years ago to write a new novel? My financial condition is no worse and no prettier than last year, so I do not want to gamble the time and effort of getting this mss. in shape unless it will really benefit me.

Bill

To Robert K. Haas — TS. RH
Tuesday [13 May 1941] — [Oxford]

Dear Bob:

I am at work on the mss. I dont know how long it will take, how much rewriting and additional material will go into it. Also, I have a nibble from California, through J. Longstreet plus Wm Herndon.[1] Dont know what will come of it, but I will keep at GO DOWN MOSES, should have it in to you by Aug. 1.

When I asked if such a book would benefit us mutually, I did not have in mind any further advance. I meant, would such a book be a worthwhile book, printable, etc. That is, I didn't think I had advance in mind, but since you mentioned the matter, a possible definite sum of advance, I will avail self of it, as, by taking it, I can go on through with this mss. instead of working at it at odd times, as I had planned. Therefore, will you send me $500.00 now, with authority to draw the other $1,000,00 later if needed? If Cal. pans out, I wont need it. But I will need $500.00 until I know about Cal. job.

And will you be kind enough to attend to the following: tell Ober of the plan, and that I am including unsold stories which he has as follows:

Story, title forgotten, beginning
"When me and Uncle Buck"[2]
THE FIRE AND THE HEARTH
DELTA AUTUMN

If he could sell any of these, for best price regardless, the book could be held back until after mag. publication.

Bill

[1] Stephen Longstreet had met Faulkner at Random House in New York. Now a Hollywood scriptwriter, he had asked agent William Herndon to determine if there was any possibility of studio employment for Faulkner. Herndon tried to find employment for Faulkner with David O. Selznick, Metro-Goldwyn-Mayer, and Warner Bros.

[2] "Almost," which would become "Was" in *Go Down, Moses.*

To Robert K. Haas
[received 5 June 1941]

TS. RH
[Oxford]

Bob:

The Hollywood agent, Herndon, thinks he might sell some of my books to pictures, wants copies. Will you please send him copies available, to

William Herndon, 9006 Sunset Blvd., Hollywood.

Bill F.

[in ink:] This is the next chapter. 1st chap. second story 'Go Down Moses'

To Robert K. Haas
[received 30 June 1941]

TS. RH
[Oxford]

Dear Bob:

Will you send $500.00 more. Thank you.

I am behind schedule with the mss. Am doing some defense work, organising Aircraft Warning Service in this county. I am getting at the script again now though. It should not take long to finish it. Nothing more from Cal. Herndon wants SOLDIERS' PAY. Can it be had? Could you send him a copy, unless it is a collector's item now. Liveright published it.

[t] bill

To Robert K. Haas
[received 30 June 1941]

TS. RH
[Oxford]

Dear Bob:

Will you please see what of my stuff you can find for Wm Herndon, 9006 Sunset Blvd., Hollywood. All I have are the last four books.

He wants Soldiers Pay particularly.

There were some you and Hal Smith published, some Hal did, and Hal and that Limey with the false teeth, whatsname.[1] Will you get in touch with Hal, see what he could dig up? Herndon thinks he might sell something; I hope to god he can.

Also he wants to see the present mss before publication. I am making but one copy. Can you let him see that? I will have to make a few minor corrections in it before you print it, but it wont be changed as far as a moom pitcher magnit is concerned.

[t] bill

[1] Faulkner is of course referring to Jonathan Cape, senior partner of the firm of Jonathan Cape and Harrison Smith.

To Prof. Warren Beck | TS. BOSTON
6 July, 1941 | Oxford, Miss.

Dear Mr Beck:

Thank you for sending the articles.[1] I agree with them. You found implications which I had missed. I wish that I had consciously intended them; I will certainly believe I did it subconsciously and not by accident.

I have been writing all the time about honor, truth, pity, consideration, the capacity to endure well grief and misfortune and injustice and then endure again, in terms of individuals who observed and adhered to them not for reward but for virtue's own sake, not even merely because they are admirable in themselves, but in order to live with oneself and die peacefully with oneself when the time comes. I dont mean that the devil will snatch every liar and rogue and hypocrite shrieking from his deathbed. I think liars and hypocrites and rogues die peacefully every day in the odor of what he calls sanctity. I'm not talking about him. I'm not writing for him. But I believe there are some, not necessarily many, who do and will continue to read Faulkner and say, 'Yes. It's all right. I'd rather be Ratliff than Flem Snopes. And I'd still rather be Ratliff without any Snopes to measure by even.'

As yet I have found no happy balance between method and material. I doubt that it exists for me. I blame this partly on my refusal to accept formal schooling (I am an old 8th grade man), but mostly on the heat in which I wrote. I have written too fast, too much. I decided what seems to me now a long time ago that something worth saying knew better than I did how it needed to be said, and that it was better said poorly even than not said. And besides, there would always be a next time, since there is only one truth and endurance and pity and courage. I discovered then that I had rather read Shakespeare, bad puns, bad history, taste and all, than Pater, and that I had a damn sight rather fail at trying to write Shakespeare than to write all of Pater over again so he couldn't have told it himself if you fired it point blank at him through an amplifier.

Excuse all the I's. I'm still having trouble reconciling method and material, you see.

Yours sincerely,
William Faulkner

[1] Warren Beck, "Faulkner and the South," *The Antioch Review*, I (Mar. 1941), 82–94; "Faulkner's Point of View," *College English*, II (May 1941), 736–49; "William Faulkner's Style," *American Prefaces*, IV (Spring 1941), 195–211.

To Harold Ober
TS. FCVA
Aug. 21, 1941
Oxford, Mississippi

Dear Mr. Ober,

I have no contract with Mr. Herndon. He wrote in the spring that he had a Hollywood offer for me, but so far nothing has come of it.

There has been some correspondence of a most unsatisfactory nature. Nothing else. However, I feel, should an authentic offer be made, then naturally I would be committed to Herndon.

Sincerely yours,
[t] William Faulkner
[s] William Faulkner

To Robert K. Haas
TS. RH
[received 25 Aug. 1941]
[Oxford]

Dear Bob:

I have been saddled with some defense work, as I wrote you. I am running behind schedule with the mss.

There is one more chapter to rewrite, the final one is all right as is. I will get at it again pretty soon. Meantime may I have the last five hundred?

Yours,
Bill

To Harold Ober
TS. FCVA
[received 27 Oct. 1941]
[Oxford]

Dear Mr Ober:

Ref rewriting my story AN ERROR IN CHEMISTRY, to simplify it. If there is a fair certainty of selling it, send it back and I will rewrite it.

[no signature]

To Robert K. Haas | TS. RH
[received 6 Nov. 1941] | [Oxford]

Dear Bob:

The rest of mss. will be in by Dec 1, sooner possibly. Am at it now. There will be a revision. I had hoped to come East for a brief holiday and do it, but see no chance now. You had better send it to me here. Send me the first chapter or section, title WAS, from page no. 1 on to beginning of section, title THE FIRE AND THE HEARTH.

[t] bill

On 5 November 1941, Harold Ober wrote Faulkner, relaying to him, at the request of The Saturday Evening Post *editors, suggestions for revision of a story entitled "The Bear," which Ober had submitted to them. They had liked the story but felt that it was "a trifle obscure" and that the last paragraph in particular should be clarified to help the reader.*

To Harold Ober | TS. FCVA
[received 10 Nov. 1941] | [Oxford]

Dear Mr Ober:

I have no carbon of the BEAR story. It was a rewritten chapter of a book under way. The story as sent you was rewritten from the chapter in the novel, first draft and in haste because I need some money badly.

In hopes that Post will take it and I can get a check next week, I am trying to make the revision desired from memory, without waiting to get back your copy. If it does not fit, please return your copy, and this revision AIR MAIL and I will get it back the same day. Please sell it for something as soon as you can. I am in a situation where I will take almost anything for it or almost anything else I have or can write.[1]

[no signature]

[1] Faulkner's rewrite was acceptable, and the story appeared as "The Bear," *The Saturday Evening Post*, CCXIV (9 May 1942), 30–31, 74, 76, 77.

In his efforts to find a job for Faulkner in Hollywood, William Herndon had talked with producer Robert Buckner at Warner Bros. It may have been as a result of this contact that Faulkner was given an opportunity to attempt to salvage a property which had thus far resulted in only an un-

satisfactory script. Harry C. Hervey's novel The Damned Don't Cry *(New York, 1939) had as its protagonist a poor-white girl named Zelda who had grown up in Savannah, Georgia. One reviewer had called the novel Zola-esque, and works such as* Sanctuary *and* The Hamlet *may have suggested Faulkner as an apt writer to treat this material.*

To Mr. Nathan — TS. WARNER BROS.
18 Nov. 1941 — Oxford, Miss.

Dear Mr Nathan:

Attached are a few suggestions re. the script 'THE DAMNED DONT CRY' which was sent to me. I was unable to get the book here and had to order it from a dealer. When it comes, I can tell more about the story, and will then air mail to you a story outline. The following are faults as I see them in the script sent me. They could be corrected by beefing up the dialog and incidents in the script as it is. But I believe a different story line would get more of the meat out of it.

As I see it, the principal fault is in the plot. It fails to state a definite problem, moral, personal, or sociological, and then proceed to solve it.

The reason for this failure lies in ZELDA, assuming that this is her story, or at least that she is the principal and therefore motivating character. She has an illegitimate child, and loves it too much to repudiate it completely. Perfectly natural. She deserves no special approbation for this. She conceals the fact. That is perfectly natural too. Unmarried, the world's moral set-up would force her to do that, unless (1) She were a woman of unusual character, or (2) She were doing it for the child's good and at sacrifice for herself, which would require character and would deserve admiration. She does it for neither of these reasons, but simply because Mrs Grundy says she must.

When the fact of the child's existence breaks, a woman of exceptional character would have risen superior to the crisis and beaten it and so have gained admiration; perhaps she would have had to choose between the child and herself and gained admiration and pity both. Or she may have been completely beaten by it and so have gained pity, even if nothing else. ZELDA does neither. She simply shrieks and faints and after a while comes to, whereupon, thanks to the frantic efforts of everybody else in the picture except her, the situation is unchanged and therefore none of it need ever have taken place. Apparently ZELDA wants a lot but she just sits and wants it until enough people rally around to attend to getting it for her.

Maybe this story is already in the script, and I just failed to see it. If this is so, and the script is an approved story line, it can be rewritten and beefed up and emphasised when necessary, changed here and there perhaps, making ZELDA consistent, and building up to a climax which she must either survive or succumb to.

DAN strikes me as being a poor sort. The worst fate ZELDA could suffer would be to marry him, even a worse fate than a woman as poor in backbone as ZELDA appears, deserves.

And there is something wrong with ENGSTAAD. He is the only man in the lot. He is almost TYLER, but ten times the man TYLER ever will be. He is the one she should have faded out with, unless something is done with DAN, either various stages of conflict shown between DAN and ZELDA, or an undeviating fidelity despite all odds as shown between DAN and ZELDA.

I would take the script and start at page 1 and rewrite it, keeping fairly close to it when possible, but changing the incidents when necessary as I went along.

When I get the book, I will try a treatment and send it to you.[1]

[t] William Faulkner

[1] In late November or early December, Faulkner apparently completed and mailed off a nineteen-page treatment of *The Damned Don't Cry*. It was the melodramatic story of the misfortunes of Zelda, a girl from the wrong side of the tracks. Her life suggested that of Caddie Compson in *The Sound and the Fury*. Handicapped further by a drunken father, a complaining mother and a no-good brother, she did the best she could despite having an illegitimate child and further unhappy love affairs. Nothing came of this treatment, but Faulkner worked on the property again at Warner Bros. in May and June of 1944.

To Robert K. Haas — TS. RH

Dec. 2 [1941] — [Oxford]

Dear Bob:

My promise re mss. Dec 1 is already broken. There is more meat in it than I thought, a section now that I am going to be proud of and which requires careful writing and rewriting to get it exactly right. I am at it steadily, and have been. If I make another definite promise, it might be broken too. But I think I will send the rest of it in by Dec. 15. Sooner of course if possible. Please have Saxe[1] acknowledge last batch: pages 250 through 295, incomplete section, to keep the record straight.

Bill

[1] Saxe Commins, now serving as Faulkner's editor.

To Saxe Commins TS. RH
Sunday [probably 7 Dec. 1941] [Oxford]

Dear Saxe:

Note received. Correct. You received last page 295, incomplete section, incomplete chapter, ending with half an incomplete word. The rest of the section and chapter will be along in a few days. (I had to drop the whole thing for a week and take a shot at a treatment for a movie job)

DELTA AUTUMN needs to be rewritten, to get matter into it pertinent to the story this mss. tells. I have it half-done. Will not take long to finish it. I hope to have the complete mss. in to you on the 15th this month.

I played hell with my team last week ago Sat. (Univ. of Miss.) I had them all ready, was in the country getting oats planted, and the bastards blew and lost to Miss. State, not only a ball game but a Sugar Bowl contract. If they are still fumbling at their other two avocations like they were doing last at football they have been chaste since and must be about starved by now.

[t] Bill

Please send me two or three of your juvenile books. For daughter Jill, 8. She has Babar, Snow-white, probably most of last few years' publication. Anything new. She is now competent for book-length continuous narrative, possibly 10 or 12 year old stuff.

To Saxe Commins TS. RH
[probably mid-Dec.]. [Oxford]

Dear Saxe:

This is all of it. The Sat eve post bought a story THE BEAR taken from the chapter by that name. I had the galleys three weeks ago, so maybe they will print soon. Will you look into it, give them a chance to print first if they want to?

I have not proof-read all this mss. If anything sounds queer, send it back. Wish I had money to come up there and go through it with you. I think it's good stuff. But then I always do.

Follow page 370 with the chapter GO DOWN, MOSES, which you already have.

[no signature]

To Harold Ober
19 January 1942

TS. FCVA
Oxford, Miss.

Dear Mr Ober:

As always, I am broke. If and when this sells, will you get the check to me as soon as you can?[1]

Sincerely,
William Faulkner

[1] The enclosure was "Knight's Gambit," which never sold but was used in expanded form as the title story of the collection *Knight's Gambit* (1949).

To Robert K. Haas
21 Jan. 1942

TS. RH
Oxford, Miss.

Dear Bob:

Here is a dedication for GO DOWN, MOSES.[1]

This world is bitched proper this time, isn't it? I'd like to be dictator now. I'd take all these congressmen who refused to make military appropriations and I'd send them to the Philippines. This day a year and I dont believe there will be one present second lt. alive.

I have organised observation posts for air raids in this county, and am a sergeant in charge of air and communications in the usual local unit. But that's not enough. I have a chance to teach navigation (air) in the Navy as a civilian. If I can get my affairs here established, I think I'll take it.

Are you still doing your staff majoring?

Yours
Bill

[1] The dedication read as follows:

To MAMMY

CAROLINE BARR

Mississippi
[1840–1940]

Who was born in slavery and who gave to my family a fidelity without stint or calculation of recompense and to my childhood an immeasurable devotion and love

To Harold Ober — TS. FCVA
Saturday [21 Feb. 1942] — Oxford, Miss.

Dear Mr Ober:

Your letter received.

I could simplify SNOW, I suppose.[1] It doesn't seem too obscure to me though.

I can take a lot of matter out of KNIGHT'S GAMBIT though, simplify it to primer class. If there is a chance yet to place it, return it to me and I will rewrite it. I dont have a clear copy here. In the case of SNOW, you might offer to have it simplified if anyone is interested in buying it provided it is worked over.

I will get to work at KNIGHT'S GAMBIT at once, though I will need the original which you have to complete the new job.

Thank you for advance two weeks ago. If you have anything else of mine which any editor ever intimated he might buy if it were simplified, send that back too. As usual, I am not quite a boat's length ahead of the sheriff.

Yours sincerely,
William Faulkner

[1] The short story "Snow" was never sold.

To Robert K. Haas — TS. RH
[received 27 Mar. 1942] — [Oxford]

Dear Bob:

GO DOWN MOSES looks very well. I looked through it and I still think it is all right. This is probably a bad time to publish anything, war and all. But I think the book is all right. It will pull its weight.

Will you please send me 4 more copies?

I am going before a Navy board and Medical for a commission, N.R. I will go to the Bureau of Aeronautics, Washington, for a job. I am to get full Lieut. and 3200.00 per year, and I hope a pilot's rating to wear the wings. I dont like this desk job particularly, but I think better to get the commission first and then try to get a little nearer the gunfire, which I intend to try to do. It will take about six weeks for comm. to go through, and orders. I am finishing a piece to send Ober, should have time for at least one more. And I am broke, as always. Can you send me $100.00 or more if you can. I think a change of environment will freshen me. I will be able to do stuff for mags. on the side and can pay the loan back in cash.

In any case, when I come to Washington I will have a chance to come up and see you.

This in confidence until the comm. has gone through. I may not pass a medical.

Bill

To Harold Ober — TS. FCVA
[received 30 Mar. 1942] — [Oxford]

Dear Mr Ober:

This is a two-part-er, apparently. The Sat. Post bought five stories about these same people back in '35. They may throw it out because of the can motif. I think it's a good funny story, and I think it has its message for the day too: of gallant indomitability, of a willingness to pull up the pants and carry on, no matter with whom, let alone what.[1]

I am going before a board for a comm. in the Navy, a desk job in the Bureau of Aeronautics. I am going to need some cash. I have written Bob H. to put the bee on him. If he wont, will you let me have $100.00? Besides, I'm the only writer I ever heard of who got advances from his agent; I wish to keep this distinction constant.

The comm. business is in confidence until I find if I can pass the board and medical.

Faulkner

[1] The story, "My Grandmother Millard and General Bedford Forrest and the Battle of Harrykin Creek," finally appeared in *Story*, XXII (Mar.-Apr. 1943), 68–86.

Faulkner had sold a story called "Two Soldiers" to The Saturday Evening Post, *CCXIV (28 Mar. 1942), 9–11, 35, 36, 38, 40. He used some of the same characters in "Shall Not Perish," but the* Post *rejected it. On Harold Ober's advice, Faulkner attempted to simplify it.*

To Harold Ober — TELEGRAM FCVA
6 May 1942 — Oxford, Mississippi

MAILING REWRITTEN STORY TO POST. WILLIAM FAULKNER

To Harold Ober
[received 14 May 1942]

TS. FCVA
[Oxford]

This is the only copy I have of the re-written story.

Hold the story 'Snow' for a while. I think I have a copy here to re-write from, but I had better put that time at something else nearer Post size, to get enough money to go on military service and leave something for dependents.

[no signature]

When the Post *rejected the new version, Faulkner rewrote the story.*

To Harold Ober
[received 25 May 1942]

TS. FCVA
[Oxford]

I think it's all right now. I should have written it this way at first; it never had tasted quite right to me. Goddamn it that's what having to write not because you want to write but because you are harassed to hell for money does.

[no signature]

Again the Post *rejected the story, and when Ober informed Faulkner he told him he thought that references to "Two Soldiers" should be omitted and perhaps the names of the characters should be changed before he offered it to another magazine.*

To Harold Ober
[received 4 June 1942]

TS. FCVA
[Oxford]

It is now condensed 5 pages more. Names are unchanged, but all direct references to incident in previous story have been removed. Maybe it will sell now.[1]

[no signature]

[1] "Shall Not Perish" was also rejected by seven other magazines before it was purchased on 19 May 1943 for $25 by *Story*, XXIII (July-Aug. 1943), 40–47.

To Bennett Cerf — TS. RH

Saturday [probably 6 June 1942] — Oxford

Dear Bennett:

Good for Don.[1] Do you know how he managed to get into the Air Force? They turned me down on application, didn't say why, may have been age, 44.

I have a definite offer from the Navy, but I want an Air Force job if possible. I still haven't given up hope. Did he get in by mere application, or did he have influence? Or was he a specialist in some line?

I'll appreciate any information, as to whether what influence I might wangle will help or harm. I was turned down after only about four weeks, so maybe there is some definite factor against me, like my age or lack of school degrees, or perhaps because I wrote my Senator and asked him to put in a word when I sent in the application. The Navy job is at a desk in the Bureau of Aeronautics in Washington. I want to stay out doors if possible, want to go to California. Incidentally, has Random House any job in California I could do?

Have seen no reviews at all yet on MOSES.

Bill

Sure enough, do you know of anyone who wants to send a missionary to California for a few weeks?

[1] Donald Klopfer.

To Whit Burnett — TS. PRINCETON

[probably mid-June 1942][1] — [Oxford]

Dear Mr Burnett:

Choose anything of mine you want to and that is convenient. I have become so damned frantic trying to make a living and keep my grocer etc. from putting me in bankruptcy for the last year that nothing I or any body else ever wrote seems worth anything to me anymore. Sorry I couldn't have helped you and best wishes for anthology. I thought I had written you before to this effect, but I have been so worried lately with trying to write pot-boilers and haunting the back door of the post-office for checks that dont come to keep a creditor with a bill from catching me on the street, that I dont remember anything anymore.

Faulkner

[1] On 8 June, Burnett had written Ober asking him to forward his request that Faulkner choose a short story for *This Is My Best,* and on 23 June he sent Faulkner a wire of appreciation.

To Harold Ober
[received 22 June 1942]

TS. FCVA
[Oxford]

Mr Ober

You had this story before.[1] As you can see from this installment, it is much longer, will run 60–75 pages, more complete and very plottified and, except for the first chapter of induction and explanation, mostly simple dialogue.

I'm sending this batch in so you can see what it is like, and to ask what chance for money. I have another shot at a comm. but haven't even r.r. fare to New Orleans to take examination. I know where the trouble lies in what I write now. I have been buried here for three years now for lack of money and I am stale. Even a military job will dig me up and out for a while. If I fail at the comm. and can get some money, I am going somewhere for a while, probably to California and try for something in pictures, even $100 a week until I get back on my mental feet. I have been trying for about ten years to carry a load that no artist has any business attempting: oldest son to widowed mothers and inept brothers and nephews and wives and other female connections and their children, most of whom I dont like and with none of whom I have anything in common, even to make conversation about. I am either not brave enough or not scoundrel enough to take my hat and walk out: I dont know which. But if it's really beginning to hurt my work, I will choose pretty damn quick. I dont think that yet; it is only my earning capacity which is dulled; possibly because I have too little fun. But if I can get some money, I can get away for a while—either in service, or out of it. Incidentally, I believe I have discovered the reason inherent in human nature why warfare will never be abolished: it's the only condition under which a man who is not a scoundrel can escape for a while from his female kin. But now the formation of these Waacs and such gives a man to blink.

Do you know of any sort of assignment that would get me to Cal. for a while, with enough to live on while I worked?

Faulkner

[1] "Knight's Gambit."

To Harold Ober
[received 25 June 1942]

TS. FCVA
[Oxford]

Mr Ober

This is also a continuation of the last plaint I sent you. What chance might I have of getting some specific assignment to write a piece that would pay my fare and keep me in Cal. for a month? That is, a drawing acct. of $1,000.00, so I can leave $500.00 here with family? If I can get to

Cal. I believe I can get myself a job at least $100.00–$200.00 a week with a movie co. I've been hoping a story might sell, for that reason. Anyway, I seem to have touched bottom as earning goes. 1 story out of 6 since January, and so to borrow a few dollars now and then to tide along is foolish. I've got to get away from here and earn more money. I know no place to do it better than Cal. if I can get hold of $1,000.00 that's what I will do. I would need that much to take up the service commission, buy uniform and transport myself to where I can report for duty and live until I draw pay, even. The comm. (if I pass board) will pay me $3200.00, but I will have to live in Washington, which will leave little over for family, and nothing at all to pay the food bills, etc. which I have run up here during the last year or so while my earnings have been falling off. I haven't even been able to pay a telephone bill in two months now and I owe the grocer $600.00 and no fuel for the winter yet. But if I can get to Cal. I believe I'll be all right in 6 mo. If you can think of any mag. article job to pay my expenses to Cal. and keep me for a month, that will do it.

Faulkner

To Bennett Cerf — TS. RH
Tuesday [probably 23 June 1942] — Oxford

Dear Bennett:

I am trying to raise $1,000.00, $500.00 to pay my grocer etc. here, $500.00 to go to Cal. on and find myself a movie job.

If I pass for the comm. it will pay $3200.00. I dont believe I can live in Washington on that and support my family here. If nothing else comes up, I will have to try it however, as I have touched bottom, spent all my savings and am in debt for food, etc. no fuel for next winter, that sort of thing.

The trouble is, I cant sell stories. Wrote 6 since Jan., sold one. I have gone stale here; I have expected it in a way, being buried here too long as I have. I have been unable to connect with Cal. by an agent, because agents think of me as a $1000.00 per week man. I believe I can go out there myself and get something, even $100.00 a week, get a change mentally and begin to earn again.

I have just written to Agent Harold Ober to see if he can get me a magazine assignment, article, something, that will get me to Cal. and keep me until I can get a movie job, or earn enough to take up the comm. with idea of writing on the side.

Right now, I cant move at all. I have 60¢ in my pocket, and that is literally all. I finished a story and sent it in yesterday, but with no real hope it will sell. My local creditors bother me, but so far none has taken an action because I began last year to give them notes for debts. But the notes will come due soon and should I be sued, my whole house here will collapse: farm, property, everything.

My best chance to earn money is Cal. Mainly I must get away from here and freshen my mental condition until I can write stuff that will sell. Am I in shape to ask an advance from the firm? if so, how much? I would like to pay the grocer something before I leave, but I have reached the point where I had better go to Cal. with just r.r. fare if I can do no better.

Bill Faulkner

To Harold Ober — TS. FCVA
Sunday [28 June 1942] — [Oxford]

Dear Harold:

Yours of yesterday received.

1932 May–Aug. Oct–May, 33	MGM.	$250–600 per week	
1934 July	Universal	$1000.00	"
1935 Dec–Jan	Fox	"	
1936 May	RKO	"	
" Aug–Dec	Fox	$750.00	
1937 Jan–Aug	"	$1000	

I believe the agents who have tried since to sell me have talked about $1000 per week. I dont think I am or have been or will ever be worth that to movies. It just took them five years to find it out. I will take anything above $100.00. I must have something somewhere, quick. For a month now I have had no cash whatever. I have borrowed a few dollars each week from my mother to pay the cook and laundry with. She has no income save what I have given to her. Her own bank balance is now less than $500.00. I can try for the comm. and be sure of $3200.00 and hope to write on the side. If I can find nothing else, I will do that. But I must find out quickly whether I can find anything else or not. If you can get me $100, per week, do so soon as you can. I have not paid my grocer in 3 months, and he cannot carry me much longer. I have nothing I can sell or borrow on anymore now, save an interest in a piece of timber. I may be able to get $500 on it. If I can, I will take that and go to Cal. and use some second-hand nepotism for something. That is, I know a director and a writer or so who might be able to find me something. But something I must have, and soon. I have cashed in my life insurance and if I were sued by anyone, all my property except my home would go and my daughter and mother and wife would have nothing. Once I get away from here where creditors cannot hound me all the time, I think I can write and sell again.

If you have anything of mine you can get $100 for, please do it. If there is any way you can get me $1000, I can go to Cal on that and try myself.

I will hold off as long as I can. Then I will try for the comm. If I am in service, I dont believe any creditor will sue me. But I cant chance even that much past July 1.

I am sending another story soon. That will be 7 in six months, 1 sale. If a man with my experience and reputation has reached that point, there is something wrong and something had better be done. I think a change of scene is the answer.

Faulkner

H. N. Swanson, Harold Ober's West Coast representative and a prominent Hollywood agent, began to look for opportunities for Faulkner at various motion-picture studios only to find himself in apparent conflict with agent William Herndon in negotiating with Warner Brothers. Ober wired Faulkner asking about his status.

To Harold Ober — TELEGRAM FCVA
15 July 1942 — Oxford, Miss.

I WIRED SWANSON YESTERDAY I DECLINED LAST YEAR TO SIGN ANY CONTRACT WITH HERNDON UNTIL HE HAD LANDED DEFINITE JOB FOR ME. I CONSIDER HE VOIDED ANY AGREEMENT BETWEEN US BY FAILING THIS. HAVE NOT HEARD FROM HIM SINCE FEBRUARY OF THIS YEAR. CAN HERNDON HOLD ME UNDER SUCH TERMS. WILLIAM FAULKNER

On 16 July, Ober wrote Faulkner that Swanson hoped the deal would go through but that Herndon was acting as agent because Faulkner had never dismissed him. Ober was unable to report any magazine sales but enclosed a check for $100 to help tide Faulkner over. On 17 July, Faulkner wired Ober that he had received a telegram from Herndon. Faulkner paraphrased the message: Herndon understood that Faulkner had authorized Swanson to close a deal Herndon felt he had made with Warner Bros. producer Robert Buckner for Faulkner, and if Faulkner did not wire James J. Geller, the head of Warner Bros. Story Department, that Herndon represented him, Herndon would take action.

To James J. Geller TS. FCVA
18 July, 1942 Oxford, Miss.

Dear Mr Geller:

Your letter of July 15 at hand. I also have Mr Buckner's letter describing the job he has in mind. It is a good idea and I will be proud to work with it and I hope and trust I can do it justice.

I am aware of the hard work Mr Herndon has done in my behalf. We had not made a contact with an actual job, so after not hearing from him in some two or three months, I asked my old New York literary agent and my publisher too to see if either could make a contact for me. The result was the authorization I gave to Mr Swanson, by request of my New York agent, to act for me. I would have protected Mr Herndon in this, and I still wish him to have some recompense for what he has done in establishing a contact for me with Mr Buckner last winter which came to nothing. But he sent me an insulting and unnecessary telegram before he had offered me any chance to see his side of the matter. So from now on please consider Mr Ober's California representative, Mr. Swanson I think, as my authorised agent. I am sending a copy of this to Mr Ober in New York, and asking him to handle all matters.

A letter to Mr Buckner goes forward today. Thanking you again for your letter, and assuring you that I am aware that Mr Herndon has worked hard in my behalf, I am

Yours sincerely,
[s] William Faulkner
[t] William Faulkner

To William Herndon TS. FCVA
18 July 1942 Oxford, Miss.

Dear Mr Herndon:

Your letter of July 14 received after I received your wire. I regret that I didn't get the letter first and I regret that you sent a wire like that at all. You accused me of deliberate underhand dealing, which is not true, and inferred that I could be forced by threats into doing what is right, which I will take from no man. I give you the benefit of the doubt to believe you were surprised at finding someone else trying for a job for me, and were worried over possible loss of a commission, and sent the wire before you had thought very clearly.

What happened is as follows. I had not heard from you since last February. You had nothing definite on the fire for me then, after working hard in my behalf for six months and better. All that while I was getting broker and broker, until in June I had exhausted all possibilities and was in very bad shape financially. I wrote in June to both my publisher and my New York agent, asking if either could manage to get me out to Hollywood, where I believed I could find a job for myself, that I would accept any salary and that I believed one reason I had not connected so far was that the people who had tried to sell me lately had asked for too much money, more than my picture record would show I was worth.

The publisher made some sort of contact through a friend, which would very likely come to nothing. The agent, Mr Ober, wrote me toward the end of June that he thought he had something lined up and to stand by. Last Saturday, June 11, he wired me that there was something pretty definite. He did not say what nor where, but asked me to wire Swanson authority to go ahead. I waited until the following Tuesday, then I wired Swanson to go ahead. After sending that wire, I received a wire from Mr Ober saying that you were holding the deal up. But I still heard nothing from you until yesterday, July 17, though you had a letter in the mail for me on July 14, describing this job with Buckner, which was the first intimation I had had about what the assignment was.

I relayed your wire of July 17 to Mr Ober in New York, before getting your letter of 7/14. He answered last night that you did not start this deal. But the last thing you had on the fire for me was a job with Mr Buckner, and because of this fact I would have protected you, not only for what you might have done in the present deal but because you had been the first to try to sell me to Buckner and Warner's. I still wish to do so, although your threatening me has left a bad taste in my mouth which I dont think I shall forget. A copy of this letter goes to Mr Ober, with a request that he make some equitable adjustment with you. Then maybe we had better part company. Without being conscious of it, I must not have had enough confidence in your ability to sell me. I see now that in all my recent money troubles I never thought of writing you to try again. I suppose I took it for granted that you had done and were doing your best and had probably given me up at last as bad merchandise. And you didn't have enough confidence in me to believe I would be just and fair with you regarding any Hollywood matter you had had anything to do with. If this is not satisfactory to you, then make good your threat and cause whatever trouble you wish.

Yours truly,
[s] William Faulkner
[t] William Faulkner

To Harold Ober | TS. FCVA
[received 20 July 1942] | [Oxford]

Dear Harold:

Attached a letter to Herndon and a copy for your files. He worked on Buckner at Warner's in my behalf on a possibility last Jan. I wrote a treatment for it, came to nothing.

Even if he had nothing to do with this particular deal and perhaps never even thought of me again until he heard somebody else was trying to sell me, there is still the fact that he brought me to Buckner's notice and the former business did exist, of which this may be a byproduct. I never saw Herndon nor heard of him until last year when a writer who knew me by name wrote me in Herndon's behalf, suggesting that H. could get me a picture job.[1] As far as I know, Herndon tried. That is, I wrote 5 20–25 page story lines for various studios or individuals, none of which came to anything. Then last Feb. I stopped that and went at short stories.

So my feeling is that, whether he actually deserves anything or not, I would rather pay his commission than have him on my mind as thinking I owed him anything. Also, if I go to Cal. to work, I would like to work in peace and not be heckled and bothered by him there. So please get me a clean slate with him. I'd rather pay his full comm. and be washed up. Something of this nature happened to me before, and I have felt better ever since because I paid a comm. which I did not feel was due, just for knowing that there's no guy saying, There goes Faulkner spending money that belongs to me.[2]

If the Herndon letter is all right, please send his copy on to him. Envelope is attached.

Faulkner

If I should go to Cal. suddenly, which you will know, will you please *NOT* SEND ANY CHECKS to my Oxford address but hold until you hear from me? But if you know a check will reach me before I leave here, send for gossake. I will try to keep you advised as to exactly when I will leave. I may have to wait for a check, as I have no money as usual. I do not want checks to come here in my absence, as they will be misapplied.

[Faulkner circled Herndon's name in the letter's first line and then drew a line down to the bottom of the letter, where he wrote:] I just received the Warner letter. My answer is attached. I will hold both the original to it and the original to Herndon. Wire me Monday as soon as possible and I will mail them airmail. That is, if they are all right, wire O.K. If I dont hear by noon Monday, I will mail Herndon's, other one too.

[1] The writer was Stephen Longstreet.

[2] Faulkner paid the commission on the film sale of *The Unvanquished* to Morton Goldman.

To Harold Ober — TS. FCVA
July 19, 1942 — Oxford, Miss.

Dear Harold:

I have at hand another letter from Herndon.

I was wrong in not getting quits with him by notifying him in advance or at the time that I had asked you to find something in pictures for me, contract or no contract. I have thought about this for several days now, and my feeling has not changed.

I have all reason to believe he was working sincerely in my behalf with various studios. I know he made a contact for me with Buckner last winter. I wrote you about this.

As he expresses it, I have failed in integrity toward him. I was not aware of this at the time, yet and strangely enough perhaps even if it is not true, I do not like to be accused of it.

But I am certainly at fault in the fact that I did not get myself discharged with him before I undertook anything else. I simply did not once think about him while I was worrying about money. I also realise that my perspective is bad here, that this may be bluff on his part to protect his commission, etc. Yet there is a certain sincerity in his letters, in all of them, a naivete almost. I know nothing else about him but his letters. But it worries me and will continue to worry me. At present I feel like throwing the whole thing up. But this will be funk, and you have done too much toward the deal for me to quit.

I have not communicated with him at all other than a wire in response to his wire in which I said I did not consider any agreement existed between us. I have not yet communicated with the studio.

What I wish to do is this, and I wish your acquiescence, for the sake of my peace of mind:

I want to wire him to go ahead and make the deal. I will pay your representative's commission, of course. I wish to wire him to make the deal, also the studio to deal with him. When I reach the coast, I will settle affairs with him. Your representative's commission I guarantee. The matter must be settled soon, and as I feel now nothing else but this will give me any peace about it.

Please wire me at once your acquiescence to this plan. I will then wire Herndon and the studio too to deal with him. Wire me at once. Thank you for the money of yesterday.

Yours
William Faulkner

To Harold Ober — TS. FCVA
[received 22 July 1942] — [Oxford]

You had this before.[1] It is rewritten, simplified, still an implied story as before, but I have tried to fill the gaps, etc. and make it explicit as well.

[no signature]

[1] "Snow."

On 20 July 1942, Ober wired Faulkner that he and Swanson were withdrawing and taking no commission. He advised Faulkner to close directly with Warner Brothers.

To James J. Geller — TELEGRAM WARNER BROS.
22 July 1942 — Oxford, Miss.

ACCEPT DEAL MADE BY HERNDON. WILL ARRIVE MONDAY SUBJECT TO TRANSPORTATION DELAYS. WILLIAM FAULKNER

To Harold Ober — TELEGRAM FCVA
28 July 1942 — Burbank, Cal.

ARRIVED MONDAY.[1] PLEASE SEND CHECK TO ME HERE AT THE STUDIO AND MANY THANKS.[2] WRITING. WILLIAM FAULKNER

[1] 27 July 1942.
[2] On 28 July, Ober sold "Shingles for the Lord" for $1,000 to *The Saturday Evening Post*, CCXV (15 Feb. 1943), 14–15, 68, 70, 71.

To Harold Ober — TS. FCVA
1 Aug. 1942 — Hollywood, Cal.

Dear Harold:

I arrived Monday and went to work that same day. Mr Swanson came out to see me Tuesday, and called me two or three times since, offered any help I needed, which was kind of him and I am grateful. I told him that as soon as I got this matter straightened out, I would come in and see him and explain the whole set-up.

It is not quite straightened out yet, but it will be in the future. Just when, depends on how I am progressing with this job. What follows must be in confidence, as will appear. I ask you to please treat it that way, as by that means I will be able to clarify myself without jeopardy.

Mr Geller told me (in private) that, if I show that I am doing all right on this job, the contract offered and signed by me will be torn up and a new arrangement made. Mr Buckner, the producer to whom I am directly responsible for this job, told me the same thing. Although I was not aware of it when I left Oxford, I was committed to the contract which they offered me. It is a long series of options, 13-13-26-26, then a series of 52 week options. I thought it over for a day. Then, feeling that I had committed myself, even though I was not aware that the deal included more than this one particular job, and on the strength of Geller's statement that, if I worked well, the contract would be voided by the studio, I decided to sign it. Afterward I talked to Buckner, who assured me that the contract would be voided. When that moment comes and the studio offers to tear it up, I will see then about making a new one to include only this one job, if possible. I am not sure this will be possible, as the studio will want to protect itself against possibility of another studio working on me. But I have Buckner's assurance that, whatever comes, I can return to Oxford when this job is finished, and any future arrangements between me and the studio will allow me to stay in Oxford practically for whatever periods of time I desire.

This of course is beside the point as regards you and myself. I agree that it will be much better if one agent handles me in all capacities. This is what I intend to arrange, and I can do it. But it will take some time, at least until the studio decides I am valuable enough to deserve a new contract. I will write you as developments come. And please keep this in utmost confidence. This is a strange and curious place and I am convinced that it will be better for me and for all of us concerned if I keep my actions uncomplicated and perfectly straight forward until the moment comes when I can clear the whole matter up with one stroke.

I will see Mr Swanson soon. I am not going to tell him of Geller's and Buckner's private assurance to me about the contract, for the reason that I dont think the studio would like it at all if I divulged such information of that private nature to an agent who does not yet represent me. If they learned I had done such a thing, they would consider it a reflection and maybe a very damaging one on my integrity, and would later harm us all to the extent that it would prevent me ever getting another job here. So please treat this as a matter between you and me. Let me explain the whole thing to Mr Swanson myself when the time is right to do so.

I will write again as things develop. Thank you again for all you have done, and again my apologies for getting things bitched up like this.

Yours,
Bill

To Robert K. Haas | TS. RH
[possibly early Aug. 1942] | [Hollywood]

Extremely sorry. I got two envelopes mixed in mailing that day. If you have time, and have not read the Mann before, read it. What an immortality that brute has got himself: an immigrant, he has expelled from his native land the foremost literary artist of his time.[1]

[no signature]

[1] The brute was of course Adolf Hitler. The Thomas Mann work may have been the pamphlet *An Exchange of Letters* (New York, 1937).

De Gaulle Story *was the title of the film on which Faulkner was working for Buckner. It treated Gen. Charles de Gaulle's career and built toward his rallying the French people to fight for victory in World War II. Faulkner usually turned in his pages of script to Story Department head James J. Geller.*

To James J. Geller | TS. WARNER BROS.
[probably mid-Sept. 1942] | Burbank, Cal.
INTER-OFFICE COMMUNICATION
Subject: 5 line description of work in progress

Dear Mr Geller:

If this dont cover the subject sufficiently, let me know and I will try again.

GIRL & 2 BOYS MEET FREE FRANCE
FINAL SCORE:
GIRL 1 BOY UP & 1 TO CARRY
1 BOY DOWN 2
1 BOY OUT
DE GAULLE 3 UP

[t] Wm. Faulkner

To Mrs. William F. Fielden[1] | MS. MRS. FIELDEN
Saturday [19 Sept. 1942] | Warner Bros. Studio
Burbank, Cal.

Dear Sister—

. . . .

I feel pretty well, sober, am writing to the satisfaction of the studio. The script I did now has the official O.K. of De Gaulle's agent and of the

Dept. of State, so nothing to do now but write in the dialogue. This is confidential, please. Dont tell publicly what I am even writing.

. . . .

Billy

[1] Faulkner's stepdaughter, the former Mrs. Claude Selby.

To Mrs. Murry C. Falkner
Sunday [15 Nov. 1942]

MS. JFSA
Warner Bros. Studio
Burbank, Cal.

Dear Moms—

I'm still counting on getting home about Dec. 15th. The studio promised me a raise, which has not come yet, so their promise that I go home Dec 15 may be the same delayed business. But I think I can make it then. I dont want to make them mad by coming anyway, because I still may get the raise, and I want a job here to come back to, since I have done pretty good for them this time. Will keep you informed of just how far I am behind the promise. What presents would you like for Xmas?

Billy

In November of 1942, Faulkner wrote a poem called "Old Ace." It was inspired by Capt. Eddie Rickenbacker, who had survived three weeks in a life raft after a plane crash in the Pacific. He mailed the poem to Ober and subsequently sent corrections. It was never sold or printed.

To Harold Ober
Thursday [26 Nov. 1942]

TS. FCVA
[Hollywood]

Dear Harold:

On the 23rd. I airmailed you a 3-page poem, 'Old Ace.' Same day I wired you to please hold it for a correction. I airmailed the second, correct draft to you today, 24th. I want to make still another correction. . . .

I am going home on 4 weeks' leave Dec. 14.

I may be able to sell as a movie my story 'Tomorrow' which you sold to Post about 2 years ago. I will write you further details. Meantime, can you send me a copy of it, to reach me not later than Dec. 5–6? Maybe I can get a Post copy of it. My only copy is at home. I would like to have a copy now. I will write a picture idea, to sell the story and picture both to a studio. Will communicate with you in advance, before I take any step, of course. I want now only to see how a treatment will come out on paper, before submitting anything.

Bill

To Malcolm A. Franklin
Saturday [5 Dec. 1942]

TS. MR. FRANKLIN
Warner Bros. Studio
Burbank, Cal.

Dear Buddy:

Your letter came today. I was glad to hear what Oxford is doing in Dec. 1942. I knew about what the picture would be, knew pretty well, but yours was the first black-and-white record I have had. So far, only Mamma and my mother and Jill have written me, and when a woman writes to her loved ones, the letter really never leaves whatever upstairs bedroom it was written in.

There is a meat, butter, etc. shortage here. I hear reports of rationing. No meat now on Tuesday; I watched a friend last night who had invited me to his home for supper, stop at seven grocery stores to find butter and found none. The street lamps are hooded from above here, wardens patrol the streets for cracks in window shades, etc. There are barrage balloons along the coast, and searchlights (and of course, A.A. batteries hidden) in all sorts of unexpected places through the city: in all the canyons, and now and then on the playgrounds of schools. They expect a bombing here. But nobody is afraid of it. Of course, people cant leave their homes, lives, businesses, just because they might be bombed. It may even be that sort of courage. I hope it is. But now and then I become concerned about these people here.

This is the reason. The strangest thing here (to me) is the attitude toward gas rationing. It's an accomplished fact; it's done, gasoline is rationed and these people were warned in advance it was going to happen. Yet they still believe it will not, that it cannot happen. They seem to get their ration books and then spend as fast as they need it, the gas coupons which are to last them for a month or more. The town is big, and it is so conditioned to going to work in cars, that the people seem to believe that somehow they will still have the cars, even though the work they are going to is not essential work to winning a war or anything else. (I'm not speaking of the aircraft factory people. They either live close, or the govt. will see that they get to work. I mean the moving picture people, and the real estate agents and lawyers and merchants and all the other parasites who exist only because of motion picture salaries, including the fake doctors and faith-healers and swamis and blackmailing private detectives who live on the people who draw motion picture salaries.)

There is something here for an anthropologist's notebook. This is one of the richest towns in the country. As it exists today, its economy and geography was fixed and invented by the automobile. Therefore, the automobile invented it. The automobile (for a time, anyway) is as dead as the mastodon. Therefore the town which the automobile created, is dying. I think that a detached and impersonal spectator could watch here what some superman in a steamheated diving-bell could have watched at the beginning of the ice age, say: a doomed way of life and its seething inhabitants all saying: Why, Jack Frost simply cant do this to us. It's not so. That's not ice we see; that's not cold we feel. We've got to be warm. We cant live otherwise.

I think you are wise to get into the service. If you wait, they'll get you anyhow. But there is a better reason. You have more aptitude for being a regimented soldier than you think, even though you have no avocation for it. You will never have that: to be a good soldier infers not only a capacity for being misled, but a willingness for it: an eagerness even to supply the gaps in the logic of them who persuade him to relinquish his privacy. And I'm afraid that the same old stink is rising from this one as has risen from every war yet: vide Churchill's speech about having no part in dismembering the Br. Empire. But it is the biggest thing that will happen in your lifetime. All your contemporaries will be in it before it is over, and if you are not one of them, you will always regret it. That's something in the meat and bone and blood from the old cave-time, right enough. But it's there, and it's a strange thing how a man, no matter how intelligent, will cling to the public proof of his masculinity: his courage and endurance, his willingness to sacrifice himself for the land which shaped his ancestors. I dont want to go either. No sane man likes war. But when I can, I am going too, maybe only to prove to myself that I can do (within my physical limitations of age, of course) as much as anyone else can to make secure the manner of living I prefer and that suits my kin and kind.

The next step opens out here, of course, and this stops being a letter and becomes a sermon. So I'll take this step in one jump, and quit. We must see that the old Laodicean smell doesn't rise again after this one. But we must preserve what liberty and freedom we already have to do that. We will have to make the liberty sure first, in the field. It will take the young men to do that. Then perhaps the time of the older men will come, the ones like me who are articulate in the national voice, who are too old to be soldiers, but are old enough and have been vocal long enough to be listened to, yet are not so old that we too have become another batch of decrepit old men looking stubbornly backward at a point 25 or 50 years in the past.

Pappy

To Harold Ober
Monday [25 Jan. 1943]

TS. FCVA
Studio

Dear Harold:

Both copies of letter received. I'm glad you finally placed the story; I still think it is amusing.[1]

The studio has taken up the second option in the contract. I intend to try for the Ferry Command in April. Failing that, or any other war work, I will try for leave of absence to go home and see to my farm. That is, I intend to remain set here until April. After that, I will know just what my position with this studio will be.

I had a pleasant time at home, hated like hell to come back. By April I hope to have enough cash backlog to make some attempt to break off, to soldier if possible, for leave to farm anyway for a while. I shant jeopardise my position with the studio though, as I apparently cannot make enough money at anything else and must resign myself to being a part-time script writer at least.

I have not spoken to the studio about leave of absence to soldier or return home for a while yet, and will not do so until later. I cant make the attempt until my bank account is in proper shape. As soon as it is, debts paid, money put aside for my family, I will broach the subject. So please hold this in confidence until I write you about it.

Yours,
Bill

[1] "My Grandmother Millard and General Bedford Forrest and the Battle of Harrykin Creek," *Story*, XXII (Mar.-Apr. 1943), 68–86.

To Robert K. Haas
February 17, 1943

TS. RH
Warner Bros.

Dear Bob:

Will you please tell me how much royalty you are reporting as paid to me for 1942.

I am well and quite busy, surrounded by snow, dogs, Indians, Red Coats, and Nazi spies.[1]

When I finish this job, I want to try for the Ferry Command. Wish me luck!

Sincerely,
[s] Bill
[t] William Faulkner[2]

[1] Faulkner was working on a film called *Northern Pursuit.*
[2] This letter was dictated and typed at Warner Bros.

Faulkner's "Shingles for the Lord" appeared in The Saturday Evening Post, *CCXV (13 Feb. 1943), 14–15, 68, 70, 71. In the story, Res Grier uses a frow so skillfully that when he hits it with the maul he not only cuts a shingle from the bolt of wood but can also aim it at the shin of Solon Quick, his adversary in a trading match. Dean F. W. Bradley wrote the editors of the* Post *that he enjoyed the story but questioned Grier's skill with the frow on the basis that bolt pieces were always split into exactly equal parts until the proper thickness of shingle was attained and that the kind of blow described might splinter the shingle. The editors forwarded the letter and the enclosed stamp to Faulkner.*

To Dean F. W. Bradley — TS. RH
March 8, 1943 — Oxford, Mississippi

Dear Sir:

Your letter r.e. misuse of frow is at hand.

I was not ignorant about frows. I just took what I thought was a minor liberty in order to tell the story. I didn't consider the liberty important and still dont. But I regret sincerely having offended anyone's sense of fitness, and I will be doubly careful from now on to be explicit in facts.

Thank you for your letter. I hope you got some pleasure from the story to balance some of the irritation. My apologies herewith to the Post too, whom I betrayed without deliberation or desire.

Yours truly,
[s] William Faulkner
[t] William Faulkner

To Harold Ober — TS. FCVA
Monday [15 Mar. 1943] — [Hollywood]

Dear Harold:

It was the man here who got the title confused. I gave him the correct one, but I thought the magazine was LIBERTY.[1]

I believe I can make a play from the story, something after BY THE SKIN OF HIS TEETH.[2] I would like to try it, when I have time. I cant afford now to buy an option on it from Mrs Fitzgerald, but I'd like very much to have the refusal of the purchase, in case any one else had the same idea.

I didn't know you had sold the story, should have thought first to mention the matter to you. Herndon is writing to you today. I imagine the

Agent Firm he is now with will want to buy this option. If, for Mrs Fitzgerald's sake, you cant refuse a money offer for the rights, can you include in the sale something stipulating that only I can use the story? I wish I could buy the option myself now. I would make the play first, then sell to movies.

When I first mentioned the story to Herndon, our agreement was that only I could write the script from it. But I dont know the firm he is now with, and dont know what they will want to do, once they come to think there is some money in it.

I wish you and I could hold on to it alone. But, as stated, I cant buy in at present.[3]

I'm getting on pretty well, but a damned dull life though. I spent Saturday at a friend's in the country, on a tremendous big roan Tennessee walking gelding, and feel better for it.

Swanson had a nibble on 2 SOLDIERS but nothing came of it so far.

Best regards,
Bill

[1] F. Scott Fitzgerald had published "The Curious Case of Benjamin Button" in *Collier's* (27 May 1922) and collected it in *Tales of the Jazz Age* (New York, 1922).

[2] A reference, apparently, to Thornton Wilder's play *The Skin of Our Teeth* (New York, 1942).

[3] On 25 Mar. 1943, Ober replied that he personally would give Faulkner an option on the story with all the time he needed, without any money down, and without Herndon's having a commission. (See Faulkner to Ober, 26 Apr. 1943.)

To Mr. and Mrs. William F. Fielden — TS. MRS. FIELDEN
Saturday evening [3 Apr. 1943] — Warner Bros.

My dear Sister and Bill:

. . . .

I have had, still have, and apparently will have for the next few decades, the damned worst bloody rotten bad cold in human captivity. I took it Tuesday, March 23. On April 4, I still have it. It is now one of triplets: lumbago, April 1, ear-ache April 3, and still going strong. There is still leprosy, bubonic, and death. But I still believe that 1 Faulkner can outlast any 1 cold. I've got used to it now. Of course I cant hear on my left side, and when I creep out in the am to go to work, I am a rachitic old man in the last stages of loco-motor ataxia. But I can still see the red lights to cross the street on, and I can still invent a little something now and then that is photogenic, and I can still certainly sign my name to my salary check each Saturday.

My best pappy's love to Vicky,[1] to you and Bill. We will all meet soon, I know. I am making a splendid collection of 25¢ paper-back whodunits to bring home. Have you seen Sayre's NINE TAILORS? It's all right, up with ABC and FER DE LANCE.[2] Am now reading Ngaio Marsh. She's too arty, I fear.

Pappy

[1] Mrs. Fielden's daughter, Victoria.

[2] Dorothy Sayers' *The Nine Tailors* (New York, 1934), Agatha Christie's *The ABC Murders* (New York, 1936) and Rex Stout's *Fer-de-Lance* (New York, 1934).

To James M. Faulkner — TS. MR. FAULKNER

Saturday afternoon [3 Apr. 1943] — Hollywood, Calif.

My dear Jim:

Your letter received this morning; also one from Chook, which I shall answer tomorrow. Also one from Miss Susan Bagget's daughter, saying how they have named the high school literary club after John.

Enclosed is a luck piece.[1] I wore it on the shoulder-strap of my overcoat. A stripe, light blue, on a khaki band, went with it to show rank: like Navy rank: one stripe, Pilot-Flying Officer (Lieut), two stripes, Flight Lieut. (Captain), two and a half, Squadron Leader, three, Wing Commander, four, Group Captain. I dont think you can wear it on your uniform, but you might ask permission from your Station Commander, tell him where it came from, your godfather, perhaps you can wear it. If not, you might have it welded onto a belt buckle, or onto your dog-tag, or clamped onto something to carry in your pocket. Anyway, keep it with you. You will probably find something else while you are flying that you will believe in, but keep them both. I would have liked for you to have had my dog-tag, R.A.F., but I lost it in Europe, in Germany. I think the Gestapo has it; I am very likely on their records right now as a dead British flying officer-spy.[2]

You will find something else, as you get along, which you will consider your luck. Flying men always do. I had one. I never found it again after my crack-up in '18.[3] But it worked all right, as I am still alive.

I think I know what a cruiser is. I believe, when this war is over, the cruisers and Cubs will be helicopters. I will have one then in the back yard, to go to the farm in, and a jeep for us to hunt and farm with. You will be on real aeroplanes soon. You should be all right, a good man. Just remember always that flying is fine, and it gets better but you've got to stay alive to enjoy it. You will have two milestones to pass, to pay back to the Govt. the cost of training you. The first one is foolhardiness. A lot of pilots dont get past that. Uncle Dean didn't. He managed to blow most of the fabric off his top wing before he found out he had done something you cannot do.

The next milestone is fear. Sometimes they happen at the same moment. This means that you fail to pass the foolhardiness milestone, and it is too late. But if the fear is not a result of foolhardiness, then you are all right. You have learned, and are capable of learning. You must know fear too. That is, you must know how to beat fear. If you cannot feel it, you are a moron, an idiot. The brave man is not he who does not know fear; the brave man is he who says to himself, 'I am afraid. I will decide quickly what to do, and then I will do it.'

That will come to you. It happens to everyone who flies and who is not a vegetable. Expect it. It is no more than a sneeze. Accept it when it comes, pass it; tell yourself, 'I am afraid. I dont like the way my heart is acting nor how my mouth tastes. But I know what my hands and feet must do, and I know they will do it, because my brain is running things for the next few seconds, and my brain is too busy to worry about what my heart is doing or my mouth tastes like.'

I want you to do well. No pilot can tell you how much you dont know. You will have to find it out, from day to day. But you can remember what good pilots have told you, so that when emergencies come, you will merely meet situations which you have already heard about. You will do things without having to think about them, that your instructors have trained you to do. You won't need to worry about that, if you have listened well. So, expect these two milestones. Pass the first one, foolhardiness, and you can take care of the next one. Expect it too, accept it and pass it, beat it. When it happens, dont forget to write me about it. Fear is an alarming experience, but I never yet knew it to kill anyone. If you are wise enough to recognize the fear, by that time you are safe. The old trained reflexes, the natural good sense, have already done the right thing.

This is a long letter, and preachified too, but Uncle Jack and your father are too old to do what you can do, and I must stay in civilian clothes to look after things for us when everybody comes back home again. So do well. Dont try to be lucky. Be happy in training, believe in yourself, believe in your ability to listen and watch and learn from instructors. I think that by now you can pretty well tell a sound instructor when you see him. Learn all you can about the aeroplane: how to check it over on the ground. Aeroplanes very seldom let you down; the trouble is inside cockpits.

Let me hear from you when you have time. I'll be here for some time yet.

Brother Will

[1] One of the lieutenant's pips from the shoulder strap of his RAF uniform.

[2] Faulkner's service with the RAF in 1918 was all in Canada.

[3] There is at present no corroborating evidence that Faulkner had a wartime crack-up.

To Harold Ober — TS. FCVA
Monday [26 Apr. 1943] — [Hollywood]

Dear Harold:

Letters received, including the check, for which thank you as always.

I want to try the Fitzgerald story as a play.[1] I am not supposed, have signed to that effect, to write anything of my own while drawing a studio's pay, and I am pretty busy at studio work also. So I dont think I will try anything else until this option is finished and I can take leave, or be fired, which will probably happen. Then I will try the play.

I had already told Herndon, as soon as I got here last Aug., that I considered him involved only in this Warner contract, and that you had been, still were, and would continue to be my partner in all writing relationships other than this contract, and that you would handle all sales of my short stories to any purchaser, also any new original material specifically intended for anyone except my novel publisher. That matter is clear to him.

I wont be satisfied until you have had a share in my motion picture venture. I will not dispossess Herndon as long as this contract, toward which he did some of the ground work a year before I ever got it, exists. But his claim goes no further. I will have a shot at the play, for you to sell it wherever you can. Will you send me a copy of the story? I think I am no good at movies, and will be fired as soon as the studio legally can. I will have to try something else then.

My best to Bob when you see him. He wrote me that his daughter is going for a ferry pilot. I would like even that, but I suppose I really am too old for anyone to want, even if I still dont believe it.

Bill Faulkner

[1] See Faulkner to Ober, 15 Mar. 1943.

To William F. Fielden — TS. MRS. FIELDEN
Tuesday [27 Apr. 1943] — [Warner Bros.]

My dear boy:

Your letter moved me very much. I too like my town, my land, my people, my life, am unhappy away from it even though I must quit it to earn money to keep it going to come back to. Can you unravel that sentence?

Yes, Big Miss[1] has done fine without me. I think she intends to have a plow horse and some gear in; I would like to see the garden so much that I dont let myself think about it.

A message for Vicki-pic[2]: I dont at all like my girls breaking their legs in Tennessee. When they want to break their bones, they must do it at Rowan Oak. When I get home, I am going to give her a spank, as well as the kiss, for breaking her leg in Tennessee.

See Air Force.[3] I wrote Quincannon's death scene, and the scene where the men in the aeroplane heard Roosevelt's speech after Pearl Harbor.

I dont know when I will come home. My contract option ends in July. If I write a good picture, I can ask for and get leave before then. If I dont, the studio will fire me when they legally can. I will stay on until I know what is what. Then, we will all meet and be together at Rowan Oak again. Until then, my love to Sister, and the message to Vicky-pic, from her ever loving

Pappy

[1] Estelle Faulkner.
[2] Victoria Fielden.
[3] A film being made by Howard Hawks.

To Jill Faulkner — TS. JFSA
Sunday [16 May 1943] — [Hollywood]

Dear Missy:

I had letters from Mama and Granny both, telling me how nice you look since you had your hair cut. Pappy misses that yellow hair that had never had an inch cut off of it since you were born, but since Pappy knows and can remember and can see in his mind whenever he wants to every single day you ever lived, whether he was there to look at you or not, why, any time he wants to he can imagine into his mind and in his sight too every single one of those days, and how you looked then. So any time he wants to think so, that hair is still long, never touched with scissors. So, that being the case, your hair can be cut like you want it, and it can still be like Pappy wants to think of it, at the same time. So I am glad you had it fixed the way you like it, and I want you to enjoy it and write me about it.

I like your letters just fine. They are the best things that happen to me. It used to be that a Negro waiter in the hotel here brought my breakfast up to my room. But since rationing started, and men got good jobs in aircraft plants, they have closed the dining-room. So I get up at seven, bathe and shave and dress, and walk down to Musso-Frank restaurant and buy a paper and have orange juice, toast, marmalade and sometimes little fellows,[1] and wait on the corner until Mr Bezzerides and Mr Job[2] come along in the car, and I go to the studio and walk into my office, and there on my desk is a letter from Mama and my Jill. That makes me feel just fine.

I am writing a big picture now, for Mr Howard Hawks, an old friend, a director. It is to be a big one. It will last about 3 hours, and the studio has allowed Mr Hawks 3 and ½ million dollars to make it, with 3 or 4 directors and about all the big stars. It will probably be named 'Battle Cry.' I'll write more about it later.

I love you very very very much.

You have two bonds now. I will send you the next one soon.[3]

Pappy

[1] Sausages.

[2] A. I. Bezzerides and Tom Job, fellow screenwriters at Warner Bros.

[3] During World War II, many employees bought government bonds, called Victory Bonds, through payroll deductions.

To Harold Ober — TS. FCVA
21 June, 1943 — [Hollywood]

Dear Harold:

I seem to have pulled something out of the hat at last here. A Miss Wallace, sister to a big shot in the studio here, who is a member of the Feldman-Blum agency, was just in, offering to take me over. So my option, which comes up Aug 1, will apparently be taken up. In which case, I will make a new agent arrangement, though Herndon, who first worked on this studio for a job for me, should still derive from me as long as my continuation here is a direct result (or is connected with) the contract in which Herndon was instrumental.

. . . I think he should derive something, as per above. I am willing to pay two commissions, if necessary, though this can be better arranged, I think, after the option has been taken up, between Herndon and me and my new agent. Is Swanson still your man? I want your coast representative, naturally. If it is still Swanson, write me by return. Please dont notify Swanson (or whoever your coast man is) yourself. Just write me who he is. I wont do anything until the option is taken up. If it is not taken up, I am free of Herndon anyhow. If it is taken up, I will call Herndon and your man both in and clear the business up. . . .

Yours,
[s] Bill
[t] William Faulkner

In late June 1943, Naval Lieutenant Robert K. Haas, Jr., a carrier-based torpedo-bomber pilot, was lost in action off Casablanca. On 1 July, Faulkner typed a draft of a letter to his father, then revised it and wrote it in pen on a single white sheet.

To Robert K. Haas — MS. MRS. HAAS
Thursday [1 July 1943] — [Hollywood]

Bob, dear boy,

Of course you dont want letters. They dont do any good. Besides, the sympathy is already yours without letters, from any friend, and some of the pride belongs to all the ex-airmen whom time has altered into grounded old men, and some of the grief is theirs too whose blood flies in this war. My nephew, 18, is about to be posted to carrier training. He will get it too. Then who knows? the blood of your fathers and the blood of mine side by side at the same long table in Valhalla, talking of glory and heroes, draining the cup and banging the empty pewter on the long board to fill again, holding two places for us maybe, not because we were heroes or not heroes, but because we loved them. My love to Miss Merle.

Bill

To Malcolm A. Franklin — TS. MR. FRANKLIN
Sunday [4 July 1943] — Warner Bros.

Dear Buddy:

Mr Robert Haas is vice president of Random House. They publish my books. During the times when I would be broke, year after year sometimes, I had only to write him and he would send me money—no hope to get it back, unless I wrote another book. He's a Jew.

He had an only son, and a daughter. In '40, the son withdrew from Yale and became a Navy pilot. In '41, the girl about 20, joined that Womens' Ferry Squadron, is now flying, ferrying aeroplanes from factories to bases. The boy was flying torpedo planes off carriers (what Jim is training for) in the Pacific. He was killed last week. The girl is still flying. All Jews. I just hope I dont run into some hundred percent American Legionnaire until I feel better.

There is a squadron of negro pilots. They finally got congress to allow them to learn how to risk their lives in the air. They are in Africa now, under their own negro lt. colonel, did well at Pantelleria, on the same day a mob of white men and white policemen killed 20 negroes in Detroit. Suppose you and me and a few others of us lived in the Congo, freed seventy-seven years ago by ukase; of course we cant live in the same apartment hut with the black folks, nor always ride in the same car nor eat in the same restaurant, but we are free because the Great Black Father says so. Then the Congo is engaged in War with the Cameroon. At last we persuade the Great Black Father to let us fight too. You and Jim say are flyers. You have just spent the day trying to live long enough to learn how to do your part in saving the Congo. Then you come back down and are told that 20 of your people have just been killed by a mixed mob of civilians and cops at Little Poo Poo. What would you think?

A change will come out of this war. If it doesn't, if the politicians and the people who run this country are not forced to make good the shibboleth they glibly talk about freedom, liberty, human rights, then you young men who live through it will have wasted your precious time, and those who dont live through it will have died in vain.

Pappy

To William Herndon — TS. RH
[possibly mid- or late July 1943] — [Hollywood]

Dear Mr Herndon:

Not having heard from you since our talk of three weeks ago, I herewith submit this letter as my request in writing that from this date you will no longer [in margin in pencil: "consider yourself as nor"] act as my agent and that on this date any and all relationship between us as agent and client, are at an end and no longer exist.

As I stated to you, I consider you to be entitled to a commission on my salary, as long as I draw a salary for work deriving from the effort and labor you contributed toward getting me the assignment of last July, 1942, until the time when the contract which you committed me to last July, shall be ended and discharged and so become void.

I had hoped that a simple statement of my desire to close our connection as agent and client would be enough for us to sever that connection amicably. But I have been thinking about your request in our last conversation for my reasons for wishing to sever this connection, and now recognise the justice of your demand and will state my reason if you still wish it.[1]

[no signature]

[1] A ribbon copy on yellow copy paper, this was apparently a draft of a letter which Faulkner may or may not have revised and sent to Herndon.

To Mrs. William Faulkner — TS. JFSA
Sunday [1 Aug. 1943] — Warner Bros.

Dear Big Miss:

. . . .

We had a meeting with the studio finance mgr. last week. Hawks asked what this picture will cost. The mgr. said $4,000,000.00. That is too much. So we must cut it down. Hawks, as a big shot, has a little house on the lot for his office. It has a kitchen, two baths, reception room, etc. I have moved my office into it, where we can work together, the whole unit of us undisturbed: director, writer, cutter, property men, etc. Hawks has set about Sept. 15th to start shooting the picture, is having sets made, an artist drawing water-color sketches of streets, characters, situations, etc. We are waiting for some official British photographs and film made in action over Europe, to complete one chapter.

I will stick at this picture until Hawks says it is finished, my part of it, I mean. He and I had a talk at the fishing camp.[1] He is going to establish his own unit, as an independent: himself, his writer, etc., to write pictures, then sell them to any studio who makes highest bid. I am to be his writer. He says he and I together as a team will always be worth two million dollars at least. That means, we can count on getting at least two million from any studio with which to make any picture we cook up, we to make the picture with the two million dollars, and divide the profits from it. When I come home, I intend to have Hawks completely satisfied with this job, as well as the studio. If I can do that, I wont have to worry again about going broke temporarily. The main problem I have now is to get myself free from the seven-year contract for a pittance of a salary. . . . I have a promise from the studio that, when I have written a successful picture, they will destroy that contract. This is my chance.[2]

I am having some trouble with the agent, Herndon. Naturally he doesn't want to let me go, now that I have written a good picture, am receiving offers from other studios. But he cant seem to understand the word 'No.' He will in time, though. Last summer, before I came out here, when the mix-up came about after I asked Ober and Bennett Cerf to get me a job, Herndon sent me letters and telegrams. . . . Then, after I had got here, without even money enough to buy a ticket back home, I found that he had committed me to a seven-year contract beginning at $300.00, so that if I worked for the studio seven years, I would at last draw $750.00 a week, ⅔ of what Fox paid me for single jobs. But that is water under the bridge now, and all that will be settled as soon as I finish this job. Hawks has promised to help me with leave, etc.

I'm so impatient to get home, I am about to bust. Thank the Lord, I have work to do, something I believe in. If I were just sitting here, waiting for a contract to expire, I reckon I would blow up.

Pappy

[1] At June Lake, Calif.

[2] Within a week after Faulkner wrote this letter, the studio halted the production of *Battle Cry*, and Faulkner's plans for a partnership with Hawks were put in abeyance.

After the demise of Battle Cry, *Faulkner entered into an informal partnership with producer William Bacher and director Henry Hathaway on a film about World War I. With a thousand-dollar advance from Bacher, Faulkner went home to Mississippi in mid-August 1943 to write a synopsis of the film.*

To Harold Ober — TS. FCVA
Saturday [30 Oct. 1943] — [Oxford]

Dear Harold:

I am in Oxford again, until about Feb. 15th. I will run out of money then and will go back into slavery for another 6 plus months.

I am working on a thing now. It will be about 10-15 thousand words. It is a fable, an indictment of war perhaps, and for that reason may not be acceptable now. I am writing it out in a sort of synopsis. I'll send it to you in that form; if anyone wants it, I'll rewrite and clean it up. I should be able to send you a copy of it in about 2 weeks. Will write you then.

Yours,
Bill F.

To Harold Ober — TS. FCVA
[received 17 Nov. 1943] — [Oxford]

Dear Harold:

Here are 51 pages of the story I wrote you about. This is the only copy I have, hence the registration to you, and please treat it the same way against loss.

The idea belongs to a diretcor in Hollywood. He told it in casual after-dinner talk to a producer[1] for whom I had done a job which the producer liked. The producer (at the time with another studio from mine) took fire, told the director I was the only man to write it, fired the director up. The three of us met, agreed that I should write the story, the other two put up the money, we would make the picture independently and own it between us, share and share alike. It was further agreed that I could write the story in any form I liked: picture script, play, or novel, any revenue from a play or novel to be mine exclusively. The picture rights of course are not for sale.

I am still under contract with Warner, pending a readjustment of which, I cannot write moving picture script for anyone else. So, to kill two birds with one stone, I am writing this story in an elaborated, detailed, explicit synopsis form, from which I can write a script later when my status with Warner is cleared up, and which I can try to turn into a play now, or rewrite as a novelette-fable, either or both of which, under my leave of absence from Warner which reserved me the right to write anything but moving pictures while off salary, I can do.

Is there enough of it here for you to show around for a sale or a reasonably definite commitment, subject to a look at the rest of it? This is about half of it. It continues on, through the Three Temptations, the Crucifixion, the Resurrection. The Epilogue is an Armistice Day ceremony at the tomb of the Unknown Soldier.

I would like to rewrite it as a magazine story, to be printed later by Bennett and Bob, and as a play. As a magazine and book piece, I will smooth it out, give the characters names, remove the primer-like biblical references and explanations, and let the story reveal its Christ-analogy through understatement. If anyone is interested, I can send the rest of this synopsis form on to you when I finish it, or you can send these fifty-one sheets back to me and I will rewrite and submit the finished product, whichever they like. If neither magazine nor theatre is interested, let Bob or Bennett have these 51 pages, to see what I am doing, then send them back to me for rewrite. *This is the only copy I have,* as I am sending the carbon duplicate to my co-owners as I make them. And *no moving picture rights are for sale or included in any sale.* If Random House does not want it either, I suggest Harold Guinzburg at Viking, granted that Bob and Bennett agree. If nobody at all wants it, send it back to me. As this form will be sufficient for later picture writing, there will be no use in my rewriting it until then.

Yours,
Bill

[in ink:] If anyone is interested and wants to see the rewritten job, send this back to me as quick as you can. This is the only copy I have to rewrite from, cant do anything until I have it back.

[1] Director Henry Hathaway and producer William Bacher.

To Harold Ober — TS. FCVA
Saturday [8 Jan. 1944] — [Oxford]

Dear Harold:

I have finished the first draft of the fable, and have started rewriting it. I go back to Cal. 10th February, hope to finish rewrite by then, if not, I'll send it to you from Cal., and arrange then for Random House to get it, let Bob read the rest of it.

I'll write from Hollywood.

Bill

To Robert K. Haas — TS. RH
Saturday [15 Jan. 1944] — [Oxford]

Dear Bob:

Your letter at hand. Thank you.

I think your feeling is wrong about the date of the fable; when you see some of it, you will agree I hope. The argument is (in the fable) in the middle of that war, Christ (some movement in mankind which wished to stop war forever) reappeared and was crucified again. We are repeating, we are in the midst of war again. Suppose Christ gives us one more chance, will we crucify him again, perhaps for the last time.

That's crudely put; I am not trying to preach at all. But that is the argument: We did this in 1918; in 1944 it not only MUST NOT happen again, it SHALL NOT HAPPEN again. i.e. ARE WE GOING TO LET IT HAPPEN AGAIN? now that we are in another war, where the third and final chance might be offered us to save him.

Very soon I will send you about 50–60 pages of the final draft. You will tell more about it then.

Thank you for your letter. All I meant was, do Random House like the idea enough to advance me cash, in case I need it before going back to Cal. Can I have from now until June to work on this book without worrying about money. Your letter answers that handsomely, as always.

If travel should get better, I'd like to come East, for a day or two, then go to Cal from there when I have to go back.

Bill

Faulkner had to return to Warner Bros. in mid-February 1944. There he was forced to put aside the fable (part of which he had sent to Ober) for studio work. Soon Howard Hawks asked for him to work on his film adaptation of Ernest Hemingway's novel To Have and Have Not *(New York, 1937).*

To Harold Ober — TS. FCVA
Saturday [22 Apr. 1944] — [Hollywood]

Dear Harold:

Yes, I am back again. I have not done anything more with the story. As soon as I got here, Howard Hawks asked for me. He is making a picture at our shop. As usual, he had a script, threw it away and asked for me. I went to work helping to rewrite it about Feb. 22. He started shooting about Mar. 1. Since then I have been trying to keep ahead of him with a day's script. I should be through about May 10–15.

I dont know when I shall get back at it, maybe then. War is bad for writing, though why I should tell you. This sublimation and glorification of all the cave instincts which man had hopes that he had lived down, dragged back into daylight, usurping pre-empting a place, all the room in fact, in the reality and constancy and solidity of art, writing. Something must give way; let it be the writing, art, it has happened before, will happen again. It's too bad I lived now though. Still too young to be unmoved by the old insidious succubae of trumpets, too old either to make one among them or to be impervious, and therefore too old to write, to have the remaining time to spend waiting for the trumpets and the lightning strokes of glory to have done. I have a considerable talent, perhaps as good as any coeval. But I am 46 now. So what I will mean soon by 'have' is 'had.'

When and if I get at it again, I will write you. After being present for a while at the frantic striving of motion pictures to justify their existence in a time of strife and terror, I have about come to the conclusion which they dare not admit: that the printed word and all its ramifications and photographications is nihil nisi fui; in a word, a dollar mark striving frantically not to DISSOLVE into the symbol 1 A.

Bill

To Mrs. William F. Fielden — TS. MRS. FIELDEN

Sunday [30 Apr. 1944] — Warner Bros.

Dear Sister:

. . . .

I think I have found an apartment, a little cubbyhole but in a quiet, convenient *not Hollywood* neighborhood, with no yard, etc. But after several years of Rowan Oak and trees and grounds, maybe Big and Little Miss will enjoy living in a city apartment, with nothing to break the silence but the shriek of brakes and the crash of colliding automobiles, and police car and fire wagon sirens, and the sounds of other tenants in the building who are not quite ready to lay down and hush at 1 or 2 a.m. They may like it. At least we will be together, I can have breakfast without having to dress and walk several blocks every morning, Big and Little can hear some music, Missy can ride with a good riding master, and I want her to take fencing lessons too, not to be a swordsman, which girls and women never are, but for the poise, co-ordination, grace in carriage and in walking, which fencing gives you.

My kindest and mostest to Vic Pic, from her good friend and admirer, and tell Bill not to talk to me about gardening. I'm homesick enough without any nudging from him on that subject.

Pappy

In early 1944, Malcolm Cowley decided to write a long essay on Faulkner which would reassess his literary achievement and give him the credit which Cowley felt was due him. He sent a letter to Rowan Oak describing his intentions and asking if he and Faulkner could meet so that he might question Faulkner about his life and aims. (See The Faulkner-Cowley File: Letters and Memories, 1944–1962, *New York, 1966.)*

To Malcolm Cowley — TS. YALE
Sunday, 7 May [1944] — Hollywood

Dear Mr Cowley:

I just found your letter of last Feb. by idle chance today. Please excuse this. During the last several years my correspondence has assumed a tone a divination of which your letter implies. My mail consists of two sorts: from people who dont write, asking me for something, usually money, which being a serious writer trying to be an artist, I naturally dont have; and from people who do write telling me I cant. So, since I have already agreed to answer No to the first and All right to the second, I open the envelopes to get the return postage stamps (if any) and dump the letters into a desk drawer, to be read when (usually twice a year) the drawer overflows.

I would like very much to have the piece done. I think (at 46) that I have worked too hard at my (elected or doomed, I dont know which) trade, with pride but I believe not vanity, with plenty of ego but with humility too (being a poet, of course I give no fart for glory) to leave no better mark on this our pointless chronicle than I seem to be about to leave.

As you can see from above, I am at the salt mines again. It would cost more to come here than to come to Miss. This town is crowded with war factory workers and troops, is unpleasant. But I have a cubbyhole which you are welcome to share until June 1, when my family is coming out. In the fall I will go back home. I dont know when I will come East, I mean to New York. I would like to, but I never seem to have that much money anymore, as I try to save what I earn here to stay at home as long as possible on.

I would like the piece, except the biography part. You are welcome to it privately, of course. But I think that if what one has thought and hoped and endeavored and failed at is not enough, if it must be explained and excused by what he has experienced, done or suffered, while he was not being an artist, then he and the one making the evaluation have both failed.

Thank you for your letter, and again excuse the time lapse.

William Faulkner

To Harold Ober
May 18, 1944

TS. FCVA
Warner Bros.

Dear Harold:

I have a new assignment, Producer Wald here.[1] It is one of the usual turkeys (a novel, good title but little else) which (God knows why) studios pay 40,000 dollars for.

I told Wald I thought it was napoo. He said all right, throw it away, that what he wanted was some 'Faulkner' in a picture. He said he wanted the story of a southern girl born on wrong side of tracks, trying to raise herself. As soon as he said that (which is the general theme in the novel) I remembered that I had already invented that character in a short story THE BROOCH, in Scribners about 1938.[2] We discussed my character, and other characters in my story, got the beginning of a story line, on which I am now working. I told Wald about my story.

I am having a copy of my story typed. I will submit it with the screen play outline. I ought to get paid for the story. If the studio paid a lot of money for the novel, and invested more money in three failed screen plays, they should pay something more to get some of the investment back.

Let this be your authorization to sell this story to them. They will have a copy of it when you receive this letter; also I think I will telephone Swanson now and inform him of what is going on, so he can begin to handle it, in case he does not think best to wait for authorization from you.

What I want, of course, is some definite understanding with the studio that they are not to use any of my material on this subject, along this story line, without buying the story from me separately from my salary. I will explain the whole thing to Swanson.

Yours,
[s] Bill
[t] William Faulkner

P.S. Just went to see Wald, told him the gist of this letter: that I wanted to sell this story. He asked how much. I said, 'Why not let the agent do that.' He said, 'Dont get the studio (I forget whether he said angry, stirred up, or what) first. Complete the treatment, submit it with the story in question, let them agree to accept or throw the whole thing out. Then have the agent come into it.'

I will follow that line. Will submit treatment, complete, and the story. Then I will communicate with you and Swanson.[3]

[1] Jerry Wald.

[2] Faulkner had apparently forgotten the work he had done on this same property two and a half years before. (See Faulkner to Nathan, 18 Nov. 1941.)

[3] Faulkner's time was charged to *The Damned Don't Cry* from 15 May to 10 June 1944. He wrote a seventy-nine-page treatment but the studio did not use it.

On 26 May 1944, Ober wrote to Faulkner quoting a letter from Whit Burnett, who wanted to recommend the story "Two Soldiers" for a radio series and who asked that Faulkner provide a sentence or two telling why he liked the story. Ober asked if Faulkner approved the idea and if he would provide the requested material.

To Harold Ober — TS. FCVA
Monday [29 May 1944] — [Hollywood]

Dear Harold:

Handle the story as you see fit.

I like it because it portrays a type which I admire—not only a little boy, and I think little boys are all right, but a true American: an independent creature with courage and bottom and heart—a creature which is not vanishing, even though every articulate medium we have—radio, moving pictures, magazines—is busy day and night telling us that it has vanished, has become a sentimental and bragging liar.

Heard from Swanson, will keep him informed about the story.[1] Apparently they have already wasted enough money on this script to pay a little more to recover, parlay.

Bill

[1] "The Brooch."

On 22 July 1944, Malcolm Cowley wrote Faulkner again about the article he wanted to do on his work, asking him particularly how much of the symbolism in his writing was deliberate. When Cowley published a part of the article,[1] he wrote Faulkner quoting a passage about the symbolism of Sutpen's Hundred in Absalom, Absalom! *and asking again how much of Faulkner's symbolism was deliberate.*

To Malcolm Cowley — TS. YALE
Saturday [early Nov. 1944] — Oxford

Dear Maitre:

I saw the piece in Times Book R.[1] It was all right. If that is a fair sample, I dont think I need to see the rest of it before publication because I might want to collaborate and you're doing all right. But if you want comments from me before you release it, that's another horse. So I'll leave it to you whether I see it beforehand or not.

Vide the paragraph you quoted: As regards any specific book, I'm trying primarily to tell a story, in the most effective way I can think of, the most moving, the most exhaustive. But I think even that is incidental to what I am trying to do, taking my output (the course of it) as a whole. I am telling the same story over and over, which is myself and the world. Tom Wolfe was trying to say everything, get everything, the world plus 'I' or filtered through 'I' or the effort of 'I' to embrace the world in which he was born and walked a little while and then lay down again, into one volume. I am trying to go a step further. This I think accounts for what people call the obscurity, the involved formless 'style,' endless sentences. I'm trying to say it all in one sentence, between one Cap and one period. I'm still trying, to put it all, if possible, on one pinhead. I dont know how to do it. All I know to do is to keep on trying in a new way. I'm inclined to think that my material, the South, is not very important to me. I just happen to know it, and dont have time in one life to learn another one and write at the same time. Though the one I know is probably as good as another, life is a phenomenon but not a novelty, the same frantic steeple-chase toward nothing everywhere and man stinks the same stink no matter where in time.

Your divination (vide paragraph) is correct. I didn't intend it, but afterward I dimly saw myself what you put into words. I think though you went a step further than I (unconsciously, I repeat) intended. I think Quentin, not Faulkner, is the correct yardstick here. I was writing the story, but he not I was brooding over a situation. I mean, I was creating him as a character, as well as Sutpen et al. He grieved and regretted the passing of an order the dispossessor of which he was not tough enough to withstand. But more he grieved the fact (because he hated and feared the portentous symptom) that a man like Sutpen, who to Quentin was trash, origin-less, could not only have dreamed so high but have had the force and strength to have failed so grandly. Quentin probably contemplated Sutpen as the hyper-sensitive, already self-crucified cadet of an old long-time Republican Philistine house contemplated the ruin of Samson's portico. He grieved and was moved by it but he was still saying 'I told you so' even while he hated himself for saying it.

You are correct; I was first of all (I still think) telling what I thought was a good story, and I believed Quentin could do it better than I in this case. But I accept gratefully all your implications, even though I didn't carry them consciously and simultaneously in the writing of it. In principle I'd like to think I could have. But I dont believe it would have been necessary to carry them or even to have known their analogous derivation, to have had them in the story. Art is simpler than people think because there is so little to write about. All the moving things are eternal in man's history and have been written before, and if a man writes hard enough, sincerely enough, humbly enough, [and, with the unalterable determination never never never to be quite satisfied with it][2] he will repeat them, because art like poverty takes care of its own, shares its bread.

I am free of Hollywood for 6 months, must go back then for the reason that when I was broke in '42 and the air force didn't want me again, I had to sign a seven year contract with Warner to get a job. Re the book offer.[3] I wrote Harold Ober, who forwarded it to me, that I would not undertake it right now. I can work at Hollywood 6 months, stay home 6, am used to it now and have movie work locked off into another room. I dont want to undertake a book of the nature suggested because I'm like the old mare who has been bred and dropped foals 15-16 times, and she has a feeling that she has only 3 or 4 more in her, and cant afford to spend one on something from outside. I am working on something now. Random House has about 70 pages of it. I will write them to let you see it, if you would like to. It's not Yoknapatawpha this time, though I explained above that I'm still trying to put all mankind's history in one sentence.[4]

[in ink:] Thank you for letter,
William Faulkner

My best to Hal Smith when you see him.

[1] Cowley's essay, "William Faulkner's Human Comedy," appeared in the New York *Times Book Review*, 29 Oct. 1944, p. 4. (See *The Faulkner-Cowley File*, pp. 8–13.)

[2] Marginal insert in ink.

[3] In November, Ober's office received a phone call and a letter from Lee Barker at Doubleday, Doran, writing on behalf of himself and a few others who wanted to rescue Faulkner from his Hollywood work. The proffered solution was a $5,000 advance for a nonfiction book about the Mississippi River. (See Faulkner to Ober, 20 Dec. 1944.)

[4] The fable, for Bacher and Hathaway.

When Faulkner left California by train on 12 December 1944, he took a copy of the script of The Big Sleep *with him. Traveling through Arizona and New Mexico, he continued to work on it, completing his rewrite in Oxford. He sent twelve typed pages to the studio with a covering note.*

To James J. Geller — TS. WARNER BROS.
[mid-Dec. 1944] — [Oxford]

The following rewritten and additional scenes for THE BIG SLEEP were done by the author in respectful joy and happy admiration after he had gone off salary and while on his way back to Mississippi. With grateful thanks to the studio for the cheerful and crowded day coach which alone saved him from wasting his time in dull and profitless rest and sleep.

With love,
[t] WILLIAM FAULKNER

At home, Faulkner continued to think about the offer of a $5,000 advance from Doubleday, Doran for a book on the Mississippi River, forwarded to Ober's office by Lee Barker in November.

To Harold Ober
20 Dec. 1944

TS. FCVA
Oxford, Miss.

Dear Harold:

Your letter received on the day I left Cal. I will be home for at least six months.

I will write you about the Mississippi River book as soon as I get my breath. I like the idea very much. That is, I am grateful to the blokes who thought of it, very pleased and comforted that such men exist, not just on my account but for the sake of writing, art, and artists, in America and the world. The reason I dont seem yet to know my own mind on the subject is as follows:

I have never done a book of that sort, never had the notion to do one, and so I dont know exactly where to begin. So in a sense that means to learn a new trade at age of 47 (assuming that for me to do such a book will be tour de force), starting 'cold,' without that speck of fire, that coal, from which a book or a picture should burst almost of its own accord. I am 47. I have 3 more books of my own I want to write. I am like an aging mare, who has say three more gestations in her before her time is over, and doesn't want to spend one of them breeding what she considers (wrongly perhaps) a mule.

So let me think about it a little longer. Maybe I will take fire myself over the idea of such a book. Let me have a month say, to get Hollywood out of my system, before I try to decide. I would not insult the men who made the offer possible by taking the money for anything less than my best; if I did that, the whole purpose of the offer would be exploded, as I would still be morally and spiritually in Hollywood.

Please express to them my gratitude, and more, my sincerest congratulations and the comfort it gives me, and through me, all writing sincere people, that good writing is not dead and will never be.

Best wishes for season.

Bill

To Bennett Cerf and Robert K. Haas — TS. FCVA

10 Jan. 1945 — Oxford, Miss.

Dear Bennett and Bob:

I am doing a thing which I think is pretty good.[1] Unless I am wrong about it, have reached that time of an artist's increasing years when he no longer can judge what he is doing, I have grown up at last. All my writing life I have been a poet without education, who possessed only instinct and a fierce conviction and belief in the worth and truth of what he was doing, and an illimitable courage for rhetoric (personal pleasure in it too: I admit it) and who knew and cared for little else.

Well, I'm doing something different now, so different that I am writing and rewriting, weighing every word, which I never did before; I used to bang it on like an apprentice paper hanger and never look back.

What I'm getting at is, this is going to take longer than I thought. I did the rough outline of it last year, Ober has a copy, or you have, I dont remember which. I left Warners Dec 15th for 6 months. As usual, I may run out of money before the six months are up. If I do, I'll either have to pot boil, or go back to the salt mine; in either case, I'll have to put this aside. Can I send you in some of this and take an advance to keep working on it with until my leave is up? That is, can I count on say 2 or 3 thousand if I need it, about March?[2]

A friend, a moving picture man in H. gave me the germ of the idea.[3] He loaned me $1000.00 last year while I was at home to work on it. So he owns part of *my* share of movie rights. He will handle all movie phases of it, if he wishes. [in ink:] In this case, I will protect your publishers' customary.

It will also make a play, I imagine. He will share in that.

He has relinquished all other profits from it, book or magazine, to me.

Am sending Ober a copy of this, to keep him posted, as I hope he can sell it to a magazine, etc.

[no signature]

[in ink:] Dear Harold[4]— This letter goes today. In case Bob & Bennett say No, could you get me advance from other source, on strength of 40-50 or so pages?

[1] The fable.

[2] Haas replied promptly that Faulkner could count on them for the money.

[3] William Bacher.

[4] Faulkner wrote this note on the carbon copy of the letter to Cerf and Haas which he sent to Ober.

To Harold Ober — TS. FCVA
Monday [24 Jan. 1945] — [Oxford]

Dear Harold:

My feeling about the River book right now is, I wont commit myself yet, even at risk of losing the offer. The reason is this present thing. It may not be any good and I may be wrong about it. But I'll have to keep at it a while yet to know. I have only six months until I am committed to go back to Cal. I dont believe I can do justice to both these books in that time.

I will carry on with this fable. I have about 60 completed pages. I will send it on to Haas, and will ask him to have a copy made and send you, in case there is a chance of a mag. or other revenue, as well as to keep your records up to date.

Bill

To Joe C. Brown — TS. FCVA
Tuesday [25 Jan. 1945] — [Oxford]

Dear Brown:

Your letter at hand. I was glad to receive it, since unless I am mistaken, you and I had a short talk on the street in front of Neilson's store one afternoon about three years ago, in which you mentioned this work. I thought then you were going to let me see it, and when I didn't hear from you anymore, I was disappointed.

The invitation[1] I offered then still holds. My hours are irregular, though I am usually at home. So I suggest that you telephone first, to make sure I am here, as it is a longish walk out here. I will expect to hear from you soon. I will read the work, then we can have a talk about it. My number is 546. In case you dont know where my home is, anybody on the square can tell you.

Yours sincerely,
William Faulkner

[1] Joe C. Brown was a young Negro who had taught at one of the Lafayette County schools. Brown had been writing poetry, and three years earlier Faulkner had invited him out to Rowan Oak to talk about it. Brown accepted Faulkner's invitation. They talked about poetry, and Brown left two of his poems with Faulkner.

To Joe C. Brown — TS. FCVA
Monday [possibly 29 Jan. 1945] — [Oxford]

Dear Joe:

I have edited, partly rewritten the first one.[1] I think this is better than trying to tell in words where your version fails.

The passion in the two poems is not controlled. Therefore, it stops being clean passion and becomes rhetoric, which a reader doubts a little.

Put the passion in it, but sit on the passion. Dont try to say to the reader what you want to say, but make him say it to himself *for* you.

I will edit the second one and send it to you when I get it right.[2]

Your idea in both is all right. Keep on practising at it until you can say it as per the second and third paragraphs above.

Your friend,
William Faulkner

[1] A fourteen-line appeal in which the poet asked America for the strong drink of true freedom and opportunity.

[2] This was a longer poem about a man who had contracted syphilis in an illicit love affair. Faulkner also reworked this poem.

To Harold Ober — TS. FCVA
Monday [19 Mar. 1945] — [Oxford]

Dear Harold:

Yes, I will go back to Warner about June 1st. I passed them my word about the contract. That is, I notified them that Herndon was empowered to act for me, though I didn't know until I got there that he had committed me to seven years. I thought it was 13 weeks. I might try to beg off my word to an equal—a literary agent or a publisher—but not to an inferior like a moving picture corp. They have been hinting ever since I got there that some day they would relieve me themselves, voluntarily, of the contract. I have never asked them to. Before I left in Dec. Geller intimated voluntarily again that when I came back, it would be done. I imagine they mean to give me more money per week to sign a brand new seven-year contract. I shall insist on a contract for one year only, no options whatever. They probably wont do it. But if they should, without haggling, I will probably feel generous enough to agree to give them the chance to match any other studio offer, before I accept it, after the year is up. Otherwise I'll finish this present one for no more money before I'll mortgage my future any longer ahead than the expiration of this one. If they had any judgment of people, they would have realised before now that they would get a damn sight more out of me by throwing away any damned written belly-clutching contract and let us work together on simple good faith and decency, like with you and Random House.

It will take some time yet to finish the mss. It may be my epic poem. Good story: the crucifixion and the resurrection. I had about 100,000 words, rewrote them down to about 15,000 now. I had my usual vague foundationless dream of getting enough money to live on out of it while I wrote and finished it. But I ought to know now I dont sell and never will earn enough outside of pictures to stay out of debt.

Bill

The Personal Narrative Office of the Army Air Corps was interested in Faulkner's doing a book on Air Force operations overseas. He was to meet Maj. Bernard A. Bergman at the Memphis airport to discuss the project on 20 April 1945.

To Harold Ober — TELEGRAM FCVA
21 Apr. 1945 — Oxford, Miss.

MET BERGMAN AS PER APPOINTMENT MEMPHIS FRIDAY. INCONCLUSIVE BECAUSE I WAS TIGHT. WRITING DETAILS. CAN ANYTHING BE DONE AS I WANT THE JOB.[1] WILLIAM FAULKNER

[1] Nothing further came of the project.

Harold Ober wrote Faulkner about a request from Whit Burnett. He offered $25 to reprint "Two Soldiers" in a high school text—with the proviso, however, that the words "hell" and "nigger" be deleted from the story.

To Harold Ober — TS. FCVA
Monday [21 May 1945] — [Oxford]

Dear Harold:

Let Burnett have the story and edit it as he likes, provided:

(1) When printed, at each change of any sort he makes, he will set an asterisk and append a footnote: 'Altered or changed from the original by (Burnett or anthologist or editor or whatever is correct).' This may be good for the children in fact; it will be teaching them at an early

and tender age to be ever on guard to protect and shield their elders and teachers from certain of the simple facts of life.

(2) I to furnish no photograph, no comment, no nothing.[1]

(3) He to pay at least fifty dollars for using the piece.

I go back to Hollywood June 4th.

Yours,
Bill

[1] The story appeared without changes in Burnett's anthology *Time to Be Young*.

To Harold Ober — TS. FCVA
Friday [25 May 1945] — [Oxford]

Dear Harold:

Yours of 22 May at hand.

I go back on the old contract, simply suspended each time I come home. I get $400.00 now. Sometime in near future, about 1 month I think after I go back on salary, option comes up and I get a raise of as I recall $50.00, will be getting $450.00 for next twelve months.

I am rewriting the fable. It's a novel now and not just a lot of rhetoric as when I sent it to Bob. Would you mind calling him, tell him I am rewriting the whole thing, ask him to send to me at Warners, *after* June 10th, the section I sent him. As soon as I type enough of the rewrite, I'll send it to him. I may need the section he now has for reference; anyway, as it is wrong, I'd like to recall it.

Yours
Bill

Nobody but Geller has ever mentioned a new and better contract to me, though he has promised about a dozen times that I am to get one. He promised again the day I left, intimated that on my return it would be done. I'll see what happens when I get there, and will write you.[1]

[1] Faulkner was not offered a new contract. His option would come up on 16 June 1945, with a raise to $500 rather than $450 as he thought. The studio would decide to exercise the option and continue the contract at the new rate.

To Mrs. Lemuel E. Oldham[1] — TS. ACLT
Thursday [28 June 1945] — Warner Bros.

Dear Miss Lida:

As the compleat letter-writer says, this leaves me well and hoping it finds you the same.

This has been a gray, wet spring here like ours was, and is still gray;

only two days of 'California' sunshine since I arrived. It has been good for the blooming things though. There is a hedge-plant here which looks like our laurel. But it has a four-petaled white bloom about the size of a dollar, looks like an enlarged Confederate jessamine, but has no odor. I intend to see if it will transplant to Miss. Also, a geranium which I never saw before, which blooms from scarlet through pink and on to pure white and then with a faint bluish tinge. I wish we had that too. Bougainvillaea everywhere as usual, much lantana ranging from yellow through the normal orange with red center which I know at home, to solid deep maroon-magenta, and a lot of blue plumbago which I like. It all looks pretty fine, a lot of magnolia blooms but the magnolia leaves are a lighter shade of green, almost sickly, not like our strong deep green.

Everybody has a garden, but they look pretty amateurish: corn too thick, etc., though tomatoes do better. Gardening people miss the Japanese, who used to do all that around private homes. They made a bad mistake in not watching their Japanese gardeners and learning something while they had the chance.

I miss home very much and am marking off the days until I get back. Am busy writing a picture, and being busy helps some. But I do miss my family in the evenings.

I hope you are feeling well. Love to Dot[2] and Mary.

Bill

[1] Estelle Faulkner's mother.

[2] Estelle's sister, Dorothy Oldham, and Mary Jenkins, Mrs. Oldham's nurse.

To William Herndon — TS. FCVA

July 25, 1945 — [Hollywood]

Dear Mr Herndon:

Please be advised as of this date, July 25, 1945, I propose to stop any further payments to you after the week ending Saturday, August 18, 1945.

Any rights to represent me which you may have enjoyed or exercised to be deemed terminated as of that date August 18, 1945.

Yours truly,
William Faulkner

To Harold Ober — TS. FCVA

26 July, 1945 — Warner Bros.

Dear Harold:

On suggestion by Mr Trilling, by advice of Mr Obringer, the studio lawyer, I have just mailed to Herndon the original of the enclosed.[1]

I send this copy direct to you, not to Swanson. Herndon seems to have some violent and fanatical hatred toward Swanson, whether on my account or not or how much so, I dont know. Partly for this reason, I had rather all official communications to Swanson came through or from you. I tried to explain to Herndon two years ago that I didn't care one way or the other about Swanson because I didn't know him, that I wanted all my writing business in the hands of one agent, particularly because that agent, yourself, had been a personal friend of long standing.

If Herndon behaves and offers to compromise, I am willing to pay him 10 weeks' commission ($500.00) as a termination, instead of the 4 ($200) which I have offered. I have not told him so yet.

I imagine he will refuse both amounts. His next step will be to attach and put in escrow or whatever you call it, my salary. The moment he does that I'm going to pack my toothbrush and return to Mississippi. I will not pay him one cent more than the $500.00. I feel that he is due that much for what work he did in getting me a job. But if he does not behave, if at any time before I begin to pay him the $200.00 offered or at any time during that period, he starts refusing and delivering warnings and threats to me, I will stop paying him then and he will not even get the $200.

Yours,
Bill

[1] Steve Trilling and Roy J. Obringer.

To Estelle Faulkner — TS. JFSA
Thursday [26 July 1945] — Warner Bros.

Dear Miss E.

Doing best I can from this distance. Missy wrote Uncle Ned is feeding too heavy, which I knew, asked me to tell him not to, as he paid no mind to her. I wrote him. You say he wouldn't let you have corn to put up. I wrote him to do so.

I have been here since June 7th. In that time I have

1. Written one complete screen play, 145 pages.[1]
2. Spent two weeks working at night and on weekends fixing up a picture for Ginger Rogers.
3. Spent two other weekends writing a 50 page story with Bezzerides which we hope to sell to Howard Hawks.

I'm doing all this to try to make enough money to get the hell out of this place and come back home and fix Missy's room and paint the house and do the other things we need.

Along with this, I attend to matters at the farm by correspondence with James, giving him directions and solving his problems.

I try to write either to you or Missy at least once every week, no matter how 'written-out' I feel. I try to write to mother at least once a week, ditto.

I have also been engaged in a battle to get rid of the agent Herndon and get myself more salary from the studio.

In addition to this, I spend 3 hours every day on buses getting back and forth from Bezzerides' house to the studio, since he is not working now and does not drive me in his car.

. . . .

Pappy

[1] *Stallion Road*, from the novel by Stephen Longstreet.

On 27 July 1945, William Herndon wrote Faulkner asking him to reconsider his decision to discontinue paying his commission. If Faulkner did not do so, Herndon would file suit immediately. If he did not hear from Faulkner in one week, Faulkner would be hearing from Herndon's attorneys.

To Harold Ober — TS. FCVA
30 July 1945 — Warner Bros.

Dear Harold:

I received the enclosed letter today.

I just talked with Mr Obringer, the studio lawyer. He says, based on my letters and telegrams to Herndon, which can be construed as a contract, that 10% of each salary check can be deducted from it and sent to the sheriff to be impounded pending a suit. But meantime, he advised me to do nothing and see what Herndon's next move will be.

If it comes to court business, there will be costs, etc., more money. I will of course have to keep on paying the commission if I lose, as long as I work for Warner, and, Mr Obringer says, very likely for any subsequent contracts, I suppose only from Warner though.

. . . .

When this mix-up happened, July, 1942, after I had asked you to find me a Hollywood job of any sort, I had a letter from Producer Robert Buckner which described a specific job: a screen play about Gen. De Gaulle. At the same time, I had a letter from James Geller of the studio, offering me, offering to me direct a guarantee of 13 weeks, salary $300.00. There was no mention of a contract at all in his letter. I dont recall whether he stated in so many words that the job was to be the De Gaulle picture. As I recall, his letter said, 'Buckner is (or has already) writing you about the job.' His letter also said, 'There is some confusion about who is representing you. Who do you want us to deal with?' or words to that effect.

By that time I had your offer to withdraw from the matter. I wired Herndon and the studio in duplicate, by Herndon's demand . . . that Herndon would represent me in this matter. I assumed, having no reason to the contrary, that this representation covered only this specific job which Geller had already offered to me myself directly.

When I reached California, I went to work at once on the De Gaulle job. I still had no reason to believe other than that I was working on one specific job, with a guarantee of 13 weeks, and that any contract presented to me would cover only this one job. I continued to believe that for two weeks, about. Then Herndon brought to my office the present contract, 7 years, with options. I said immediately: 'I wont sign it.' He said, 'But you authorised me to represent you. I have already committed you to it.' In effect, though I dont recall that he actually said it, 'You are already drawing salary on it.'

. . . .

I dont think I have a case in court. I offered to try to reach some compromise with him at the end of the contract's first year. He declined. . . . He is prospering lately, probably can afford lawyers. So I still think my best 'out' is to clear out of here as soon as he makes the first legal move. The studio will suspend me, but it may be worth it to my peace of mind.

I will let you know what the next step is. If you have any suggestion, send it along. I'm inclined to think though my course is to draw what free checks I am able to, then pack up and clear out.

Yours,
Bill

On 9 August 1945, Malcolm Cowley wrote Faulkner a long letter telling him that he had received approval at Viking Press to put together a collection to be called The Portable Faulkner. *He asked Faulkner's advice about selections to be included. (See Cowley, pp. 20–24.)*

To Malcolm Cowley — TS. YALE
Thursday [16 Aug. 1945] — [Hollywood]

Dear Cowley:

The idea is very fine. I wish we could meet too, but that seems impossible now. I will do anything I can from here.

By all means let us make a Golden Book of my apocryphal county. I have thought of spending my old age doing something of that nature: an alphabetical, rambling genealogy of the people, father to son to son.

I would hate to have to choose between Red Leaves and A Justice, also another one called Lo! from Story Mag. several years ago. The line dividing the Chickasaw and Choctaw nations passed near my home; I merely moved a tribe slightly at need, since they were slightly different people in behavior.

Yes, there is difference between magazine and Hamlet 'Spotted Horses.' One is a magazine story, shorter and more economical: it is a story made from several chapters of The Hamlet, reduced to their essentials. What is lacking in it is the justice of the peace al fresco trial regarding the damage done.

What about taking the whole 3rd section of SOUND AND FURY? That Jason is the new South too. I mean, he is the one Compson and Sartoris who met Snopes on his own ground and in a fashion held his own. Jason would have chopped up a Georgian Manse and sold it off in shotgun bungalows as quick as any man. But then, this is not enough to waste that much space on, is it? The next best would be the last section, for the sake of the negroes, that woman Dilsey who 'does the best I kin.'

AS I LAY DYING is simple tour de force, though I like it. But in this case it says little that Spotted Horses and Wash and Old Man would not tell.

THE HAMLET was incepted as a novel. When I began it, it produced Spotted Horses, went no further. About two years later suddenly I had THE HOUND, then JAMSHYD'S COURTYARD, mainly because SPOTTED HORSES had created a character I fell in love with: the itinerant sewing-machine agent named Suratt. Later a man of that name turned up at home, so I changed my man to Ratliff for the reason that my whole town spent much of its time trying to decide just what living man I was writing about, the one literary criticism of the town being 'How in the hell did he remember all that, and when did that happen anyway?' Meanwhile, my book had created Snopes and his clan, who produced stories in their saga which are to fall in a later volume: MULE IN THE YARD, BRASS, etc. This over about ten years, until one day I decided I had better start on the first volume or I'd never get any of it down. So I wrote an induction toward the spotted horse story, which included BARN BURNING, and WASH, which I discovered had no place in that book at all. Spotted Horses became a longer story, picked up THE HOUND (rewritten and much longer and with the character's name changed from Cotton to Snopes), and went on with JAMSHYD'S COURTYARD.

The Indians actually were Chickasaws, or they may so be from now on. RED LEAVES actually were Chickasaws. A JUSTICE could have been either, the reason for their being Chocktaws was the connection with New Orleans, which was more available to Chocktaws, as the map herewith will explain:

[MAP][1]

At this time the Tallahatchie, running from the Chickasaw across the Chocktaw nation, was navigable; steamboats came up it. Wish to hell we could spend three days together with these books. Write me any way I can help.

Faulkner

[1] See Cowley, p. 27.

To Prof. A. P. Hudson[1] — TS. PROF. HUDSON
16 Aug. 1945 — Warner Bros.

Dear A.P.

A writer here, Thomas Reed, has a mss. It has a love story in it, but the idea is what I am writing you about. It is the story of the Confederate States Naval Academy, mainly from the day in 65 when Lee notified the Richmond govt. the city could not be held, and the cadets took what there was of govt. gold and tried to save it.

Nobody has touched that story that I know of, in any form. I think it should have a more literate outlet than moving pictures, at least for its initial appearance: movie later if necessary.

Will you read the mss. if he sends it to you? I suggested the Chapel Hill Press as the best outlet for its first appearance, before the idea is ruined by some publisher's demands—that sort of thing.

If you are too busy, can you suggest someone to send it to?

I dont like this damn place any better than I ever did. That is one comfort: at least I cant be any sicker tomorrow for Mississippi than I was yesterday. I see Phil Stone when I am at home, and Doctor Bishop and Dr Brown.[2] But the place is changing fast these days. Dr Brown resigned last month.

My best respects to Mrs Hudson.

Your friend,
[s] Bill
[t] William Faulkner

[1] Faulkner had known Prof. Hudson, who was now teaching at the University of North Carolina at Chapel Hill, when he resided in Oxford.

[2] Profs. D. H. Bishop and Calvin S. Brown of the University of Mississippi.

On 8 August 1945, William Herndon wrote Faulkner following a conversation two days earlier in which Faulkner had asked him to fix a price which would free him of their contract. Herndon informed Faulkner that the last option in the Warner Bros. contract called for $750 a week and that total commissions under the remaining five years of the life of the contract would total $21,320. Herndon was willing to sell his contract with Faulkner to another agent for that amount, but he set forth tentatively a sum for which he might be willing to forfeit Faulkner's contractual obligations to him. It was $10,000, to be paid at the rate of $100 per week. He said that this counteroffer remained only a suggestion until they talked again.

To Harold Ober — TS. FCVA

Monday [20 Aug. 1945] — [Hollywood]

Dear Harold:

Enclosed is the last from Herndon.

Apart from this Herndon matter, I think I have had about all of Hollywood I can stand. I feel bad, depressed, dreadful sense of wasting time, I imagine most of the symptoms of some kind of blow-up or collapse. I may be able to come back later, but I think I will finish this present job and return home.[1] Feeling as I do, I am actually becoming afraid to stay here much longer. For some time I have expected, at a certain age, to reach that period (in the early fifties) which most artists seem to reach where they admit at last that there is no solution to life and that it is not, and perhaps never was, worth the living. Before leaving here, I will try to make what contacts I can in hopes to do work at home, as this seems to be the easiest way I can earn money which I must have or at least think I must have. Meanwhile, have you anything in mind I might do, for some more or less certain revenue? My books have never sold, are out of print; the labor (the creation of my apocryphal country) of my life, even if I have a few things yet to add to it, will never make a living for me. I dont have enough sure judgment about trash to be able to write it with 50% success. Could I do some sort of editorial work, or some sort of hack-writing at home, where living wont cost me so much as now, where I support a divided family, that is myself here in hotels, etc., and a house at home whose expenses dont alter whether I am there or not.

I think mainly though that I am not well physically, have lost weight, etc., though nothing serious that I know of or anticipate. Only, if I pull out of here now, I may leave myself in such bad odor that it will be hard to come back, even to Warner's who of course will put me under suspension, unless something can be done about this contract, from which they have declined to release me. I will probably try once more before I leave here though, insist on a release, see what comes of it.

I have considered this, let me hear from you about it: to get a statement from Herndon in writing that I will owe him ONLY the money stated: that is, the commission on this present contract until it ends, the sum which he calculates as $21 thousand something (see his letter) then have Swanson try for a better contract and pay Swanson commission also, in hopes that Swanson can get me a contract good or better enough to pay both commissions and also net myself more money. At even $1000.00 a week I could pay $150.00 commissions and be better off, and he might even get me more since I believe I am doing good work for these people now. Have about finished script on a book at which several before me failed, that sort of thing.[1]

Let me hear from you. I wont be able to get away from here at any rate before Oct 1 probably.

Bill

[1] *Stallion Road.*

To Estelle Faulkner — TS. JFSA
Saturday [25 Aug. 1945] — Warner Bros.

Dear Miss E:

....

Bezzerides are all well, the little boy is growing like a weed. They have been mighty kind to me. I have been trying ever since I got here to find a place to move to, cant even find a hotel room which will keep me longer than 5 days. I eat at restaurants to keep from using up their ration points, but even at that I know having a guest in the house this long is not too good. I hope I'll be starting for home soon though, and so relieve them of me. I went home yesterday afternoon with Tom Reed, a writer here. He lives on a cliff above the ocean at Palos Verdes, has two girls a little older than Missy, but not so much so that there was not so much difference that I didn't get a new twinge of homesickness just from talking with the younger one.

Much love to my dear ladies.

Pappy

To Richard Wright
Tuesday [probably 11 Sept. 1945]

TS. *New Letters,* 38 (Winter 1971), 128
[Hollywood]

Dear Richard Wright:

I have just read *Black Boy.*[1] It needed to be said, and you said it well. Though I am afraid (I am speaking now from the point of view of one who believes that the man who wrote *Native Son* is potentially an artist) it will accomplish little of what it should accomplish, since only they will be moved and grieved by it who already know and grieve over this situation.

You said it well, as well as it could have been said in this form. Because I think you said it much better in *Native Son.* I hope you will keep on saying it, but I hope you will say it as an artist, as in *Native Son.* I think you will agree that the good lasting stuff comes out of one individual's imagination and sensitivity to and comprehension of the suffering of Everyman, Anyman, not out of the memory of his own grief.

A friend of yours lives in my town, Joe Brown. He has shown me his verse. I have (I hope) helped him to learn what you learned yourself: that to feel and believe is not enough to write from. He has not read enough. He has taken my advice lately. The things he has sent me since I have been here (since June) are improving. I am returning to Oxford, Miss. next week, when I shall see him.

Yours sincerely,
William Faulkner

[1] *Black Boy: A Record of Childhood and Youth* (New York: Harper & Row, 1945).

To Harold Ober
Monday [17 Sept. 1945]

TS. FCVA
[Hollywood]

Dear Harold:

Your letter at hand. I will ask Reed to send his mss. on to you at once, with many thanks from us both. I dont know his mss. but he is a good man, an amateur sailor. I've found that any man with an active hobby like sailing or hunting or horses or whiskey is pretty liable to be all right, whether he can write or not. I hope Reed can; he wants to, is humble enough about it, does not need the money.

Yes, I have thought about the Doubleday matter.[1] I still feel the same. I would like to do it, if I believed I could do a first rate job. I would have no qualms about the first rate job, if I had thought of the idea myself. But as I have not thought of such a book in my 47 years, perhaps the job is not for me. I'll sell myself here to do what I am not sure I can do, but

I have too much respect for my ancient and honorable trade (books) to take someone's money without knowing neither of us will be ashamed of the result. I will keep it in mind though. I will probably need money, as I leave here with the intent of staying away until my affairs are in much better shape here. I will write you from home just what I am doing, what plans, etc.

So please keep the Doubleday matter in status quo until I have been at home and have got myself together. That is, dont refuse or accept it either until you have heard from me later.

Yours,
Bill

[1] The offer of an advance on a book about the Mississippi River.

To Malcolm Cowley — TS. YALE
Thursday [20 Sept. 1945] — [Hollywood]

Dear Cowley:

Yours of 17th at hand.

If you wish to print 'THE HOUND' and 'SPOTTED HORSES' for the sake of their simple content, use the magazine versions, also 'BARN BURNING' which I think was Harpers, spring 1938 or maybe '39, also in the O HENRY memorial collection, I think they call it, either one of those years or the next, maybe as late as '40. It won a prize, the only damned prize or anything else I ever got for free.

But if you want to use them for their implications of a complete novel (novels) with its (their) particular style, etc., better lift them from the novels, as they were conceived in that form. I like them better in the novel forms, though you have length to watch.

'BARN BURNING' as a story bears the same relation to it as the beginning of 'THE HAMLET' as the other two do to their respective origins. In the mag. 'THE HOUND,' Snopes's name was Cotton. Change it.

Suppose you used the last section, the Dilsey one, of SOUND & FURY, and suppose (if there is time: I am leaving here Monday for Mississippi) I wrote a page or two of synopsis to preface it, a condensation of the first 3 sections, which simply told why and when (and who she was) and how a 17 year old girl robbed a bureau drawer of hoarded money and climbed down a drain pipe and ran off with a carnival pitchman.

Warren Grimm does hold together, whole.[1] If I recall him aright, he was the Fascist galahad who saved the white race by murdering Christmas. I invented him in 1931. I didn't realise until after Hitler got into the newspapers that I had created a Nazi before he did.

I'll write to Hemingway.[2] Poor bloke, to have to marry three times to find out that marriage is a failure, and the only way to get any peace out of it is (if you are fool enough to marry at all) keep the first one and stay as far away from her as much as you can, with the hope of some day outliving her. At least you will be safe then from any other one marrying you—which is bound to happen if you ever divorce her. Apparently man can be cured of drugs, drink, gambling, biting his nails and picking his nose, but not of marrying.

Faulkner

[in pencil:] Will be in Oxford about next Sunday.

[1] Cowley had proposed using the Percy Grimm segment of *Light in August*, referring to him as Warren Grimm.

[2] Cowley had told Faulkner how Hemingway had praised his work to Sartre, and how he had written Cowley that he felt lonely now. Cowley had suggested that Faulkner write Hemingway. (See Cowley, pp. 27–30.)

To Malcolm Cowley — TS. YALE

Friday [5 Oct. 1945] — [Oxford]

Dear Cowley:

Yours at hand this morning. I am getting at the synopsis right away, and will send it along.

The idea about the other volume is pretty fine.[1] There are some unpublished things which will fit it that I had forgot about, one is another Indian story which Harold Ober has, the agent I mean. It is the story of how Boon Hogganbeck, in THE BEAR, his grandfather, how he won his Chickasaw bride from an Indian suitor by various trials of skill and endurance, one of which was an eating contest. I forget the title of it.[2] There is also another Sartoris tale, printed in STORY two years ago, about Granny Millard and General Forrest, told by the same Bayard who told THE UNVANQUISHED.[3] There is an unpublished Gavin Stevens story which Ober has, about a man who planned to commit a murder by means of an untameable stallion.[4] You may have seen these. If you have not, when you are ready to see them, I will write Ober a note.

Yes, I had become aware of Faulkner's European reputation. The night before I left Hollywood I went (under pressure) to a party. I was sitting on a sofa with a drink, suddenly realised I was being pretty intently listened to by three men whom I then realised were squatting on their heels and knees in a kind of circle in front of me. They were Isherwood, the English poet and a French surrealist, Hélion;[5] the other one's name I forget. I'll have to admit though that I felt more like a decrepit gaffer telling stories than like an old master producing jewels for three junior co-laborers.

I'll send the synopsis along. It must be right, not just a list of facts. It should be an induction I think, not a mere directive.

Faulkner

[1] Cowley had written Faulkner suggesting a volume of his short stories organized by cycles: the Indian stories, the town stories and the like. (See Cowley, p. 34.)

[2] "A Courtship," which would appear in *The Sewanee Review*, LVI (Autumn 1948), 634–53.

[3] "My Grandmother Millard and General Bedford Forrest and the Battle of Harrykin Creek."

[4] The title story of *Knight's Gambit* (1949).

[5] Christopher Isherwood and Jean Hélion.

To Col. J. L. Warner — TS. WARNER BROS.
15 October, 1945 — [Oxford]

Dear Colonel Warner:

Referring to my last talk with Mr McDermid[1] before leaving the studio on 18th Sept., I still feel that I should not sign the leave-suspension agreement. That I should not commit myself further to studio work, and that if possible I should sever all my existing studio commitments. The reasons being as stated to Mr McDermid:

I feel that I have made a bust at moving picture writing and therefore have mis-spent and will continue to mis-spend time which at my age I cannot afford. During my three years (including leave-suspensions) at Warner's, I did the best work I knew how on 5 or 6 scripts. Only two were made and I feel that I received credit on these not on the value of the work I did but partly through the friendship of Director Howard Hawks. So I have spent three years doing work (trying to do it) which was not my forte and which I was not equipped to do, and therefore I have mis-spent time which as a 47 year old novelist I could not afford to spend. And I dont dare mis-spend any more of it.

For that reason, I am unhappy in studio work. Not at Warner's studio; my connection with the studio and all the people I worked with could not have been pleasanter. But with the type of work. So I repeat my request that the studio release me from my contract. I admit that I am making the request this time not so much to the head of the studio, as to that same fairness which you have shown before in such situations, two of which I have specific knowledge of since friends of mine were involved. So I know my request will receive fair consideration, and I hope favorable.[2]

Waiting to hear from you, I am

Yours sincerely,
[s] William Faulkner
[t] William Faulkner

[1] Finlay McDermid.
[2] One week later, the request was denied.

To Malcolm Cowley — TS. YALE
Thursday [18 Oct. 1945] — [Oxford]

Cher Maitre:

Here it is.[1] I should have done this when I wrote the book. Then the whole thing would have fallen into pattern like a jigsaw puzzle when the magician's wand touched it.

NOTE: I dont have a copy of TSATF, so if you find discrepancies in chronology (various ages of people, etc) or in the sum of money Quentin stole from her uncle Jason, discrepancies which are too glaring to leave in and which you dont want to correct yourself, send it back to me with a note. As I recall, no definite sum is ever mentioned in the book, and if the book says TP is 12, not 14, you can change that in this appendix.

I think this is all right, it took me about a week to get Hollywood out of my lungs, but I am still writing all right, I believe. The hell of it though, letting me get my hand into it, as was, your material was getting too long; now all you have is still more words. But I think this belongs in your volume. What about dropping DEATH DRAG, if something must be eliminated? That was just a tale, could have happened anywhere, could have been printed as happening anywhere by simply changing the word Jefferson where it occurs, once only I think.

Let me know what you think of this. I think it is really pretty good, to stand as it is, as a piece without implications. Maybe I am just happy that that damned west coast place has not cheapened my soul as much as I probably believed it was going to do.

Faulkner

[in ink:] I may get up east some time this fall. Will let you know.

[1] Instead of the page or two of synopsis to introduce the Dilsey section of *The Sound and the Fury*, which Faulkner had proposed in his letter to Cowley on 20 Sept. 1945, he had composed the Compson genealogy. Cowley used it, and it was also published with subsequent editions of the novel as "Appendix/ Compson: 1699–1945."

To Harold Ober | TS. FCVA
Friday [26 Oct. 1945] | [Oxford]

Dear Harold:

I am at home since 25 Sept.

I dont have a complete list of my stories. I have forgotten where some of them were printed, and even that I wrote some of them: vide the mystery story Queen bought.[1] Until I had read through the first page, I didn't even recognise it, thought for sure I had finally caught my impersonator.

I will try to remember as best I can, or reconstruct, and send you a list.

[no signature]

[1] "An Error in Chemistry."

To Malcolm Cowley | TS. YALE
Saturday [27 Oct. 1945] | [Oxford]

Dear Cowley:

Letter received. I hope this catches you before you have returned the mss.

I know it's *de l'homme*.[1] I made it incorrect mainly because I decided no one would care especially. That is, it seemed righter to me that Ikke., knowing little of French or English either, should have an easy transition to the apt name he gave himself in English, than that the French should be consistent. Maybe Soeur-Blonde de Vitry deliberately warped his own tongue so Doom could discover his English name. Change it as you see fit.

Jason would call $2840.50 '$3000.00' at any time the sum was owed him. He would have particularised only when *he* owed the money. He would have liked to tell the police she stole $15,000.00 from him, but did not dare. He didn't want the money recovered, because then the fact that he had stolen $4000.00 from the thief would have come out. He was simply trying to persuade someone, anyone with the power, to catch her long enough for him to get his hands on her.

(In fact the purpose of this genealogy is to give a sort of bloodless bibliophile's point of view. I was a sort of Garter King-at-Arms, heatless, not very moved, cleaning up 'Compson' before going on to the next 'C-o' or 'C-r.')

Re Benjy. This Garter K/A didn't know about the monument and the slipper. He knew only what the town could have told him: a) Benjy was an idiot. b) spent most of his time with a negro nurse in the pasture, until the pasture was deeded in the County Recorder's Office as sold. c) Was fond of his sister, could always be quieted indoors when placed where he could watch firelight. d) Was gelded by process of law, when and (assumed) why, since the little girl he scared probably made a good story out of it when she got over being scared.

My attitude toward Benjy and Jason has not changed.

Re expulsion of Indians. As I recall I said (approximately) . . . 'the time was 1840 now . . . and Ikkemotubbe's people were gone from the land too' (Indefinite: implied: might have been last year, 10 years ago, since the preceding established date was within a few years of 1810, or when Jason I rode up Natchez Trace. Compson domain . . . etc. etc.

Then you can still date Red Leaves 1845.

I dont say take out DEATH DRAG, I just thought of this to make room for the genealogy. If room for both, leave it.

Faulkner

About Sound & F. Someone at Random House has my copy. About 10 years ago we had notion to reprint, using different color inks to clarify chronology, etc. I underlined my copy in different color crayons, sent it to Bennett, never got it back. Will you try telling him you need it? Maybe they can dig it up.[2]

[1] Cowley had suggested that Ikkemotubbe's title should be *de l'homme,* not *du homme,* and went on to note discrepancies between the book and the new material. (See Cowley, pp. 41–43.)

[2] This book has never been found.

To Malcolm Cowley — TS. YALE

[received 7 Nov. 1945] — [Oxford]

I never made a genealogical or chronological chart, perhaps because I knew I would take liberties with both—which I have.

Issetibbeha was the chief who conveyed the patent from which all the land sales to whites derived. He owned the slave who was pursued to complete his suttee.

Moketubbe was his son, the dropsical man in the too-tight shoes, who followed the pursuit of the fleeing slave in a palanquin.

Ikkemotubbe, Doom, was Issetibbeha's sister's son, who frightened Moketubbe into abdicating.

Hence RED LEAVES would have to precede A JUSTICE, by actual chronology.

I assume you plan to 'date' by specific year each story as it appears. If you wish to put A JUSTICE first, what about simply leaving the date off RED LEAVES when it appears? granted that you wish to cover the approximate decade 1840 plus by so dating Red Leaves. All these grants (deeds) were recorded before 1840, by which time this country had become 'white' country, though a few Chickasaws still retained holdings under the white man's setup. (the patent for my home is 1833)

Had-Two-Fathers was the son of Doom and the slave woman in A JUSTICE. Sam Fathers was actually Had-Two-Fathers' son, and hence the *grandson* of a king.

I realised some time ago that you would get into this inconsistency and pitied you. I suggest you make dates, when you state them, as vague as possible. Say, in these Indian pieces, when you state a date, call it '18-' or 'ante 1840.'

I think your plan of sequence is the right one. If I were doing the book, I would keep your plan, simply not date specifically the pieces, or give them their correct date regardless. I would date A JUSTICE when it happened, then date RED LEAVES when it happened, regardless of whether it preceded A JUSTICE in time. Or I would specify a date *only* for each section: like this.

Section I. THE OLD PEOPLE. 1800-1860.
" 2. THE UNVANQUISHED. 1860-1874.

I agree with your plan of inserting words to establish who and when and where, wherever you wish.

'Walked up' is used by any hunter or woodsman in this country. The dog 'finds' the birds, or when the dog fails, the gunner 'walks them up' by accident or hope. The deer hunter 'walks up' a deer. It means the hunter steals through the woods skilfully enough to get close enough to the game to flush it within shooting range.

THREE BASKET was one of ISSETIBBEHA'S men (Warriors), probably a minor leader. The country was getting overrun by white men about then. Herman Basket was Three Basket's son with a halfwhite name, a young blood, a wild companion of young Ikkemotubbe, who became Doom.

Sutpen's deed would derive from Issetibbeha's grant, since Issetibbeha as the chief granted all the land, that is, made treaty to surrender the patent, though the white purchaser's deed from the govt. might be dated years later. Ikkemotubbe, (Doom), as Issetibbeha's inheritor, would have sold land still under his uncle's patent.

All right about SPOTTED HORSES.[1]

Dont worry either about chrn. in EVENING SUN.[2]

OLD MAN. By all means. The story ends with: 'Here's your boat' etc. Stop it there.[3]

PERCY GRIMM. All right.[4]

DELTA AUTUMN. All right.[4]
Will rewrite portions of the APPENDIX.[5]

[no signature]

[1] Cowley planned to use the longer version from *The Hamlet* with cuts rather than the shorter version in *Scribner's*.

[2] Cowley had decided not to worry about the fact that Quentin was telling this story at age twenty-four though he had died in *The Sound and the Fury* before reaching twenty-one.

[3] Because of space limitations, Cowley had first wanted to omit the last chapter of the "Old Man" portion of *The Wild Palms* but later included it.

[4] Cowley had suggested minor changes for clarification.

[5] Cowley was concerned about discrepancies of dating relating to Ikkemotubbe, Jason Lycurgus Compson and Miss Quentin Compson. (For all the above see Cowley, pp. 46–53.)

To Robert K. Haas — TS. RH
Friday [2 Nov. 1945] — [Oxford]

Dear Bob:

This is a belated reply to your letter received last Friday about the watch. I delayed, hoping to have the watch itself. As it has not arrived yet, I imagine it is in Oxford, Massachusetts, waiting for me. Then it will go to Oxford, Missouri, then back to New York, where it will start over again, this time to Mississippi. It sounds like a good job. If it is the large size, very likely I can have the dial (telemetre) scribed later in 1–20, which not only converts miles into kilometers but I used my old one for all sorts of things: a slide rule in surveying ditches on the farm, for counting English money, etc. I am anxious to see the watch, which may arrive yet by any mail. I will write Betty my many thanks.[1]

I left Warner, refused to sign any suspension agreement. They threatened that, if I did not, they would prevent me selling any work to anybody, 'any editor' they put it. After reaching home, I wrote J L Warner personally asking to be released from the contract, got the same answer, not from him but from his legal dept. As a result, for the reason I wrote you last year, that another man owns movie rights in this present work, I cannot release it until my Cal. business is settled. I will probably keep working at the novel though, even before I am free of Warner. I may have to go back again, as I will run out of money in about 6 months as usual. If Warner really intends to try to starve me into fulfilling the contract, I may be able to make enough stink through publicity over it to free myself.

Meanwhile, say nothing officially about this: only that you heard from me in a private way that Warner seems to insist he owns everything I write, and so Faulkner wont do any writing until he finds out just how much of his soul he no longer owns.

As soon as the watch arrives, I will write you and Betty both, and thank you both very much.

Bill

[1] Faulkner had asked Haas to purchase a watch for him, and Haas's daughter, Betty, had selected it.

To Robert K. Haas | TS. RH
Tuesday [probably 6 Nov. 1945][1] | [Oxford]

Dear Bob:

The watch is here. It is a damned fine handsome instrument; I couldn't have chosen better myself out of a thousand of them. I am not only amazed that Betty found it, but that she ever reconciled herself to letting it get out of her own possession.

I had set aside the money to buy it. I hadn't thought about Random House carrying the charge of it. Will you let remain so, until royalties pay it off? As I wrote, I am faced with some Warner trouble and may have to go back. So I can use this $125.00 here, if it is all right with you.[2]

Thank you again for your effort.

Bill

[1] The watch had been sent on 29 Oct. 1945.

[2] On 26 Nov. 1945, Haas wrote Faulkner that he had requested the Bookkeeping Department to cancel the charge against Faulkner's account for the watch and asked him to accept the watch with their "best wishes and genuine affection."

To Robert K. Haas | TS. RH
Tuesday [probably 4 Dec. 1945] | [Oxford]

Dear Bob:

I found your kind note on returning from a two weeks' deer-hunt. I accept with gratification and pleasure, not just the gift but its commemoration of a long and happy relationship which is to continue for three or four times these fifteen years, since we are all still young men yet.

I had a good hunt. We use dogs and horses in this country, so the getting of meat is incidental. I saw seven deer, all does, and did not shoot my rifle one time. But we ran every day, fine sport, hell-for-leather on a strong horse through the woods after the dogs, ran one old buck almost fifty miles, from 7 a.m. until the dogs gave out about 3 p.m., came back to camp after dark, leading the horse and striking matches to read the compass. The buck got away, I was glad to know, was shot at three times but he still ran.

I have spent the fall doing whatever he would let me to get Malcolm Cowley's Viking Faulkner into shape. It is going to be a good book.

I thank the shop again for the present. My best wishes of the season to all of you, my very best to you and Miss Merle and Betty.[1] My nephew, the Marine pilot, is on his way home.[2] He has Air Medal, though he wont tell how he got it. A friend who knew him on service tells us it had something to do with Kamikazi. His younger brother or his sweetheart will probably get it out of him.

Bill

[1] Mrs. Robert K. Haas and her daughter.
[2] James M. Faulkner.

To Malcolm Cowley — TS. YALE
Saturday [8 Dec. 1945] — [Oxford]

Dear Cowley:

You should have the map by now.

You are right, the phrase wont do, out of regard to Random House. Could it read something like this:

. . . saga of . . . county . . .
A chronological picture of Faulkner's apocryphal
Mississippi county, selected from his published
works, novels and stories, with a heretofore
unpublished genealogy of one of its principal
families.
Edited by M. Cowley

It's not a new work by Faulkner. It's a new work by Cowley all right though. If you like, you might say 'The first chronological picture' etc.

The name is 'Falkner.' My great-grandfather, whose name I bear, was a considerable figure in his time and provincial milieu. He was prototype of John Sartoris: raised, organized, paid the expenses of and commanded the 2nd Mississippi Infantry, 1861–2, etc. Was a part of Stonewall Jackson's left at 1st Manassas that afternoon; we have a citation in James Longstreet's longhand as his corps commander after 2nd Manassas. He built the first railroad in our county, wrote a few books, made grand European tour of his time, died in a duel and the county raised a marble effigy which still stands in Tippah County. The place of our origin shows on larger maps: a hamlet named Falkner just below Tennessee line on his railroad.[1]

My first recollection of the name was, no outsider seemed able to pronounce it from reading it, and when he did once pronounce it, he always wrote the 'u' into it. So it seemed to me that the whole outside world was trying to change it, and usually did. Maybe when I began to write, even though I thought then I was writing for fun, I secretly was ambitious and did not want to ride on grandfather's coat-tails, and so accepted the 'u,' was glad of such an easy way to strike out for myself. I accept either spelling. In Oxford it usually has no 'u' except on a book. The above was always my mother's and father's version of why I put back into it the 'u' which my greatgrandfather, himself always a little impatient of grammar and spelling both, was said to have removed. I myself really dont know the true reason. It just seemed to me that as soon as I got away from Mississippi, I found the 'u' in the word whether I wished it or not. I still think it is of no importance, and either one suits me.

I graduated from grammar school, went two years to highschool, but only during fall to play on the football team, my parents finally caught on, worked about a year as a book-keeper in grandfather's bank, went to RAF, returned home, attended 1 year at University of Mississippi by special dispensation for returned troops, studying European languages, still didn't like school and quit that. Rest of education undirected reading.

The above I still hope can remain private between you and me, the facts are in order and sequence for you to use, to clarify the whos who piece. The following is for your ear too. What I have written is of course in the public domain and the public is welcome; what I ate and did and when and where is my own business.

I more or less grew up in my father's livery stable. Being the eldest of four boys, I escaped my mother's influence pretty easy, since my father thought it was fine for me to apprentice to the business. I imagine I would have been in the livery stable yet if it hadn't been for motor car.

When I came back from RAF, my father's health was beginning to fail and he had a political job: business manager of the state University, given to him by a countryman whom my grandfather had made a lawyer of, who became governor of Mississippi. I didn't want to go to work; it was by my father's request that I entered the University, which I didn't want to do either. That was 1920. Since then I have: Painted houses. Served as a 4th class postmaster. Worked for a New Orleans bootlegger. Deck hand in freighters (Atlantic). Hand in a Gulf of Mexico shrimp trawler. Stationary boiler fireman. Barnstormed an aeroplane out of cow pastures. Operated a farm, cotton and feed, breeding and raising mules and cattle. Wrote (or tried) for moving pictures. Oh yes, was a scout master for two years, was fired for moral reasons.

Faulkner

[1] The assertions that Col. William C. Falkner died in a duel, that the county raised his monument and that the family originated in the hamlet of Falkner are among the several inaccuracies in Faulkner's account.

To Robert K. Haas — MS. RH
[received 12 Dec. 1945] — [Oxford]

Dear Bob—

Here are 65 pages.[1] I rewrote and edited them 3 times and I think they are about right. I think it's pretty good and I'd like for Ober to see it. A copy would cost me about 25¢ a sheet, and we dont need a copy yet. Could you let him read this? Then if all agree he should have a copy right away on chance of mag. or other sale before you print it, we can have a copy made.

I think it's all right, maybe good enough for me to quit writing books on, though I probably wont quit yet.

Best to all.
Bill

[1] The fable.

To Malcolm Cowley — TS. YALE
Monday [24 Dec. 1945] — [Oxford]

Dear Cowley:

The piece received, and is all right.[1] I still wish you could lead off this way:

WHEN the war was over—the other war—William Faulkner, at home again in Oxford, Mississippi, yet at the same time was not at home, or at least not able to accept the postwar world.

Then go on from there. The piece is good, thoughtful, and sound. I myself would have said here:

'or rather what he did not want to accept was the fact
that he was now twenty-one years old and therefore was
expected to go to work.'

Dear Bob—

Here are 65 pages. I rewrote and edited them 3 times and I think they are about right. I think it's pretty good and I'd like for Ober to see it. A copy would cost me about 25¢ a sheet, and we don't need a copy yet. Could you let him read this? Then if all agree he should have a copy right away on chance of mag. or other sale before you print it, we can have a copy made.

I think it's all right, maybe good enough for me to quit writing books on, though I probably won't quit yet.

Best to all.

Bill

But then, that would be my piece and not yours. It is very fine and sound. I only wish you felt it right to lead off as above, no mention of war experience at all.

Best season's greetings and wishes. I hope to see you some day soon, thank you for this job.

Faulkner

[1] Cowley's introduction to *The Portable Faulkner*.

To Malcolm Cowley
[early Jan. 1946]

TS. YALE
[Oxford]

Dear Cowley:

Herewith returned, with thanks.[1] It's all right, sound and correct and penetrating. I warned you in advance I would hope for no biography, personal matter, at all. You elaborate certain theses from it, correctly I believe too. I just wish you didn't need to state in the piece the premises you derive from. If you think it necessary to include them, consider stating a simple skeleton, something like the thing in Who's Who; let the first paragraph, Section Two read, viz:

> Born (when and where). (He came to Oxford as a child, attended Oxford grammar school without graduating, had one year as a special student in modern languages in University of Mississippi. Rest of education was undirected and uncorrelated reading. If you mention military experience at all (which is not necessary, as I could have invented a few failed RAF airmen as easily as I did Confeds) say 'belonged to RAF in 1918.' Then continue: Has lived in same section of Miss. since, worked at various odd jobs until he got a job writing movies and was able to make a living at writing.

Then pick up paragraph 2 of Section II and carry on. I'm old-fashioned and probably a little mad too; I dont like having my private life and affairs available to just any and everyone who has the price of the vehicle it's printed in, or a friend who bought it and will lend it to him. I'll be glad to give you all the dope when we talk together. Some of it's very funny. I just dont like it in print except when I use it myself, like old John Sartoris and old Bayard and Mrs. Millard and Simon Strother and the other Negroes and the dead airmen.

I don't see too much Southern legend in it. I'll go further than you in the harsh criticism.

The style, as you divine, is a result of the solitude, and granted a bad one. It was further complicated by an inherited regional or geographical

(Hawthorne would say, racial) curse. You might say, studbook style: 'by Southern Rhetoric out of Solitude' or 'Oratory out of Solitude.'

Re. literature (songs too) in the South 1861–65. It was probably produced but not recorded. The South was too busy, but the main reason was probably a lack of tradition for inventing or recording. The gentlefolk hardly would. For all their equipment for leisure (slavery, unearned wealth) their lives were curiously completely physical, violent, despite their physical laziness. When they were not doing anything—not hunting or superintending farming or riding 10 and 20 miles to visit, they really did nothing: they slept or talked. They talked too much, I think. Oratory was the first art; Confederate generals would hold up attacks while they made speeches to their troops. Apart from that, 'art' was really no manly business. It was a polite painting of china by gentlewomen. When they entered its domain through the doors of their libraries, it was to read somebody else's speeches, or politics, or the classics of the faintly school, and even these were men who, if they had been writing men, would have written still more orations. The negroes invented the songs and their songs were not topical nor even dated in the sense we mean. So there was no literate middleclass to produce a literature. In a pastoral cityless land they lived remote and at economic war with both slave and slaveholder. When they emerged, gradually, son by infrequent son, like old Sutpen, it was not to establish themselves as a middleclass but to make themselves barons too. What songs and literature they possessed back home were the old songs from 15th–16th century England and Scotland, passed from mouth to mouth because the generations couldn't write to record them. After they emerged prior to and during and after the War, they were too busy to record anything or even to sing them, probably, were probably ashamed of them. Pass the eighty years, the old unreconstructed had died off at last, the strong among the remaining realised that to survive they must stop trying to be pre 1861 barons and become a middle class, they did so, and began to create a literature. Reason for the vital Southern one re the War and no Northern one is, the Northerner had nothing to write about regarding it. He won it. The only clean thing about War is losing it. Also, as regards material, the South was the fortunate side. That war marked a transition, the end of one age and the beginning of another, not to return. Before it in his wars man had fought man. After it, machine would fight machine. During that war, man fought bare handed against a machine. Of course that doesn't explain why the North didn't use the material too. It's not enough to say that perhaps the machine which defeated his enemy was a Frankenstein which, once the Southern armies were consumed, turned on him and enslaved him and, removing him from a middle class fixed upon the land, translated him into a baronage based upon a slavery not of human beings but of machines; you cant say that because the Northerner writes about other things. Maybe the carpetbagger is to blame, maybe it is the new blood which he brought into the South after 61 which produced the literature, and as soon as something happens to cause vast throngs of Southern middle class to move into the North, a belated Northern literature about the Civil War will spring up. Or maybe the South will be able to write all the literature about the Civil War we need and what we want is a new war, maybe a group of Dismal Swamp or Florida Everglades Abolitionists will decide to free the country from machines and will start a movement to do so, followed by a vast influx of Tennessee and Mississippi and Virginia carpet-baggers, and then the North will have a war to write about.

Thank you for seeing the piece. It's all right. The 'writing in solitude' is very true and sound. That explains a lot about my carelessness about bad taste. I am not always conscious of bad taste myself, but I am pretty sensitive to what others will call bad taste. I think I have written a lot and sent it off to print before I actually realised strangers might read it.

William Faulkner

[1] Cowley's introduction to *The Portable Faulkner*.

To Harold Ober

TS. FCVA

5 Jan. 46

[Oxford]

Dear Harold:

Enclosed is my copy of my present contract. That is, I asked for and received a sum of money, in return for which I signed this contract engaging a novel when I wrote one. I am careless about such, hate the very idea of them like very hell. This may not be the last one even. My present belief is, I have taken an advance on a contract for a yet unwritten novel, and am engaged to supply that novel when I write it, with I suppose an option on the NEXT SUCCEEDING NOVEL after this first unwritten one. For this reason I am sending Bob Haas a copy of this letter, which is my request to him to give you any and all information about my commitment with Random House.

Other commitments I have none, except the contract with Warner, which they will not release me from, and regarding which, when I left the studio after refusing to sign a 6 month leave of absence stating that I took the leave in order to write a novel on which they would have the studio claim, I was vaguely threatened with all sorts of reprisals, to the effect that if I wrote and submitted anything anywhere, the buyer of it would buy at his peril.

Thank you for the Ellery Queen check. What a commentary. In France,

I am the father of a literary movement. In Europe I am considered the best modern American and among the first of all writers. In America, I eke out a hack's motion picture wages by winning second prize in a manufactured mystery story contest.[1]

Malcolm Cowley has done a fine job in Spoonrivering my apocryphal county, to be a Viking Portable, they call them. Be sure to see it.

Bill

[1] "An Error in Chemistry" had won the prize in a contest sponsored by *Ellery Queen's Mystery Magazine*.

To Robert K. Haas — TS. RH
Wednesday [16 Jan. 1946] — [Oxford]

Dear Bob:

I have your note about the Mercury prize.[1] Thank you for sending the word along. Our Uncle Sam in Washington will not sneeze at even a mere 500$ prize.

I wish I could tell you how much I enjoy the possession of the chonometer, the satisfaction of owning and using a firstrate instrument, even though at present its main purpose is to notify me when to drive in to the village and fetch my daughter from school. I am also using it to clock a new mare, a pretty fast quarter horse I brought her from California last fall.

I hear by the radio I am having a nervous breakdown, in expensive privacy.[2] It's nice to be rich, even if only on the air waves.

You have the carbon of my letter to Harold Ober. He just wants information regarding my contracts, to answer inquiries with.

Best to all of you.
Bill

[1] "Honor" appeared in *The American Mercury*, LXIII (Oct. 1946), 485–93, with the notation "This magazine, indeed, was perhaps the first national periodical of its class to print [Faulkner's] fiction. This story, first published in the issue for July 1930, is the second in a series of reprints of outstanding material from past issues of the *Mercury*."

[2] A report broadcast by Walter Winchell on one of his Sunday night news programs.

To Malcolm Cowley
Monday [21 Jan. 1946]

TS. YALE
[Oxford]

Dear Cowley:

Yours at hand. You're going to bugger up a fine dignified distinguished book with that war business. The only point a war reference or anecdote could serve would be to reveal me a hero, or (2) to account for the whereabouts of a male of my age on Nov. 11, 1918 in case this were a biography. If, because of some later reference back to it in the piece, you cant omit all European war reference, say only what Who's Who says and no more:

Was a member of the RAF in 1918.

I'll pay for any resetting of type, plates, alteration, etc.

I dont think I can come up East this spring. I'll have to go back to Warner by 15 Mar. or have his legal dogs on me. He has already made vague though dire threats about warning any editor to buy my stuff at his peril, if I dont come back.

If Thomas[1] is taking up farming cold at his age, even with 372 acres, I hope he's rich; he'll need to be. He'd better move his decimal point and start with 3.72 acres. If he really wants a farm, I'll sell him mine, including 4 span of mules and 11 head of niggers.

I'm really concerned about the war reference. As I said last, I'm going to be proud of this book. I wouldn't have put in anything at all about the war or any other personal matter.

Yours,
Faulkner

[1] Cowley's friend Thomas Mabry.

To Malcolm Cowley
Friday [1 Feb. 1946]

TS. YALE
[Oxford]

Dear Cowley:

Yours of 26th at hand. I see your point now about the war business, and granting the value of the parallel you will infer, it is 'structurally' necessary.[1] I dont like the paragraph because it makes me out more of a hero than I was, and I am going to be proud of your book. The mishap was caused not by combat but by (euphoneously) 'cockpit trouble'; i.e., my own foolishness; the injury I suffered I still feel I got at bargain rates. A lot of that sort of thing happened in those days, the culprit unravelling himself from the subsequent unauthorised crash incapable of any explanation as far as advancing the war went, and grasping at any frantic straw before someone in authority would want to know what became of the aeroplane, would hurry to the office and enter it in the squadron records as 'practice flight.' As compared with men I knew, friends I had and lost, I deserve no more than the sentence I suggested before: 'served in (or belonged to) RAF.' But I see where your paragraph will be better for your purpose, and I am sorry it's not nearer right.

I just had a letter from Linscott about the proposed re-issue. I may write him, suggest your idea of TSAF alone, plus the Compson thing you have. He wants an introduction for it, for $250.00. I'll do almost anything for $250.00 or even $25.00, but I dont know how to write introductions. I dont recall ever seeing one, except the one I wrote for B Cerf about 10 years ago when he thought he would reprint TSAF and didn't or forgot it or whatever.

I would like to come up East, but I am about to run out of money and will have to go back to Cal. I am afraid. But if I can come up, I'll certainly let you know.

How much land will you work? If you are now a tractor man, it must be more than just a shirt-tail of it.

Faulkner

[1] Earlier, Cowley had argued that some knowledge of Faulkner's wartime experiences was necessary to prepare the reader for his reaction against the postwar world. (See Cowley, p. 75.)

To Robert N. Linscott[1] TS. RH
4 Feb. 1946 Oxford, Miss.

Dear Mr Linscott:

When you reprint THE SOUND AND THE FURY, I have a new section to go with it. I should have written this new section when I wrote the book itself, but I never thought of it until Malcolm Cowley let me help him getting together his portable Faulkner volume that Viking has.

By all means include this in the reprint. When you read it, you will see how it is the key to the whole book, and after reading it, the 4 sections as they stand now fall into clarity and place. He has the only clean copy of this new section. I will write him today to have a copy of it made and sent to you. When you issue the book, print the sections in this order, print this appendix first, and title it APPENDIX. This will be anachronic but no more so than the other sections:

1st section: APPENDIX
Compson

Then continue with the sections as they now are. I dont have a copy of the book and cant cite correctly, but they follow:

Benjy's section:
APRIL 5 (I think)
Quentin's section
June 2, 1910
Jason's section
APRIL 6
Author's section
APRIL 7

Be sure and print the appendix *first*, but call it as I titled it:

APPENDIX
COMPSON

I had never thought of TSAF and AS I LAY DYING in the same breath.[2] I never wrote but one introduction (seriously) which was when Bennett had a notion about 10 years ago to make a special edition of TSAF, which came to nothing. This introduction (along with my only copy of the book incidentally, which I marked up in colored crayon, since the idea was to print the different time transitions in different colors, and sent to him with the introduction,) may be somewhere in the office now, since I never got either of them back. So the introduction will have to cover both stories. I never read introductions either, and know little about them. But I will do a lot for $250.00. But I'll have to think about it, try to think up something. Maybe I cant. Maybe I could subcontract the introduction to somebody. What would you like to have in an introduction to these two stories? If you could give me some idea, that might be quicker than for me at my age to back up and do a course in introduction reading.

I will write Cowley at once about getting a copy of the appendix section to you.

[no signature]

[1] Random House's new senior editor.

[2] Random House planned to publish *The Sound and the Fury* and *As I Lay Dying* together as one Modern Library volume.

To Malcolm Cowley — TS. YALE
Tuesday [5 Feb. 1946] — [Oxford]

Dear Cowley:

I have a letter from Linscott about the combined TSAF and LAY DYING. I wrote him to include the new material in the appendix which you have. I dont have a clear copy of it. Could you have a copy made, I will pay the score, and send it to Linscott? Damn to hell, I have never yet been able to afford a secretary; I never missed one much until these last few years. Now I dont know where about half of what I have is, nor even (at times) whether I ever wrote it or not.

Let me hear if possible to get a copy of the appendix.

[no signature]

Cowley had finally sent Faulkner a revision of the introduction to The Portable Faulkner *in which the only reference to Faulkner's military career noted that he had served in the Royal Air Force in 1918. (See Cowley, pp. 83, 85.)*

To Malcolm Cowley — TS. YALE
Monday [18 Feb. 1946] — [Oxford]

Dear Brother:

I feel much better about the book with your foreword beginning as now. I saw your point about (and need for) the other opening all the time. But to me it was false. Not factually, I dont care much for facts, am not much interested in them, you cant stand a fact up, you've got to prop it up, and when you move to one side a little and look at it from that angle, it's not thick enough to cast a shadow in that direction. But in truth, though maybe what I mean by truth is humility and maybe what I think is humility is really immitigable pride. I would have preferred nothing at all prior to the instant I began to write, as though Faulkner and Typewriter were concomitant, coadjutant and without past on the moment they first faced each other at the suitable (nameless) table.

I cant write an introduction; I hope to hell Random House cant find the other one I did. What about doing it yourself? or would that be too much Cowley plus F? let me know about it. I will then write Linscott and ask for someone to do it. I dont want to read TSAF again. Would rather let the appendix stand with inconsistencies, perhaps make a statement (quotable) at end of the introduction, viz: the inconsistencies in the appendix prove that to me the book is still alive after 15 years, and being still alive is still growing, changing; the appendix was done at same heat as the book, even though 15 years later, and so it is the book itself which is inconsistent: not the appendix. That is, at the age of 30 I did not know these people as at 45 I now do; that I was even wrong now and then in the very conclusions I drew from watching them, and the information in which I once believed. (I believe I was 28 when I wrote the book. That's almost 20 years.)

I will return your volume carefully.

Faulkner

To Robert K. Haas — TS. RH
Monday [18 Feb. 1946] — [Oxford]

Dear Bob:

Yours of 14th at hand. The trouble is, as I tried to explain, Warner has threatened me verbally through the studio man who manages the writers dept. that the studio owns everything I write and that anyone else buys it at his or her peril. In the case of this novel, the moving picture claim already belongs to the man about whom I wrote you two years ago, who had the germ of the idea. So I cant release any of it until I am free of Warner. And it looks like I cant even get free of Warner by serving out my biblical seven years servitude, as I cannot find a place in Los Angeles to live. I spent the 4 months last summer guest of a friend, where I slept in a passage way in a house where the man's wife and his mother fought all the time. It was just about unbearable; I managed to stick it 4 months. I am now out of money again, I would go back; I can stay as guest with another friend who lives 2 hours from Burbank by car, so that I would have to have a car to go to work in (if I could find or afford to buy one). He lives on the coast, in the country, where not even busses run. I dont know what to do, much. I still have $500.00, I may take that and go on out to Cal. with a return ticket back here, and see what can be done.

You wrote me date 12-30 something about a $500.00 prize from Mercury I won. Do you know any more about it? I hadn't heard, have not received any $500.00 from Mercury, though I did receive a $500.00 prize from Ellery Queen Mystery Magazine. Could this be the same?[1]

I'm glad the firm has a nice house.[2] Maybe I can get a furlough from the poorhouse someday and see it.

Bill

. . . .

[1] It was the same prize.

[2] Random House had moved from 20 E. 57th St. to new offices in one wing of a large brownstone building with a courtyard which faced onto Madison Avenue between 50th and 51st sts. Faulkner liked the ornate rooms with their high ceilings and paneled walls softened with heavy drapes.

To Harold Ober
Monday [18 Feb. 1946]

TS. FCVA
[Oxford]

Dear Harold:

Maurice Coindreau is one of my French translators: SOUND & FURY, AS I LAY DYING, LIGHT IN AUGUST, etc. I may have told him it was all right about the piece; I dont remember. I usually refer all this to you, and am inclined to think I would not have made any such agreement in this case. I dont recall having heard from him since I wrote the piece, but if he says I authorised this through him, I will accept his statement. I cant imagine any other way in which I might have.[1]

Do you know anything about the enclosed from Bob? Is this the same Ellery Queen business?[2]

. . . .

Had I better hold this cashiers check until you find what's up?[2]

Bill

[1] By late spring of 1937, Faulkner had written a comic story called "Afternoon of a Cow." He had read it to friends in Hollywood, and Maurice Coindreau seemed the only one amused by it. He gave a souvenir copy to Coindreau, whose French translation, "L'Après-midi d'une Vache," had appeared in *Fontaine*, 27–28 (June–July 1943), 66–81, and had subsequently come to Harold Ober's attention. It would be published in the United States in *Furioso*, II, 4 (Summer 1947), 5–17.

[2] See Faulkner to Haas, 18 Feb. 1946.

To Harold Ober
Saturday [23 Feb. 1946]

TS. FCVA
[Oxford]

Dear Harold:

In this week's Post, Feb. 30, a story, OLD MAN IN A SHOE.[1] I see a movie in it, for the child star, Obrien[2] I think, and a man who can play the sort of comedy with her as Robert Young (I think) did in CANTERVILLE GHOST. They will reform (politically) a small city.

I would like to do it. I am still committed to Warner, and therefore to the agent Herndon. Do you see any way to use this story:

1. As a lever to get me free of Warner, and hence Herndon. That's first.
2. To enable me to earn some money while staying here, even though Herndon shares in it, from Warner or anyone else.

I am broke, must go back on salary in March. Have been trying to find a place to live in Cal. Cant do it. If I have to go back, the only room I have found yet is in home of a friend who lives 2 hours away from studio by car, no busses at all. I cannot even get to work without buying a car.

I now have only about 500$ cash. Am writing the studio today I will be there about Mar 15 if they will find me a place to live. They probably wont; they have never yet done anything for me.

Did you receive rewritten KNIGHT'S GAMBIT piece?

Bill

[1] The author of the *Saturday Evening Post* story was Douglass Welch.
[2] Margaret O'Brien.

To Robert K. Haas — TS. RH

Sunday [probably 24 Feb. 1946] — [Oxford]

Dear Bob:

Yours at hand.

I cant find my Warner contract. I lost or mislaid it sometime between the day I received it, in Aug. 1942, and when I returned home that Xmas. I have not seen it since, and have hunted for it since last winter, in vain. I will get a copy from the studio when I return there next month.

When I notified the studio I was coming back here last Sept., they drew up a suspension agreement stating that I was taking six months leave in order to write a novel, the rights of which they would own under the contract. I refused to sign it, came home anyway.

The threat was verbal, from McDermid, the studio superintendent of writers, who advised me to sign it, that if I didn't, the studio would fix it so that any editor would buy any material of mine at his risk.

As you know, the movie rights to this novel are already the property of the man I spoke of, who loaned me $1,000.00 which enabled me to stay here long enough to do the synopsis I sent you the copy of 2 years ago.

Yes, I had Harold's letter about his lawyer. I did not avail myself of his offer because the studio had already promised me voluntarily, through James Geller, the then superintendent of writers (he was fired overnight by Warner last year) that once I got a credit, this present contract would be torn up and a new one offered me. I believed him, felt that that was the best way to extricate myself: get the old contract destroyed, since I did not want to dodge or evade anything I had voluntarily assumed. When I asked last Aug. for the studio to make good Geller's promise, they refused.

I notified McDermid yesterday I would return 15 Mar if the studio would find me a place to live. If they wont, I can go back and stay with a friend, though he lives too far from the studio for me to make Warner's daily 9:30 deadline without a car. As soon as I can, I will get a copy of my contract and find exactly what rights I have signed to Warner. But I think the only thing that will free this novel is for Warner to release the movie rights, as he will claim them as soon as I release the novel.

I have no recollection of any such letter mentioned in this cable. It must refer to book rights.[1] Will you wire them, my expense, to send you a copy of the letter, and deal with it? If it should refer to a short story you dont have, Ober will have it and you can turn the matter over to him.

I have discussed my situation with several friends in Hollywood, veteran movie writers. They all say my only hope is to get the contract abrogated, get myself fired somehow, that legally I am helpless, that the contract, and Herndon's arrangement, which is based on the contract and is automatically a part of it, will stand in court, and the only way I can get out of the contract is by means of someone who can say privately to Warner: 'Let this guy go today, and I'll scratch your back tomorrow.' That sort of thing. I dont know anybody in Hollywood who can do that, who for me will, not yet anyway. My only hope is to get fired. But I'll get a copy of the contract and see exactly what I have committed myself to.

Thank you for your last sentence. I knew that already. I am trying to stop borrowing money which I dont see any way of returning. I'd borrow like a shot to get myself out of the hole I'm in. But not just to put off going back to Hollywood another month or so.

[no signature]

[1] Arnoldo Mondadori Editore of Milan had cabled asking for a response to a letter sent 13 Nov. 1945. The firm would become Faulkner's Italian publisher.

On 3 November 1945, Eugenio Vaquer wrote Faulkner asking if he had any objection to the publication of Vaquer's translation of "Turn About" in an Italian literary magazine. On 22 January 1946, he wrote again thanking Faulkner for sending permission through Mr. Hodge, chief of the United States Information Service book section. Vaquer reiterated his original request and asked permission to include "Lo!" in an anthology he was preparing.

To Harold Ober — TS. FCVA
Thursday [28 Feb. 1946] — [Oxford]

Dear Harold:

Re enclosed. I cannot remember any Mr Hodge. I cannot remember authorising anyone to transmit to any third party any permission to reprint anything, as I (so I think) invariably submit all this to you, usually without even reading the letter.

Though I may have done so. Anyway, the thing is done now, and I am willing to acquiesce, or accept it. I would have done that, anyway.

I agree to his other request. Will you communicate with him, find who Mr Hodge is, and other circumstances about this matter. You can write Sr. Vaquer that I am happy to acquiesce, but will he kindly refresh my memory about Mr Hodge and what is U.S.I.S.

Re Warner contract. I dont remember seeing my copy of it since I signed the thing Aug. 1942. I will ask studio for a new copy.

I have written studio I will be there as soon as they can find me a room to live in.

In 6 months there I can save enough to live six months here. This is a hand to mouth existence, but I seem to have reached the age where I no longer have the courage to face the prospect of borrowing advances against what I have not yet done, or of beating out what is to me hack work on speculation. If I accepted $5000.00 advance on that river book, I would spend all the time worrying about what I would do when that was spent. I have at least one book in mind that I want to write too much to do justice to one I dont particularly want to write.

I am sending you today a 40 page synopsis, movie idea. A part of it belongs to another man, who will agree to whatever I do. He says it is rotten, has no chance of sale.[1] I still think so. Can you sell it? I am willing for Warner to have first claim, if he will meet price.

I consulted Obringer, studio lawyer, at suggestion of Trilling, Warner's man Friday. Obringer says that legally Herndon will be construed as having a claim on me as agent, based on my Warner contract and my wire to Herndon authorising him to make the original deal.

As I am about broke again, I may go on out to Hollywood anyway. I can stay with a friend, though he lives 2 hours from Burbank, in a rich section with no busses, so that I will need a car to get to work. I may be able to find a place to live while on the spot.

It's a bloody awful hell of a note. I never in my life knew anyone who needed as badly to belong to the unearned increment classes as me.

Bill

[1] Faulkner was probably referring to a thirty-seven-page double-spaced synopsis which he typed and dated 1946. It was entitled *Continuous Performance*, and a sequence which began on p. 15 was tagged "This idea belongs to Tom Reed." Under the title, Faulkner had listed two possibilities for starring actors, first Cary Grant and then Fred MacMurray. The story dealt with a recently married couple, very much in love but plagued by the bride's extravagances. It was an attempt at light comedy which never sold.

To Robert N. Linscott — TS. RH
13 March [1946] — [Oxford]

Dear Mr Linscott:

Here is the SOUND & FURY appendix. I hope you agree with me that it should come first, though still titled APPENDIX, then the book itself should follow in its original order. As you will see, this appendix is the key to the whole book; after reading this, any reader will understand all the other sections. That was the trouble before: the BENJY section, although the most obscure and troublesome one, had to come first because of chronology, the matter it told. And to title this new section FOREWORD seems bad to me, as a deliberate pandering to those who wont make the effort to understand the book. Also, it actually is an appendix, not a foreword.

Cowley suggests you will do better to find someone else to write the preface, if possible, and I agree with him. I have done the best I could for the book; there is nothing else I can say or add to it. He suggests that perhaps Conrad Aiken will consider it.

I dont agree with you about printing TSAF and AS I LAY DYING together. It's as though we were saying 'This is a versatile guy; he can write in the same stream of consciousness style about princes and then peasants,' or 'This is a universal writer; he has written about all the kinds of people in Miss. in the same style.' I would like to see TSAF and THE WILD PALMS section from that book, the part of it about the doctor who performed the abortion on his own sweetheart.

As you know, this appendix section belongs to VIKING PRESS. This is the only copy Cowley and I have. Could you make another?

Please tell Mr Haas that I am leaving for California Mar 21st, and will communicate with him from there. Ask him to inform Mr Ober.

Yours sincerely,
William Faulkner

In mid-March, Haas wired Faulkner suggesting that he delay his departure for California in the hope that Haas and Ober could persuade Warner Bros. to modify their stand about Faulkner's working on the fable and their potential rights in the work.

To Robert K. Haas — TS. RH

Wednesday [20 Mar. 1946] — [Oxford]

Dear Bob:

Your wire was cheering. My hope is to be able to stay here and write the book, in which case I will have to have advance. So maybe best will be to free it, so I can earn money in Cal. while doing it. But how you will ever get Warner to agree to such, I dont know.

If the negotiations take longer than Apr. 1, can I have some advance, as I am now down to $500.00 total assets. Also, let me know as soon as possible if I am to try for another train reservation.

Will you please do this for me. On 6 March the mainspring of my chronometer broke. I sent the watch, insured parcel post of that date, back to Black, Starr and Gorham, with a covering letter. They have not acknowledged receipt of the watch yet. (By their records, a Mathy-Tissot strapwatch, ordered by Miss E. Haas and sent to me by express in Nov. 45) Will you please call them, see if they have received the watch, what chance to repair it and send it back to me before I go to the Coast (if I go).

I think I told you: William Bacher and Henry Hathaway had the germ of the idea. Bacher decided I was the one to write it. I am to write it in any form I like, script or novel, he and Hathaway to have the movie privileges (that is, they are to make the movie) the 3 of us to share alike in all profits. Bacher loaned me $1,000.00 in 1943 while I was at home to work on it.

I will appreciate your effort in regard to the watch. I miss it a lot; if I am to go to Coast without it, I would like time to instruct Black Starr etc, where to send it to me there.

Incidentally, I can go back to coast, stay away from Warner, and earn some money under the rose. I could pay my way in this fashion while writing the novel perhaps. I wish I could see you in person now. Explain fully these ramifications. If you think it a good idea and will lend me the money, I can come up for 2–3 days so we can get together re my affairs. But you will know best. Let me know what more information I can supply.

Bill

To Robert N. Linscott — TS. RH

Friday [22 Mar. 1946] — [Oxford]

Dear Mr Linscott:

I am opposed to asking Hemingway to write the preface. It seems to me in bad taste to ask him to write a preface to my stuff. It's like asking one race horse in the middle of a race to broadcast a blurb on another horse in the same running field. A preface should be done by a preface writer, not a fictioneer; certainly not by one man on another in his own limited field. This sort of mutual back-scratching reduces novelists and poets to the status of a kind of eunuch-capon pampered creatures in some spiritual Vanderbilt stables, mindless, possessing nothing save the ability and willingness to run their hearts out at the drop of Vanderbilt's hat.

The woods are full of people who like to make a nickel expressing opinions on the work of novelists. Cant you get one of them?

If you like having in AS I LAY DYING better, I am agreeable.[1]

Faulkner

[1] Instead of "The Wild Palms" segment of *The Wild Palms*, as Faulkner had suggested.

To Harold Ober — TS. FCVA
Friday [22 Mar. 1946] — [Oxford]

Dear Harold:

Yours of 20 Mar at hand.

I cannot do the book in 3 months. If I stay here that much longer to work on it, I will get that much further in debt to Random House, and delay the end of this Warner contract and this whole intolerable situation that much more.

So it seems to me the best thing I can do is to go on back to the coast and get on salary again, do as I have done before, stick it as long as I can, then come back here and stay until the money runs out and then go back.

Bacher has the moving picture claim on this book. For the very reason that there is no sort of written contract between us, I will do nothing whatever that will jeopardise his rights and wishes in the matter. If he makes an arrangement with Warner about it, I will agree to anything he likes. I myself have made the only request of Warner I intend to make of him, which was to cancel my contract. I took this step mainly because his studio had been lying to me ever since I got there in 1942, about destroying this contract and giving me a better one.

Please talk to Bob and let me hear from you as soon as possible, so I can put in for another reservation to the coast.

Bill

To Robert K. Haas — TS. RH
Sunday [24 Mar. 1946] — [Oxford]

Dear Bob:

Yours received. I wrote Harold yesterday, in answer to him.

As I understand it, the best you hope for is a further leave of absence in order to write or finish a novel.

I cant finish a novel in that time, even if this present one were free as regards movie rights. Even if I could, I would have to borrow money, get further in debt.

So, as I wrote Harold, the best thing I see is for me to go on back and get on salary again. The sooner I get back on pay, the better. It takes some time to get another reservation, so let me hear from you as soon as possible, in order to try for the ticket. Having put you to all this trouble already, I dont want to bugger up things by going back without your approval, and Harold's. But if I must go, and apparently I must, the sooner the better.

Please find out about the watch, so I will know how to direct them to send it to me in California, if I cant have it before I leave.

I think you know I am grateful for all you are doing in this matter.

Yours,
Bill

On 26 March 1946, Ober sent to the New York representative of Warner Bros. sixty-four pages of the fable, now tentatively entitled Who?, *and asked that Warner permit Faulkner to finish the novel. Two days later, Ober wired Faulkner that Warner Bros. thought it best for him to finish the novel. The same day, Ober wrote Faulkner that Warner Bros. agreed that they had no rights in* Who? *and that Random House wanted the novel and would provide money for Faulkner to finish it in Mississippi; then Faulkner would be expected to return to complete his film contract.*

To Robert K. Haas — TS. RH
Saturday [30 Mar. 1946] — [Oxford]

Dear Bob:

On receipt of Harold's wire Friday, I got to work on the mss. I think it will go all right but I cant undertake to say yet how long it will take.

About money. I will try to hold myself under $400.00 per month, and stick to the mss. If I cant, I'll have to put the mss. down and try to boil pot from time to time.

I have a $250.00 income tax payt, due 15 June, another 15 Sep. and 15 Dec. I have other outstanding debts which I can pay off by degrees, until I finish mss. and get back on Warner salary.

Can you send me $1000.00 now, $500.00 May 1st, another $500. June 1st. By then I should know where we are with mss. and date to go back on Warner salary. Without doubt I will need more after June, but will ask for it later.

I feel fine, am happy now, thanks to Harold and you. Will you please call Black, Starr and Gorham and instruct them to send the watch to me here.

I imagine you know of correspondence between Mr Linscott and me re. introduction to my reprint. I dont like the idea of asking any fiction writer to stop his own work to write an introduction to another man's fiction. At present I dont have any pressure of my own to do an introduction with, though if necessary I will try to bull something through. Ask Mr Linscott if the new appendix material wont do as introduction, with perhaps a paragraph over my name explaining how it came about: that I should have written this when I wrote the book, and failed to see its need or perhaps at that time I too didn't know my own characters as well as their creator should, that perhaps the characters themselves grew up after they escaped the nest, as human beings do—that sort of thing.

Thanks for attending to the watch business. My best to all.

Bill

On 2 April 1946, R. J. Obringer of Warner Bros. wrote Faulkner a letter setting forth Faulkner's contract status, stating that the studio had no claim on his novel in progress and noting that Faulkner would return to the studio to work after completing the novel. Before signing to indicate his acceptance of these terms, Faulkner sent the letter to Ober.

To Harold Ober — TS. FCVA
[received 18 Apr. 1946] — [Oxford]

Dear Harold:

I send you the enclosed for your look-see. They seem all right to me in substance, but the second paragraph is mostly wrong, viz. I have been in default since Sept 20 1946. But I haven't been writing a novel since that time. While on leave in 1943, I laid out notes and a synopsis, but I did not start work on it for publication (in a form to be printed) until after I received your wire saying Warner had waived any rights he might attempt to claim in it. This was about Mar 25 of this year, wasn't it? Also, it will not be called WHO.

The rest is all right, only I dont think I shall be able to finish it before I will have to go back to work. That is, I dont know that Bob will feel Random House can underwrite me that long, as this is going to be a lot of book, something new for me, really not a novel. It may go slow at times; it may take me two years to get it right. I shant release it until it is right. In which case, I may have to go back on studio salary about next Sept.

If you think the second par. or any other should be altered or amended, do so and return to me.

Bill

To Malcolm Cowley
TS. YALE

Tuesday [23 Apr. 1946]
[Oxford]

Dear Cowley:

The job is splendid.[1] Damn you to hell anyway. But even if I had beat you to the idea, mine wouldn't have been this good. By God, I didn't know myself what I had tried to do, and how much I had succeeded.

I am asking Viking to send me more copies (I had just one) and I want to sign one for you, if you are inclined. Spotted Horses is pretty funny, after a few years.

Random House and Ober lit a fire under Warner, I dont know how, and I am here until September anyway, on a dole from Random House, working on what seems now to me to be my magnum o.

Faulkner

[1] *The Portable Faulkner*, edited by Malcolm Cowley (New York, 1954), in the Viking Portable Library series.

To Robert K. Haas
TS. RH

Sunday [5 May 1946]
[Oxford]

Dear Bob:

Yours at hand. I should have kept you informed. I got at the mss. as soon as I had Warner's assurance about claiming it. It is going all right, I think it is a big book myself.

Here is a batch of it. I will send more as I get it cleaned up, and typed.

The central idea has not changed, it just has more in it than I knew at first.

I'm not so certain I will be able to finish it within the length of time Random House will want to continue to finance me. So I am more or less planning on having to go back to studio for a time about Sept. Yet in those 4 months I might do it. As I begin to see the whole plan of it though, it looms too big in size to be finished in that time. I'll keep you informed.

Cowley's portable Faulkner pleases me very much. Could you have your girl telephone Viking to send me a dozen of it C.O.D.

If Ober should want to see this mss. I hope you'll let him, as part of my thanks for putting his shoulder to the wheel to help you get me the chance to work at it. To repeat, I think it is all right. It may be my best. It's not a novel at all. I think it's more than just a fable.

Bill

Please tell Mr Linscott I'll try again on the preface as soon as I can get straightened out in my mind just what I think he wants. I'm not a preface man, never read one and dont intend to, dont see why for them. But I think I know what he wants and will try again.

When the Russian writer Ilya Ehrenburg visited New York in the spring of 1946, he told Cowley that he wanted to meet Faulkner and Cowley agreed to write him.

To Malcolm Cowley — TS. YALE
[early or mid-May 1946] — [Oxford]

Dear friend:

Thank you for warning me. What the hell can I do? Goddamn it I've spent almost fifty years trying to cure myself of the curse of human speech, all for nothing. Last month two damned Swedes, two days ago a confounded Chicago reporter, and now this one that cant even speak english. As if anything he or I either know, or both of us together know, is worth being said once, let alone twice through an interpreter. I swear to Christ being in Hollywood was better than this where nobody knew me or cared a damn. I hate like hell to be in this state, I can even put up with mankind when I have time to adjust. But I do like to have the chance to invite people to come to look at me and see where I keep my tail or my other head or whatever the hell it is strangers want to come here for.

Thank you again for warning; I'll just have to bull through it someway.[1] The book received. Yours in mail tomorrow. Maybe the b hasn't realised he's in America now; I still own my home.

Faulkner

[1] When a U.S. State Dept. representative accompanying Ehrenburg phoned from Chattanooga, Tenn., on 17 May, Faulkner avoided a visit by offering to give Ehrenburg one hour.

On 22 May 1946, Robert Linscott wrote Faulkner that they had found the introduction to The Sound and the Fury *which he had written in August 1933 for the special edition Random House planned to publish. Linscott proposed using it in the forthcoming Modern Library edition and suggested adding a postscript to it based on a one-page revision, which he enclosed, of two paragraphs Faulkner had written in a letter to him about the Compson appendix.*

To Robert N. Linscott — TS. RH
[probably late May 1946] — [Oxford]

Dear Mr Linscott:

Bless you for finding the introduction and sending it back to me.[1] Random House paid me for it and I remembered writing one, but I had forgotten what smug false sentimental windy shit it was. I will return the money for it, I would be willing to return double the amount for the chance of getting it out of danger and destroyed.

I realise you cant reconcile to not having an introduction, so we'll have to compromise. I am busy on this new book, it is hot now. I will try to pull away and do an introduction from this old one and the new single page by editing, rewriting; it wont be as long. I dont know how long it will be. So if you still insist and cant wait, arrange with whomever you like to write one. When I get this one done, I will send it in. If it is too late, you will have sent the other one to printer and nothing lost. Perhaps I can take a day off about this weekend and rewrite this one, if you can wait that long.

Meantime, have the House charge me with what they paid me for this other one, I think it was $500.00 though I hope less.

Yours,
Faulkner

I'm certainly glad to have it back. I knew all the time. I had no business writing an introduction, writing anything just for money. Now I am convinced of it and cured.

[1] Published in *The Southern Review*, 8 (N.S., Autumn 1972), 705–10.

Faulkner sent Linscott a short introduction as he had promised. On receipt of it, Linscott apparently asked for a balancing introduction to As I Lay Dying.

To Robert N. Linscott — TS. RH
[late May 1946] — [Oxford]

Dear Mr Linscott:

This seems to be harder to get at than either of us hoped or feared.

I reckon I wrote TSATF for fun. The one before that had been turned down by everybody I sent it to and so I was disabused of hopes of printing; had never had any about making money writing anyway. I wrote the first section, found there was a little more in it, wrote the second section, found there was still more, etc., etc. Didn't think anybody would print it and was correct, until Hal Smith who had tried to get Harcourt to take it, set up for himself and printed it.

Somewhat the same with Dying book. I asked Smith for $500.00 loan, said I would write him a book, really didn't expect the loan but got it, spent it, time passed and I remembered I had promised a book, finally took myself by scruff of neck and wrote him a quick one, 6 weeks for it, got in under the promised wire by a hair.

This doesn't make an introduction though; neither would the truth help: that I am trying to write something that will pass muster in order to get the fee for it. And if you put into my mouth what I am to say, we will be losing the time it takes for the letters to go back and forth, since you could do it yourself.

Could you use the page I sent you, follow it with the appendix, follow the appendix with TSATF, then a page as above re. the writing of AS I LAY DYING, follow it with the book?

As you see, I'm no good at this. To me, the book is its own prologue epilogue introduction preface argument and all. I doubt if any writing bloke can take seriously this or any other manifestation of the literary criticism trade. But if a par. about how I wrote DYING as above will do, let me know and I'll fire it in.

Yours,
Faulkner

To Robert N. Linscott — TS. RH
[late May or early June 1946] — [Oxford]

Dear Mr Linscott:

I am for no introduction. If I who wrote it cant think of what to put into an introduction, there must not be an introduction for it. It's 20 years old now; if it cant stand alone yet, no crutch can help it.

I wrote my opinion about one carpenter writing a piece about another carpenter's hen-house, so I still vote no about Miss Gordon too.[1]

FIRST,

If you print the appendix, then follow with the novel of Sound & F., that will clear up its obscurity. I dont remember that AS I LAY DYING was obscure to readers; only the other one.

Also, Viking titled the appendix

The Compsons.

It should be, simply:

COMPSON
1699 1945

Because it's really an obituary, not a segregation.

Faulkner

[1] Linscott had suggested Caroline Gordon to write the introduction. On 3 June 1946, he wrote capitulating: there would be no introduction unless Faulkner changed his mind and decided to write one. The book would appear with only the Compson appendix.

To Robert K. Haas — TS. RH
[received 3 June 1946] — [Oxford]

Dear Bob:

Yes, this is it. I believe now it's not just my best but perhaps the best of my time. I cant tell you in a letter where it's going because that's what I'm trying to do by writing it in the 1 or maybe 2 hundred thousand words it may take: tell where it's going. I'll send it in as done.

It's going to take longer than any 6 months. I imagine it's out of the question to plan to finish it before returning to Warner. Random House cant underwrite me that long, can it?

I would like to plan to stay here until Jan. 1, work at it until then, then go back to Warner for a while, they will probably insist on a whole year I suppose.

That means you will have paid me by then: $500 per mo. 9 mo equals $4500.00. To stay here until then, I will have to have 3 $285.00 income tax payts. say $900.00 more, $5400.00, also very likely another $1000.00 for things I cant even anticipate yet. Does Random House want to get in as deep as $6000.00, still with no finished mss. possibly?[1] Let me know about this, I will understand, am perfectly willing to go back to studio if I have to, finish the mss. later. Let me have as much notice as possible.

I believe I see a rosy future for this book, I mean it may sell, it will be a War and Peace close enough to home, our times, language, for Americans to really buy it. You understand this is a confidential letter to the firm, the House; dont quote me outside please.

[no signature]

[1] By return mail on 3 June, Haas told Faulkner that Random House would provide the money he needed.

To Harold Ober — TS. FCVA

[received 24 June 1946] — [Oxford]

Dear Harold:

You may have received already a novel mss. from Emily Whitehurst Stone.[1] If so, she has told you its chronicle to date.

I haven't seen it. I have known her husband many years, have confidence in his judgement about books, I mean literary. I gave him your address, told him you would look at it. It may not be salable but I dont believe it will be trash.

My present job is going all right. Haas has about 150 pages of it. If you have time, look at it. Thanks a good deal to you, I have the chance to work at it. Maybe some of it might be sold to a mag. now. Bob has agreed to carry me on the cuff until Jan. 1 anyway, so he will agree to let some of it be printed in mags. to ease his bank roll. He already has two sections, 40 or 50 pages each, which are almost complete long short stories, will have soon a third similar one which will probably stand alone even better.

[no signature]

[1] The wife of Phil Stone.

To Harold Ober TS. FCVA
[received 3 July 1946] [Oxford]

Dear Harold:

I'm glad you'll see the stuff even if it may not sell. Maybe some precious literary quarterly might take some.

Here are some pages to substitute at the end.

In a few days I'll have another section typed. Why not hold what you have and I'll send this new batch straight to you, you can notify Random House. You'll have more material then, and this new section may be easier to place.

[t] Bill

To Lambert Davis[1] TS. YALE
25 July [1946] [Oxford]

Dear Mr Davis:

I received Warren's book. Thank you for it.

The Cass Mastern story is a beautiful and moving piece. That was his novel. The rest of it I would throw away. The Starke thing is good solid sound writing but for my money Starke and the rest of them are second rate. The others couldn't be bigger than he, the hero, and he to me is second rate. I didn't mind neither loving him nor hating him, but I did object to not being moved to pity. As I read him, he wanted neither power for the sake of his pride nor revenge for the sake of his vanity; he wanted neither to purify the earth by obliterating some of the population from it nor did he aim to give every hillbilly and redneck a pair of shoes. He was neither big enough nor bad enough. But maybe the Cass story made the rest of it look thinner than it is. The Cass piece was beautiful and moving. '. . . couldn't bear the eyes watching me.' That's all right. It's fine the way Warren caught not only the pattern of their acts but the very terms they thought in of that time. There are times when I believe there has been little in this country since that time—1860—'70 etc. good enough to make good literature, that since then we have gradually become a nation of bragging sentimental not too courageous liars. We seem to be losing all confidence not only in our national character but in man's integrity too. The fact that we blow so hard so much about both of them is to me the symptom.

But this has got away from Warren's book. He should have taken the Cass story and made a novel. Though maybe no man 75 years from that time could have sustained that for novel length.

William Faulkner

[1] Editor Lambert Davis of Harcourt, Brace had sent Faulkner a prepublication copy of Robert Penn Warren's new novel, *All the King's Men.*

In July 1946, Famous Artists Agency, Inc., with which William Herndon had become affiliated, sent Faulkner for signature a contract to represent him as a screenwriter.

To Harold Ober TS. FCVA
Friday [2 Aug. 1946] [Oxford]

Dear Harold:

The enclosed is self-explanatory. I assume that Herndon still has a claim that will hold legally on me so long as Warner holds my contract.

The following will be advantageous to me in this extent. Howard Hawks is Feldman's partner in this outfit. Hawks has carried me in pictures, seen that I got credits I really did not deserve, that sort of thing, also he has given me chances to pick up extra money.

Feldman, I know, gets along very well with him. Out of friendship he made an effort to get me loose from Warner, unofficially of course. He is one of the top agents there, *if he handles a client himself*. Because of Hawks I believe he will do that in my case.

But I want it clearly understood that you are my agent in all things except the making of contracts to write pictures from studio materials. You to have the final say in all my short story and original material of mine to all purchasers. As regards pictures, with Feldman representing me I will be in so much better condition that you and he will both profit. I can afford what I would wish anyway: to pay double commissions at any time our office and his conflict. Excuse bringing up the money matter, I just want it clear that when I better myself, which I think this will do, your establishment is to benefit too.

I am sorry you and Feldman are not directly connected. In my own case I would like you to be, I will pay any additional freight.

Please look over this, see that you remain my agent for anything not written directly on assignment for pictures. I would like for you and Feldman to contact each other before I sign this but that's for you to decide. Let me hear as soon as possible.

Bill

. . . .

On 6 August 1946, Ober wrote Faulkner suggesting that he should not sign the Famous Artists contract. He offered to write Feldman to tell him that Faulkner was now on leave to write a book and that before Faulkner had to return they would take up the matter of the contract.

To Harold Ober
Thursday [8 Aug. 1946]

TS. FCVA
[Oxford]

Dear Harold:

Yours of today at hand.

I wrote Feldman he would hear from you. I'll be all right with his agency. If it can be worked out that way it will please me, I think benefit me. I want you to share in the benefits though.

The novel is all right, slow now as I have been busy out of doors with farming. I dont think I will finish it before Jan 1 though, will then go back to the Coast.

Bob was to send me $500.00 per mo. while I am here working on it. Have had no check since June 1. Maybe he thinks the movie thing is through and I have money from that. What about the movie stories?[1] Had I better write Bob to remind him? I was already one month in the red when I got your check last week.

Here is another section. Nothing in it to sell I imagine. Shall I keep on sending it to you or shall I send the rest in to Bob?

Bill

[1] RKO Studios had been negotiating with Ober for the purchase of film rights to "Death Drag" and "Honor," and Cagney Productions for those to "Two Soldiers."

To Robert K. Haas
Tuesday [probably mid-Aug. 1946]

TS. RH
[Oxford]

Dear Bob:

Check received. Thank you. It was all right. I knew what had happened, especially after Harold mentioned you had gone to Vermont. I had hoped something would come of a moving picture nibble at some stories and I would not need more cash. But apparently nothing has.

The mss. going all right, slow as I anticipated. I sent the two last batches to Harold, through page 199. Where shall I send it from now on?

Will be harvesting crops to Nov. now but will still get a few pages done each week. I'd like to come up for a week or so this fall. I've been buried six years now.

Bill

To Robert K. Haas — TS. RH
[probably early Oct. 1946] — [Oxford]

Dear Bob:

. . . .

Mss. is all right, slow now because I am gathering crops. Will send next batch to Ober soon, now at about 250 pages.

Please send me 1 copy Modern Lib. Sanctuary. An Army recruiting sergeant wants it. For that sorry lost occupation (nothing nearer oblivion than a military policeman in peace time) every one should bend every effort to alleviate. Though god knows what he wants with a book. Should think a 10 cent address book for girls' telephone numbers would be his meat.

Bill

To Robert K. Haas — TS. RH
Nov. 10 [1946] — [Oxford]

Dear Bob:

3 weeks ago I found a chance to pick up some extra money, which will perhaps enable me to put off going back to Cal. for some time past Jan. 1.; I dont want to go back and find myself in the middle of labor trouble, picket lines to cross, that sort of thing.[1] I dont intend to dodge brickbats etc in order to draw Warner salary, nor do I want to go to Cal. and not be able to draw pay while there.

To do this work, I have stopped the novel for two months. I have not cashed the last check. Shall I hold it, or send it back to you? Also, dont send one Dec 1. unless you prefer to continue with the agreement to send them until Jan. 1, and let me make up the two months after I finish this other job. I have not drawn any pay for this present job, had not intended to until I finish it. I can cash your checks, reimburse you for the time lost when I am paid for this other job, or get off your cuff and stay off until I go back on the novel—which ever you like.

As I wrote, the novel will take nearer a full 12 months than the six. I may be able to put off going back to Cal for some time yet by means of these extra jobs like the present one. Incidentally, this is a private matter which Warner had probably better not know about, or he will maybe demand my presence at the studio. So dont mention it. As far as he is concerned, I am merely working on a novel and drawing no pay from him.

Let me know what you prefer about the checks.

. . . .

Bill

[1] See the following letter.

To Harold Ober | TS. FCVA
[received 18 Nov. 1946] | [Oxford]

Dear Harold:

. . . .

Four weeks ago I found a chance to earn some extra money by working over a movie script. I put my novel aside for that purpose, wrote Bob I had done so and will get off his cuff if he likes during this period. I will not draw any money until I finish it, which should be in another 4 weeks. I think under my W. contract my name must not appear in this, so dont mention it anywhere. As far as W. is concerned, I am at home finishing a novel. I want as much cash reserve as possible; if labor troubles continue in Hollywood I may not be able to go back on salary even if I return in Jan. When I collect for this, I'll send you your commission, not to make you an accessory but because if it hadn't been for your stout effort I would not be in position to earn it. But please keep the matter private; officially you had probably better know nothing about it.

I will get back on the novel as soon as I finish this.

Bill

To Harold Ober | TS. FCVA
Thursday [5 Dec. 1946] | [Oxford]

Dear Harold:

I have finished the other job and am back at the novel again.

What is my status re Warner at present? Am I due to go back there at any specific deadline, or is my stay indefinite, as long as I keep at the novel? Somehow I have it in my head that we have promised me back there in Jan, which will be 9 months from when I did not return on schedule in March.

Bill

Let me know. If I am to go back, I have got to begin finding somewhere to live. . . .[1]

[1] On 13 Dec., Ober wrote Faulkner that Warner Bros. understood he was to stay at home until he finished his novel. He also informed him that the sale of the film rights to "Death Drag" and "Honor" had been completed.

To Robert K. Haas | TS. RH
Sunday [8 Dec. 1946] | [Oxford]

Dear Bob:

I finished the other job and am back at my own again. I have just written Harold to find what my status is about returning to Warner. I have it in my head that I am to report back after Jan. 1. The novel is not done yet.

I would rather stay here and work on it but I am not certain I can afford to. That is, I will have to draw on you if I stay—unless Harold turns up something else. If I can find a place in Hollywood to live, I might better go back for six months or so, save some more money, come back and take up the novel again. I will wait to hear from him. Have had no pay yet for the other job, unless I get it by Jan. will begin to run dry again since I must save against next year's income tax—unless I can go back on Warner salary to pay it with.

Harold now has 250 pages of novel, but it has done no more than set the stage; I haven't even got into the story yet. It seems to be longer than Tom Wolfe.

Returned the Nov 1 check last week. Went deer hunting last week in Nov., lived in a tent, shot a small buck, missed a magnificent stag twice. He was a beautiful creature, broke out of a thicket 100 yards away running like a horse, perfectly flat, not jumping at all, doing about 30 mph, ran in full view for 75 yards, I picked two perfect openings in trees and shot twice. I left my customary 30-30 carbine at home for my boy to use and was shooting a .270 bolt action. I think the first bullet hit a twig and blew up. The second one missed him clean, over or maybe behind him; he was just running too fast. He was a beautiful sight. I'm glad now he got away from me though I would have liked his head.

Bill

Merry Xmas to Bennett, Don, Saxe and all. My best to you and Miss Merle as always.

To Malcolm Cowley — TS. YALE
Sunday [Dec. 1946] — [Oxford]

Dear brother:

Thank you for sending the Chinese thing.[1] Will see about it. I am still here in Miss. since Sept 1945 now. Am on Random House's cuff, to write a book, wont go back to Cal. until Random House gets tired and money ceases. I shall get back to work at it, now that the weather's too bad here to hunt. I missed a beautiful stag last fall. He had what you call 6 points and we here 12, since we count both horns of the antlers. He broke out of a thicket at full speed; I just heard a stick crack and looked around and there he was, running flat like a horse, not jumping at all, about 30 mph, about 100 yards away. He ran in full sight for 50 yards. I think perhaps the first bullet (it was a .270) hit a twig and blew up. But the second shot I missed him clean. He was running too fast for me. He was a beautiful sight. Now it's done, I'm glad his head is still in the woods instead of on a plank on the wall.

It's a dull life here. I need some new people, above all probably a new young woman. But if I leave here I will spend in two weeks money I can live here for two months on, and then I'd have to go back to Cal. At 30 you become aware suddenly that you have become a slave of vast and growing mass of inanimate junk, possessions; you dont dare look at any of it too closely because you'll have to admit there is not one piece of it you really want. But you bear it for the next eighteen years because you still believe you will escape from it someday. Then one day you are almost 50 and you know you never will.

Faulkner

[1] In Dec. 1946, Cowley appealed to Faulkner to contribute to funds to be distributed in China by the Chinese Writers' Association.

To Harold Ober — TS. FCVA
[received 30 Dec. 1946] — [Oxford]

Dear Harold.

I got 35 hundred for the job. Here is yours. Best season wishes and all that.

Bill

On 20 January 1947, Ober wrote Faulkner quoting a letter from Reed Whittemore, who had obtained a copy of "Afternoon of a Cow" from Maurice Coindreau and now offered $5 a page (between $75 and $100, he thought) for the right to publish it in Furioso.

To Harold Ober — TS. FCVA
[received 27 Jan. 1947] — [Oxford]

Dear Harold:

It's all right with me about the story. I dont have a copy of it. I wrote it one afternoon when I felt rotten with a terrible hangover, with no thought of publication, since the story is a ribald one. I dont have a copy. If Whittemore has one, maybe you had better look at it first and decide yourself about letting him print it. I have tried it on various people (Americans) who seemed to think it not funny at all but (apparently, as I realise now, they thought it was true) in bad taste. Also, I have already used it in THE HAMLET. But I leave it to you. Though it might be better to keep its amateur standing unimpaired.

The last pages of mss. 229 on through 251 are not right. I have left out an element. Please send them back to me at once. I am rewriting them now, want the others out of circulation immediately.

Bill

To Harold Ober — TS. FCVA

[received 25 Feb. 1947] — [Oxford]

Dear Harold:

Sell the piece if you can.[1] Maybe it is funny, as I thought myself. I suppose I tried it on the wrong people. Anyway, they all reacted as one from a single premise: that it had really happened to me and that in telling it I had committed two crimes: 1, against reticence, 2, against good taste: from which point the process really becomes involved, to wit: It is funny as long as it was imaginary but since no refined mind would imagine such a thing, let alone tell it, it is not funny.

Bill

[1] "Afternoon of a Cow" appeared in *Furioso*, II (Summer 1947), 5–17.

To Harold Ober — TS. FCVA

[received 24 Mar. 1947] — [Oxford]

Dear Harold:

Here is the rewritten section. The conviction is growing on me that this book is going to be a book.

I am toying with the notion of coming up there so I can tell you and Bob what it is to be. If I tried to write you in a letter, I wouldn't need to do any more on the book because it would be finished then.

I think Bob is entitled to know, as I will soon need to draw on him as before. I took the money you earned for me, gave my mother $1000.00 and cleaned up for good two matters which I had intended to amortise over several years. I decided the cheapest thing I could buy at this time was my signature on a note.

Maybe I can get hold of a trained secretary-stenographer and dictate to her what I would say if I came to New York. It would be say a 25 page letter, maybe more.

I know every word in the book now but I dont write as fast as I used to. It will take another year, probably two. Bob has told me not to worry about money and I shall take him at his word. Do you have any trouble keeping Warner off of me?

Bill

To Robert K. Haas
Monday [possibly 24 Mar. 1947]

TS. RH
Oxford

Dear Bob:

I think it is about time that Random House knew more about this present job, since it is going to take some time yet to finish it, and I will be on your cuff again without I go back to Hollywood for a while.

I have about 300 correct pages. I now know where the rest of it is going, and how. Later on in the spring, next month perhaps, suppose I come to New York and go over it with you. I have what I think is a good reason. (I mean, more than just wanting a vacation.) It has to do with the locale and the matter. If the book can be accepted as a fable, which it is to me, the locale and contents wont matter. Perhaps they wont anyway. But then you might not want to publish it. I may be wrong about this, probably am. I could write the reasons, but that's what I'm trying to do in getting the book down. That is, to explain what I mean by correspondence will take about as much space as writing the book itself.

So the best thing is for me to come up, take a whole evening and tell you all the story, get your reaction, and then plan between us about advance for me for some specific time ahead—say a whole year, maybe more.

(What I mean by locale and contents is: the villain is historically the French army or all the allied armies of 1918, and the principal ones are (still historically though to me fabulous and imaginary) Foch, Haig, Pershing, et al.)

Enclosed a note to Miss Ruth Ford. She had a part in a translated French play (Sartre I think) called 'No Exit.' It was on during the winter, may still be on. Will you please try to locate her and forward this to her? I want to have her address when I come up, or be able to find her then.

Will let you know later when to expect me. I think this is a sound idea, to tell you what this thing is fully at this point. What do you think?

Bill

To Harold Ober
Tuesday [25 Mar. 1947]

TS. FCVA
[Oxford]

Dear Harold:

Here are 2 more impositions on your kindness.

I realised last night that the course of my present story pays off too fast. I am doing a few pages of rewrite back toward p 25 etc.

Apparently I shall continue to see errors after the fact, like this. The main thing with me is to know whom to send these corrections to. I am still assuming that you have or are custodian of the mss. That is, shall I send corrections to you or Random H.

Bill

To Robert K. Haas — TS. RH
Monday [probably 31 Mar. 1947] — [Oxford]

Dear Bob:

Have a note from Harold who says there is no trouble to be expected from Warner, as I am to finish this job before considering returning. So I shall settle down to at least another year at the mss. and I had better go back on the $500.00 monthly.

Harold writes that you are willing to take my word about the script, that is, best to get it written rather than hold up to tell you the story. I would still like a few days in New York but I'll probably finish the spring here with the farm planting and the script, come up later if possible.

Will you begin right away with the monthly $500.00? I'll try to keep inside it.

Bill

To Harold Ober — TS. FCVA
Thursday [24 Apr. 1947] — [Oxford]

Dear Harold:

I have just found another serious bug in the ms. No wonder nobody seems to have any definite idea about it. Seems to have taken me longer than I imagined to get movie scripting out of my reflexes.

Please send back to me pages 1 (one) through 121. This time I think it will be all right and competent to be shown when I return it. From 121 on is right now. The other has a lot of junk in it because I myself was not certain of the line then.

Bill

To Robert K. Haas — TS. RH
[spring 1947] — [Oxford]

Dear Bob:

The Penguin books received. It looks all right, only I wish we could keep biographical stuff and literary opinions out of all of it and let the work itself stand. I dislike more and more seeing my name and picture in print.[1]

I have realised lately how much trash and junk writing for movies corrupted into my writing. Just asked Harold to send me back part of the mss. I will clean that up, then the first 250 pages will be all right; from then on it should give no trouble though it will be a slow thing compared to the speed I had once. I am a little stale; I would like to come up East for a week or so. If mss goes all right through summer, I will come up then.

Bill

[1] The first Penguin edition of a Faulkner novel was that of *Soldiers' Pay*, with a preface by Richard Hughes, published in England in Jan. 1938. For subsequent Penguin editions of Faulkner novels, see James B. Meriwether, *The Literary Career of William Faulkner: A Bibliographical Study* (Princeton, 1961).

Between 14 and 17 April, Faulkner met with six literature classes at the University of Mississippi for question-and-answer sessions with an honorarium of $250. They were to be informal, but several of the students took notes and two of them used theirs as the basis for a projected magazine article. This was done with the encouragement of Marvin M. Black, the University's Director of Public Relations, who issued a news release quoting some of Faulkner's statements. English Department Chairman W. Alton Bryant asked instructor Margaret Parker to show Faulkner her composite notes and assured him that there would be no magazine article; he also declared the program "a smash hit" and hoped for a repeat performance.

To Prof. W. Alton Bryant — TS. PROF. JAMES W. WEBB
Monday [12 May 1947] — [Oxford]

Dear Dr Bryant:

Thank you for your letter. I never had any doubt but that our ideas were one regarding the purpose of the plan. Thank you for going on record also, and along with the gratitude, my apologies for having put you on a spot (if I did so) where you felt it necessary to do so.

I went over the material with Miss Parker. It is fairly correct now (I mean by 'fairly' that it is not complete, still informal) and it is yours to do with as you like. I just hate like hell to be jumbled head over heels into the high-pressure ballyhoo which even universities now believe they must employ: the damned eternal American BUY! BUY!! BUY!!! 'Try us first, our campus covers ONE WHOLE SQUARE MILE, you can see our water tank from twelve miles away, our football team almost beat A.&M., we have WM FAULKNER at 6 (count them: 6) English classes.' That sort of thing I will resist with my last breath. But if the English department, not the publicity dept., uses the material, I shall have no qualms and fears.

You may be interested and pleased with the enclosure. I mean, that undergraduates really are—or believe they will be—boosted by this sort of thing, and that the word of your trial of it has already spread to neighboring universities.

If you decide on a 'repeat,' let me know.

Thank you for the check.

Yours sincerely,
William Faulkner

To Harold Ober — TS. FCVA
Monday [received 9 June 1947] — [Oxford]

Dear Harold:

Here are pp 1–73-J. I believe they are now correct.

The idea of having it all typed again is pleasing, but to me not so good. I have a copy and you have one. To type it again will cost I imagine 25 cents a page. I cant afford that at present; in fact for that money I might better stop writing it and retype it myself and pick up that much.

I have my usual batch of pleas from writers asking how to get published. I have 2 in particular, dont know the people, haven't and dont intend to read the mss. Do you want to look at them? If so, I'll write them to send the mss. and all information about where they have tried to place it, to you.

re. my mss. You will see that I have filled it with plus pages, a,b,c., etc. If you and Bob insist on a new typing, you might ignore my numbers and number anew in sequence.

Bill

It's getting right now. It was a tragedy of ideas, morals, before; now it's getting to be a tragedy of people.

On 11 May 1947, the New York Herald Tribune *had carried excerpts from Marvin Black's press release based on Faulkner's classes at the University of Mississippi in which Faulkner was quoted as saying Hemingway had no courage. Hemingway began a reply to Faulkner but abandoned it and instead asked his friend Brig. Gen. C. T. Lanham to write Faulkner, telling him only what he knew about Hemingway under fire. A month later, Lanham did so.*

To Brig. Gen. C. T. Lanham
28 June 1947

TS. PROF. CARLOS BAKER
Oxford, Mississippi

Dear General Lanham:

Thank you for your letter.

The statement as you [re-quoted] it is not correct because apparently it was incomplete as you saw it, and in its original shape it had no reference whatever to Hemingway as a man: only to his craftsmanship as a writer. I know of his record in two wars and in Spain, too.

In April, on request from the English department of the University of Mississippi here (my alma mater) I met six English classes, answering questions about literature, writing. In one of them I was asked to rate the greatest American writers. I answered, I wouldn't attempt it since I believed no man could, but (after further insistence) I would give my own personal rating of my own coevals: the men whose names were most often connected with mine since we began to write. I named Hemingway, Wolfe, Dos Passos, Caldwell. I said:

'I think we all failed (in that none of us had yet the stature of Dickens, Dostoevsky, Balzac, Thackery etc.). That Wolfe made the best failure because he had the most courage: to risk being guilty of bad taste, clumsiness, mawkishness, dullness: to shoot the works win or lose and damn the torpedoes. That Dos Passos was next since he sacrificed some of the courage to style. That Hemingway was next since he did not have the courage to get out on a limb as the others did, to risk bad taste, overwriting, dullness, etc.'

This was elaborated of course. I spoke extemporaneously, without notes, as I believed at the time, informally, not for publication. Your letter was my first intimation that it had been released, and from what you re-quoted, garbled and incomplete.

I'm sorry of it. A copy of this goes to Hemingway, with a covering note. Whatever other chances I have to correct it, I shall certainly take.

Thank you again for your letter.

Yours sincerely,
William Faulkner

To Ernest Hemingway
28 June 1947

TS. PROF. CARLOS BAKER
Oxford, Mississippi

Dear Hemingway:

I'm sorry of this damn stupid thing. I was just making $250.00, I thought informally, not for publication, or I would have insisted on looking at the stuff before it was released. I have believed for years that the human voice has caused all human ills and I thought I had broken myself of talking. Maybe this will be my valedictory lesson.

I hope it wont matter a damn to you. But if or when or whever [*sic*] it does, please accept another squirm from yours truly.

Faulkner

re letter from Brigadier Lanham who commanded (then) an infantry regiment you were with. He sounds like they had a good mess.

To Harold Ober — TS. FCVA
Sunday [13 July 1947] — [Oxford]

Dear Harold:

From now on, when I cant discourage them, I will tell people to write you and ask if you will read mss.

The book is going all right, but slow. Am now in middle of an entire new section (chapter) which follows page 120. When I realised I had left it out I thought it would run about 15–20 pages. It is going to run nearer 50–75. When I finish it, it picks up with old page 120, runs on to the last you have.

The rev. dept. have disallowed all exemption claims I made covering the cost of my 1944 California residence. Apparently I am going to have to pay them about $1000.00 more tax for that year. In consequence, I dont see how to avoid going back to Warner about Jan. 1. I am making plans now on that assumption. I dont feel I can ask Random House for an additional sum of $1000.00 when they are sending me $500.00 per mo. already, and no possibility of finishing this mss. by Jan. 1.

My return to work there should be handled through you, shouldn't it, as you handled the leave of absence? I will be able to say definitely I will come back about November, to report at studio after Jan. 1. I'll put it off as long as I can but I see no other out at present. I could work on the book while at Warner's, though I dont think they would agree to it. At present I have about 400 consecutive pages, plus notes. I believe the book will run at least 1000. At this rate, that means another year after 1947. Maybe the best thing will be to go back Jan 1, work there for 6–8 months, or until Nov. say.

Let me know if you are to notify Warner that I will come back.

Yours,
Bill

To Harold Ober TS. FCVA
Friday [18 July 1947] [Oxford]

Dear Harold:

Yours at hand. The day I got the letter from the Rev Dept that demand for additional tax would be made on me, a friend from Hollywood had stopped here on a visit.[1] I told him about it, that I had always made my own returns. He laughed at me for a sap, told me to get all the papers together and send to him and he would give them to his own consultant, a specialist in movie writers' taxes, who, he guaranteed, would attend to the whole thing successfully. I didn't think of consulting you, in New York, and sent the papers to him last week. I hope to hear from the matter soon.

I have graduated from trying to make my own returns now. Have you someone in your office who does that sort of thing? From what the Hollywood friend told me of his own case, I have been paying more than I should for years; from now on I shall pay a specialist consultant to do it for me.

Will let you know what I hear from Cal. I will put out of mind going back to Cal. until I have to plan on it. It might be done this way. Warner seems to know I am dissatisfied with the present contract, since he has intimated I am to be offered a better one. It might be suggested to him that I want to come out for one specific job, consultations if possible, a quick treatment, then to work on the script here. When he says No, Faulkner must come back here because we are going to give him a better contract, then we say, Faulkner is satisfied with this one, will complete it. He just wants to come out for one specific job, the rate and amount of pay to be on Warner's terms, the work to be done on Faulkner's.

Thank you for the letter.

Bill

[1] A. I. Bezzerides.

To Robert K. Haas TS. RH
Sunday [24 Aug. 1947] [Oxford]

Dear Bob:

Yours received. Whatever you do is right here.

The mss. is going all right. Slow though but so far I have not let that worry me much, I mean having to write it on credit like this. I am now in the middle of a hundred page new chapter which itself is a good story, a complete novelette,[1] about a white man and an old Negro preacher and the preacher's 14 year old grandson who stole a crippled racehorse and healed its broken leg and spent a year dodging from one little back country track to the next racing the horse before the police ever caught them, then the white man shot the horse. They did it not to win money but because (the horse was a valuable champion) its owner would have retired it to stud because of its ruined leg while the thieves knew that what the horse wanted to do was to run races: a champion: a giant among horses.

. . . .

Best to everyone. My kindest to Miss Merle and Elizabeth.

[no signature]

[1] Published as *Notes on a Horse Thief* (1951) and revised for inclusion in *A Fable* (1954).

In the omitted portions of the letter above, Faulkner asked Haas to check for him on a watch he had sent to New York for repairs and requested that Saxe Commins or someone else procure for him a pipe he had tried unsuccessfully to obtain through a local dealer.

To Robert K. Haas | TS. RH
[received 4 Sept. 1947] | [Oxford]

Dear Bob:

The watch came all right.

I dont really want the damn pipe, I have just got my back up about it. I saw the colored ad. last December, tore out the page, sent it to Kaywoodie and asked for the pipe. They wrote back they dealt only through authorised retailers, didn't send the picture back. I hunted around until I found another Sat Eve Post of Dec 7, got another picture, hunted around until I found a retailer, had him send the picture, Kaywoodie sent a pipe I never saw before. I sent it back with a frantic plea for the one they advertised, got the pipe at last with a crack in the bowl, sent it back and was in the groove again when they sent the wrong pipe again. All this took 7 months, going on 9 now. That's a symptom of what's wrong with this country. People have to make too many pipes to sell to too many people to pay too much tax to support too much government which we really can no longer afford: to pay for which people have to make too many pipes to sell to too many people, etc.

The section of the mss. is a flash back I suppose. It describes what caused a man to do or be capable of doing one single act which carries on the story of the mss. itself. The reason may be 1. This is perhaps the last book I'll write and I am putting all the rest of it into it, or 2. It may contain the germs of several more books. I see no chance of finishing it this year. Perhaps after Xmas I had better have another session on Warner salary. I think I'll come up this fall and have a talk with you.

Bill

To Robert K. Haas — TS. RH
Sunday [21 Sept. 1947] — [Oxford]

Dear Bob:

The pipe arrived. Thank you very much for bothering with it. I believe it will turn out a satisfactory smoke.

My inclination is to stay here and work on the mss. too. But I am going to need more money; our corn and hay crop was cut here this season by drouth and heat after a late (June) flood. I will have to buy some feed. I will probably have to pay some back 1944 income tax though I have a good man working on it. I will have to pay some advance 1947 tax soon. Also I want to buy another horse since pretty soon now I shall be too stiff in the joints for anything except old man's riding. I dont intend to ask Random House for extra money because you will let me have it and I will be getting that much deeper not only into an unfinished book but into about all I have which might be called capital.

So maybe I had better take another Hollywood hitch. I think I can still keep at the mss. there. I am writing to Harold, for him to feel out what arrangement might be made; Warner will probably want me to stay a full year at least, after 2 years away. He wont commit me right away, until he has heard from them and communicates with me again. If you wish to, discuss it with him. By Jan 1, when I should go out to coast, I should have a section or block of this mss., about 500 pages, which might be printed as is, of an incomplete work. You might consider that.

We just finished having the fringe of a hurricane here. No damage.

Bill

To Robert K. Haas — TS. RH
Friday [3 Oct. 1947] — [Oxford]

Dear Bob:

Yours at hand today.

(1) The five hundred pages if published would not be a complete work, such as the first volume of a trilogy, etc., but would be an incomplete section, a craftsman's item sort of thing, as when the old Dial I think printed

some of Ulysses.[1] It may be though that this section would be evocative enough to make reader want to see the rest. But I realise that this opinion is a craftsman's opinion. I dont particularly want to print it yet; I thought of the idea for Random House's sake, who already have a considerable sum invested in it.

The horse story section though is fairly complete. There will be about half of it, about 75 pages, which could stand alone, which Ober might be able to place. He has 30 pages of it, I am just finishing the next 40–50 pages, should send them in to him soon.

(2) I dont think I can guess how much longer it will take. I seem to write so slowly now that it alarms me sometimes; now and then I think the stuff is no good, which is the reason it takes so long. Yet I wont stop it; when I stand off a moment and bring to mind the whole pattern, I have no trouble in believing in it. One reason it goes slow, maybe the main one, is conditions here. Negro servants in this country have all quit. The men draw army G.I. money; also there is a great construction wave at the University here, common labor gets 75 cents an hour; we have to pay 5.00 per hundred for cotton pickers. For two years now I have had no house servants except a doddering old man and a 12 year old boy who must go to school too. An amazing amount of my time is taken up in things which are really not important yet have to be done if a household is to get along—things which I must get up from my typewriter to attend to, which is bad. That is, the typewriter is the least important thing in my daily life. I dont believe 12 months more will do it.

(3) A demand has been made on me for additional $900.00 income tax for 1944. I have a lawyer working on it now, hope to reduce it.

I will have to pay soon estimated tax for 1947, about $1500.00 I imagine. Except for this, the 500.00 seems to do. In other words, if this is a fair sample, the 500.00 is enough except for about 2500.00 more.

Maybe the best thing for you to do is to take what I have sent Ober which is correct, and read it. Then maybe my old thought is a good one and I ought to come up and tell you the rest of it. This may give you an idea: 3 years ago I sent you a sort of synopsis. The story began with a meeting of the principals in the office of the commander in chief, as a result of a mutiny of a French regiment. The synopsis continued from there. Ober has about 400 odd pages, at the end of which I have just reached the scene in the office where the story actually begins. That is, I have not yet quite finished the introduction. This introduction is all new stuff; maybe when I finish it and begin to fill in the old synopsis, which is the story, it will go faster. Maybe a year will do it, but I have been wrong before in estimating it.

Have just re-read paragraph (2). That's wrong. There's nothing wrong with this book; I am just getting older and dont write fast anymore. I always did do a lot of rewriting; I just make my mistakes slower now—

and correct them slower. I've probably written a million words on it to date, but the 12,000 app. which Ober has are all right. But I dont know how much longer; just be assured that any time Random H. feels this has gone far enough, so do I.

Bill

[1] The magazine was *The Little Review*, not *The Dial*.

To Harold Ober — TS. FCVA
Sunday [5 Oct. 1947] — [Oxford]

Dear Harold:

No more do I want to go to the coast. Nothing suits me better than to stay here and work. The question is, can I—or we—afford it. . . .

. . . .

Under my contract with Warner, I cant very well take on any other assignment of any other nature, since I am on leave only to write this particular book.

Incidentally, I think best to let this present contract alone. I will fulfill it; this way I can do so on my own terms, accepting no further obligations which I should have to do in courtesy for rearrangement, etc. That is, under this one I would feel freer to go back when I wish, stay 6–8–10 months, then notify them I am off salary again as I have done before. What more money they might give me income tax would consume and I'd be no better off. What I need is to get an additional 4 or 5 thousand dollars from somewhere, then continue on Random H. 500 per mo. and keep on at the novel.

I wont do anything until you and Bob have another talk. Writing him today.

Bill

On 14 October 1947, Haas wrote Faulkner urging him to stop worrying about Hollywood and assuring him that his financial needs did not seem excessive and that Random House would be glad to back him. Haas would send the $900 for the 1944 income tax now if Faulkner needed it and the other $1,500 whenever that became necessary. Haas hoped that Faulkner would keep at the book but he would, of course, be very welcome to come to New York to talk about it at any time.

Robert K. Haas — TS. RH
Saturday [18 Oct. 1947] — [Oxford]

Dear Bob:

Yours received yesterday. The reason I keep on talking about coming up there is to tell you about this book, the whole idea. I seem to be afraid you cant have faith in it to keep on letting me have money against it without knowing more about it than you do. I believe it is a tremendous idea; some of the trouble I seem to have getting it written to suit me is because of its size and (myself) being so close to it all the time. It's like standing close to an elephant; after a while you cant see the elephant anymore at all.

Maybe the best news I could have is a definite refusal or advice from H.[1] that I could not get on salary for a year at least. This stuff is taking me much longer than I ever had to take writing before; I get tired, stale, begin to worry about its slowness while I am drawing money against it and I begin to worry about the money (unearned). Then I think of Hollywood; that after all, I can go back there and get out of arrears again. Maybe I need to know that is out; i.e. instead of a bale of hay in the safe distance ahead of him maybe what the mule needs is a stick behind him.

I dont know why I keep on fretting and stewing this way. You wrote me years ago not to worry about the money but to write the book; I dont know why I cant remember it.

I think I will attend to 1947 income tax at once. As soon as I count it up, I'll send the payment for it. I have enough in my account to pay it I think, as soon as I write the check I will ask you for some part or all of the $1500.00. Then 1947 will be off my mind for 12 months. Then when my man settles for the 1944 tax, I will pay that and if necessary call on you again. That is, I assume I can have $2400.00 extra, will take only what I need when I need it. If Harold could give me some fairly definite assurance that I couldn't get on salary if I wanted to at Warner, I will settle down to the mss., then when I need extra cash or feel stale, take a week or so off and write a short story. That is, with H. out of mind, I might stop worrying myself and you too.

Will send the rest of the horse piece in as soon as I finish this section of it. Only about 10 pages, when they come right, and a printable section will be ready.

[no signature]

[1] Hollywood.

To Harold Ober
Thursday [30 Oct. 1947]

TS. FCVA
[Oxford]

Dear Harold:

Yours received. Here are pages to 120-Z-42 inc. of the horse piece. There are about 10 more pages, when it reaches a point where this part can be printed by itself and make sense, that is come to an end. I should have had these 10 pages finished but they wont quite come right yet. I can do them in 1 day as soon as they jell properly. This whole horse piece is a monotone, sustained on one note; it will have to finish that way; I cant slough it off. The ten pages are this:

The lawyer takes the five guards back to the courtroom where the crowd is waiting. He has every confidence; he has only to hold the crowd's attention for five minutes, until the turnkey and the Negro can reach the car and get out of town. The lawyer begins a political speech, the sort of thing which has held American crowds for a hundred years, full of rhetoric and meaning nothing. But as soon as the crowd realises what it is, they rise up and run politely over him, no anger, rage, they just push him out of the way and overtake the turnkey and the Negro and set the Negro free, tell him to keep his money and get out of town and stay out, that they dont like rich niggers there. But it's got to be right. What about showing what you have, explain what the end is to be and that I'll get it in soon as I can.

Bob has said I can have more money for the tax etc, about $2400.00. I can stay here another year at that. I would rather work on the mss., that is you and Bob and I agree here. His last intimated you might be able to find out, committing nothing, whether Warner will put me on now; maybe he wont. Any case, I will go on with the mss., see how things look financially about Dec 1. My trouble is simply, I dont want to be broke in my old age when I cant earn anything more, as so many artists do at the end of their lives. I dont save anything much in Hollywood but I at least dont spend now what Random House will advance me.

Bill

To Harold Ober
[received 14 Nov. 1947]

TS. FCVA
[Oxford]

Dear Harold:

Here is the rest of this episode which can be printed as a more or less complete piece. It is 90 pages app., pretty long for a mag.

Also I am not stubborn about the 2 paragraphs you mention as introduction, may be dense but I dont know what to put in them other than the statement 'Portion (or from) an unfinished work'

If a mag will print it this length, I suggest a new opening sentence, say this: 'In 1912 the groom went to America in charge of . . . a horse etc'

If this is too long as is, suppose it begins with death of the horse and the capture, I will write a synopsis to bring the story up to the moment when the federal deputy visited the groom in jail and let the printed story be what happened in the town after the thief was arrested.

I have proof-read these pages here but not the previous ones; there may be typographical errors, repetitions etc. but the punctuation is right. However, if the editor who buys it wishes, he might eliminate italics and even punctuate and put in caps if he insists though my version will go into the book since all this is really one single adjectival clause describing a man.

Attached here is an amendment to page 120-Z–39., for the purpose of inserting the business about *hanging up the telephone* since the lawyer has already stated he will telephone and have the car ready when the turnkey and the prisoner reach the hotel, which he has obviously done since later he hears a car and assumes the prisoner has escaped safely.

Bill

In mid-October, Robert Linscott had told Ober that The Partisan Review *would probably be willing to pay a thousand dollars or more for the horse race story, and Ober submitted it. Faulkner went off to hunting camp and upon his return found that the magazine would not take the story in its present form.*

To Harold Ober — TELEGRAM FCVA
28 Nov. 1947 — Oxford, Miss.

LET PR EDIT AND CUT BUT NOT REWRITE IT. LETTER FOLLOWS. BILL

To Harold Ober — TS. FCVA
Friday [28 Nov. 1947] — [Oxford]

Dear Harold:

I just got back last night from hunting camp.

Let Partisan Review cut and edit the piece as they like, so long as what they do print is the original matter in its original form.

As I wrote before, it could well begin with the lawyer's arrival in the town, and what he found there and tried to do with it. I could write a page or so of synopsis, explaining who stole the horse and what his reason seemed to be, and what became of him and the horse up to the moment when the lawyer reached the town, then let the piece carry on from there. This would cut the piece to 60 pages. If this is still too long, I suggest they simply lift what they wish where they wish and print it simply as a fragment or fragments from a work. Though the last 60 pages are a complete story in a way: an anecdote anyway of a mob (man at his basest) performing an act of right and justice despite himself, because of base motives. They freed two thieves not because of pity for them but because they would defend at all costs man's right to get that much money, no matter how.

Let me hear soon as possible and I will get at the induction.

Meanwhile I will get on with the script. Will pay this year's advance income tax, ask Bob for more money, about $1500.00 I suppose it will be.

Bill

[in ink:] Yes. I have a copy. Shall I have another made here of this section?

To Harold Ober — TS. FCVA
Friday [5 Dec. 1947] — [Oxford]

Dear Harold:

Yours received. Did PR give a reason for turning the piece down?[1] I would like to know. I have a notion they were disappointed in it. Did they find it dull as written?

I never have had an opinion from you and Bob cum Random House about it, other than to go ahead: than which an artist could ask no more. What is your opinion of this section in question? Dull? Too prolix? Diffuse?

I have an idea that this may have been PR's reason: The world has been so beat and battered about the head during the last few years that man is in a state of spiritual cowardice: all his bottom, reserve, strength has to go into physical stamina and there is nothing left to be very concerned with art. That that magazine does not exist now which would have printed sections from Ulysses as in the 1920's. And that the man crouching in a Mississippi hole trying to shape into some form of art his summation and conception of the human heart and spirit in terms of the cerebral, the simple imagination, is as out of place and in the way as a man trying to make an Egyptian water wheel in the middle of the Bessemer foundry would be.

What is your opinion of this stuff? Will anybody read it in the next say 25 years? Are Random House by taking me on absolute faith as they have, wasting their money on it? My own time doesn't count; I dont believe I am wasting it or I would have stopped before now. There is nothing wrong with the book as it will be, only it may be 50 years before the world can stop to read it. It's too long, too deliberate.

Might be worth while trying some of it in some 'precious' publication like school quarterlies or some such amateur payless medium. I had hoped to get $1000.00 to pay income tax with, but will ask Bob for it.

Bill

[1] Harold Ober apparently did not tell Faulkner Philip Rahv's reason for rejecting the piece: not only was it too long, but they thought it read like a first draft—it just wasn't ready for publication.

To Harold Ober — TS. FCVA

1 Feb. [1948] — [Oxford]

Dear Harold:

....

On Jan 15th I put the big mss aside and I now have 60 pages on an approximate 120 page short novel[1] set in my apocryphal Jefferson. The story is a mystery-murder though the theme is more relationship between Negro and white, specifically or rather the premise being that the white people in the south, before the North or the govt. or anyone else, owe and must pay a responsibility to the Negro. But it's a story; nobody preaches in it. I may have told you the idea, which I have had for some time—a Negro in jail accused of murder and waiting for the white folks to drag him out and pour gasoline over him and set him on fire, is the detective, solves the crime because he goddamn has to to keep from being lynched, by asking people to go somewhere and look at something and then come back and tell him what they found.

I should finish it in another 3 weeks. Please tell Bob about it; it might make him feel better about me. Tell him I suggest sending it first to you for possible magazine serial sale, then he will have it for a book. 120 pages is short, but it will make a book wont it?

I hope the idea will please Bob. I've been on Random H's cuff a long time now.

Bill

[1] *Intruder in the Dust* (1948).

To Robert K. Haas | TS. RH
Sunday [probably 22 Feb. 1948] | [Oxford]

Dear Bob:

I have finished the first draft of the new mss. Am rewriting it now, a little more of a book than I thought at first so the rewrite will actually be the writing of it, which will take some time yet. I wont set a date; I'll just work at it.

Am arguing with Rev dept over 1944 additional income tax. They owe me about $2200.00, claim I owe them $3900.00. I may have to pay the 3900 before they pay me the 2200.00. Also, must pay state income 1947.

I imagine I can put the feds off for a while even after assessed, though the int. will climb. But if necessary, can I have this 3900 plus about 500 for state? or (2) can I have difference between 39 and 22 hundred, plus 500 for state?

In either case, can I have extra 500 before March 15th to pay state? Will need this regardless.

Can you do anything about the enclosed from Mencken?[1]

Bill

[1] H. L. Mencken had written asking if Faulkner could send a few of his novels to a German professor preparing to lecture on his work in his seminar at the University of Berlin.

To H. L. Mencken | TS. NYPL
Sunday [probably 22 Feb. 1948] | [Oxford]

Dear Mr Mencken:

Yours received. I dont have any of my books except ones in foreign translations. They get borrowed or just taken or I gave them away maybe which though it proves that Mississippians dont read foreign languages, they do read English despite New York critics.

I am sending your note on to Random House to see what they can do.

I am looking forward to the new *American Language Supplement*. It's good reading, like Swift or Sterne. You and they seem to have the same problem: there are just too goddamn many of the human race and they talk too much.

William Faulkner

To Robert K. Haas — TS. RH
Monday [1 Mar. 1948] — [Oxford]

Dear Bob:

Of course, do as you like about my account.[1]

I have a legal tax expert on the income business. He says we can get some reduction. The only question is, will I receive the 2400$ they owe me *before* they finally demand the 3000 plus I owe them.

Hodding Carter and an old friend of mine, Ben Wasson, have what they call the Levee Press, at Greenville, Miss. Three times a year they get out an issue, which is a sort of colophon thing: a single story or article, limited number. I am letting them have the section of the big mss. which Ober offered to Partisan Review and was declined. It will resemble a special edition pamphlet, bound of course, signed by me, to sell at $2.50. I get 25%. This is all right with Random House, isn't it? The section is about 80–100 pages typescript. They will call it Section (of from) Work in Progress I think. I want to do it mainly to confound the people who say nothing good out of Miss. The Press is less than a year old, is already getting known even though in slightly precious circles, like Yale reviews etc. Its foundation is Carter's Greenville daily newspaper. His name is familiar to you, probably: lecturer, liberal, champion of Negro injustice though no radical, no communist despite Bilbo and Rankin.[2]

New mss is bigger than I thought. Is a good story, not just a document. It's going to be longer than I thought, possibly over 200 pages in place of 130. It's going all right.

Will put off asking for the money as long as I can.

Yours
Bill

[1] Haas had referred to specific accounting procedures for advancing to Faulkner the sums he had requested.

[2] As outspoken editor of the Greenville *Democrat-Times*, Hodding Carter had been attacked by Sen. Theodore G. Bilbo and Rep. John E. Rankin.

To Robert K. Haas[1] — TS. RH
[received 15 Mar. 1948] — [Oxford]

Yes, all right about the contract.[2]

This novel should certainly be ready for fall list. See no reason why you should not have it say by June 1st, but I seem to write so much slower, have to do so much more rewriting before sentences come exactly right than I used to, that I am a little afraid to commit myself.

By the way, first time in my experience, I cant find a title. I want a word, a dignified (or more dignified) synonym for 'shenanigan,' 'skulduggery; maybe legal-quasi-latin word, for title like this:

Shenanigan }
Skullduggery } IN THE DUST
Jugglery }

Maybe Saxe can think of one. The story is: a murdered man is buried. When someone digs him up to prove how he was killed, another man's body has been substituted for him. When the law opens the grave to find out what goes here, there is nobody in the coffin at all.

[1] Haas had written Faulkner on 3 Mar. 1948 and received this reply, without salutation or signature, typed at the bottom of his own letter.

[2] The contract provision was that Faulkner's royalty on new books would be a flat 15% of the retail price.

On 16 March 1948, Haas wrote Faulkner suggesting titles for the new novel. The first was Imposture in the Dust; *then he offered four more with varying initial nouns:* Masquerade, Stratagem, Pattern *and* Cabal.

To Robert K. Haas — TS. RH
Sunday [possibly 21 Mar. 1948] — [Oxford]

Dear Bob:

No, I mislaid the original of suggestions. I like CABAL for its shortness, but the substitution wasn't a mutual plot. This is true of MASQUERADE.

Temporarily will hold to Imposture, but make it:

IMPOSTOR IN THE DUST.

? INTRUDER IN THE DUST ?

SLEEPER IN THE DUST Sleeper in the sense of the forgotten chip on the poker or roulette table, only slumber and death too synonymous; nobody would recognise the other significance

? MALFEASANCE IN THE DUST ? too long.

? SUBSTITUTION IN THE DUST ?

Since looking at it, I am beginning to like MALFEASANCE.

? MALAPROP IN THE DUST ? too esoteric?

MALPRACTICE IN THE DUST

TROUBLE IN THE DUST

6 hours later: I believe INTRUDER IN THE DUST is best yet. I cant think of a single good synonym for sleight of hand, which is actually what we want. If anyone thinks of anything better, do so.

[in ink:] Tuesday—Still like

INTRUDER IN THE DUST.

Bill

To Robert K. Haas — TS. RH
Wednesday [7 Apr. 1948] — [Oxford]

Dear Bob:

Yours received. The short story volume is all right.[1] I agree, better be stuff not in a book yet. I will go over your list carefully later; think a few changes in your starred list, one or two on it I dont consider first rate and I think one or two omitted which I do. Will attend to that later for this reason.

I'm on the last chapter in the present mss. It will be about 275 pages in all, maybe more. I believe I will have it in to you before May 15th, so it can be the next published. Then the short stories.

I thought first this one would be about 120 pages. It has grown with rewriting, which is why it has taken longer than I thought, as I finished first draft in 6 weeks. You should have it in plenty time for next spring, as your letter fixed, that is, '49 pubn.

I will see to proper copyright of Levee Press piece.

[no signature]

[1] On 30 Mar. 1948, Haas had written Faulkner proposing a new collection and listing stories for possible inclusion.

To Robert K. Haas — TS. RH
Tuesday [20 Apr. 1948] — [Oxford]

Dear Bob:

The mss. is finished and goes to you by express within the next day or so.

I'm sending it to you instead of Ober because I still dont have a title, haven't found that word yet which means substitution by sharp practice IN THE DUST.

Please think again, ask Saxe, Don, Bennett, anyone, think of other titles besides IN THE DUST if necessary. JUGGLERY is nearest I know, but harsh ugly word. Just thought of IMPOSTURE, not too it.
INTRUDER? in the etc.

Let me know what you think of the book. It started out to be a simple quick 150 page whodunit but jumped the traces, strikes me as being a pretty good study of a 16 year old boy who overnight became a man.

Will take a few days off from writing, then will write you about what I had better do, that is if Random H. will continue to carry me on the other mss. or what to do.

Bill

Robert K. Haas | TS. RH
Wednesday [28 Apr. 1948] | [Oxford]

Dear Bob:

Your wire just came. These two enclosures explain themselves. I agree to any publication date you like of course. But would like the extra money from a magazine sale if possible. The letter to Harold explains itself regarding such a sale. If you agree to let him try to sell it for mag. publication before you print, forward the letter to him on to him when you send him the mss. This is of course in case a mag. ed. will want the mss. changed, simplified to bare story.

I'm glad you like the mss.

I will assume you will continue to send the monthly check until we have a chance to get together about it.

I will not get seriously or steadily back at the other mss. until this year's planting, farming, is done, about July 4th, though I shall work at it from time to time.

I hope Bennett will like it too. He must be mad at me. I haven't heard hide nor hair of him in years.

Am inclined for INTRUDER IN THE DUST.

Bill

To Harold Ober | TS. FCVA
Tuesday [possibly 27 Apr. 1948] | [Oxford]

Dear Harold:

I sent Bob the finished mss. last week, asking him to let you see it with idea of magazine serial sale.

As it is now, it is a mystery story plus a little sociology and psychology. If a mag wants a simple story, we can eliminate chapter IX, take the story from where old Gowrie says '. . . . take our son home.' and go straight to the jail that night when the boy and his uncle see the sheriff and Lucas leave to trap the murderer, cut out all except the essential story line of the three people waiting in the lawyer's office, as it is written as the lawyer explains and sums up just what happened. The book can end with that chapter, X, with Miss Habersham's speech: 'That will be nice.' or the last Chapter, XI, can be included as is, or pared down to its essential story matter, which is to show that the sheriff and Lucas were successful, Lucas vindicated, murderer caught, etc.

I suggest this as a point you can offer if editors balk at mss. for popular consumption as is. This paring, editing, as you see, will leave it a simple story of movement.

You can add that I will do this work myself.

Will you telephone Bob and tell him the jist of this?

Bill

To Harold Ober — TS. FCVA

Sunday [2 May 1948] — [Oxford]

Dear Harold:

Let them have the story COURTSHIP, only change the man's name from Calicoat to Hogganbeck, David Hogganbeck.[1] I wrote that story before I had my Yoknapatawpha genealogy straightened out. The steamboat pilot, David Hogganbeck, was the grandfather of the hunter, Boon Hogganbeck, in GO DOWN MOSES. Please be *sure* that they make this change.

Sent to Bob a letter to you regarding selling of the new novel to a magazine. I suppose he has communicated by now.

Bill

[1] After "A Courtship" had been offered to six magazines without success, Albert Erskine obtained an offer of $200 from *The Sewanee Review*. It appeared in Issue LVI (Autumn 1948), 631–53.

To Bennett Cerf — TS. RH

Wednesday [possibly 5 May 1948] — [Oxford]

Dear Bennett:

I dont quite like BEAT FOUR as title.

Beat Four was only incidentally the villain and was not the hero; it was no concerted assault by Beat Four on humanity.

Secondly, every county is divided into what corresponds to beats in Mississippi and other states too; it would be like renaming Grand Hotel Floor Ten.

BEAT FOUR doesn't strike my ear in this case, anymore than Range Four or Township Four would. COUNTY would come nearer fitting.

I wish we could think of a pleasanter word than JUGGLERY. But lacking any short word for substitution, swap, exchange, sleight-of-hand, I think INTRUDER IN THE DUST is best. I am not bound to it, but I dont think Beat Four is right at all. As it is, it means nothing. Then if you let the story give it a significance, you foist the wrong significance on it. Beat Four did no more than all the rest of the county would have in those circumstances.

Bill

To Bennett Cerf — TS. RH

Saturday [possibly 8 or 15 May 1948] — Oxford

Dear Bennett:

As Bob probably told you, I was victim of additional income tax assessment for 1944 recently, and Bob agreed that rather than me going back to Cal. on movie pay, I would stay here and keep at mss. and stall the people off. I will owe them $360 or 70 odd June 15th. The whole sum is about $2000.00 but for now they demand the 370 by 15th. Will you send me additional say $375.00 to meet that one?

I would like to come up this fall, haven't seen anybody to talk to in 8 years now. I will have to borrow money to come on though, unless a studio buys the book. No, I have never even seen Mrs Cerf. Dont know how you are as a husband but Random House has been a good papa to me so maybe you are all right in that capacity just as the least porter in the vatican partakes a little of heaven too.

Yours,
Bill

Bennett Cerf was exploring possibilities for the sale of film rights to Intruder in the Dust. *Warner Bros. and Cagney Productions appeared to be the most interested prospective buyers, though the rights would be purchased and the film produced by Metro-Goldwyn-Mayer.*

To Bennett Cerf — TS. RH
Tuesday [18 May 1948] — Oxford

Dear Bennett:

re my wire: I think Warner should have first shot at buying the book. I dont know if you are up to date about my status, but Bob and Harold Ober know, as all communication was through Ober. Warner agreed to hold no claim on what I did while on leave, but my relations have been amicable with them, about getting time away when I insisted, no great fuss about it. And since they did not become stuffy about relinquishing claim to movie rights on what I do while off their pay, I would like to give them the refusal, then let Cagney see it.

What do you think? I suggest you talk to Ober about it before you talk to Cagney's people.

Bill

To Bennett Cerf — TS. RH
Tuesday [probably 13 July 1948] — Oxford, Miss.

Dear Bennett:

I forgot this when reading the galley.

In the chapter when Miss H. and the two boys reach the country church that night and throw the flashlight on the tombstone. The tombstone should read:

AMANDA WORKITT
wife of
N. B. Forrest Gowrie
(date) (date)
birth death

Will you have the change made?

You did fine about the movie sale.[1] All I wanted was, that Warner be notified from me (us) that the book was finished and for sale, with time to make an offer as soon as anyone else had time to do it. Since this was done, I'm satisfied and immensely pleased over your stout effort with the other party.

I'll be able to come up this fall with no strain on Random House bank balance now.

Bill

[1] Metro-Goldwyn-Mayer bought the film rights to *Intruder in the Dust* for $50,000.00.

To Harold Ober — TS. FCVA
Friday [16 July 1948] — [Oxford]

Dear Harold:

Yours received. Sorry you didn't see mss. I thought you had. I sent it direct to Bob, mainly as some concrete return on their advances to me, assuming that you would see it immediately. The letter I had in reply, I think from Bob, said as I recall that it had been decided the chance for magazine sale was so slight that they would go ahead with immediate book printing at once. In fact, I wrote Bob and offered to edit the mss. for a mag., with brief synopsis of what I would delete.[1]

He may be right and there is no chance of sale. I hope so, however, so you can share in the spoils, since it was your effort with Warner that gave me the freedom to write it in recess from the other, which I will now get back at.

Will see you this fall I think. I want to come up and consult you and Bob both about what to do with this money so my friends and kinfolks dont or cant borrow and spend it.

Bill

[1] Faulkner had, of course, written this information in a letter to Ober dated "Tuesday" (possibly 27 Apr. 1948), then apparently enclosed it in a letter to Haas dated "Wednesday" (28 Apr. 1948) for transmission by Haas to Ober if Haas agreed to let Ober seek magazine publication before book publication. At Albert Erskine's suggestion Ober did try, without success, to sell the first section of *Intruder in the Dust* to *Harper's* and the *Atlantic*.

To Malcolm Cowley — TS. YALE
16 July [1948] — Oxford, Miss.

Dear Brother Cowley:

I had a letter from a Mr Pearson at New Haven about coming there to make a talk, something.[1] I have lost it and cant answer. He spoke of you in the letter; will you either send me his address or if you correspond write him my apologies for losing the address and that I dont think I know anything worth 200 dollars worth talking about but I hope to be up East this fall though I still dont believe I will know anything to talk about worth 200 dollars so I would probably settle for a bottle of good whiskey.

If I come up, I would like to see you.

Faulkner

[1] Prof. Norman Holmes Pearson of Yale University. Faulkner did not give the talk.

To Robert K. Haas — TS. RH
Saturday [received 16 Aug. 1948] — [Oxford]

Dear Bob:

I have been more or less out of circulation for the last two weeks. So I didn't get your word about a dedication. I dont have one and anyway you did quite right to go ahead since you didn't hear. This is just to say I didn't ignore it.

As you may recall, I still owe govt. 1944 income tax (additional—they say). On the strength of the book sale I am asking them to bring the matter to a head, give me a hearing with a lawyer in New Orleans, and save interest. If they agree and will hold the hearing, may I count on you for the money, in case MGM check not yet in?

Bill

To Emmanuel Harper[1] — TS. RH
16 Aug. 1948 — Oxford, Miss.

Dear Mr Harper:

Us country folks in Miss. dont know very much about these long fine-print contracts.[2] We just pass our word and have done.

So my notary may have mixed things up too much. Maybe you can get enough clean pages by shuffling them about, and let me have the buggered up one.

Or maybe they will be all right. In any case, here they are. I signed where you indicated anyway, though Miss McCoy's notarising may have gone astray here and there.[3]

I think we all did mighty well on this book. I have not read the contract, since your legal staff has checked it and I couldn't make head nor tail of it anyway; too much verbiage for me.

Yours,
Bill Faulkner

[1] Secretary of Random House.
[2] Contract for the film rights to *Intruder in the Dust*.
[3] Miss Ruby McCoy was bookkeeper of the First National Bank of Oxford, whose first president was Faulkner's grandfather, J. W. T. Falkner.

To Robert K. Haas — TS. RH
Wednesday [Aug. 1948] — [Oxford]

Dear Bob:

Yours received. No, I wasn't sick. I was spending most of the time on water. Govt. built a big flood control dam in local river here, we have a big pond 11 miles long.[1] A retired army man and 2 friends built a houseboat, 44 x 14, lugger engine.[2] I am his only help in sailing it, I supervised the launching and since have been busy helping them learn to sail a biggish craft, set out two cans to moor between, marked channels, etc., getting her shaken down.

About the money. I signed my part of the contracts and sent them back to Harper, so maybe that money will be along soon. Anyway, I shall push the income business, get it done so I can come up East this fall.

Yours,
Bill

[1] Sardis Reservoir.
[2] The M.S. *Minmagary*, built by Col. Hugh Evans with Dr. Ashford H. Little and Ross Brown.

To Robert K. Haas — TS. RH
Sunday [probably 12 Sept. 1948] — [Oxford]

Dear Bob:

I am going to New Orleans Wednesday with a lawyer to try to argue with the income tax people about the 1944 additional assessment.

I may need more money, perhaps $2000.00. If so, I will wire you at once so I can cover my check to them.

I hope I wont need it but I found a chance to buy an almost new, only 2500 miles, Ford Station wagon, my other car being a 1936 Ford and about used up, which cost me 2300.00$, which I had not intended to spend until 1949, leaving me too short to take care of the possible assessment of 3500$ by govt.

I dont want to draw any more money in 1948 than possible, because of income tax, but I may have to ask for more.

I still hope to come up for a week or so this fall, probably Oct.

Bill

[in ink:] Just inclosed a note to Saxe, book looks fine, asking him to send me 6 more copies.

To Robert K. Haas — TS. RH

Saturday [18 Sept. 1948] — [Oxford]

Dear Bob:

Yours at hand.

The income tax thing was successful. They reduced the assessment a thousand dollars, so I shall need only 1 thousand instead of 2. Please send it when convenient, $1000.00.

About the short story collection, yes by all means. I have mislaid the list you sent me. I dont have copies of all these pieces, so I must use my memory. Please send me a copy of this list. I would like to mull over it, try to give this volume an integrated form of its own, like the Moses book if possible, or at least These 13.

The big mss. is coming, but slow at present. I will probably not get seriously at it until winter and the bad weather. With four years ahead free of money worries, that is, having to borrow ahead from you as I did for 3 years, I will get a lot done on it; I may get hot and finish it next year. I got thrown for a slight loss last month with an ulcer which still bothers me a little. But it is getting better and next month I hope to feel like coming up for a week or so; then I will get back at the big mss. in earnest.

Please remind Saxe to send me the 6 copies of Intruder In Dust.

Yours,
Bill

Faulkner apparently found the list of stories Haas had proposed for the new volume in his letter of 30 March 1948. He retyped the list with comments, and someone, presumably in New York, wrote "9/23/48" at the top. Haas replied on 4 October 1948.

To Robert K. Haas TS. RH
[late Sept. or early Oct. 1948] [Oxford]

MULE IN THE YARD—	Will be a chapter or incident in the further SNOPES saga.[1] I say Yes.
GOLDEN LAND—	Yes.
CENTAUR IN BRASS—	Also a part of the Snopes saga, when and if I get the two other volumes done.[2] Yes, include it.
THAT WILL BE FINE—	Have you a good reason for not including this?
LO!	Yes.
GOLD IS NOT ALWAYS—	No. Already in a book.[3]
UNCLE WILLY—	Yes. I like this one.
LION—	No. Already in book.[4]
MONK	Not too good, but will be included nowhere else, and there will probably not be enough more to make a volume, provided all my pieces are to be reprinted in book form.[5]
A BEAR HUNT	Yes. [in ink:] Let me have this for a correction of locale
PENNSYLVANIA STATION—	Am willing to omit, but see MONK above.
THRIFT	OMIT it if you like. Not too good.
THE BROOCH	See MONK and PENN STATION above.
MY GRANDMOTHER MILLARD ETC.—	Yes.
BARN BURNING—	No. Was in first chapter of THE HAMLET, wasn't it?[6]
TOMORROW—	Dont remember it, but include.[5]
THE TALL MEN	Yes.
TWO SOLDIERS	YES
SHINGLES FOR THE LORD—	Yes, but let me have it to make a minor necessary change.
SHALL NOT PERISH—	No. Topical, not too good.
AN ERROR IN CHEMISTRY—	Yes, except that some day I might collect or finish out a series of Gavin Stevens detective pieces.[5]
SNOW	Omit if you like, not too good, good idea somewhere in it but it didn't come off that time. May do it later.

[in ink:] WITH CAUTION & DISPATCH—Let me think about this one.

KNIGHT'S GAMBIT— Omit it.[5] See AN ERROR IN CHEMISTRY above.

A COURTSHIP— Yes. I like this one.

Also you might consider:

HAND UPON THE WATERS— Sat. Eve. Post, somewhere between 1935–1940, maybe earlier. But see AN ERROR IN CHEMISTRY and KNIGHT'S GAMBIT above.[5]

SMOKE Harpers I think, somewhere about 1930. But see AN ERROR IN CHEMISTRY, KNIGHT'S GAMBIT, HAND UPON THE WATERS above.[5]

A Gavin Stevens story about a juryman who refused to convict a killer. This may be TOMORROW which I cant recall, was in Post about that time. If so, see AN ERROR IN CHEMISTRY etc above.

These are all I can recall which you dont list.

If you want to include the Gavin Stevens pieces, they could be in a section to themselves and if I add to them, they could still be included again in another volume.

I am not too clear about BARN BURNING, on second thought. Maybe I rewrote it for THE HAMLET, from a new point of view. If not too similar, include it.

[in ink:] On second thought, wasn't 'SMOKE' in DR MARTINO?[7]

[no signature]

[1] Incorporated in *The Town* (1957).

[2] *Ibid.*

[3] First published in the *Atlantic*, CLXVI (Nov. 1940), 563–70, the story had become Chapter Two of "The Fire and the Hearth" in *Go Down, Moses.*

[4] This story was written from a segment of "The Bear" in *Go Down, Moses.*

[5] Collected in *Knight's Gambit* (1949).

[6] Faulkner had attempted without success to sell the short story "Barn Burning." He then thought of using it to open *The Peasants*, which would become *The Hamlet* (1940). Later, he decided on a different approach to the material of *The Hamlet*, and "Barn Burning" was published in *Harper's*, CLXXIX (June 1939), 86–96.

[7] "Smoke" had been published in *Harper's*, CLXIV (Apr. 1932), 562–78, reprinted in *Doctor Martino* (1934).

On 15 September 1948, Hamilton Basso, whom Faulkner knew when he lived in New Orleans in 1925, wrote that The New Yorker *had asked him to write a "profile" of Faulkner. Basso asked if he would consent, and Faulkner wrote his reply on the bottom of Basso's letter.*

To Hamilton Basso — MS. MRS. HAMILTON BASSO
[postmarked 23 Sept. 1948] — [Oxford]

Oh hell no. Come down and visit whenever you can, but no piece in any paper about me as I am working tooth and nail at my lifetime ambition to be the last private individual on earth & expect every success since apparently there is no competition for the place.

Bill

To Bennett Cerf — TS. RH
Tuesday [28 Sept. 1948] — Oxford

Dear Bennett:

Thank you for your invitation to stop with you when I come up. I look forward to meeting your family but one purpose of my expedition is vacation from the nest-and-hearth business. I will stay at a hotel (granted of course they still exist in the sense that I used to know them).

Has the Algonquin changed too much? If it has, what would you suggest, knowing my taste and habits? I think I will come up about Oct 15–20, for a week or so.

Yours,
Bill

To Robert K. Haas — TS. RH
Tuesday [28 Sept. 1948] — Oxford

Dear Bob:

Good news about the extra 1000 sale. I am trying to hold my drawing of cash down so income tax wont be so much. I am assuming you will continue to send me $500.00 each month; this will total for 1948 5 x 12, $6000.00 plus the $7000.00 I have drawn since book sale. At last in Miss we have community property law, so the rate wont be so high. So I think I will draw more; I want to buy a small garden tractor and gear, and put a roof on my house. So will you send along the $1000.00 from handibook sale.

I think I shall come up about Oct. 15–20, soon as squirrel and dove shooting is over here. I'll bring some of the big mss. and give Random House a chance to see what goes.

I just wrote Bennett about a hotel. Malcolm Cowley was kind enough to offer the Harvard Club but being an old Yale man (vide the two days I spent at the Yale club on your cuff in 1935) this might be lese majesty, unless it may be considered post graduate work.

Yours,
Bill

Faulkner spent 18–23 October in New York City. From 23–26 October, he recuperated at the home of Malcolm and Muriel Cowley in Sherman, Connecticut, after which he returned to New York. He flew home on 30 October.

To Saxe Commins — TS. RH
Sunday [31 Oct. 1948] — Oxford

Dear Saxe:

Herewith the two corrected stories.[1]

On the way down yesterday, I kept on thinking about the table of contents page; something about it nagged at me. I kept on thinking, why *Indians* when we had never said The Country *people* and the Village *people*, but only the *Country* and the *Village*. Then I thought, not *Indians* but *Wilderness*, and then suddenly the whole page stood right, each noun in character and tone and tune with every other and I imagine that now you have divined the word for the war section too: The Wasteland: like this:

The Country
The Village
The Wilderness
The Wasteland
The Middle Ground
Beyond

I believe that's it. We could use *Desert* or *Barren* but I believe Wasteland is the right one.

I may get to work on the foreword pretty soon now even if there is no hurry.

Bill

[1] "Shingles for the Lord" and "A Bear Hunt."

To Malcolm Cowley — TS. YALE
Monday [1 Nov. 1948] — Oxford

Dear Malcolm:

I had a slow uneventful trip down on a flight which stopped everywhere there was an airport big enough, but I was home in my own bed by midnight Saturday.

It wasn't too dull because I spent the time thinking about the collection of stories, the which the more I think about, the better I like. The only book foreword I ever remembered was one I read when I was about sixteen I suppose, in one of Sienckewicz (maybe that's not even spelled right), which, I dont even remember: Pan Michael or what, nor the actual words either: something like 'This book written in . . . travail (he may have said even agony and sacrifice) for the uplifting of men's hearts.'[1] Which I believe is the one worthwhile purpose of any book and so even to a collection of short stories, form, integration, is as important as to a novel—an entity of its own, single, set for one pitch, contrapuntal in integration, toward one end, one finale.

I think I have this one about right though you may not be familiar with all these pieces.

It is divided into sections, like this, with these section-designations:

I THE COUNTRY
- Barn Burning
- Shingles for the Lord
- The Tall Men
- A Bear Hunt
- Two Soldiers[2]

II THE VILLAGE
- A Rose for Emily
- Hair
- Centaur in Brass
- Dry September
- Death Drag
- Elly
- Uncle Willy
- Mule in the Yard
- That Will Be Fine
- That Evening Sun

III THE WILDERNESS
- Red Leaves
- A Justice
- A Courtship
- Lo!

IV THE WASTELAND
- Ad Astra
- Victory
- Crevasse
- Turnabout
- All the Dead Pilots

V THE MIDDLE GROUND
- Wash
- Honor

Dr Martino
Fox Hunt[3]
My Grandmother Millard
Golden Land
There Was a Queen
A Mountain Victory

VI BEYOND
Beyond
Black Music
The Leg
Mistral
Divorce in Naples
Carcassonne

I will write a foreword[4] for it.

I went to Abercrombie and thought I had a corduroy coat that would do but when I got home and looked at it, it was wrong, too snappy, collegiate. I sent it back. I still want one like yours, white or nearwhite corduroy, bellows pockets and a loose belt and a vent in back so I can ride a horse in it. Brooks said they had not had them in two years. The next time you are in there, will you see if they can get the corduroy and make me one like yours?

My best most grateful remembrances to Muriel.

Bill F.

[1] Henryk Sienkiewicz (1846–1916) of Poland was awarded the Nobel Prize for Literature for 1905. The quotation Faulkner remembered came at the end of the novel *Pan Michael* (1887–88): "Here ends this series of books, written in the course of several years and with no little labor, for the strengthening of men's hearts." The novel completed a trilogy which included *With Fire and Sword* (1883) and *The Deluge* (1886). Faulkner would adapt this quotation for his Nobel Prize acceptance speech of 1950.

[2] When *Collected Stories of William Faulkner* appeared in 1950, the contents were as Faulkner outlined them here, with the addition of "Shall Not Perish" at the end of this section and the three other stories listed below.

[3] Here were inserted "Pennsylvania Station," "Artist at Home" and "The Brooch."

[4] There was no foreword in the published volume.

To Robert K. Haas — TS. RH
Thursday [11 Nov. 1948] — Oxford

Dear Bob:

Thank you for the sonnets and the photograph. I shall keep them. You ought to write more verse, I mean for the sake of the verse itself. The only difference between you and the sonless griefless natural poet is, the poet is capable in his imagination alone of all grief and degradation and valor and sacrifice.

I am working at the big mss.[1] though not too hard as our deer hunting camp opens next week and due to the deaths this past year of the two senior members, most of the work—getting the dogs and horses sent up, cook, tents, feed etc., has fallen to my lot.

I have remembered still another story which ought to go into the collection, granted the volume is to be comprehensive of all my short pieces except those previously allotted to other complete volumes in future. I'll communicate with Saxe about it.

My love to Miss Merle and regards to all the vinyardists and tenantry and thank your honeychild daughter for sending the reviews.

Bill

[1] A *Fable*.

To Saxe Commins — TS. RH

Wednesday [possibly 24 Nov. 1948] — [Oxford]

Dear Saxe:

Please discuss this with Bennett and Bob.

Ever since I got home I have been thinking about our collected volume. Something nagged at my mind. I have decided (or admitted) that what I seem to be hottest on now, would like first, is another volume. Maybe we are too previous with a collected Faulkner.

I am thinking of a 'Gavin Stevens' volume,[1] more or less detective stories. I have four or five short pieces, averaging 20 pages, in which Stevens solves or prevents crime to protect the weak, right injustice, or punish evil. There is one more which no one has bought.[2] The reason is, it is a novel which I tried to compress into short story length. It is a love story, in which Stevens prevents a crime (murder) not for justice but to gain (he is now fifty plus) the childhood sweetheart which he lost 20 years ago. It will probably run about 150 pages, which should make a volume as big as INTRUDER.

This is the story I seem to be hottest to write now. Talk it over and let me hear.

Also, tell Bennett and Bob (I will write them soon) that I have been thinking of the reprint suggested. I think LIGHT IN AUGUST is available now in a reprint, isn't it? So I would rather see ABSALOM, ABSALOM! printed again, not only because it is out of print but because I think it's a better job.

Let me hear from you. If you all agree about Stevens book, I will get at the rewrite job after Xmas, should be ready for fall pubn.

Yours,
Bill

[1] *Knight's Gambit* (1949).
[2] "Knight's Gambit," the title story.

To Robert K. Haas — TS. RH
30 Dec. 1948 — [Oxford]

Dear Bob:

Yours at hand. Since the estimated tax is not due until Jan 15th, I am all right.

As soon after Jan 1st as practicable, will you send me $4,000.00. This will leave $6,000.00 of the next MGM payment, or $500.00 per month. 12 months.

I thought of you and Miss Merle Xmas, had a drink to you both *in absentia,* and will do the same tomorrow night.

Yours,
Bill

A member of the National Institute of Arts and Letters since 1939, Faulkner was elected to the American Academy on 23 November 1948. He did not acknowledge notification of the honor, and at the end of the following month Felicia Geffen, assistant to the president of the Academy, wrote him asking word of his acceptance.

To the president of the American Academy — TS. AMERICAN ACADEMY OF ARTS AND LETTERS
31 Dec. 1948 — Oxford, Miss.

Dear Sir:

The letter must have become mislaid after it reached my home, since I did not receive it. I was in a deer hunting camp Nov. 23. Telegrams are a casual business here; the office in town telephones them out and if you are not there to answer the phone, nothing else is done about it unless the operator happens to meet or pass you in the street and happens to remember to tell you a telegram came for you two or three weeks ago; did you get it?

I would have acknowledged otherwise, and take this opportunity to express my awareness of the honor.

Yours sincerely,
William Faulkner

While Malcolm Cowley was working on a profile of Ernest Hemingway for Life *in the summer of 1948, his editor had asked if he would do a companion piece on Faulkner. When Faulkner stayed with the Cowleys in October, Cowley proposed the idea and received the impression that Faulkner reluctantly consented. He talked about his work and himself at some length, and Cowley made notes for future use. (See* The Faulkner-Cowley File, *pp. 103, 127–28.)*

To Malcolm Cowley — TS. YALE
Wednesday [5 Jan. 1949] — [Oxford]

Dear Malcolm:

I have waited two weeks, and am still no nearer getting into the dentist's chair. About 10 years ago I had no little difficulty in convincing Life[1] (or somebody) that I didn't want a piece about me in their mag. and two years ago it took six months and a considerable correspondence and telegrams to convince Vogue that I would have no part of their same project.

I still dont want it, I mean, me as a private individual, my past, my family, my house. I would prefer nothing about the books, but they are in the public domain and I was paid for that right. The only plan I can accept is one giving me the privilege of editing the result. Which means I will want to blue pencil everything which even intimates that something breathing and moving sat behind the typewriter which produced the books.

I imagine this wont go down with LIFE. I imagine the last thing on earth they will pay their good money for is a piece about somebody's mere output even though art, since I imagine they dont care two whoops in the bad place about art but only about what they would call 'personalities.' But I am still trying to think of some workable approach so you can collect on it. I haven't done it yet, since I cant know what or how much you can do keeping me out; that is, how much material suitable to Life will be left.

This is a damned bastardly clumsy letter. I'm trying to say No, but in a ten-page polysyllable since conscience, heart, liking and what dregs of gratitude I might possess, forbid that simple rapid word. Write me again, let's see if we cant work out something Life will take.

My best to Muriel.

Bill

[1] Faulkner may have been recalling the cover story, in connection with the publication of *The Wild Palms*, in *Time*, XXXIII (23 Jan. 1939), 45–48.

To Saxe Commins — TS. RH

Wednesday [19 Jan. 1949] — [Oxford]

Dear Saxe:

I am working at the Gavin Stevens volume.

I dont have copies of these stories. I can recall only 4, though there seems to me to have been 5. But for my life, I cant recall another title nor even what it was about.[1]

SMOKE—In Dr. Martino.

HAND UPON THE WATERS[2]—SAT EVE POST.

Can you get a copy? some time about 1940

TOMORROW[3] (I think; am not even sure about title; Ober sold it) Sat Eve Post, about 1940

AN ERROR IN CHEMISTRY[4] (Ober sold it)—

Ellery Queen mystery mag. 1945

Ask Ober if he has record of any other.

KNIGHT'S GAMBIT—unpublished. Am rewriting, will be about 100 or 150 page novella.

Bill

[1] This story was "Monk," *Scribner's*, CI (May 1937), 16–24.

[2] *The Saturday Evening Post*, CCXII (4 Nov. 1939), 14–15, 75–79.

[3] "Tomorrow," *The Saturday Evening Post*, CCXIII (23 Nov. 1940), 22–23, 32, 35, 37–39.

[4] *Ellery Queen's Mystery Magazine*, VII (June 1946), 4–19.

Harold Ober had read that the Valerie Bettis ballet based on As I Lay Dying *was a sellout. He wrote Faulkner as part of an effort to ensure that he receive any royalties due him.*

To Harold Ober — TS. FCVA
Friday [21 Jan. 1949] — Oxford

Dear Harold:

My recollection is, this Bettis thing happened or was done through Random House. Bob should know, or Saxe Commins. Either a letter came to me in person, care Random House, or to Random House, asking permission, no money involved since the spectacle would be noncommercial. I said it was all right with me, to which Bob or Saxe or whoever it was, acquiesced. I initialled a page of the letter, as I recall, there in the office, my recollection being that whoever it was I consulted with at the time undertook to send the letter to whoever wanted it.

I'm sorry I am so hazy on it. Get in touch with Bob or Saxe; ask Saxe to comb Random House and try to find out more. I do remember initialling a letter which stated the thing was noncommercial.

Yours,
Bill

On 10 January 1949, Haas had written Faulkner that the plates of Go Down, Moses, The Hamlet *and* The Wild Palms *were intact and that Random House now wished to reissue the novels. Haas asked if Faulkner wanted to make any minor changes. Because Faulkner had emphasized to Albert Erskine that* Go Down, Moses *was not a collection of stories but a novel, Haas asked if Faulkner would like to have chapter numbers in addition to the titles of the individual sections.*

To Robert K. Haas — TS. RH
Wednesday [26 Jan. 1949] — Oxford

Dear Bob:

I dont know what has happened to your recent letters. I never had them. I hunted about, and found a copy of Intruder from you, but no return carton or instructions. I have written on the title page, and it goes back to you today, with my apologies for the delay.

I did not receive the copy of the MOSES jacket. Moses is indeed a novel. I would not eliminate the story or section titles. Do you think it necessary to number these stories like chapters? Why not reprint exactly, but change the title from GO DOWN, MOSES and other stories, to simply: GO DOWN, MOSES, with whatever change is necessary in the jacket description. We did THE UNVANQUISHED in this manner, without either confusion or anticipation of such; and, for that matter, THE WILD PALMS had two completely unrelated stories in it. Yet nobody thought it should be titled THE WILD PALMS and another story. Indeed, if you will permit me to say so at this late date, nobody but Random House seemed to labor under the impression that GO DOWN, MOSES should be titled 'and other stories.' I remember the shock (mild) I got when I saw the printed title page. I say, reprint it, call it simply GO DOWN, MOSES, which was the way I sent it in to you 8 years ago.

No, dont know of any changes in the three sets of plates. But if we ever reprint INTRUDER, I left something out of it which I would like very much to put in. A single page, or 3 to make the smooth insert, will do it. I remembered it last year only after the book was in press.

Yours,
Bill

To Malcolm Cowley — TS. YALE
Friday [11 Feb. 1949] — Oxford

Dear Malcolm:

I saw the LIFE with your Hemingway piece. I didn't read it but I know it's all right or you wouldn't have put your name on it; for which reason I know Hemingway thinks it's all right and I hope it will profit him—if there is any profit or increase or increment that a brave man and an artist can lack or need or want.

But I am more convinced and determined than ever that this is not for me. I will protest to the last: no photographs, no recorded documents. It is my ambition to be, as a private individual, abolished and voided from history, leaving it markless, no refuse save the printed books; I wish I had had enough sense to see ahead thirty years ago and, like some of the Elizabethans, not signed them. It is my aim, and every effort bent, that the sum and history of my life, which in the same sentence is my obit and epitaph too, shall be them both: He made the books and he died.

But I still owe you a drunk. I will hold it on demand at sight draft, not transferable of course since you and Muriel will have to be present. But I will furnish someone to do the actual drinking; not myself this time.

Yours,
Bill

To Harold Ober — TS. FCVA
Saturday [19 Feb. 1949] — [Oxford]

Dear Harold:

Yours at hand. I am not likely to stop and write a piece for Burnett[1] or anybody, and if I do naturally it will go to you for selling.

I found what was wrong with the KNIGHT'S GAMBIT piece. It's not a short story, but a novella. I am rewriting it, into a 100 plus page novella, to be included in a collected volume of the Gavin Stevens detective stories. So if you can, please call it back from Burnett and hold it or send it to me. I have the carbon to work from, so dont need your copy. But the rewrite will invalidate yours. When I complete the rewrite, you can look at it and fix your commission on Random House printing of it.

I hope you can recall it and no harm done, since (in its new form) it will be one heretofore unpublished piece in the volume and its novella size, approximately half the proposed volume, may help sales.

Yours,
William Faulkner

[1] Whit Burnett, editor of *Story* magazine.

To Eric J. Devine — TS. MR. DEVINE
Friday [23 Feb. 1949] — [Oxford]

Dear Jim:

Here is the belated letter. I intend to catch Buddy[1] before mailing it and make him thank you for the book, which I am now reading.

Naturally I found plenty of use for the leather box. It carries rifle ammo, I have a razor, soap, steel mirror, etc. which fits it, but I use it mainly for my 'navigator's' kit on our home-made steamboat, the flat-bottomed houseboat I told you about that my ex-colonel hunting mate built in his back yard. The navigator's kit being 1 small rat-nosed pliers, 1 collapsible screwdriver, 1 tin of mosquito ointment, waterproof matchbox and a corkscrew beer bottle opener. Last Sunday we took 42 people aboard, one sheep and one shoat, two cases of whiskey, hung up two lanterns on cypress snags for markers and sailed into a cove across the lake and had a barbecue. Good fun, poker and crap game, one fight. Evans and I are by now probably the best flat-bottom boat sailors in the world.

Let me hear from you now and then. Will be up east again next fall, I hope. Much excitement here, since they are making a movie of my book in Oxford.[2] It's too bad I'm no longer young enough to cope with all the local girls who are ready and eager to glide into camera focus on their backs.

Yours,
Bill

[1] Malcolm A. Franklin.
[2] *Intruder in the Dust.*

To Saxe Commins — TS. RH
Saturday [5 Mar. 1949] — [Oxford]

Dear Saxe:

The pipe came today, the glass a few days ago, both in excellent shape, for which I thank you; I am sorry you dont need a pipe yourself, though I shant hold it against you.

I am at work on the long Stevens story. The volume will be: MONK, SMOKE, HAND UPON THE WATERS, AN ERROR IN CHEMISTRY, TOMORROW, and the new unpublished one, KNIGHT'S GAMBIT—that's correct, isn't it?

I dont remember MONK too well, though I think it is told from the outside, isn't it? in the 3rd person? Or does the nephew-protagonist tell it? In either case, I say, lead off with SMOKE, which is 3rd person, the boy not in it at all; also SMOKE is the first one I wrote. Then MONK, then HAND UPON THE WATERS, which is in its chronological order, also contains a murder, then TOMORROW, still in chronology but only incidentally concerned with a death, then ERROR IN CHEMISTRY, which is a murder, then KNIGHT'S GAMBIT, the long one, not published yet, in chronology, a long, the longest, piece, also marking the end of a phase of Stevens' life, since he gets married; that is, he prevents a murder not for the sake of justice, etc., but to gain his childhood sweetheart whom he had lost.

If you will get the first 5 into shape, I will work at the last one. I see no reason why you shant have it by May 15th, perhaps earlier.

I haven't got a title yet. I think of something legal, perhaps in workaday legal Latin, some play on the word *res*, like *res in justicii* or *Ad Justicii*.

Bill

To Robert K. Haas — TS. RH
Monday [probably Mar. 1949] — [Oxford]

Dear Bob:

I dont seem to know my own strength with a pen and a check book. I need more money. I am going to buy a sailing dory hull, in good shape except for caulking, scraping the stick, new canvas soon, to sail in our reservoir lake.

Also, draining my bottom farm land ran higher than I thought.

With your permission, I will draw the balance of the $10,000.00 from the movie for this year. I have had $4, then $3, so will you please send the other $3,000.00.

The new volume material is coming along all right. I will keep Saxe posted.

Yours,
Bill

To Valerie Bettis
23 April, 1949

TS. FCVA
Oxford, Miss.

Dear Miss Bettis:

Remain calm. You have a letter bearing my permission to use the material noncommercially.[1] You now have two.

I have written to Mr Ober today, sending him a copy of this. He is not only my agent but my good friend, was merely protecting me.

I wish you all success with your interesting project, and wish I could see it.

If it ever should show a profit, I would be happy to have 5%. But dont bother about that until it does—if or when.

I mean what you mean by noncommercially: as long as it only pays expenses until it is underwritten or produced or financed by someone whose intent is to make a little money out of it, which I think is the least of your concern right now.

Yours truly,
William Faulkner

[1] *As I Lay Dying* adapted as a ballet.

To Harold Ober
Saturday [23 Apr. 1949]

TS. FCVA
[Oxford]

Dear Harold:

Just had a letter from Miss Bettis, enclosing the lawyer's one about 5% royalty.

I dont imagine she is getting rich at this, and I like to assume she is an artist, trying to make something new, rather than to hit a jackpot.

Since I already gave her permission, on an initialled letter to Random House, to use the material non-commercially, I suggest letting her go on with no more strings than an agreement to share if the thing should build into a commercial property.

That is, as long as she is just paying expenses, actors, etc. and even a few dollars over, let her go unhampered, with her agreement that the author is to share if the material is ever used with the intent to produce a profit, and does begin to produce that profit.

Enclosed is a copy of my letter to her today.

If any expenses are incurred by the lawyer to date and in stopping any further steps, let me know and I'll reimburse you.

Bill

To Saxe Commins — TS. RH

Sunday [1 May 1949] — [Oxford]

Dear Saxe:

I am near the end of the rewritten piece, will send it in as soon as finished. It is running around 150 pages mss.

I cant remember if I wrote or not about a title and make-up. What do you think about

KNIGHT'S GAMBIT (title for book)

Then the stories in this order, each with its own title as you did Go Down, Moses, but if you like, set these titles in smaller type, more like chapter headings, except for chapter numbers, which we dont need.

Smoke
Monk
Hand Upon the Waters
Tomorrow
Error in Chemistry
Knight's Gambit

Bill

On 24 April 1949, Mollie Darr, a student at Northwestern University, wrote reminding Faulkner that she had previously requested permission from him to present a dramatic adaptation of As I Lay Dying. *She asked him to sign an enclosed form which specified only that he gave permission to her and three other students to present their adaptation of his novel at any time. Faulkner typed in an amendment and signed immediately below it:*

To Mollie Darr and others — TS. FCVA

[2 May 1949] — [Oxford]

I assume you are students, or connected with the University, and therefore amateurs. I assume the project is non-commercial. In that case, all right and I wish you luck. If it becomes commercial, that is, shows profit above normal expenses, let me know and let us make a new agreement.

William Faulkner

Faulkner sent Mollie Darr's covering letter to Ober with the following note at the bottom:

To Harold Ober — MS. FCVA
[2 May 1949] — [Oxford]

Here is another Bettis. It's all right as long as it is non-commercial, and until it begins to show profit above expenses. Then a new arrangement will have to be made.

On the same day, Faulkner sent both documents to Ober with his own covering letter.

To Harold Ober — TS. FCVA
Monday [2 May 1949] — [Oxford]

Dear Harold:

Here is another Bettis thing. This is all right with me; I am glad to have people using the material; would give them plenty of leeway about royalty. I would not expect royalty at all when the show is only paying its way; would not worry the parties until it exhibited symptoms of growing into a valuable property. Then we should have a new arrangement, or agreement, or a renewal of this one.

Maybe the best thing will be to draw up a form for this, stating that as long as the people are more or less amateurs, just making expenses and a few cigarettes and manicures Greenwich Village tabledhotes over, it is all right. But if it begins to grow, anyone becomes interested with the aim of making a profit, we should have an accounting with a royalty idea.

Please glance over the enclosed agreement which I have amended, and send it to Miss Darr.

Bill

On 4 May, the long-suffering Ober sent Faulkner a stiff letter telling him that they did have a form which reserved to Faulkner all professional rights. He had written Mollie Darr a letter which he was sure Faulkner would agree represented a wiser course and enclosed a copy. He also said he had sent Faulkner's letter to Valerie Bettis though he thoroughly disapproved of it. He regarded her as a well-paid professional. She had been doing sellout performances, he said, and Faulkner should receive part of her receipts.

To Harold Ober — TS. FCVA
Friday [6 May 1949] — [Oxford]

Dear Harold:

Yours re Bettis at hand. The harm is done now, or rather ratified, since my letter repeated the gist of what I initialled in the one through Random House.

Suppose I write her again, ask her to send you a weekly accounting for all performances for record?

Yours,
Bill

To Saxe Commins — TS. RH
Wednesday [possibly 18 May 1949] — [Oxford]

Dear Saxe:

The ms.[1] is finished, 148 pages, but I am not quite satisfied with parts. I am doing some rewriting, I dont know how much yet. I should send it in by next week-end, that is, by June 1st.[2] But you can go ahead with necessary publishing schedule, as this chore is merely rewriting certain pages for clarity, and we are agreed about title, set-up, etc., and you know the exact number of pages.

I wont waste any time with it.

Bill

1 "Knight's Gambit."

2 On 2 June 1949, Commins wrote Faulkner that he had just finished reading "Knight's Gambit."

To Saxe Commins — TS. RH
[mid-June 1949] — [Oxford]

Dear Saxe:

I see in the catalogue you announce Knight's Gambit as a novella and four stories. Aren't there five stories, besides the long one:

MONK, SMOKE, HAND UPON THE WATERS, TOMORROW, AN ERROR IN CHEMISTRY.

re 'Epenemide.'[1] It's Greek, isn't it, means 'Diary,' daily record, the substance of one's past. Might consult a Greek scholar, which I am not. I believe though 'ephemeride' is the correct form. Might italicise it if you like. But consult authority, anyway.

Bill

[1] In his letter of 2 June 1949, Commins had quoted a phrase on p. 15 of Faulkner's TS. of "Knight's Gambit": "A protagonist of a young girl's ephemeride." Commins suggested "ephemera" but consulted his friend, Prof. Whitney J. Oates, of the Classics Department of Princeton University. In the printed novel, the word would appear in its singular form, on p. 145, as "ephemeris."

To Robert K. Haas TS. RH
5th July [1949] Oxford

Dear Bob:

I'm going to run out of money, as usual. Can I draw more? Can I have $5000.00?

I'm having a fine time with my sloop,[1] am become a fair fresh water lake sailor, where a dozen different weathers can happen in 30 minutes: rain and thunder squalls this time of year, and pretty exciting for five or ten minutes. Have blown off a few stays, but no mast or canvas yet. I seem to have done a really expert caulking job on her hull; ten years old when I bought it, and out of water for four; 19 feet, 7 foot beam; a New England dory in fact, with about 200 ft of sail, not supposed to be fast, but she runs away from a standard Snipe which, I understand, does five and a half knots. She will carry 8, and two can sleep in the cockpit. I have a coleman stove, water-butt, a bottle of rum. She sails in very little wind, and can sail in and out of any hole she can turn around in. Two neighbor boys and my 16 year old daughter are my crew.

Am saving a stamp with this. The enclosed is for Saxe. Please tell him that 'ephemeris' is probably the form we want, and to thank his friend for me.

Bill

[1] Faulkner named it *The Ring Dove*.

To Manuel Komroff TS. FCVA
27 July, 1949 Oxford, Miss.

Dear Manuel

Please forgive. I'm the world's rottenest correspondent. All I remember about the other letter was about the letter Anderson gave me for you.[1] Only I dont remember that letter. I knew Anderson in New Orleans. When I left him there, I went to Europe, so I dont think he could have given me a letter to someone in New York. When I saw him next in New

Orleans, he had taken umbrage at me in the meantime; I never did know why, and wouldn't even speak.[2] Though I ran into him in New York several years later, and everything seemed to be all right again. Spent an afternoon with him, and never saw him again.

Was there something else in your first letter? I never keep correspondence. If there was, and I can answer it, please write me.

Bill

[1] Sherwood Anderson had written Horace Liveright advising him to take Faulkner's first novel, which Boni & Liveright published as *Soldiers' Pay*. On Faulkner's way home from Europe in Dec. 1925, he stopped in New York and visited the firm, where he talked with Manuel Komroff, one of the editors. In 1949, when Komroff was planning a retrospective essay, he remembered two letters from Anderson (the second, he thought, was possibly about *Mosquitoes*, Faulkner's second novel), but Faulkner remembered only one.

[2] There were several possible causes of the rupture, some of which Faulkner must have known but forgot or chose not to remember. See Blotner, *Faulkner: A Biography, passim.*

To Saxe Commins MS. RH
Wednesday [probably 5 Oct. 1949] [Oxford]

Dear Saxe—

Book received.[1] Beautiful job; we are all to be congratulated. Thank you.

Bill

[1] *Knight's Gambit,* which would be published 27 Nov. 1949.

To Samuel Marx TS. INDIANA
12 Oct., 1949 Oxford, Miss.

Dear Sam:

Ever since our mild fiasco of twenty years ago,[1] I have felt that accounts between me and MGM were not at balance, and my conscience hurt me at times. But since seeing Clarence's[2] 'Intruder in the Dust' here last night, the qualms have abated some. I may still be on MGM's cuff, but at least I am not quite so far up the sleeve.

Yours,
[s] Bill
[t] William Faulkner

[1] On 7 May 1932, Faulkner had reported for work at MGM Studios, where Sam Marx was head of the Scenario Department. Almost immediately Faulkner fled the studio and did not return for more than a week. During this first Hollywood stint, neither he nor the studio found his work very satisfactory, and it was only under director Howard Hawks that Faulkner contributed much of value or achieved much satisfaction.

[2] Director Clarence Brown.

Composer Virgil Thompson wrote Faulkner that he wanted to compose an opera based on The Wild Palms, *but ultimately nothing came of it.*

To Virgil Thompson — TS. FCVA
14 Oct., 1949 — Oxford, Miss.

Dear Mr Thompson:

Yours of 5th at hand. I am pleased and flattered by the idea. I am sending your letter today to Mr Harold Ober, 40 East 49th St., New York, asking him to communicate with you.

Yours sincerely,
William Faulkner

To Harold Ober — TS. FCVA
Friday [14 Oct. 1949] — [Oxford]

Dear Harold:

Herewith two letters, with my replies.[1]

Big hurrah here this week, with what is known as 'World Premiere' of Int. Dust. It is a good picture, I think.

Knight's Gambit will be out soon. Will you ask Bob at Random House to send you a copy as soon as possible, then you can count pages or calculate the unpublished piece, the long one titled Knight's Gambit which I withdrew from you and rewrote, so we can figure some commission for you on it? Do it any way you like; have Random House pay your commission out of my royalties, or I will pay it from here myself.[2]

Yours,
Bill

[1] Besides the Virgil Thompson proposal, there was another concerning film rights to the Valerie Bettis ballet based on *As I Lay Dying*.

[2] The Ober files do not reveal acceptance of Faulkner's proposal.

Harold Ober turned over to Robert Haas the proposal by Virgil Thompson that he compose an opera based on The Wild Palms *and the inquiry about film rights to the Valerie Bettis ballet based on* As I Lay Dying. *On 26 October 1949, Haas wrote Faulkner mentioning these inquiries and others that Haas had forwarded to him. Ober discussed with Haas the matter of the many items of miscellaneous rights to Faulkner works which had been raised with him over the years. Ober was willing to continue processing such inquiries, but because most of these rights were controlled by Random House, both he and Haas felt they should go there, and Haas asked for Faulkner's concurrence. Ober would continue to handle short stories, essays, letters and serial rights to novels.*

To Robert K. Haas — TS. RH
Saturday [5 Nov. 1949] — [Oxford]

Dear Bob:

The answer to your letter is Yes, Certainly, By All Means. I have mislaid it, or I would annotate the letter itself for your files; I hope this will suffice. I have been so amazingly fortunate in publishers and agents, that I dont even read contracts, just sign them. I imposed on Harold through ignorance, and I now realise I imposed a lot. From now on, of course I will refer all these things to Random House. When I received such communications, I simply sent them on to Harold, as *his* agent, to keep his records straight. I will now do the same with Random House.

I still hope to come up to town some time. Two of the old members died, so I have inherited the secretaryship of our deer hunting club, and will be engaged with it until after the deer season is over, Dec. 1. That is late to come up, and besides, I am trying to stay within a budget for this year on money. But I may come up for a week or so early in Dec., as I want to have a talk with you, imposing again on your kindness, about sticking away some of next year's money into something like an annuity, which will depend of course on how much I can draw for next year. It can be done by mail, but I would rather talk to you in person, besides a few days in town with all of you who have been my good friends for many years and whom I see seldom enough as is. I'll write later about coming up.

Please forgive delay. I repeat, anything you do in Faulkner book affairs has already received my ok.

Yours,
[s] Bill
[s] William Faulkner

To Saxe Commins — TS. RH
Wednesday [probably 16 Nov. 1949] — Oxford

Dear Saxe:

Yours at hand. I have looked for the pages, but cant find them.[1] They must be here somewhere; as soon as I can locate them, I will attend to the matter. Please excuse me.

Will you send me 10 copies of Knight G.

Leaving Friday for a week in deer hunting camp; while I'm gone they will overhaul my work-room, and the sheets will turn up then I know.

Still hoping to see you this year or winter.

Bill

[in crayon:] Also, one Intruder in Dust

[1] Commins had sent sheets which Faulkner was to autograph for a special limited edition of *Knight's Gambit*.

To Robert K. Haas — TS. RH

Tuesday [29 Nov. 1949] — [Oxford]

Dear Bob:

I had a good hunt this year, but missed my stag, three times, easy shots, couldn't get the rifle on him somehow. But it wasn't much of a head, so it was not too bad.

I will need a thousand dollars to finish this year; will you please send it at once, as I am about overdrawn already.

I'm glad you liked the picture.[1] I thought it pretty good, myself. Last night, lying in bed, I suddenly realised that I was bored, which means I will probably go to work on something soon.

Because of finances, I probably wont come up to town until after 1950 new year.

yours,
Bill

[1] *Intruder in the Dust.*

To Dayton Kohler — TS. FCVA

10 Jan. 1950 — Oxford, Miss.

Dear Mr Kohler:

Thank you for sending the piece from College English.[1] I agree with it; I mean, re Faulkner's aim. You and Cowley have both seen it, along with Prof. Warren Beck of Wisconsin[2] and one twenty-one-year-old Tennessee school girl,[3] and who knows, maybe a dozen or a hundred others; I have not wasted time and ink after all; not that that's important, since first and last, a man really writes simply because he likes to; it is his cup of tea.

I think he also discovers pretty soon in his career that having nothing to his hand but language, he is doomed to about the damndest clumsiest frailest awkwardest tool he could have been given. But it also proves that if you just keep on trying to say a thing long enough and hard enough, it will emerge; someone will hear it; though this, the fact that someone capable of hearing it sooner or later does, may actually only prove man: his soul, divinity. In either case, it's a good workable excuse for Faulkner's writing style.

Thank you again for the piece.

William Faulkner

re opening. Am proud to have belonged to RAF even obscurely. But had no combat service nor wound.

[1] Professor of English at the Virginia Polytechnic Institute, Kohler had published "William Faulkner and the Social Conscience," *College English,* 11 (Dec. 1949), 119–27.

[2] See Warren Beck, "Faulkner and the South," *Antioch Review,* I (Spring 1941), 82–94, and "Faulkner's Point of View," *College English,* II (May 1941), 736–49.

[3] Joan Williams of Memphis, a student at Bard College.

In August 1949, Mr. and Mrs. John Reed Holley of Oxford had invited Mrs. Holley's cousin, twenty-one-year-old Joan Williams, to come from her home in Memphis and visit them. Determined on a writing career since high school, Miss Williams asked Holley if she could meet William Faulkner, whose work she admired greatly. Holley, a one-time playmate of Faulkner's stepdaughter and stepson, arranged a meeting, but the visit of the Holleys and Miss Williams to Rowan Oak to see Faulkner was brief and unsatisfactory. Upon returning home, Miss Williams wrote Faulkner, attempting to explain her hopes and aims and asking questions she felt he, as a successful writer, might be able to answer. Thereafter they occasionally exchanged letters and met briefly. During her junior year at Bard College, Miss Williams had entered Mademoiselle's *short-story contest and had been named one of the winners. Her story was "Rain Later,"* Mademoiselle *(Aug. 1949), 229, 331–35.*

To Joan Williams — TS. FCVA

Sunday night [postmarked 13 Jan. 1950] — [Oxford]

. . . .

I read the piece in Mlle. It's all right. You remember? 'to make something passionate and moving and true'? It is, moving and true, made me want to cry a little for all the sad frustration of solitude, isolation, aloneness in which every human being lives, who for all the blood kinship and everything else, cant really communicate, touch. It's all right, moving and true; the force, the passion, the controlled heat, will come in time. Worry because it's—you think—slow; you've got to worry; that's part of it: the suffering and the working, most of all the working, the being willing and ready to sacrifice everything for it—happiness, peace, money, duty too if you are so unlucky. Only, quite often, if you are really willing to sacrifice any and everything for it, everything will not be required, demanded by the gods.

I think I ought to see something more, what do you think, whether you consider it all right or not. . . .

Faulkner

On 2 February 1950, Faulkner arrived in New York for a ten-day visit. Joan Williams came down from Bard, and he talked with her about a play he had in mind which would eventually bear the title of a short story Faulkner had begun on 17 December 1933 but never completed: Requiem for a Nun. *He had been encouraging her to strike out on her own if necessary to further her writing career, and he hoped to aid her in finding a job with a magazine. He also invited her to collaborate with him on the play. Departing for Oxford on 12 February, he began the play on the train home. The next day, he sent Joan three pages of notes penned on Hotel Algonquin stationery, in sketchy form setting forth the opening curtain for Act One as a defendant named Nancy heard a murder charge read against her and replied, "Guilty, Lord."*

To Joan Williams — MS. FCVA
[13 Feb. 1950] — [Oxford]

You can begin to work here. This act begins to tell who Nancy is, and what she has done. She is a 'nigger' woman, a known drunkard and dope user, a whore with a jail record in the little town, always in trouble.[1] Some time back she seemed to have reformed, got a job as nurse to a child in the home of a prominent young couple. Then one day suddenly and for no reason, she murdered the child. And now she doesn't even seem sorry. She seems to be making it almost impossible for the lawyer to save her.

So at the end of this act, everybody, sympathy is against her. She deserves to hang, a sentiment which reflects even on the lawyer defending her.

. . . .

[no signature]

[1] This Nancy Mannigoe was much like the Negro prostitute and supposed cocaine addict named Nancy whom Faulkner had portrayed in "That Evening Sun Go Down," *American Mercury,* XXII (Mar. 1931), 257–67, revised as "That Evening Sun" in *These 13* and reprinted in *Collected Stories of William Faulkner* (1950). In the unfinished short story entitled "Requiem for a Nun" and dated 17 Dec. 1933, a black couple stood before Gavin Stevens in his office, the woman's throat bandaged.

To Joan Williams MS. FCVA
Friday [possibly 17 Feb. 1950] [Oxford]

. . . .

Anything we do on this first draft may have no connection at all with the finished one. Let it change itself in either your hands or mine while we are getting it on paper; we expect that.

So herewith is not only a few pages of play, but (as I see it now) a kind of synopsis of it. I wont remind you of your school work again; I'll just leave it with you to work—think—on the play when you feel you can. Rewrite this first scene if you want to, write any of the rest of it; this is just *first* draft; all we want is to get something on paper to pull apart and save what is good and right.

. . . .

[no signature]

To Mrs. Robert K. Haas MS. MRS. HAAS
Monday [probably 20 Feb. 1950] [Oxford]

Dear Merle—

This is to thank you—try—again for my pleasant stay in town.

The paints have not come yet, though they are in the post office today, and maybe I can send you a sample effort soon.[1]

I had such a nice time at your house, the lunch, the shopping, the talking. Am writing the play now, began it on the train last Sunday; have almost one act.

Tell Bob I will write soon, and my best to Priscilla and her nice husband.

Bill

[1] Mrs. Haas had helped Faulkner to select some watercolors and brushes.

To Joan Williams TS. FCVA
Wednesday night [22 Feb. 1950] [Oxford]

. . . .

I dont know anything about the Nobel matter. Been hearing rumors for about three years, have been a little fearful. It's not the sort of thing to decline; a gratuitous insult to do so but I dont want it. I had rather be in the same pigeon hole with Dreiser and Sherwood Anderson, than with Sinclair Lewis and Mrs. Chinahand Buck.[1]

. . . .

I have got the first act laid out, rough draft of about twelve pages. You had better get your own work along before you look at it though, hadn't you? Anyway, I wont send anything until you write for it.

. . . .

Bill

[1] The Nobel Prize for Literature had been awarded to Sinclair Lewis for 1930 and Pearl S. Buck for 1938.

To Joan Williams — MS. FCVA
Thursday night [2 March 1950] — [Oxford]

. . . .

I tell you again, the play is yours too. If you refuse to accept it, I will throw it away too. I would not have thought of writing one if I hadn't known you[1]. . . . I have the notes you sent: they are all right, so all right there is no need to comment on them. The thing now is to get *everything* down on paper, even, written of course, to be cleaned and made right later, which it will be or neither of us will be content with it. You will help, you will do your own work too of course; that should come first: you do that, and I will keep on at the play until you can take up on it; no hurry.

. . . .

[no signature]

[1] In 1933, Dean Faulkner had brought Ruth Ford, then a graduate student in philosophy at the University of Mississippi, to Rowan Oak to meet William and Estelle Faulkner. In 1943, Ruth Ford was an actress under contract at Warner Bros. Faulkner was working there as a script writer, and they met again. One day, she said to him, "The one thing I want most in the world is for you to write me a play." He was noncommittal, but it may have occurred to him, as he worked on Warner Bros. screenplays, that there were dramatic possibilities in the sequel to *Sanctuary* which he had meditated.

To Joan Williams — TS. FCVA
Wednesday [22 Mar. 1950] — [Oxford]

Dear Joan,

You wrote you will reach home 5th–6th, until the following Tuesday; wasn't that it? We should be able to meet twice, anyway. Your family will want most of your time probably, but maybe you could come down here one day, and I will come up one day. That is, we will do one or the other as soon as you are home. Talk, lay out work, then you can work, telephone me when you need, until the last day of visit, then we will meet again and plan how to carry on when you are back at school.

. . . .

Bill

[in ink:] 2nd act going slow but it moves. Maybe you can write the 3rd one while you are at home.

Marjorie Lyons was reading Faulkner while her husband was doing graduate work at Indiana University. Puzzled that the reporter in Pylon *was not referred to by a proper name, she wrote Faulkner.*

To Marjorie Lyons MS. MRS. LYONS
[postmarked 28 Mar. 1950] [Oxford]

What reporter? The only one I can think of in connection with my work is the one in Pylon. He had no name. He was not anonymous: he was every man. I think that every young man, no matter how ugly—dwarf, freak, cripple, halitosis, all—has once in him the capacity for one great love and sacrifice for love, to a loved one, a beloved. But most of us miss it. We are dumb ourselves and fail to get it across, or we choose (if there is choice) the wrong one, either unworthy, or too big, too strong for us, out of our class anyway. That: what he did. Tragic, sad, true; but better than nothing. In fact, the best is not to be loved, but to love; if you have read far enough, you will remember another character of mine who said 'Between grief and nothing, I will take grief.'[1]

Faulkner

[1] Harry Wilbourne in *The Wild Palms*.

In the spring of 1950, Mark Van Doren informed Faulkner that he had been chosen to receive the Howells Medal by the American Academy, which bestows it once every five years for distinguished work in American fiction. Van Doren invited Faulkner to accept the medal at the Joint Ceremonial of the Institute and the Academy on 25 May.

To Mark Van Doren
1 April 1950

TS. AMERICAN ACADEMY
OF ARTS AND LETTERS
Oxford, Miss.

Dear Mr. Van Doren:

Thank you for your letter. I deeply appreciate this honor; nothing makes a man feel better than for his fellow craftsmen publicly and concretely to depose that his work is all right.

I would like to be present, of course. I am very sorry that right now I cant even say No. I am a farmer this time of year; up until he sells crops, no Mississippi farmer has the time or money either to travel anywhere on. Also, I doubt if I know anything worth talking two minutes about.

But you cant hang half fast and half loose just because I do, so perhaps the best is for me to say I will not be able to come up in May, and in great pride for the honor and gratitude for the letter, I am

Yours truly,
William Faulkner

Ben Wasson had been waiting for Faulkner to send the excerpt from his fable, the piece about the horse race which was to be published in Greenville by the Levee Press.

To Ben Wasson
Tuesday [18 Apr. 1950]

MS. *Delta Review,*
2 (July–Aug. 1965), 45
[Oxford]

Ben. please excuse this delay. am busy farming now; also writing a play at odd times, and just forgot it. Come over and see me when you can.

Bill

To Robert K. Haas
[received 15 May 1950]

TS. RH
[Oxford]

Dear Bob:

Unless something happens at the last minute, I wont come up for that affair the 25th.[1] Busy getting some farming done this time of year.

Have two acts on my play. I realise more than ever that I cant write a play, this may have to be rewritten by someone who can. It may be a novel as it is. Will know more when finished, and you and Ober can look at it. Maybe we can print it as a book first, let me reserve right to try a play first, that sort of thing.

. . . .

Bill

[1] Presentation of the Howells Medal by the American Academy.

To Bennett Cerf — TS. RH
Monday [probably 15 May 1950] — [Oxford]

Dear Bennett:

Celebrating your birthday would fetch me up where the academy business wouldn't move a peg. But I dont think I can come up now. I am busy farming and trying to stretch out my money as usual; also I am 2 acts away on a play which, as I just wrote Bob, may not be a play at all and I will have to write it first as a novel. Will finish the first rough draft and know more about it.

My best to Phyllis,[1] and I wish I could come up. If I do, it will be at the last minute. I have already told the ac. I dont think I will be there, and I probably will stick to it.[2] Too many people for one thing, if no other reason.

Yours,
Bill

[1] Mrs. Bennett Cerf.
[2] Faulkner stayed home and received the medal by mail.

To Joan Williams — TS. FCVA
Friday [19 May 1950] — [Oxford]

The enclosed explains itself.[1] Bob's note of yesterday, mentioned here, said for us to let him know when you are ready to hunt a job, and he would lend a hand too.

I suggest you write Mrs Rosin at once. You will know what to say; if you are not quite ready to commit yourself now, you could ask her permission to get in touch with her when she comes back from Europe, when you will know better how to arrange your affairs at home, to come to New York for permanence: you know the sort of thing.

. . . .

You will have two 'clubs' to hold over your Memphis ties now: Mrs Rosin, and what Haas will be able to do. You could come home, acquiesce to what extent, and pull out after your people are more reconciled. While you are at home in Memphis, you can work on the play. If it comes off, it will be enough to get you back east. If it doesn't then you can use Bob or Mrs Rosin. Or, if you are not too sure you can break away, once you are back in Memphis, we can try Haas and Mrs Rosin now, and you can make the break with your people before they get you back here. But you have got a lot more time than you think you have got. They cant keep you in Memphis when you really want to get out. Remember that. Dont take my advice too hard. There may be more in your background than I know about; all I can answer is what you write to me.

I will not come up for the medal thing.

Am about done with my version of 3rd act. It is not a play, will have to be rewritten as a play. It is now some kind of novel, can be printed as such, rewritten into a play. Of course, we'll make no commitment until after we decide together, we'll just finish it and hold until we get together on it.

. . . .

[no signature]

[1] A letter from Haas to Faulkner saying that Mrs. Axel Rosin, the daughter of Harry Scherman, head of the Book-of-the-Month Club, would be delighted to try to help Joan and suggesting that Joan write her as soon as possible.

On 25 January 1950, Saxe Commins had written that he and Donald Klopfer were thinking about issuing the proposed volume of Faulkner's selected short stories in August. He asked for a response from Faulkner.

To Saxe Commins — TS. RH

Saturday [probably mid-May 1950] — [Oxford]

Dear Saxe:

You and Don were both right about the collection and I was wrong;[1] I mean, about the time and the place for it. I was worse than wrong; stupid; I didn't seem to understand what 'collection' meant. It's all right; the stuff stands up amazingly well after a few years, 10 and 20. I had forgotten a lot of it; I spent a whole evening laughing to myself about the mules and the shingles.[2]

My best to all. Hope I can come up this winter.

Bill

[1] Meditating *Knight's Gambit,* Faulkner had felt that the publication of a volume of selected stories would be premature.

[2] "Mule in the Yard," *Scribner's,* XCVI (Aug. 1934), 65–70, and "Shingles for the Lord," *The Saturday Evening Post,* CCXV (13 Feb. 1943), 14–15, 68, 70, 71.

To Robert K. Haas — TS. RH
Tuesday [probably mid-May 1950] — Oxford

Dear Bob:

The present mss. is coming all right. I have finished first draft of the story, the play, and am now writing the three introductory chapters which hold the 3 acts together. I could finish it in two weeks if needed, but dont feel the need to have it in to you until next year, for next fall printing at earliest; besides, it will be something to work on during the bad weather this winter.

Just wrote Saxe that I was badly wrong about the collected volume, and he and Don were right.

Want to buy a new tractor; old one has finished its fifteenth year, and should be retired. So I want to draw $5000.00 more, please.

My best to everybody. I hope I can come up this winter sometime.

Bill

To Robert K. Haas — TS. RH
Monday [22 May 1950] — [Oxford]

Dear Bob:

I have your letter. I'm sure Mrs Rosin is right; I wrote Joan and suggested that she write Mrs Rosin.

I have finished first draft of the play. I will rewrite it. That is, my version or complete job will be a story told in seven play-scenes, inside a novel; it will run about 200 typed double-spaced pages. This summer, I will set Joan at it, see if she can lift the play scenes and condense the long speeches into a workable play script. Then get advice from some playwright who knows how to do it. Mine will print as a book, will be—to me—an interesting experiment in form. I think it's all right.

Got caught in a squall Friday and blew my sloop over, lost my toolbox and my pants containing wallet with hundred and ten dollars just collected from sale of pigs. Sat on hull 5 hours until drifted close enough to shore to swim in. Got boat up next day, dried out and no harm done except loss of rudder, and all the battens blew out of the mainsail. Was short handed and couldn't get it down fast enough. Also found when the hull rolled bottom-up that the centerboard was jammed and had never come down, which may have been why she failed to luff in time.

No, I haven't opened a tube of the paints yet, just haven't got around to it, I suppose, between farming and writing and training a colt for my daughter, helping her that is.

I put away the $5000.00 and I imagine will run out of money before long.

I can draw on you again, cant I? Do you notice this new typewriter ribbon? Dont look like me, does it?

[in ink:] My love to Miss Merle.

Bill

To Harold Ober TS. FCVA
Saturday [1 July 1950] Oxford

Dear Harold:

The enclosed is a by-product of my play.[1] I would like to have a Sat Eve Post price for it. But I feel that every writer (old bloke) owes some gesture to the Harper golden issue, whatever they call it, planned for this fall.

In case you dont get a good price anywhere, I suggest them. I suppose they wouldn't think about meeting Post price.

Bill

[1] "A Name for the City," *Harper's*, CCI (Oct. 1950), 200–14, would become the prologue to Act I of *Requiem for a Nun* (1951) under the title "The Courthouse (A Name for the City)."

To Joan Williams TS. FCVA
Thursday [3 Aug. 1950] [Oxford]

. . . .

What do you think of this? This is what sends Temple back to Jefferson. If this were film, we could show the scene: a California beach say. But in a play, Temple had probably better tell Gavin (the lawyer) this: she and the little boy on a beach, Temple reading perhaps, the boy with a toy shovel and pail.

CHILD

Mama, we're a long way from Jefferson now, aren't we?

TEMPLE (reading)

Yes, a long way.

CHILD

How long are we going to stay here?

TEMPLE

As long as we want to.

CHILD

Will we stay here until they hang Nancy?

TEMPLE (reacts now, listening, probably knows what's coming but it's too late to stop now.)

CHILD

Where will we go then?[1]

[no signature]

[1] See *Requiem for a Nun*, p. 78.

To Joan Williams — TS. FCVA

Friday night [29 Sept. 1950] — [Oxford]

Yours today. I have an idea for you. . . . A young woman, senior at school, a man of fifty, famous—could be artist, soldier, whatever seems best. He has come up to spend the day with her. She does not know why, until after he has gone. They talk, about everything, anything, whatever you like. She is more than just flattered that a man of fame has come up to see her; she likes him, feels drawn to an understanding, make it wisdom, of her, of people, man, a sympathy for her in particular; maybe he will of a sudden talk of love to her. But she will know that is still not it, not what he came for; she is puzzled a little; when he gets on the train, she is sad, probably worried; she does not know why, is uncomfortable because she is troubled. There is something inconclusive, yet she cannot imagine what conclusion there could be between the two of them. But she knows he came for some reason, and she failed to get it, whether he thought she would or not or is disappointed that she didn't. Then she finds why he came, what he wanted, and that he got it. She knows it the next day; she receives a telegram that he is dead, heart; she realises that he knew it was going to happen, and that what he wanted was to walk in April again for a day, an hour.[1]

Write that one, fairly short, objectively, from the outside, 3rd person, but of course from the girl's point of view. You can do it. . . .

. . . .

Bill

[1] Cf. Col. Cantwell and Renata in Ernest Hemingway's *Across the River and into the Trees*, published that month.

Joan Williams continued to encounter problems arising out of the conflict between her own career aims and the claims of her family.

To Joan Williams — TS. FCVA
Friday [3 Nov. 1950] — [Oxford]

. . . .

. . . People need trouble, fret, a little of frustration, to sharpen the spirit on, toughen it. Artists do; I dont mean you need to live in a rathole or gutter, but they have to learn fortitude, endurance; only vegetables are happy.

. . . .

Bill

In March 1946, Faulkner was visited at Rowan Oak by Thorsten Jonsson, who had worked in New York during the war as the correspondent of Dagens Nyheter, *Stockholm's biggest daily newspaper. Returning home at the war's end, Jonsson was one of the first in Sweden to translate Faulkner's stories and to introduce his work with warm praise to his countrymen. On a tour of the United States with a group of Swedish newspapermen at the time of this visit, Jonsson told Faulkner, "Someday you will receive the Nobel Prize for Literature." Thereafter, Faulkner heard similar predictions, and in early November of 1950 newspaper stories appeared listing him as one of the leading contenders for the award. It had actually been voted to him by fifteen of the eighteen members of the Swedish Academy the previous year, but because the vote had to be unanimous, it was resolved that there should be no award for 1949. The three dissenters subsequently decided to vote for Faulkner, but it was too late to award the prize for that year. On the morning of 10 November 1950, Sven Ahman, New York correspondent of* Dagens Nyheter, *telephoned to tell Faulkner that he had been named Laureate in Literature for 1949.*

To Sven Ahman — TS. MR. AHMAN
16 Nov. 1950 — Oxford, Miss. U.S.A.

Dear Mr Ahman:

The following is a statement which is an explanation of my reply to the formal notification from the Secretary of the Swedish Academy of the Nobel award to my work, which the Secretary should have and perhaps should receive directly from me. I make it to you, since your predecessor, Mr Jonsson, was my first personal contact with Sweden, and because it was your thoughtful kindness which first intimated to me from Sweden of the award, but with the further request on your kindness that you submit it first to the Academy Secretary and have his authorization to print it, if it should be public, any part of it, that is.

The notice from the Secretary included an invitation to be present at the festival in Stockholm. I replied that I would be unable to be present.

It may be impossible for the canons of procedure of the Academy in these circumstances to accept that statement; certainly I will do nothing to violate its canons or show anything but respect to the Academy and the Swedish people.

This is the elaboration of the statement. I hold that the award was made, not to me, but to my works—crown to thirty years of the agony and sweat of a human spirit, to make something which was not here before me, to lift up or maybe comfort or anyway at least entertain, in its turn, man's heart. That took thirty years. I am past fifty now; there is probably not much more in the tank. I feel that what remains after the thirty years of work is not worth carrying from Mississippi to Sweden, just as I feel that what remains does not deserve to expend the prize on himself, so that it is my hope to find an aim for the money high enough to be commensurate with the purpose and significance of its origin.

I leave to your discretion the printing of this; I ask only that you first ask the authority of the Academy.

Thank you again for your kindness in communicating with me.

Yours truly,
[s] William Faulkner
[t] William Faulkner

One of those involved in persuading the reluctant Faulkner to go to Sweden to receive the prize was Hon. Erik Boheman, Swedish Ambassador to the United States.

To Erik Boheman
27 Nov. 1950

TELEGRAM SWEDISH ROYAL MINISTRY
FOR FOREIGN AFFAIRS
Oxford, Miss.

RETURNED HUNTING TRIP TODAY. RECEIVED YOUR LETTER NOV 21ST. WILL BE PLEASED TO JOURNEY STOCKHOLM. APPRECIATE VERY MUCH YOUR UNDERSTANDING. WILLIAM FAULKNER

In a characteristic response to an apparently insoluble dilemma—not wanting to go to Stockholm but being pressured into it by his government, his family and his friends—Faulkner had begun to drink heavily in hunting camp. In addition, he had caught a serious cold. Neither condition improved with his return home. By the time he and Jill reached New York on 6 December, however, he was drinking less but suffering from a high fever and other symptoms of the grippe. He managed to work on his Nobel Prize acceptance speech nonetheless and had a complete draft by the time their plane landed in Stockholm on 9 December. The high point of the strenuous three-day visit came on 10 December with the presentation of the awards and the acceptance speeches. Faulkner's delivery was almost inaudible, but when his text was published the next day the effect was tremendous, and the much-reproduced speech would be regarded by many in Stockholm as perhaps the most memorable ever given by a Laureate in literature. The American Embassy sent back to Washington enthusiastic accounts of Faulkner's performance and the public reaction to it. After a three-day stopover in Paris and two days in London, Jill and her father returned to Oxford on 18 December—she ill with the grippe and he enormously relieved to be home.

To Erik Boheman
27 Dec. 1950

TS. SWEDISH ROYAL MINISTRY FOR FOREIGN AFFAIRS
Oxford, Miss.

Your Excellency:

Please accept my thanks for your kindness in making even more pleasant my daughter's and my most pleasant visit to your country in December.

I hope that it was within my power, and that mine and my daughter's conduct was such, to leave as high an opinion of Americans in Sweden as the regard and respect for Sweden which we brought away.

Respectfully,
William Faulkner

To Mrs. Robert K. Haas
Wednesday, 27 [Dec. 1950]

TS. MRS. HAAS
[Oxford]

Dear Merle:

This is belated, though the sincere wishes are not, were in existence long before the day to offer them.

We are at home again, lots of family, plenty of Xmas. Missy is still trying to adjust herself to her experience, get things sifted into order so she can tell people all she saw and did.

I dont at all regret going to Stockholm now; I realise it was the only thing to do; you can commit mistake and only feel regret, but when you commit bad taste, what you feel is shame. Anyway, I went, and did the best I knew to behave like a Swedish gentleman, and leave the best taste possible on the Swedish palate for Americans and Random House. I hope to see you soon, and tell you all about it.

My best to Bob and the children, and please accept the seasonal wishes which are not seasonal from me to you, because seasons dont have anything to do with them; they are constant.

Bill

To Robert K. Haas — TS. RH
Monday [1 Jan. 1951] — [Oxford]

Dear Bob:

Thank you for your note. The piece[1] was what I believe and wanted to say, though I might have said it better with more time to compose it. But then, maybe not; I might have lost its thread in trying to make literature out of it.

I found your letter here. The section of the big work will take some cleaning up. Now, I want to finish the Requiem for a Nun mss. so I wont divert to the other one until this is done. I have about a month's farm work, building new pasture, etc.; that and the mss. will keep me busy until March probably. As soon as I finish the mss. I would like to bring it up, ask Bob Sherwood[2] maybe to look at the play part of it and tell me whether it is a play or whether I can write a play or not. In either case, we can print it as a book, a novel, next fall, cant we?

I have put aside my prize money while I learn enough about finance to decide how to use it as I plan. I shant touch it at all until I have decided.

May I have $10,000.00 from my account?

I still have the damned cold, which I carried from deer camp to N.Y. to Europe and back. I aim to keep it now until Easter: a record. Otherwise, I feel fine, and am anxious to get back to work. Jill sends her respectfullest and kindest.

[in ink:] The dress suit came. Will write Bennett soon.

Bill

[1] Faulkner's Nobel Prize acceptance speech.
[2] Playwright Robert E. Sherwood, three-time Pulitzer prizewinner in drama.

To Phillip E. Mullen[1] TS. MR. MULLEN
[probably Jan. 1951] [Oxford]

Dear Phil:

Thank you for letter and pictures. Enclosed is a clipping from Ben Wasson, Greenville, and a letter. The letter is interesting. I fear that some of my fellow Mississippians will never forgive that 30,000$ that durn foreign country gave me for just sitting on my ass and writing stuff that makes my own state ashamed to own me.

Yours
Bill

[1] Associate editor, the Oxford *Eagle*.

To Joan Williams TS. FCVA
Sunday [28 Jan. 1951] [Oxford]

You will write, some day. Maybe now you haven't anything to say. You have to have something burning your very entrails to be said; you dont have that yet but dont worry about it; it is not important whether you write or not; writing is important only when you want to do it, and nothing nothing nothing else but writing will suffice, give you peace.

. . . .

I'm leaving Thursday,[1] by air. I would like to have our act three section—you have it: two or so pages, first pages, not carbons, the scene in the jail. That's the only copy I have. If you can get in the mail—No, I was about to say send it to Oxford. But just hold it, I will send you a California address and you can send it to me there. If you send it here, it might not reach me before I leave. I am getting the mss. in good shape I think, though this job will interrupt it for a while. I should be done with Cal. by April though.

. . . .

Bill

[1] On or about 1 Feb. 1951, Faulkner went to Hollywood to work for Howard Hawks on the script of the film *The Left Hand of God.*

To Joan Williams MS. FCVA
[11 Feb. 1951] The Beverly-Carlton
Beverly Hills [Cal.]

Here I am now until about March 1st. Fantastic place, fantastic work, almost worth the 2000 a week they pay me. Send the 3rd act to me here. I wish I could see you. Talked to your mother when I passed through Memphis that day. Tell me about the job.

Bill

To Joan Williams — MS. FCVA
Sunday [4 Mar. 1951] — The Beverly-Carlton

This one is very belated. I have been very busy, I was to get a bonus by writing the script within 4 weeks which I successfully accomplished this morning, with one day to spare. I will go back home in about a week—10 days. Will be in New York some time between April 10–May 1.

. . . .

This is a nice town full of very rich middle class people who have not yet discovered the cerebrum, or at best the soul. Beautiful damned monotonous weather, and I am getting quite tired of it, will be glad to farm again. . . .

Bill

Faulkner planned to resume work on his fable as soon as he had finished with Requiem for a Nun. *He was now planning a trip which would take him to places such as Verdun, where he could see scenes he would describe. Before departing for New York on the first leg of the trip, he sent what Commins called "the second section" of the work. It arrived on 2 April. The introduction or prologue within Act One he had called "THE COURTHOUSE (A Name for the City)." In the printed volume, the prologue to Act Two would be called "THE GOLDEN DOME (Beginning Was the Word)." With the material Faulkner sent was a query about the parenthetical phrase.*

To Saxe Commins — MS.[1] MRS. SAXE COMMINS
[late Mar. 1951] — [Oxford]

Re title—Act II—The Golden Dome
(Beginning Was——)
What I wanted here was to paraphrase Eliot,
'In the beginning was the Word,
Superfetation of τὸ ἕν.'[2]
I dont know Greek.
Can we use
(Beginning Was τὸ ἕν)?
If not, (Beginning Was the Word)

[no signature]

[1] Faulkner wrote the note in ink. It is set in type in Meriwether, *The Literary Career*, p. 36.
[2] From T. S. Eliot's "Mr. Eliot's Sunday Morning Service."

In New York, Faulkner concluded some business before leaving for Europe on 15 April 1951.

To Robert K. Haas — TS. RH
April 13, 1951 — Random House, Inc.

Dear Bob:

I would like it understood between us that in the event of my death Random House is to continue as the publishers of all my literary work, previously published as well as what may remain unpublished.

It is my wish that Saxe Commins have the final authority in connection with all material submitted for publication after my death. By this I mean authority as to what is to be published; how it is to be edited; deletions, corrections, etc. I would also like him to act in an advisory capacity in connection with any manuscripts of mine to be sold or given to museums or libraries. In other words, I would like Saxe to act as my literary executor and as editor for all my past and future literary work.

If this is agreeable to you and to Saxe, I would appreciate your signing the copy of this letter for Random House and Saxe's signing it as to the duties which I have requested him to perform.

Yours very sincerely,
[s] William Faulkner
[t] William Faulkner

[s] Robert K. Haas, V.P.
[s] Saxe Commins

At the Nobel ceremonies, Faulkner had met Else Jonsson, the widow of Thorsten Jonsson. An employee of the house of Bonniers, Faulkner's Swedish publisher, she helped to entertain Faulkner during his stay in Stockholm and they became friends.

To Else Jonsson — TS. MRS. JONSSON
[23 May 1951] — [Oxford]

Mss. going pretty well. It will be a good book. I have one more to do, the big one (Verdun) and then I have a feeling that I shall be through, can break the pencil and cast it all away, that I have spent 30 years anguishing and sweating over, never to trouble me again.

. . . .

Bill

To Else Jonsson | TS. MRS. JONSSON
[4 June 1951] | [Oxford]

The mss. is about finished. I'll be glad; I am tired of ink and paper; I have been at it steadily now since New Year's, look forward to spending the summer planting dirt, raising crops and cattle and training horses; have a perfectly beautiful new foal, a filly (mare), born last week, out of Jill's gaited saddle mare, Peavine's Jewel, and a stallion of a friend, named Ridgefield Rex. The baby's name is Ridgefield's Temptress.

. . . .

Bill

To Else Jonsson | TS. MRS. JONSSON
[9 June 1951] | [Oxford]

I finished the mss. yesterday.[1] I am really tired of writing, the agony and sweat of it. I'll probably never quit though, until I die. But now I feel like nothing would be as peaceful as to break the pencil, throw it away, admit I dont know why, the answers either.

. . . .

Bill

[1] *Requiem for a Nun.*

To Saxe Commins | TS. RH
[probably early June 1951] | [Oxford]

Dear Saxe:

What do you think about setting up the mss. as I did? Like this:

ACT I
The Courthouse
(   )
The prose etc.
Scene I
The Courtroom etc.
Scene II
The Living room etc.
Scene III
The Living room

ACT II
The Golden Dome
(   )
Scene I
Governor's office
Scene II
Temple's sitting room
Scene III
Governor's office

ACT III
The Jail
(   )
Scene I
Int. Bull pen etc.

By the galleys, the words Act 1, 2, 3 precede the actual play scenes, *not* the prose prologue, as I did them, since to me the prose is not at all a prologue, but is an integrated part of the act itself.

[no signature]

To Saxe Commins — TS. RH
[probably early June 1951] — [Oxford]

Saxe:

The paragraph indentations, etc. for the narrative part should be consistent, if possible.

In Act 2 and 3, the narrative is one single sentence, no period until the end, each par. ends with ; , no indentation for the first word, Cap. letter.

Act 3, sent you today, is set up by me the same.

What do you think about setting Act 1 that way, no indentation except for the *dialogue* in quotes, each par. of narrative to begin with Cap letter, end with ; , no indent. unless the indent begins with ' ?

Note re subtitle Act 2, attached to that galley.

This is a good piece. If I were only older, and had the big book behind me, I would be almost tempted to break the pencil here and throw it away.

[no signature]

During his spring visit to Paris, Faulkner had been entertained by Gaston Gallimard, head of his French publisher, Éditions Gallimard.

To Gaston Gallimard — TS. GALLIMARD
le 14 Juin, 1951 — Oxford, Mississippi U.S.A.

Monsieur:

Priere de pardonner ce longue temps que je ne vous envois pas mes remerciements pour votre amite constantement pendant ma visite en France et a Paris. Mon excuse c'est seulment que j'etais engage completer un roman lequel sera digne, on espois sincerement, de la generosite de votre pardon.

Priere d'expresser a monsieur votre fils mes complements and mes remerciements aussi.

Tout le monde doit bien aimer la France; ici en Mississippi c'est un homme qui aime la France et Paris un petit peu encore parce qu'il se donne l'honneur croire qu'il possedois l'affection mutuel de la Maison Gallimard.

Avec mes hommages sincerements,
William Faulkner

To Joan Williams — TS. FCVA
Monday [18 June 1951] — [Oxford]

I am coming to NY in about two weeks for a few days. I have a bona fide offer from the man who produced Kiss Me Kate,[1] to produce what I still think of as our play, even though you have repudiated it. He seems to mean business about it, the galley of the novel was shown to him without my knowledge;[2] that is, I had given up trying to make a play out of it for the time being. I am coming up about a week after next, to see him; will telephone Random House tonight to learn more about it.

. . . .

Bill

[1] Lemuel Ayers.
[2] Ruth Ford had shown her set of galleys of the book to Ayers.

To Ruth Ford — TS. MISS FORD
Monday [probably 18 June 1951] — [Oxford]

Dear Ruth:

I telephoned Saxe Commins at Random House, told him about your call, and that I would consult with your producer. He agreed that Random House would keep hands off, only that he, Commins, would like to see any contract, to which I agreed. He also said that Random House, and Ober, my agent, had received inquiries about a play I was rumored to be writing. He agreed, voluntarily, to my request that Random House answer No to any subsequent inquiries on the subject.

I will come up to town, and talk the matter over. I realise the whole second act should be rewritten, that the husband should be in it too, maybe the third. I may not be playwright enough to do it. But I would like to try.

I have some farm work here this week, a part of next week, Cho Cho[1] and her husband and daughter will be here for a visit. I would like to stay here for that. Suppose I come up at the end of their visit, which will be the end of next week, say, the Monday, which will be about July 1st or something? Will that do?

Tell your man (I was so excited that I didn't remember his name) not to bother about sending me a contract, the play, part, was written for you, so no contract is needed until we have talked and decided if anything can come of the matter.

I have already thought of how to get the husband into the second act, and so break up the long speeches.

Let me know if around June 30th will be all right. I will come up as soon before then as I can, of course, for 3 or 4 days or whatever, to plan future course. It will be pretty fine if we can make a good vehicle for you. I would like to see that title in lights, myself. It's one of my best, I think: Requiem For A Nun.

Bill

[1] Victoria Fielden.

To Else Jonsson — TS. MRS. JONSSON
[22 June 1951] — [Oxford]

My new novel contains a full length play, written as a play, a producer has taken it, I am going East to consult with him next week. If it goes over, it will be in Europe next year, 1952, or anyway I may be able to wangle a workable reason to go to Europe, maybe before next year.

I was busy finishing the mss. until June 15th, will get busy again fixing up the play part of it soon, I think.

. . . .

Bill

Faulkner arrived in New York in early July and wrote short synopses of each of the acts of Requiem for a Nun. *He rewrote after conferences with Ruth Ford and Lemuel Ayers, and they went over the material again.*

To Else Jonsson — TS. MRS. JONSSON
[early July 1951] — Hotel Algonquin, New York

. . . .

Am going back home Wednesday.[1] I have done all I can for the play at present, will get back to farming, though I shall probably have to be in and out of New York later, if they begin to rehearse it when they say.

Bill

[1] 11 July 1951.

To Else Jonsson — TS. MRS. JONSSON
[19 July 1951] — [Oxford]

Dear Else,

I am at home again, spent the two weeks in NY working very hard on the play script, I'm still at it here, with plan to start rehearsal as soon as I am done, I think; I mean, that is the producer's plan, I know so little about theatre myself. Very hot here, I am farming too, changing old cotton land to pasture, have some more beef cattle now, little calves being born every now and then.

. . . .

Bill

On 20 May 1951, Malcolm Cowley had written Faulkner that Robert Coughlan, of Life *magazine, was preparing to do a piece on him. Haas and Harrison Smith interceded in Coughlan's behalf, but Faulkner remained adamant in his determination not to cooperate and to prevent the article if possible.*

To Robert K. Haas — TS. RH
Friday [3 Aug. 1951] — [Oxford]

Dear Bob:

Yours received. My point of view re. publicity piece has not changed. I still contend that my printed works are in the public domain and anyone can bat them around. But my private life and photographed face are my own and I will defend them as such to the end. I have deliberately buried myself in this little lost almost illiterate town, to keep out of the way so that news people wont notice and remember me. If, in spite of that, this sort of thing comes down here, I not only wont co-operate, I will probably do whatever I can to impede and frustrate it. You'd think, with as many people as they seem to be in this country willing to pay any price to get themselves in the public print, that they would let be one insane and eccentric enough not to want to, wouldn't you?

Am now swotting away at the play, am close to having another draft done. Farming going well, good corn and fine hay prospect. Hot as hell here though.

Please tell Saxe that everything arrived, the linen jacket is very handsome and fits perfectly. Will he please telephone Dunhill's and ask them to send me a pound of tobacco A10528, also stop in the place on Madison and get a pound of John Cotton 1 & 2 blended.

My best to everyone. Jill's school is lined up. We will leave here by car Sept 9th, should be in town about 14th or so.

Bill

To Harrison Smith — TELEGRAM RH
13 Aug. 1951 — Oxford, Miss.

PLEASE ASK HIM NOT TO COME. WILL DO ALL I CAN TO PREVENT THIS. BILL

To Else Jonsson — TS. MRS. JONSSON
[13 Aug. 1951] — [Oxford]

Dear Else,

I shall be busy with the farm here until Sept. 10th, when I will take Jill up to her Mass. school, and have a conference with the play people about that, to plan on getting it into production which I imagine will mean more re-writing, patching. I will know then just where I will do it, whether back here, or near New York. That is, after I reach New York in Sept–Oct, I will know just what I am to do from then on, where I will be.

. . . .

Bill

To Robert K. Haas — TS. RH
20 Aug.[1] — Oxford

Dear Bob:

I am thinking about writing my memoirs. That is, it will be a book in the shape of a biography but actually about half fiction, chapters resembling essays about dogs and horses and family niggers and kin, chapters based on actual happenings but 'improved' where fiction would help,[2] which will probably be short stories. I would like to use some photographs. Maybe some of my own drawings. It would probably run about novel length, it will ramble some but will mostly be confined between Rowan Oak, my home in town here, and the farm, Greenfield. What do you think of the idea?

Bill

[1] At present, it is impossible to date this letter precisely. It might have been written at almost any time after the purchase of Greenfield Farm in 1938 when Faulkner was not preoccupied with other material.

[2] Cf. the semiautobiographical "Mississippi," *Holiday*, 15 (Apr. 1954), 34–47.

To Else Jonsson — TS. MRS. JONSSON

[27 Aug. 1951] — [Oxford]

This is the beginning of harvest. We are harvesting hay, for horses and cattle. It is very hot, with thunder storms about, which may descend at any time. So you watch the sky, the weather, you gamble on weather, because the hay must not become wet between cutting and the barns, risks. So you try to guess three days ahead, lay off a section of the grass, which is clover, bean vines, etc., decide on a certain portion which you can risk, then mow it, with a tractor and a mower blade, my tractor driver, a Negro, running the machine, I watching, until he has cut what I decided to risk, the cut grass lies on the ground through one day of sunlight, then on the third day we have the full crew—the baling machine, which is run by the tractor, a broad raking thing drawn by two mules, another raking machine run from a jeep, which I drive, and five men to put the grass into the baling machine, take out the finished bales, load them onto a wagon drawn by mules, and carry them to the barn and stow them away—all in the hot sun, temperature about 95—all chaff and dust and sweat, until sundown, then I come back to the house, have a shower and a drink and sit in the twilight with another drink until supper, then bed in the heat full of the sounds of bugs, until daylight, when I get up again and go back to another section of grass, to guess again whether I can cut it before it rains or not. Then, when the hay is off the ground, the field, the earth is plowed and more seed is sown for grazing for the cattle during the winter months. In November, the corn is ripe; the same process for it; the gathering, stowing away, and always the cattle, to be vaccinated, inoculated, nursed.

. . . .

Bill

To Random House
September 25, 1951

TS. RH
[Oxford]

Gentlemen:

I hereby authorize Harold Ober to act as my agent in all matters pertaining to my play *REQUIEM FOR A NUN*. It is understood, however, that this in no way alters your participation in the earnings from dramatic, moving picture, and other rights as stipulated in the contract between Random House and myself.

[s] William Faulkner
[t] William Faulkner

To Else Jonsson
[30 Sept. 1951]

TS. MRS. JONSSON
[Oxford]

I am all over the U.S. at present, or half of it. I took Jill up to Massachusetts[1] Sept 12th, returned here last Tuesday to attend to farm work, am going back to Boston next Tuesday, Oct 2nd, to begin rewrite on the play, for rehearsal in November, opening Jan 10th if we can get it ready. Will be in Boston until Oct 15th, when I am to go to New Orleans to receive my formal Legion of Honor from the French Consul General, then probably back to Boston to work at the play.

. . . .

Bill

[1] Jill was entering Pine Manor Junior College, in Wellesley, Mass.

To Joan Williams
Wednesday [28 Nov. 1951]

TS. FCVA
[Oxford]

I cant write the story outline down; it will take too long, and I will miss too much. I will have to tell it to you. It's not a short story anyway but a short novel really; you will have to work at it. Do you want to? Dont decide now; I will have to see you and tell you first. Maybe sell it to you. . . .

It's a good idea, a good story. It has a line, a plot, now. This is a reversal, isn't it? I failed to persuade you to help me write a play; now I seem determined to help you write a novel whether you want to or not.

. . . .

[no signature]

To Else Jonsson | TS. MRS. JONSSON
[30 Nov. 1951] | [Oxford]

. . . in deer hunting camp 17th to 23rd. saw no deer, in New Orleans Nov 24th, command attendance to be sponsor for a Tulane professor who was raised from chevalier to officier of Legion, home Nov 27th, farming again, waiting (I suppose) to go back to Boston or somewhere to rewrite the damned play again, of which I am quite sick now, except that as soon as it works, the producer has agreed to take it to Europe which is to be in the spring.

. . . .

Bill

To Joan Williams | TS. FCVA
[20 Dec. 1951] | [Oxford]

. . . .

The trouble with the short story is, it doesn't move. It's static. You can write about a lazy, inner character, but the character must be told in motion. Why not start the story when she is sent to pick up Ben, instead buys the dress, lets Ben get wet because she deviated to buy the dress, show all this in action, dialogue which carries action, tell the story from the OUTSIDE instead of INSIDE. This is not an essay, remember.

Start off by seeing if you can tell the story orally to me, for instance, in one sentence. Any good story can be told in one sentence, I mean, the line, the why of it. Try it that way. About the other one. Rewrite that first letter you sent me, a young woman, girl, writing to a famous poet say, whom she called on against his will probably, and wrote to apologize: 'I didn't intend to bother you, interfere, I just wanted, hoped, you would tell me why life is, because you are wise and you know the answers.' You wrote that once, more or less; write it again, send it to me, I will answer it and outline your next letter. This story will be a series of letters.

. . . .

[no signature]

To Lemuel Ayers | TS. FCVA
29 Dec. 1951 | Oxford, Miss.

Dear Lem:

I realise that producing a play is not a one- or two-man job, nor even just a ten man job, and that signed recorded statements of agreement and intention are necessary.

This being so, I want to include in the agreement between us one other specific, specifically recorded understanding and agreement: that this play is for Ruth, the part, character-part, is hers until she herself refuses it. I'm sure you know what I am trying to say: that whatever mutations and shifts of design and control and ownership the rights to it as a play might pass through, Ruth will be protected in her first claim to this part, or an equity in the play.

I am sending a copy of this letter to Ober, you and he can work out the phrasing of it. Any way in which you and he work it out and phrase it, will be all right with me.

I have just written Ruth, as chairman of the Faulkner lost-and-found dept., my thanks for the pipe and pouch, also my promise not to lose this one.

Yours,
[t] William Faulkner

Faulkner had made a copy of his letter to Lemuel Ayers, and he sent it with a covering letter to Harold Ober.

To Harold Ober — TS. FCVA
[received 4 Jan. 1952] — [Oxford]

Dear Harold:

The enclosed copy of letter to Ayers explains what I mean. Will you attend to it? I have known Miss Ford a long time, admire her rather terrifying determination to be an actress, and wrote this play for her to abet it. Will you add a phrase or paragraph protecting her, as a part of my equity, if you like. As I will have to sign or initial that too, I am sending everything back and you can return all for my signature.

Happy New Year to you.

Bill

To Albert Marre[1] — TS. MR. MARRE
29 Dec., 1951 — Oxford, Miss.

Dear Albie:

I have just written Ruth, as chairman of the Faulkner lost-and-found, my thanks for the pipe and pouch and my promise not to lose it this time.

I have not approached Lovett[2] re the transport business, and I am convinced at last that my instinct not to do so was right. For the reason of all the mink coat deep freeze stink in govt. now.[3] I would have to approach him as a friend, asking what might be construed as a favor at govt. expense, and I dont think I should do it because it might blow up the whole plan. It should be you or the producer in your official capacities. Then, if Bob should open the matter to me from his end, I can put my shoulder to it.

My respectful duties to Miss Jan,[4] and cheer-o to Dave, and no heel taps.[5]

Yours,
Bill

[1] The director with whom Faulkner had worked on the stage version of *Requiem for a Nun* in Cambridge, Mass., in Oct. and Nov. 1951.

[2] A friend whom Faulkner had first met in New York in 1931, Robert A. Lovett had enjoyed a successful career in business and government and was now serving as Secretary of Defense.

[3] Allegations of influence-peddling with rewards of items such as mink coats and freezers had recently been made against government officials.

[4] Mrs. Marre.

[5] "Heel taps" refers to the shape of the residue left in a glass that has not been drained.

To Saxe Commins — TS. RH
Sunday [probably Jan. 1952] — [Oxford]

Dear Saxe:

Will you consult with Bob, Bennett, etc. on this, and give me your advice and information as soon as possible?

I had heard nothing about the play from Ayers or Marre either, since November, when I did the last rewriting. I heard rumors from time to time: that it was to open Jan. 10th, to open Feb. 20th, that it had already opened in fact in Cambridge.

Then Marre telephoned me last week, the play was to open in Paris May 30th. and that he would come down to see me. He is here now. He tells me that the situation is this:

Ayers was unable to raise enough money from his backers, due to the fact that the publication of the book had taken the original 'shine' off the thing. Ayers then planned to open it in Sept. this year.

Ruth, Marre, Ayers and I had talked about taking it to Europe first, last November. All favored Europe except Ayers. Ruth, who because of her known commitment to the part, had had a pretty hard winter, missing radio and t.v. jobs because her known commitment to the play had removed her from availability in people's minds, went to Ayers recently and asked, first, if he wanted any part of taking it to Europe in order to open this spring. Ayers said he didn't. Ruth then said, will you let us do it? Ayers said, yes, only to leave him out.

Marre then contacted the people in charge of the Paris festival[1] for this spring. They will accept the play into their official auspices, to open June 1st. They will put up the equivalent of $7,000.00. We will have to put up the remaining $15,000.00 which Marre estimates as top to run the play for one week, rehearsal, salaries, etc. The old-Russian painter, [Pavel Tchelitchew], will design the sets, getting back to my original version of the script. If the play runs a week, Marre believes (the French people will give us all the gate receipts) it will earn 10 or 12 thousand dollars in francs. If it is that successful, Marre has promise of 'second money' to carry it on, perhaps to London. If it is that successful, we will own the whole job, sets, tried play and all, to sell to an American producer.

The problem is this. I will have to put up the $15,000.00. Under the auspices of the festival, it will run at least a week, earn the estimated $10,000.00 back, but in francs, which I cant take out of France. That is, if it fails, I will have swapped $15,000.00 dollars for its equivalent in francs, which I cant use except in France. If it is a success, of course that wont matter.

I am inclined to risk it, since the Russian's idea sounds like me, but mainly on Miss Ford's account, who to an extent has suffered because of the delay. That is, she is shooting the works on this, her last—best—chance to make tops as an actress.

I dont mind risking the money, and even losing it, since this idea of the staging of the play sounds like me, instead of a conventional run-of-the-mill American play. But to draw this much, will run my income tax out of sight. I would risk and even lose the money, but I dont want to have to pay Uncle Sam about half of it again for the privilege.

Is there any way this can be avoided? that I could take it as a loan, to be amortised at an increase on my income of a thousand a year for fifteen years, instead of 15 thousand in one year?

The French people will have to have an answer pretty quick from me, to make their own schedule. All we need to do is, pay for the transportation, the salaries, of the American troupe, the sets, living expenses in France. The festival does the rest: rents the theatre, pays the French hands, etc., will give us all the gate.

Perhaps you had better telephone me, wire me what hour, etc. Marre will leave here about Monday, he says, but you can telephone me here, I imagine it will be about Wednesday. Think it over well.

Bill

[1] The French government was planning a festival for the spring: *Oeuvres du XXe Siècle,* which would comprise not only plays, ballets, concerts and cultural exhibits, but also a writers' conference.

To Joan Williams
Tuesday [15 Jan. 1952]

TS. FCVA
[Oxford]

The story is better now. It doesn't quite suit me, but I see now that the only way for it to seem exactly right to me, is for me to rewrite it, which I think you dont want.

. . . .

The piece is better now. You have got to write the first sentence of a story so that whoever reads it will want to read the second one. That is a good rule.

[no signature]

When Faulkner had visited England in April 1951, he was entertained by Harold Raymond, senior partner of his English publisher, Chatto & Windus.

To Harold Raymond
22 January, 1952

TS. CHATTO & WINDUS
[Oxford]

Dear Mr Raymond:

Thank you for your letter, and the enclosure. Naturally a bloke is pleased and proud that his words should be considered worth printing, though it was the letter from you which moved me most, reminding me of my most pleasant short two days with you, dinner with Mr and Mrs Cochrane and the port he gave us, and the lunch with you and Piers[1] and the honor of being presented to Mrs Raymond, and the invitation to see something of the Kentish countryside, which I still hope to avail myself of someday soon.

Wasn't it Mrs Smallwood[2] who was at Mrs Cochrane's[3] that evening? Please give my remembrances to her, and my regards to your son, and my respectful duties to Mrs. Raymond.

I snaffled his copy of W. C. Closterman's THE BIG SHOW from Saxe Commins, at Random House, last summer. A very fine job, though I still think the best of the flying ones, and (to me) the best of the war books, was Victor Yeates's WINGED VICTORY.

I have also read Mr Greene's[4] THE END OF THE AFFAIR; not one of yours, but for me one of the best, most true and moving novels of my time, in anybody's language.

Yours sincerely,
William Faulkner

[1] Harold Raymond's son, Piers.
[2] Norah Smallwood, one of the partners of Chatto & Windus.
[3] Mr. and Mrs. J. A. Cochrane gave a dinner party for Faulkner at their home in Chelsea. Cochrane was at that time a director of Chatto & Windus.
[4] Graham Greene.

To Else Jonsson — TS. MRS. JONSSON
[2 March 1952] — [Oxford]

. . . .

I stay busy, working at my big book, also farming. Am very interested now in training Temptress. She is big and strong, jerked me off her mother's back last week, because of my carelessness mainly. I didn't dare turn her or her mama's bridles loose, or they might have stepped on me or kicked me. So there I was, lying flat on my back in a mud puddle, with a frantic horse in each hand. No harm though; I learned years ago how to fall off horses.

The play is to open in Paris in May, I understand. The director is coming down next week to make plans.

Bill

To Harold Ober — TS. RH
Friday [28 March 1952] — [Oxford]

Dear Harold:

This is why I have not returned contracts.

I sent first ones back (sent all back, I cant find any extra one here) to have Ford clause included.

Albert Marre, the director, came down to see me, he said Ayers had failed to raise money, Marre had arranged to put it on in Paris May 30th, Ford had gone to see Ayers, who had declined to have any part of European production, gave Ford and Marre freedom to raise the money and produce themselves. I declined to put up 15 thousand dollars to produce in France, Marre went back N.Y. to see what he could do, telephoned he had 7500, what could I do, I wired him I would put up 2 at present.

Received second (revised) contracts from you, have held them waiting to hear from Marre. I dont know whether the play is to be put on in Paris or not. I dont know whether I am still to sign the contract with

Ayers or not, whether his okay to Ford for her and Marre to go ahead in Paris meant, with the contract to him, or if he was waiving contract with me. Will you find out about this, before giving him the contract? He has my word about it, and the papers are now signed. I just do not know what the whole understanding between him and Ford and Marre is, and what they expect me to do about it.

I have heard nothing from Marre since my wire promising 2 thousand. I assume this is not enough, but I dont know, dont want to botch his and Ford's plan by signing too quick. Marre said, if we produced ourselves, in Paris, we would own all rights to it.

I will follow your instructions.

Bill

To Else Jonsson — TS. MRS. JONSSON
[9 Apr. 1952] — [Oxford]

Dear Else,

The play in Paris has failed. The trouble was, to raise the money, U.S. money, put into a play in France, would be sunk there. It can not be taken out, but must be spent there in francs. Income tax is so high here now, that nobody will take the loss.

. . . .

Bill

On 25 March 1952, President Rufus C. Harris of Tulane University wrote Faulkner that the University wished to confer the Doctor of Letters degree upon him and invited him to attend the commencement exercises on 27 May.

To Rufus C. Harris — TS. TULANE
11 April, 1952 — Oxford, Miss.

Dear Dr. Harris:

I received with pride and humility too your letter of last month, and with regret I answer it.

I feel that, for one who did not even graduate from grammar school, to accept an honorary degree representative not only of higher learning but of post-graduate labor in it, would debase and nullify the whole aim of learning.

Please transmit to the University Senate my true appreciation of the honor offered me.

Yours sincerely,
[s] William Faulkner
[t] William Faulkner

To Robert K. Haas — TS. RH
Saturday [probably Apr. 1952] — [Oxford]

Dear Bob:

This sounds like a nice idea to me.[1] I'll be glad to discuss it further with them, re my co-operation, if they want it. How immediate is it? At present, I am trying to wangle a trip to France, the details of which Saxe can give you. I will go May 18th, until June 10th. Until that time, I will be pretty busy here farming. After June 10th, I will have plenty of time.

It's too bad about our Derby plan. Fielden, the son in law who was the Louisville resident and had the house, is now in Manila with his new company, where his family will join him this summer, so the Random H. syndicate will have to play this year via cigar stores.[2]

If the Paris trip goes through, I will see you about May 17th.

Speaking of horses, my last spring's foal is going to be a dandy, best I ever raised. She works already in harness, draws a light weight, next year a rider and I'll gait her. I have six low hurdles in the pasture and have been running Jill's quarter horse over them. The colt takes them too now.

My love to Miss Merle, and best to everyone.

Bill

[1] A proposal for a documentary film on Faulkner's work, under the auspices of the Ford Foundation.

[2] In May 1951, Faulkner had attended the Kentucky Derby and placed two-dollar bets for himself and Haas on the winner, Count Turf. The two had planned to go to the Derby this year and stay at the home of William F. Fielden.

To Else Jonsson — TS. MRS. JONSSON
[19 Apr. 1952] — [Oxford]

. . . I will not be too involved in Paris. I decline to be a delegate to anything; the words 'delegate' and 'freedom' in the same sentence are, to me, not only incongruous but terrifying too. I will not accept any commitment. I will pay my own way, give that time to the festival which will meet my conscience. That is, I will be a free agent in Paris, as far as I believe now. I will attend what meetings I wish, will leave when I want to.

. . . .

Bill

To Joan Williams TS. FCVA
Friday [possibly spring 1952] [Oxford]

. . . .

Have looked through it again. You are learning. All you need is to agonise and sweat over it, never be quite satisfied even when you know it is about as right as it can be humanly made, never to linger over it when done because you dont have time, you must hurry hurry to write it again and better, the best this time. Not the same story over again, but Joan Williams, who has the capacity to suffer and anguish and would trade it for nothing under heaven.

Write me when you have time. I am interested to know what you are doing. Are you happy, are you finding something you did not know yesterday, all about it. . . .

Saturday

You know: something new, so that it was worth living through yesterday in order to reach today; and since you know you can, will, find something new still, it will be worth living through today in order to reach tomorrow.

The mss. is still too prolix. It needs to be condensed. There is more writing than subject; you see, I read it again last night. A child's loneliness is not enough for a subject. The loneliness should be a catalyst, which does something to the rage of the universal passions of the human heart, the adult world, of which it—the child—is only an observer yet. You dont want to write just 'charming' things. Or at least I dont seem to intend to let you.

[no signature]

To Joan Williams TS. FCVA
[7 May 1952] [Oxford]

. . . .

Yes, I will make a speech at the Cotton Council meeting in Cleveland, Miss. the 15th, go to NY the 16th, to Paris 19th, home about June 15th. . . .

I'm leading a dull, busy, purely physical life these days, farming and training a colt and working every day with a jumping horse over hurdles, a long time now since I have anguished over putting words together, as though I had forgotten that form of anguishment. Which probably means that I am getting ready, storing up energy or whatever you want to call it, to start again. Which, I believe, is what is happening to you. To have written something once which you dont need to hate afterward is like having cancer; you dont really ever get over it. . . .

[no signature]

Upon arriving in New York, Faulkner found that renewed plans for taking the play to Paris had collapsed. Nevertheless, he flew to Paris via London as planned on May 19. After suffering back pain and illness in Paris, he went to England on 31 May and left there on 4 June to recuperate near Oslo, whence he would fly to New York on 14 June.

To Saxe Commins — MS. RH
Sunday [8 June 1952] — [near Oslo]

Dear Saxe—

Will cross Sat. night, arrive N.Y. Sunday. Will you see at New Weston[1] that reservation is for *Sunday*, not Saturday. Discovered in Paris that I have a broken back.[2] Will tell you about it next week.

Bill

[1] A hotel formerly at Madison Avenue and 50th Street, near Random House.
[2] X-rays taken in Paris on 27 May 1952 showed old compression fractures of the 12th dorsal and 1st lumbar vertebrae. X-rays four months later would reveal more old injuries: mild compression fractures of dorsal vertebrae 8, 9 and 10.

When Faulkner had visited Paris in April 1951, novelist-editor Monique Lange was one of those at Gallimard charged with entertaining him. In May 1952, he spent time with her and her husband, Jean-Jacques Salomon, though he did not see her on his departure because she was in the hospital for the birth of her daughter.

To Monique and Jean-Jacques Salomon — TS. MLLE. LANGE
Monday [16 June 1952] — New York

Dear Monique and Jean-Jacques

I am almost home, will be home tomorrow. I feel much better. In Oslo I found a very fine Swedish masseur, who loosened the muscles in my back and then pressed the bad vertebra back into place, so that I have no back pain at all any more, the first time in years, I realise now.

. . . In London I suffered another collapse, had an English doctor there, felt so bad when time came to go to Oslo that I could not find this ticket where I had stowed it away. I found it in Oslo but they would not redeem it there. It must be redeemed in Paris. So I send it to you. In my haste and illness, we did not attend to the gift for my god-daughter. I want you to take this money and buy something for her, in silver if you like or anything else. If silver, hers and my names can be engraved on it, to my god-daughter from son beau papa, or what you like.

. . . .

William Faulkner

In 1950, in the wake of the criticism which had greeted the serial publication of Ernest Hemingway's Across the River and into the Trees, *Evelyn Waugh had written the editor of* Time *attacking the critics who had panned the book. Faulkner then wrote the editor applauding Waugh and adding his own defense of Hemingway in a letter which appeared on 13 November 1950. On Faulkner's return from France in June 1952, his friend Harvey Breit, of the New York* Times Book Review, *asked him if he would review Hemingway's new novella,* The Old Man and the Sea. *Faulkner said he would not know how to do a review but took the book to Mississippi with him. There he wrote a statement which embodied ideas and phrases from his earlier letter and sent it to Saxe Commins to forward to Breit.*

TS. HARVEY BREIT

20 June, 1952 Oxford, Mississippi

A few years ago, I forget what the occasion was, Hemingway said that writers should stick together just as doctors and lawyers and wolves do. I think there is more wit in that than truth or necessity either, at least in Hemingway's case, since the sort of writers who need to band together willy nilly or perish, resemble the wolves who are wolves only in pack, and, singly, are just another dog.

Because the man who wrote the MEN WITHOUT WOMEN pieces and THE SUN ALSO RISES and A FAREWELL TO ARMS and FOR WHOM THE BELL TOLLS and most of the African stuff and most of all the rest of it, is not one of these, and needs no pack protection.

So he does not need even this from another writer. Maybe he doesn't even want it. So he gets this for free from one who, regardless of how he rated what remained, has never doubted the integrity of it, and who has always affirmed that no man will be quicker and harsher to judge what remained than the man who wrote MEN WITHOUT WOMEN and

THE SUN ALSO RISES and A FAREWELL TO ARMS and FOR WHOM THE BELL TOLLS and the best of the African stuff and most of the rest of it; and that if even what remained had not been as honest and true as he could make it, then he himself would have burned the manuscript before the publisher ever saw it.

[t] William Faulkner

To Saxe Commins — TS. RH
Sunday [22 June 1952] — [Oxford]

Dear Saxe:

I send the enclosed to you, since I dont know whether Harvey Brite [*sic*] has left the Times yet or not. Please send it to him, or if he is gone, maybe to send it to Hemingway's publisher would do.[1]

Here is a list of Jill's summer required reading. Will you please locate them for us and have them sent down?

Hot as hell here. I can ride, but Jill is working the horses in good shape while I sit on the rail and supervise. All are well and send love.

Bill

[1] Harvey Breit passed Faulkner's letter on to Hemingway, telling him that he planned to use it in the piece he was writing. To his dismay the letter made Hemingway furious, as he concluded that Faulkner was calling him "just another dog."

On May 15, before the Delta Council in Greenville, Mississippi, Faulkner gave a speech extolling individual independence and criticizing government policies. It was later published as an eight-page pamphlet.

To Billy Wynn — TS. *Delta Review*,
June 20th [1952] — 2 (July–Aug. 1965), 33
Oxford

Dear Billy:

I just got home two days ago, which explains delay in answering you.

The speech belongs to the Council; by all means do as you like with it. If you make the copies, will you please send me one, as I seem to have mislaid the one I had?

Thank you for your letter. Thank all the kind Delta people who made the unaccustomed ordeal of speech-making so pleasant, that it can well become a habit.

No, I didn't get a bottle of whiskey. I got twelve of them. The first drink out of each one of them is a salute to the 15th of May.

Yours sincerely,
Bill Faulkner

To Harold Raymond
28 June, 1952
Dear Mr Raymond:

TS. CHATTO & WINDUS
Oxford, Miss.

This is to thank all of you again for the pleasant dinner and evening, and to ask you to transmit my duties and remembrances to Mrs Raymond and Piers and Miss Smallwood and Mr and Mrs Lewis for the kindness I received at your hands.

My back is all right now. In Oslo I found a first rate Swedish masseur. I was with him daily for a week, until he relaxed the muscles and with his hand, set the bad vertebra back into place; the discomfort vanished at once and will continue so if I am careful for a few months, he says. I must stop away from horses for a while, which is not too high a price for being free of the back after three months of it.

I am sorry about neglecting this. I was in some pain at the time, and was not thinking too well. So I enclose herewith my check in blank, and ask you to be kind enough to discharge the doctor's fee, and any other obligations which I left behind; I think I still owe you something more in our exchange of checks for the hotel bill.

Again my thanks and best regards.

Yours sincerely to command,
William Faulkner

While he was in England, Faulkner had talked with Antony Brett-James of Chatto & Windus about the English edition of Requiem for a Nun. *Now he provided information to be used in its flap copy.*

To Antony Brett-James
8 July 1952

TS. CHATTO & WINDUS
Oxford, Mississippi

Dear Mr Brett-James:

It is not Missouri, which us folks here consider a Northern state, but Mississippi.

He considers his connection with the Royal Air Force to be, in comparison, too minor a one to warrant or bear more than the simple statement 'belonged to the Force in the First War.' After armistice, returned to Oxford, Mississippi, did odd jobs, painter, paperer, carpenter, was crew member in a Gulf of Mexico fishing trawler, did newspaper work in New Orleans, was a deck hand in Atlantic merchant freighters, returned to Oxford, became married and had really to go to work, coal heaver in power plant, barn-storming aircraft about country cow-pastures, was writing all the time, is now more farmer than writer, that is, breeds beef cattle and a few horses, does some shooting and the sort of non-pink-coat hunting of our local fashion.

That about covers him.

Yours sincerely,
William Faulkner

To Joan Williams — TS. FCVA
[11 July 1952] — [Oxford]

I think I have something for you, it may be the key to your freedom. An executive[1] I worked with at Warner's in '42 is now in television. He wants ideas, plots, not the finished actable script but just the idea, 6 or 7 pages, will pay $500 plus 3% of the net returns. He wants names of course now, but if you and I could invent something, let him have the first one under my name, I can and will work you into the picture, maybe you can establish yourself as a television writer or rewriter, you know: hack work, for pay, while you do your own writing. . . .

[no signature]

[1] James J. Geller.

Faulkner and Joan worked on a story line which Faulkner sent to Geller, who called it "The Graduation Dress." Joan's major involvement at the time, however, was with a story called "The Morning and the Evening" in which she dealt with a forty-year-old "loony" named Jake. Faulkner went over it and sent it back to her, together with a letter he intended to use to submit the story to Harper's *if she would permit it.*

To Joan Williams — TS. FCVA
[possibly 14 July 1952] — [Oxford]

Here is the story. It will have to be typed again, to be cleaned up, neated. You could either rewrite, copy it into your language, or use what of it in mine, whatever you like. I will probably still meet resistance in you which

I will hope to vanquish by seeing you face to face, since to do it by letter is too difficult. . . . I am only trying to help you become an artist. You owe me nothing in return for what I try to do or succeed in doing for you. . . .

What I am trying to say is, whatever your first reaction to what I have done with your story, dont do anything about it, I mean, adverse to the agreement that we would rewrite it together, until we have talked. . . .

[no signature]

To the editors, *Harper's* — TS. FCVA

14 July, 1952 — Oxford, Miss.

Dear Sirs:

As is probably obvious, the enclosed was written by a student of Faulkner. It is the first one I have seen in advance, which in my estimation warranted the covering letter, which letter is written and sent more or less over the protest of the author.

I hope you will look at this twice, if necessary.

Return postage enclosed; the mss. or any communication regarding it, please send to the author,

Miss Joan Williams
1243 East Parkway South,
Memphis, Tenn.

Yours sincerely,
William Faulkner

To Joan Williams — TS. FCVA

Tuesday morning [29 July 1952] — [Oxford]

. . . we now have $500.00, the check came from Mr Geller for the nine yellow pages, he calls it GRADUATION DRESS and seems to like it. . . .

. . . How is the Sat Eve Post piece coming? We might make this a business, except for the good ones like Jake; you remember, you suggested it once? Send the Sat Eve Post one in under my name for the bigger price, do others the same way, build up a back-log?

. . . .

[no signature]

To Joan Williams TS. FCVA
Friday [8 Aug. 1952] [Oxford]

. . . I still felt so rotten yesterday morning that I had to do something,[1] so suddenly I dug out the mss. of the big book[2] and went to work at it; suddenly I remembered how I wrote THE WILD PALMS in order to try to stave off what I thought was heart-break too. And it didn't break then and so maybe it wont now, maybe it wont even have to break for a while yet, since the heart is a very tough and durable substance or thing or whatever you want to call it. Did a good stint on the mss. and yesterday went sailing along all afternoon, not much wind, so I lashed sheets and tiller and stretched out on the deck looking up the mast. . . .

Read Jake again.[3] It's still all right, but maybe I shall keep it a while and think about it again. I know that in time you will do it better, and maybe that time will be soon; you may even decide yourself to write JAKE again. You must learn more. Where I beat you was, I set out to learn all I could sooner in my life than you did. I mean, the reading. . . .

[no signature]

[1] During the month of August, Faulkner reinjured his back in a boating accident.

[2] The fable.

[3] Entitled "The Morning and the Evening," the story had been rejected by *Harper's*.

To Joan Williams TS. FCVA
Tues. am. [12 Aug. 1952] [Oxford]

Ober says to send him the story. Re your analysing a story: that works with the hospital sort: not with Jake. You have to learn how to do ones like Jake from inside yourself, because JAKES are not commercial tricks, which is all anyone, Col[lege] or correspondence or anyone else, can teach from the *outside*. You have to feel Jake from inside, as you did. To write him properly, you must have not instruction nor criticism, but imagination, which you had to have to invent him, and observation and experience. Which you will get partly from reading the best which others have done, and from watching people, accepting everything. You have got to break your wall. You have got to be capable of anything, everything, accepting them I mean, not as experiments, clinical, to see what it does to the mind, like with drugs or dead outside things, but because the heart and the body are big enough to accept all the world, all human agony and passion. . . .

Am going to read Jake again now. May send it to Ober unless I can find some glaring fault which I can point out to you. But Jake is too good for that, even for me to touch. . . .

The big book going well. . . .

[no signature]

To Else Jonsson — TS. MRS. JONSSON
[19 Aug. 1952] — [Oxford]

Back not much better; probably impossible with my nature and occupation—natural nervousness, inability to be still, inactive, and the farmwork, to take care of, though I am off horses, not been on one since I got home. Though probably the great trouble is unhappiness here, have lost heart for everything, farming and all, have not worked in a year now, stupid existence seeing what remains of life going to support parasites who do not even have the grace to be sycophants. Am tired, I suppose. Should either command myself to feel better, or change life itself, which I may do; if you should hear harsh things of me, dont believe all of them. . . .

Bill

To Harold Ober — TS. FCVA
20 Aug. 1952 — Oxford, Miss.

Dear Harold:

Here is Miss Williams' story which Harper saw. I think it was truely conceived, with imagination and compassion, though possibly the fire did not quite come through onto the pages. I can be wrong about this. I felt the heat myself, though this might have been because I was biased to the extent of knowing what she was trying to do. I think she will do it, maybe next time, if she keeps trying.

I dont especially want to go to Hollywood for any reason. Re pictures, I am still primarily committed to Hawks, since he is the only one I have any success with, which means, through him, Feldman. But I will have to do hack work of some sort soon, or be broke and a nuisance to my friends again. I have the POST in mind still, but nothing of it yet. Maybe I shall have to cut completely away from my present life, at least for a time. I seem to have lost heart for working. I cant find anything to work, write, *for*. I failed to form the habit of letting money be sufficient, or even a factor, and I am not likely to earn any more glory at 55, and that doesn't leave much.

Let me know what you think of Miss W's. story. She doesn't want money: she needs the encouragement of seeing herself in print, in a mag. she will be proud of, no matter how small in circ. etc. If this one is not ready yet, tell me so.

Bill

To Joan Williams — TS. FCVA

[21 Aug. 1952] — [Oxford]

. . . .

Sent JAKE to Ober yesterday.

Why not do another tv thing for Geller, six or seven pages. You know the trick now, do one on your own, your own name alone on it, see what he says. If he wants my name too, let him have it. But try first with just yours. If he would take one from just you alone, and Ober places JAKE, then you could throw F. away too. . . .

[no signature]

To Joan Williams — TS. FCVA

Saturday [27 Sept. 1952] — [Oxford]

. . . .

. . . I have a lot to do. The Ford Foundation history of my apocryphal county,[1] a moving picture record of it, and a TV piece, from one of my stories,[2] already written. . . .

[no signature]

[1] In November, a film crew would arrive at Rowan Oak to do a documentary on Faulkner and his work. Produced under the sponsorship of the Ford Foundation, it would later be telecast on the program *Omnibus*.

[2] Probably "The Brooch," for *Lux Video Theatre*.

Working in New York for Look *magazine, Joan Williams had gone, at Faulkner's suggestion, to see his friend and former publisher, Harrison Smith.*

To Joan Williams — TS. FCVA

Saturday, 2 pm [27 Sept. 1952] — [Oxford]

. . . .

Smith is a good man for you to have seen. He will do a great deal for me that doesn't cost actual cash money. Dont hesitate to demand of him nor of anyone at Random House in my name.

. . . .

[no signature]

Harold Ober sent Faulkner a copy of a letter accepting Joan's story "The Morning and the Evening." It would appear in the Atlantic, *191 (Jan. 1953), 65–69.*

To Harold Ober — TS. FCVA

Monday [29 Sept. 1952] — [Oxford]

Dear Harold:

Thank you for sending the copy of Miss Williams' Atlantic letter. She has been my pupil 3 years now, when nobody else, her people, believed in her. I am happy to know my judgment was right.

She is shy and independent, will ask no help. But for my sake, do whatever you can for her.

Yes, I am interested in the Mississippi piece.[1] I have a fractured vertebra which has been giving me trouble since I fell off a horse last spring, and have been in hospital[2] the past week. Have done some work on the big book, and shall probably keep at it. But I will think about the Mississippi piece and write either it or you later. Is there a deadline?

I still feel pretty bad, but should improve from now on.

Bill

[1] A semiautobiographical essay requested by *Holiday*, it would appear as "Mississippi," *Holiday*, XV (Apr. 1954), 33–47.

[2] The Gartly-Ramsay Hospital in Memphis, Tenn.

Thomas H. Carter, the editor of Washington & Lee University's journal, Shenandoah, *wrote Faulkner asking him to review* The Old Man and the Sea.

To Thomas H. Carter — TS. MRS. THOMAS H. CARTER
29 Sept. 1952 — Oxford, Miss.

Dear Mr Carter:

I may be a snob, but I am not literary at all. But I did do a 3 paragraph piece on Hemingway's new book, which was honest and (I thought) about right. I sent it to critic Harvey Breit, New York Times. Would you consider writing him for a copy of that, or had you rather have a fresh one?[1]

The reason I suggest this is, that one said it and I dont want to repeat.

I have been sick is why this delay.

William Faulkner

[1] Carter did ask for a fresh one, and Faulkner sent him one paragraph which appeared in the Autumn 1952 issue of *Shenandoah* and is reprinted in *William Faulkner: Essays, Speeches & Public Letters*, p. 193.

To Else Jonsson — TS. MRS. JONSSON
[24 Oct. 1952] — [Oxford]

I have been sick. Another collapse, this one pretty bad, since September first, in hospital in Memphis, until last Monday night.[1] I am still sick, am having a brace made for my back, which may help some, I should feel stronger and less nervous and depressed by next week, and will write you a better letter then.

Bill

[1] Faulkner had returned to Gartly-Ramsay during Oct. 7–21.

To Joan Williams — TS. FCVA
Saturday 10 PM. [1 Nov. 1952] — [Oxford]

. . . .

I would hate to be marooned on an island with Ober too, but he is a fine agent and a good person. I never see him, because we have nothing to talk about. We correspond, but that is all. Let that be your attitude toward him. He is all right, just horribly shy, and I mean horribly.

. . . .

It's splendid you are working on the book.[1] I'm not surprised, of course; you are lost now; Jake will never let you stop, even if I would. You wont stop now, you dont belong to the middle class anymore, Jake freed you. . . .

If I were you, I wouldn't bother about changing Jake. The point is minor; Jake is there, you can do no more for him. Suppose his overalls dont quite fit this time. So what? If you have not changed him, I'd let him stand as he is. When I read it the first time, I knew it was all right, as I told you.

. . . .

[no signature]

[1] This would become Joan Williams' first novel, *The Morning and the Evening* (1960).

To Joan Williams — TS. FCVA
Thursday [6 Nov. 1952] — [Oxford]

. . . .

. . . you are faced with a choice too. I think you have already accepted it: the choice between art and the middle class; as I wrote, Jake freed you. You cant be both, and being an artist is going to be hard on you as a member of the human race. You must expect scorn and horror and misunderstanding from the rest of the world who are not cursed with the necessity to make things new and passionate; no artist escapes it. . . .

[no signature]

To Else Jonsson — TS. MRS. JONSSON
[4 Dec. 1952] — New York, N.Y.

I have been here, or in Princeton,[1] for two weeks, getting work done on a novel. . . .

I finally decided to try simply ignoring my back. It hurts now and then, but I try to pay no attention to it, the surgeon in Memphis said I must either try surgery, or just make up my mind to live with the back. Which is what I have decided to do, when I go back home next week, I shall get back on a horse.

. . . .

Bill

[1] Faulkner stayed first in Princeton, N.J., at the home of Saxe and Dorothy Commins and then at the Princeton Inn.

To Harold Ober — TS. FCVA
19 Dec. 1952 — [Oxford]

Dear Harold:

Enclosed are two telegrams. I dont understand the one from THE FREEMAN.[1] I answered it as follows, as soon as I got it yesterday:

CANNOT RECALL WHAT PIECE YOU HAVE. PLEASE ADVISE TITLE OR DESCRIPTION BEFORE PUBLISHING.

Will you look into this? Can it be a communist stunt?

re the one from Ruth Ford. I wrote the play with her in mind. I want her to have it. If Ayers has dropped option, will you handle the matter for Miss Ford?

Also the enclosed letter. I had forgot about this story.

Merry Xmas and happy New Year to all of you.

Bill

[1] A request to reprint the Delta Council Speech, which appeared under the title "The Duty to Be Free" in *The Freeman* (26 Jan. 1953), 304–06.

To Harold Ober — TELEGRAM FCVA
23 Dec. 1952 — Oxford, Miss

ANSWERED FREEMAN MYSELF. IT IS ALL RIGHT. BILL

To Joan Williams — TS. FCVA
Wednesday [31 Dec. 1952] — [Oxford]

What I expected seems to have happened. I have run dry, I mean about the writing. It began three days ago, what I put down on paper now is not right and I cant get down what I know is right. I cant work here, I found that out before, but I hoped I would have enough momentum to carry on while I have to stay here. But I am afraid that hope is no good, and I will be able to do nothing until I get away.

. . . .

[no signature]

To Joan Williams — TS. FCVA
Friday 10 pm [2 Jan. 1953] — [Oxford]

I was wrong. The work, the mss. is going again. Not as it should, in a fine ecstatic rush like the orgasm we spoke of at Hal's[1] that night. This is done by simple will power; I doubt if I can keep it up too long. But it's nice to know that I still can do that: can write anything I want to, whenever I want to, by simple will, concentration, that I can still do that. But goddamn it, I want to do it for fun again like I used to: not just to prove to bill f. that I still can. . . .

[no signature]

[1] Harrison Smith's New York apartment.

To Saxe Commins
5 Jan. 1953

TS. RH
[Oxford]

Dear Saxe:

Please send me $5000.00. I will begin to pay up all small current debts here at once.

Am working at the mss. daily. The initial momentum ran out, and it is getting more and more difficult, a matter of deliberate will power, concentration, which can be deadly after a while. I must get away as soon as I can.

Have made a tentative arrangement about my registered cattle, to let my nephew,[1] who owns a small farm, have them, to pay me on demand in calves. Will probably rent the farm itself to the people who live on it, to take care of it, pay the taxes, etc. for a year or until I decide what to do. I hope to be able to come up between 15–30 Jan. Who would be a good agent to write to re an apartment in Princeton?

This is a very incoherent letter; forgive it. Please send the money, and any suggestion about how to locate an apt. Princeton, about Feb 1st.

Love to Dorothy. Had a charming note from Frannie,[2] bless her.

Bill

[1] James M. Faulkner.
[2] Saxe and Dorothy Commins' daughter, Frances.

To Joan Williams
Thursday [8 Jan. 1953]

TS. FCVA
[Oxford]

I have Jake. Keep my copy for me until I get home again. . . .

Who told you you cant write short stories? A short story is a crystallised instant, arbitrarily selected, in which character conflicts with character or environment or itself. We both agreed long since that, next to poetry, it is the hardest art form. But they are all three short stories, not character studies. . . .

Work is going damned well. Very hard to do here, and slow. Am doing new stuff now: it is all right. I still have power and fire when I need it, thank God. . . .

[no signature]

On 31 January 1953, Faulkner left Oxford for New York. He stayed in Harrison Smith's apartment, but soon his illnesses flared up again and he was hospitalized twice during the first two weeks of February.

To Malcolm A. Franklin
Monday [16 Feb. 1953]

TS. MR. FRANKLIN
Mr Saxe's office

Dear Mac:

I am distressed at heart very much to have caused all this worry. I know that I have not been quite myself since last spring, I mean, these spells of complete forgetting. I have had three of them, one in Paris for two days last spring, two here. The idea has occurred to me that maybe, when Tempy snatched me off Sunny last March, that when I hit the ground so hard on my back, that I might have struck my head too. Mr Haas has found a good doctor here, and I am going to see him this week and find out if that is so. Meanwhile, dont tell Mamma, to alarm her, just tell her that I am well now, Mr Saxe takes good care of me, am at work on a piece for the New Yorker (I think), then one on Mississippi for HOLIDAY.

Believe me, I am all right now, will see the doctor, am getting started on Missy's commencement address speech.[1] Mr Hal Smith, one of her godfathers, is going to come up with us to the commencement.

Tell Mamma I am all right, since I have an idea what the trouble might be, I will take better care of myself. I want you to be fond of me always, but I dont want you to worry, to let worry over me interfere with your work. *Dont worry.* I am earning money again, first time in two years almost now, and have every reason to keep on at a gait which wont give anyone reason to worry. Am glad you called Saxe. Reassure Mamma, as he has tried to do. Remember, he will not lie to you about me. When anything serious happens, he will tell you.

Yours,
Pappy

[1] Jill Faulkner would graduate from Pine Manor Junior College on 8 June 1953.

To Else Jonsson
[22 Feb. 1953]

TS. MRS. JONSSON
[New York City]

I have been in New York since Feb 1st, may stay on here until June. Not much happier here but am working, busy: a piece last week for a magazine,[1] have just finished a foreword for Sherwood Anderson's published correspondence,[2] will make a television play of one of my stories this week,[3] then a piece on Mississippi for another magazine.[4] Meanwhile, I work too on my novel.

I still have back trouble. Am seeing another doctor this week. Because something is wrong with me; as you saw last spring, my nature has changed. I think now that when I fell off the horse last March, I may have struck my head too. I will know this week.

Bill

[1] This was probably the short story "Weekend Revisited," which he had referred to in his letter of 16 Feb. to Malcolm Franklin as intended for *The New Yorker*. It was rejected by that magazine and two others and would be published posthumously as "Mr. Acarius," *Saturday Evening Post*, CCXXXVIII (9 Oct. 1965), 26–27, 28, 29, 30, 31.

[2] This essay would appear not in the book but as "Sherwood Anderson: An Appreciation," *Atlantic Monthly*, CXCI (June 1953), 27–29.

[3] The "Old Man" portion of *The Wild Palms*.

[4] *Holiday*.

To Else Jonsson — TS. MRS. JONSSON

[31 Mar. 1953] — [New York City]

Am writing television scripts now, to have money to go somewhere and get at my own novel again. I do not see yet where I can go. I wish I could come to Stockholm, promise to come at this time, for the summer. I just cannot tell yet. I have had a great deal of doctor, medical expense. I had two more spells like that in Paris, in which I would not know what happened until I would wake up in a hospital, and have just finished a series of examinations for a possible skull injury when I fell off the horse. There is no skull injury. According to the doctor, the tests show that a lobe or part of my brain is hypersensitive to intoxication. I said, 'Alcohol?' He said, 'Alcohol is one of them.' The others are worry, unhappiness, any form of mental unease, which produces less resistance to the alcohol. He did not tell me to stop drinking completely, though he said that if the report had been on him, he would stop for 3 or 4 months and then have another test. He said that my brain is still normal, but it is near the borderline of abnormality. Which I knew myself; this behavior is not like me.

Otherwise I feel all right, am working steadily, making television scripts, shows. I will go home about June 1st, see about the farm, drive back up to Jill's school where I am to make the graduation address June 9th, then take her back home. By that time, I will know what I will be able to do this summer, whether I can come to Europe or not.

Last week I recorded the Stockholm speech, to be broadcast in Europe by the VOICE OF AMERICA.

Bill

To Joan Williams — TS. FCVA
Wednesday [29 Apr. 1953] — [Oxford]

. . . .

Working at the big book. . . . I know now—believe now—that this may be the last major, ambitious work; there will be short things, of course. I know now that I am getting toward the end, the bottom of the barrel. The stuff is still good, but I know now there is not very much more of it, a little trash comes up constantly now, which must be sifted out. And now, at last, I have some perspective on all I have done. I mean, the work apart from me, the work which I did, apart from what I am. . . . And now I realise for the first time what an amazing gift I had: uneducated in every formal sense, without even very literate, let alone literary, companions, yet to have made the things I made. I dont know where it came from. I dont know why God or gods or whoever it was, selected me to be the vessel. Believe me, this is not humility, false modesty: it is simply amazement. I wonder if you have ever had that thought about the work and the country man whom you know as Bill Faulkner—what little connection there seems to be between them. . . .

[no signature]

A frugal man, Faulkner often used the blank sides of pages from earlier typescripts for letter drafts and new work. The verso of p. 126 of the typescript of The Town *(1957) is one such page. On 4 May 1953, it was announced that Hemingway's* The Old Man and the Sea *had been awarded a Pulitzer Prize for fiction. Faulkner apparently drafted a congratulatory telegram, which he may or may not have actually sent.*

Probably to Ernest Hemingway — TS. FCVA[1]
[probably May 1953] — [Oxford]

Splendid news. stop not that quote the old man unquote needs more accolade than it already has from us who know the anguish it took and have tried to do it too.

[t] Bill Faulkner

[1] See Eileen Gregory, "Faulkner's Typescripts of *The Town*," *Mississippi Quarterly*, XXVI (Summer 1973), 362–86.

To Else Jonsson — TS. MRS. JONSSON
[15 May 1953] — [New York City]

. . . Mrs F . . . is better now, and I came back here this week, to work again until time to go to Jill's school and I am to make the graduation address.[1] Then we will go back home. . . . I have accepted another job, a long one, to make a full-length moving picture for an actress, Julie Harris, from one of my books.[2] I shall go away somewhere to have peace and quiet to work in; I hope it might possibly be Europe for the time or at least some of it, but still I cannot say yet.

I have a polo player's belt which I wear occasionally, though after a time it is more uncomfortable than the back itself. . . .

Bill

[1] Published as "Faith or Fear," *Atlantic Monthly*, CXCII (Aug. 1953), 53–55.

[2] This project was not carried through.

To Joan Williams — TS. FCVA
Tuesday night [possibly 16 June 1953] — [Oxford]

Never be afraid, of anything, ever.

Least of all, dont be afraid about money. That is death to an artist. I know, we are alike in so many ways, especially this one: never accept money unless you give something for it. I will help you find another job. . . .

Will write more about the colony. What held me back is, the big book I am on. I could not do justice to a group which trusted me, and do my own work too. Two of us, you and I, could work together and I could still do the big one, but not the group. If I stay with big book, the group will have to wait until next year, when I am free. . . .

[no signature]

To Joan Williams — TS. FCVA
[18 June 1953] — [Oxford]

Written from the approach which you have chosen, the point of view, this is Howard's story. It is actually a character sketch of him, as much as JAKE was a character sketch of Jake. But Howard cant keep on telling Doakes what he is by repeating himself: he must tell Doakes what he is by letting Doakes see his actions and the reactions of the other people in the story to his actions. Everything revolves around him: even Ottis's character emerges from what people say to Howard.

This is all overemphasised, burlesqued almost. But from this distance, I dont know how else to do it; I must write almost as many words explaining what I mean, as I would need to write the story itself, which would be much easier. And I hate to send the letter, because I am afraid [of its] result on you: will discourage or depress you, because we dont agree on what you have done. It should not, I hope it does not, because it is not the best you can do. You worked hard at this story. I know that. Where you didn't work hard enough was in using the time I was with you to learn from me the best point of view to approach a story from, to milk it dry. Not style: I dont want you to learn my style anymore than you want to, nor do I want to help you with criticism forever anymore than you want me to. I just want you to learn, in the simplest and quickest way, to save yourself from the nervous wear and tear and emotional exhaustion of doing work that is not quite right, how to approach a story to tell it in the manner that will be closest to right that you can do. Once you learn that, you wont need me or anybody.

I learned to write from other writers. Why should you refuse to? You could even do this: when I think you need help, take the help from me. Then, if your conscience troubles you because the story is, as you feel, not completely yours, just remember what you learned from that one and burn the story itself up, until you can use what you have learned, without needing to turn to me. The putting of a story down on paper, the telling it, is a craft. How else can a young carpenter learn to build a house, except by helping an experienced carpenter build one? He cant learn it just by looking at finished houses. If that were so, anyone could be a carpenter, a writer.

. . . .

Isn't this a copy? can I keep it, or shall I send it back? Let me edit it. I wont touch it until you say though, of course.

LATER. READ THIS ONE FIRST

I may be completely wrong about the story, and you may be right. What do you think about this: show it to Ober, ask him if it is salable, right as it is, see what he says. It may be that, with one who is himself a writer, since his own work never quite is right, good enough, nobody else's can ever be.

Dont tell him anything I said about it until he has read it.

[no signature]

To Joan Williams — TS. FCVA
Friday night [3 July 1953] — [Oxford]

. . . .

Yes, am working at big book. The expected happened, it ran dry after about two days, I was miserable, kept at it, the stuff was no good, I would destroy it every night and still try again tomorrow, very bad two weeks. . . .

Have heard nothing about OLD MAN thing. Have an offer to come out to Cal. when it suits me, for a conference about a job. . . .

I will keep at the big book until I hear from you again, until it runs dry again, which it will do. . . .

Of course this version is not the best you can do. I know that. So do you, you have proved it, not just this time, but before. So far, you dont take the work seriously. You take Joan Williams seriously, but not the work. You wont like that, because nobody would. But remember this: if I did not believe in the talent, I would not say it. . . .

Have read it twice. It is not right yet, but so close. Not the story: the way it is told. The story is there, but it is told too gently. Jake was a gentle story, it had to be told gently. This is not a gentle story. It is a story of violence. It is the story of a stiff-necked, hard-headed opinionated, powerful man, an anachronism, years behind his time, living in a time when the time he intends to live in, is years dead, bent on moving inexorably towards his doom, with three women doing everything they can to stop him.

The first sentence should tell Doakes that something bad is going to happen. It should be such a sentence that Doakes has got to read it, then read all the rest of them, until he cannot put the story down until he finds out what happened.

It should begin like this, with the second paragraph: As soon as Mr Howard left the bedroom and reached the head of the stairs, he knew that something was wrong.

From that first sentence on, the story and dialogue should be the two negro women, knowing what is wrong and knowing what Howard will do about it, and what will happen if he does, trying to keep him from finding out what is wrong until they can get rid of Ottis, even though they know they cant do that either.

But he is the boss, a white man, they cant keep him from finding out from them.

Then Mrs Howard should find out what is going on; the negro women in desperation may tell her, knowing that, another woman, she will side with them to prevent tragedy. Or she may extract it from them as Howard himself did. That she will try to stop him, she may even try to telephone the law and he wont let her, he will not let anyone interfere, show him how to run his plantation.

The end of the story may be, her first chance to get to the phone is after he leaves the room with the gun. She is running toward the phone when she hears the shot and knows it is too late.

The tension should increase from that first sentence that says, as soon as Howard reached the stairs, heard the unusual silence, he knew that something was wrong. Everything should build the tension up: the flowers etc., the women should react to the flowers, only Howard ignores their significance.

[no signature]

On 3 August 1953, Saxe Commins wrote Faulkner that the New American Library had proposed two paperback editions: one would include Sanctuary *and* Requiem for a Nun; *the other would print "Wild Palms" and "Old Man" consecutively rather than alternating their chapters as Faulkner had done in* The Wild Palms. *Commins recommended this plan and asked Faulkner's approval. Faulkner typed his answer at the bottom of Commins' letter.*

To Saxe Commins — TS. RH
[early Aug. 1953] — [Oxford]

Of course I agree,[1] appreciate the notice, which you never fail to give me anyhow. Dismembering THE WILD PALMS will in my opinion destroy the over-all impact which I intended. But apparently my vanity (if it is vanity) regarding my work has at last reached that pitch where I consider it does not need petty defending. Am so near the end of the big one that I am frightened, that lightning might strike me before I can finish it. It is either nothing and I am blind in my dotage, or it is the best of my time. Damn it, I did have genius, Saxe. It just took me 55 years to find it out. I suppose I was too busy working to notice it before. . . . You and I will need about 2 weeks to go through this mss. and get everything out of it that it will spare. It will be about 700 typed pages.

[no signature]

[1] The two parts were printed consecutively as proposed.

To Saxe Commins — TS. RH
Friday [Aug. or Sept. 1953] — [Oxford]

Dear Saxe:

One more chapter, and the mss. will be finished. So now I feel that I can draw more money. I plan to invest $2500.00 in a business which I will explain when I see you. How much can I draw this year?

As soon as I finish the mss. I will get in touch with Ober and try to earn more outside as I did last spring, or the OLD MAN script may materialise.

The Europe job with Hawks[1] is out until next year because of Cooper's operation.

I will probably be up East about Sept 1st or so. Will let you know later.

Will fix finances for J & E in Mexico Sept to Dec.[2]

Please send $10,000.00 now.

Bill

[1] A film planned by Howard Hawks and Gary Cooper.

[2] Jill planned to study during the fall term at the University of Mexico, her mother to accompany her.

Near the end of August, learning that Saxe Commins had suffered a heart attack, Faulkner wired him in Princeton.

To Saxe Commins
29 Aug. 1953

TELEGRAM MRS. COMMINS
Oxford, Miss.

GLAD TO HEAR IT. BEGGED YOU LAST SPRING TO REST AND LET JOINT EXPLODE. MAYBE YOU WILL NOW. LOVE TO DOROTHY. BILL

On 28 September 1953, Life *published "The Private World of William Faulkner," the first half of Robert Coughlan's long essay. The second half, entitled "The Man Behind the Faulkner Myth," appeared on 5 October.* Oxford Eagle *associate editor Phillip E. Mullen had helped Coughlan to gather material, and now he wrote Faulkner to tell him that he had not supplied the personal details about the Faulkner family.*

To Phillip E. Mullen
October 5, 1953

TS. MR. MULLEN
[Oxford]

Dear Moon,

Thank you for your letter. No, I haven't seen the piece in LIFE yet, but if you had anything to do with it, I know it is alright and I hope you make a nickel out of it.

Yours,
Bill

To Phillip E. Mullen — TS. MR. MULLEN
Wednesday [possibly 7 Oct. 1953] — [Oxford]

Dear Phil:

I haven't seen the LIFE thing yet, and wont. I have found that my mother is furious over it, seems to consider it inferentially lies, cancelled her subscription.

I tried for years to prevent it, refused always, asked them to let me alone. It's too bad the individual in this country has no protection from journalism, I suppose they call it. But apparently he hasn't. There seems to be in this the same spirit which permits strangers to drive into my yard and pick up books or pipes I left in the chair where I had been sitting, as souvenirs.

What a commentary. Sweden gave me the Nobel Prize. France gave me the Legion d'Honneur. All my native land did for me was to invade my privacy over my protest and my plea. No wonder people in the rest of the world dont like us, since we seem to have neither taste nor courtesy, and know and believe in nothing but money and it doesn't much matter how you get it.

Yours,
Bill

This time I wasn't even consulted, didn't even know it was being done, nor did my mother. She knew she was being photographed and specifically asked the photographer not to print the picture anywhere.[1]

This seems to me to be a pretty sorry return for a man who has only tried to be an artist and bring what honor that implies to the land of his birth.

[1] In mid-September, *Life* had sent a photographer to Oxford to take additional pictures. The magazine carried one of her which had been made in 1941 when an article on John Falkner was being planned.

To Malcolm A. Franklin — TS. MR. FRANKLIN
Tuesday [Oct. 1953] — New York

Dear Mac:

. . . .

Am feeling fine, working again on my mss. which ran dry on me at home in August, which may have been partly responsible for my—and your—trouble. It's going all right now though.

Will talk to Mr Hawks over telephone this afternoon, then I will know what I am going to do. I dont want to go to Europe until after New Year's, as I want to finish this mss. then edit the Book of the Month mss.[1] Also a rumor that my play will go into production this fall. Will try to persuade Howard to put his job[2] off until next year. Will let you know of course.

Love to both of you. I think often of Ria's[3] kindness and good sense.

Pappy

[1] *The Faulkner Reader* (1954).

[2] Hawks was planning a new film which would be released in 1955 as *Land of the Pharaohs*.

[3] Malcolm's wife, Gloria.

To Malcolm A. Franklin — TS. MR. FRANKLIN
Saturday [possibly 17 Oct. 1953] — New York

Dear Buddy:[1]

After a considerable cabling and telephoning to Mr Hawks in Paris, I know my plans now. I will stay here till 1st Dec. to finish the book, edit it with Mr Saxe, edit the Book of the Month club volume. Dec. 1st I will go to Paris to do Mr Hawks' job, will stay until job is finished which will probably be in Feb. I will [lose] Xmas at home but otherwise I would have had to go to Europe Nov. 1st, come back Dec. 1st, then go back to Europe Jan. 1st, which is too much.

Am writing Mamma tonight.

. . . .

Pappy

[1] Malcolm had been called Mac, but after Jill's birth she and the other members of the family called him Buddy. Faulkner used both names.

Mrs. Murry C. Falkner — TS. MR. JAMES M. FAULKNER
Monday [19 Oct. 1953] — Random House

Dear Moms:

I finally got straightened out. I will stay here until Dec. 1st, finish my novel. I will meet Mr Hawks in Paris Dec 1st or 2nd, to stay until the job is finished, which means I will [lose] Xmas at home, will be back I hope in February. I cant turn Mr Hawks down because he has been too good to me, besides the $15,000.00 and expenses; the trip will cost me nothing.

I am well, I believe the book is a good one. All the people here like what they have seen of it.

I will write again soon, to make all arrangements you and Dean[1] will need before I get back. I love you.

Billy

[1] Dean Faulkner, the daughter of Faulkner's youngest brother, Dean, who had died in a plane crash in 1935.

To Saxe Commins TS. RH
Saturday [probably Oct. or Nov. 1953] [Oxford or New York City]

Dear Saxe:

The enclosed came yesterday, registered mail, asking for a receipt. I dont understand it. Have I a title 'Monkey Money' or any title which could be translated that way?[1] Also, I dont remember this publisher, B. Arthaud, of Grenoble. Also, all my European translations have been through you; I have never before had a direct communication regarding business.

I spoke to Bennett about a power of attorney for you to sign a contract Ober may have after I leave. I think you already have one, dont you? Contact Ober about this matter.

Bill

[1] Available records show no such title.

Mrs. Murry C. Falkner TS. JAMES M. FAULKNER
Monday [Nov. 1953] [New York City]

Dear Moms:

I finally heard from Mr Hawks again, and Warner Bros. sent my ticket, so I leave Monday Nov. 30th, cant get out of it. I dont want to go at all, dont want a movie job, but Mr Hawks has been too good to me.

My address in Paris: care Librairie Gallimard,
17, rue de l'Universite,
Paris.

They will forward to me. I dont know how long it will be, Hawks usually takes three months, and I promised to stay until he is done with me. Though I hope, or try to believe, I might get back in Feb. I dread going very much, hoped until the last something would happen and I would not have to. But it may not be as bad as I think. I will telephone home during this coming week end, will telegraph, maybe you will be near the phone too.

Much love
Billy

Before leaving for Europe, Faulkner expressed to Joan his concern about her finishing her novel and about her friends.

To Joan Williams | TS. FCVA
Saturday [possibly 27 Nov. 1953] | [New York City]

. . . these people you like and live among dont want the responsibility of creating. That's what I meant by sophomores: they are like people still in school, irresponsible parasites, who now dont even have to pass courses in order to stay there. They go through the motions of art—talking about what they are going to do over drinks, even defacing paper and canvas when necessary, in order to escape the responsibility of living.

. . . .

[no signature]

To Mrs. Murry C. Falkner | MS. JAMES M. FAULKNER
[postmarked 30 Nov. 1953] | [New York City]

On the way today. Will write you. I love you.

Billy

On 4 December 1953, Hawks and his party arrived at Stresa, Italy, for a two-week stay. There he would work with Faulkner and Harry Kurnitz on the script of Land of the Pharaohs.

To Mrs. Murry C. Falkner | MS. JAMES M. FAULKNER
12 Dec 1953 | [Stresa]

Dear Mother—

This is Stresa, where I stayed for a while one summer back about 1924[1] I think it was. Weather is good, cold, foggy in morning but warms later.

We live in a 'palace' belonging to an Egyptian millionaire who turned it over to us. 3 servants. Elegant.

We go to St Moritz, Switzerland next week. Will write there.

Much love
Billy

[1] The year was 1925.

To Mrs. Murry C. Falkner
Sunday [probably 20 Dec. 1953]

MS. JAMES M. FAULKNER
Suvretta House
St. Moritz, Switzerland

Dear Moms—

This is right in the middle of the Alps, snow on them and moonlight, very beautiful, much ski-ing and bob-sledding, place full of American movie people, plus King Farouk of Egypt—Gregory Peck, Charles Feldman, my California agent, many others—actors, writers, etc. I dont like it. I am going to England then Paris for Xmas and New Year's,[1] wish I was home, which is the only place to spend Xmas. I love you all and miss you all. Want very bad to see Missy and little Jimmy and Dean and Vicki and all my children. Will be here until about 15 January, then Rome, then Cairo. Will always let you know where I am. I love you. I have my camera, and will make pictures.

Billy

[1] On 26 Dec. 1953, Faulkner flew to Stockholm, where he stayed until New Year's Day, when he flew to England. He returned to St. Moritz on 6 Jan. 1954.

To Joan Williams
Monday 11th [Jan. 1954]

TS. FCVA
Suvretta House

. . . .

Stockholm Xmas was pleasant; I had forgot how in Europe the artist is like the athletic champion at home. I tried to stay obscure, in a small hotel, but in two days reporters with cameras followed me, and every morning there would be gangs of schoolchildren, and older people in the snow at the hotel door, asking for autographs. I was at Mr Harold Raymond's (he is Chatto and Windus) country place, Biddenden House, in Kent during last of Xmas, which lasts here until 12th Night, which is 4th Jan., and was back here at work last Monday. Had the masseur in Sweden, and my back has not troubled me since.

. . . .

Bill

To Harold Raymond
Friday [15 Jan. 1954]

MS. CHATTO & WINDUS
Suvretta House

Dear Harold—

Thank you for taking care of the pipes. I go tomorrow to
Hotel Ambassador,
Via Veneto,
Rome.

If duty is not too much, please send the pipe to me there; we should be in Rome about 1 week. If duty is very much hold the pipe until spring, when I hope to see all of you again.

You should love Kent. I do, even after only 2 days. My best and warmest remembrances to Mrs. Raymond and all the children.

Sincerely and gratefully,
Bill

Chatto & Windus were now preparing to bring out a volume of Faulkner's work comprising one novel, excerpts from other novels, short stories, and the Nobel Prize speech. It would be called Faulkner's County *(1955).*

To Harold Raymond
January 23rd. 1954

TS. CHATTO & WINDUS
Ambassadors Hotel,
Via V. Veneto,
ROME

Dear Harold,

Yours of the 20th is at hand. I assume you want to keep all the short stories which come to 52,000 words. We will assume that you want to keep 'AS I LAY DYING.' If I may say so, I would like to think of this volume as representative to your readers, not so much of my work as of my imaginary county.

'THE BEAR,' 65,000 words, has a section—number 3 as I remember[1]—which is concerned, not with the boy and his pursuit of the bear, but with a section of Isaac McCaslin's past or ancestry. Assuming that this section is a fourth of the 65,000 words, by dropping it 'THE BEAR' will be 50,000 words.

I suggest dropping 'THE OLD MAN,' 45,000 words, completely, since it does not take place in my imaginary county.

I would like to keep 'SPOTTED HORSES' if possible. 'AN ODOUR OF VERBENA' is already a part of another volume which you have printed and we could drop that. 'THE COURT HOUSE' is also a part of another volume which you have printed, if possible I would like to keep that, though of course I leave this decision to you.

'THE BEAR,' 65,000 words, less section 3, 15,000 words, and 'THE OLD MAN,' 45,000 words, would leave a net gain of 5,000 words. 'SPOTTED HORSES,' 23,000 words, would increase the gain to 28,000 words. 'THE COURT HOUSE,' 12,000 words, would be 40,000 words. Would this bring the volume under the wire?[2]

I dont know how much longer we shall be here, I think perhaps a week. As soon as I know our next address and what day we leave here I will write to you.

Thank you very much for taking care of the pipe and my best and sincerest remembrances to all the family and always to yourself.

Bill

[1] Faulkner was thinking of section 4.
[2] Raymond followed his suggestions.

To Joan Williams
24 Jan. [1954]

MS. FCVA
Albergo Palazzo e
Ambasciatore,
Roma

We will be here about a week longer, I think, not long enough for a letter to reach me though a cable will. I will send you Egypt address as soon as I know it, and date.

I like this city. It is full of the sound of water, fountains everywhere, amazing and beautiful—big things full of marble figures—gods and animals, naked girls wrestling with horses and swans with tons of water cascading over them. Am mailing pictures.

Damned glad to have left Switzerland. I have seen enough snow to last me the rest of my life.

Love,
Bill

To Saxe Commins
January 29th, 1954

TS. RH
Albergo Palazzo Ambasciatori
Roma

Dear Saxe:

It is splendid to have a letter from you bearing all the earmarks of the old shop and business as usual again.

The passage on galley No. 59, the word is 'trips' though, on thinking about it, maybe 'tours' is better. If you agree, change the phrase to read—Marlborough's Continental Tours.

Galley No 87, the word 'relusive' should have been 'refusive' which is one of my own inventions again, and if you dont like it change it to 'revoltive' which is a new word too of course, but it does say what I tried to express, which was a combination of pity and shock, in which you might say 'What a pitiful sight. Hide, conceal it.'

Since these are the only two that you mention I'm quite sure that you can take care of the others yourself.

Give my best to Mike and Virginia[1] and my love to Dorothy and children.

Yours,
Bill

[1] Prof. and Mrs. Whitney J. Oates.

In a short acknowledgment at the beginning of A Fable, *Faulkner wrote that William Bacher and Henry Hathaway "had the basic idea from which this book grew into its present form. . . ." As publication approached, Bennett Cerf was concerned about Bacher's claim on any motion-picture sale of the book.*

To Saxe Commins — TS. RH
4 Feb. 1954 — [Rome]

Dear Saxe:

Yours at hand this morning. I think that the acknowledgement will have to stand. I dont want to claim anything that is not absolutely mine. As you remember, Bacher and Hathaway approached me in Cal. with the idea of a moving picture script based on this idea—that is, who the unknown soldier might be. The idea of making a book first, then the picture, they—Bacher, who was the leading one—agreed to, the book to be completely mine, Bacher and I (with Hathaway if he should direct it) to share equally in the picture. Since I was under contract, I could not work on the book mss. while drawing pay from Warner. I began work on the mss. only after returning home without pay: while I was working on it, Bacher even advanced money on request, $1000.00, I sent him a copy of the same general outline-synopsis which I sent to Ober and, I think, to Random House.

But to me, none of this is a binding in any legal sense, nearly as strong as the moral one which I feel and assume and, of course, will defend. Bennett may have forgotten all this, since it was with you and Bob that I discussed it, as I recall.[1] Perhaps you had better bring him up to date at once, since the only release [from] Bacher's first claim on its moving picture side, which I can accept, is one voluntarily from Bacher himself. I would first relinquish to him my own picture rights and leave all picture rights between Random House and him.

You can understand my position. I love the book, gave ten good years of my life to it: if any part of it should taste like dust on the tongue, I had better never have done it. If Random House wants a written agreement with Bacher, let it be like that: Random House and I to own the book as a book, all four of us—Random H., Bacher, myself and Ober, who advanced me money and help at times when I needed it, to share in the picture side, until any one of the four voluntarily withdraws. Let it be like that. Let it be so that no man alive will be sorry of the book, have any bad taste in the mouth because of it. Will you accept this and act on it at once? I am unhappy about it now. I dont want to be, must not be: that book must not be blemished by a squabble over rights. I would take my own name off it first and give it to anyone who would defend it from that.[2]

Will be here about one week, maybe longer but uncertain, best wait for the Egyptian address. But you could cable me here RECEIVED CONCURRED and I will feel all right again. Love to Dorothy and the children and always to you, Bob, Don, Bennett, all.

. . . .

Bill

[1] Faulkner had specified the details of the arrangement in his letter of 10 Jan. 1945 to Cerf and Haas. Other letters concerning it went to Ober and Haas over an extended period.

[2] In the end there was no problem. Cerf rightly concluded that the book was not a very likely film prospect, and Faulkner's acknowledgment, like the original understanding about first film rights, remained unchanged.

At a party they gave in St. Moritz, Charles and Jean Feldman introduced a young friend of theirs to Faulkner. The daughter of Jules Stein, founder of the Music Corporation of America, Jean Stein was studying that year at the Sorbonne. She admired Faulkner's work greatly. They would see each other occasionally thereafter and correspond.

To Jean Stein — TS. MISS STEIN
[14 Mar. 1954] — [Cairo]

Worked very hard all this past week . . . finished script again, for the second time, yesterday. Hawks went to Aswan Thursday, to look at locations; will be back Sunday, tomorrow; Monday he can tear the script up again. . . .But just maybe, maybe, he wont, by March 23rd I may, just may, be done with it. . . .

Bill

On 29 March 1954, with his part of the film writing done, Faulkner flew from Cairo to Paris. Despite a collapse similar to one he had suffered when he first arrived in Egypt, he continued to think about A Fable *and even to meditate revisions.*

To Saxe Commins — CABLE MONIQUE LANGE
12 Apr. 1954 — Paris

FORGOT JUDAS MISERY DESIRE REWRITE ONE SECTION PLAN ARRIVE 20 APRIL OR WILL CABLE TO SEND SECTION HERE.[1] BILL

[1] On 19 Apr., Faulkner departed from Orly, arriving in New York the next day.

To Jean Stein — TS. MISS STEIN
Thursday [22 Apr. 1954] — [New York]

I wrote this on the typewriter because I have just finished signing my name 1100 times on autograph sheets for the book. By now, I not only cant hold the pen anymore, I hate Wmfaulkner almost as much as mccarthy.[1]

. . . .

Bill

[1] Joseph R. McCarthy, U.S. Senator from Wisconsin, 1947–57.

To Saxe Commins — TS. RH
Sunday [probably late Apr. or early May 1954] — [Oxford]

Dear Saxe:

Before the mss. FABLE is shopped around to movie prospects, be sure everybody understands about Bacher, that he is to have first chance to refuse it. I agree with Bennett, there is no movie in it that I can see now, but Bacher must have first chance to buy or use or have a share in making the movie.

As I told you, we agreed that I would do it as a book, to belong to me completely; then he and I together would share in it when it became a film.

I dont know how you can do this. That is, can you ask for bids, and take the best offer? If so, we might give him the chance to meet the best offer, if he wishes to, inside a limit of time—hours or days. Or if he had rather let Random House sell it, and he to share in the price—my part of the money of course, not Random House's. Would it be better for you to do this—Random H.—or shall I get in touch with him by mail? Or has R.H. a representative in Los Angeles, to handle it.

That is, to me, he has a moral claim to the first refusal, provided Random House and I get the top price. If he cannot meet the top price, or does not want to, or cannot handle the matter without delaying things, to our cost, then he can have a share of my part of the sale price. That is, Random House is not to suffer, and neither is he.

Talk this over, and let me hear from you.

He may be able to work along with you or your agent in selling it, and work himself into the producing deal, we to get our price, and he to get his share without cost to us, which would settle everything.

Am well, too damned hot here. Will write you later re Missy as soon as the thing is formally announced, etc.[1] Love to all in shop, and to Dorothy and the children.

This business is going to cost, so I will need money probably.

Yours,
Bill

[1] Jill's engagement to Paul D. Summers, Jr., would be announced on 10 June 1954, with the wedding set for 21 Aug.

To Jean Stein — TS. MISS STEIN
Monday 10th [May 1954] — [Oxford]

. . . I am busy out of doors all day now, trying to get back into proper physical condition again, already sunburned a little, farming, building fences, training a colt and so forth. But mainly to get time passed. . . .

Bill

To Jean Stein — TS. MISS STEIN
Saturday [29 May 1954] — [Oxford]

Here is a snap of Lady Go-lightly[1]. . . .

I have rented the farm for next year, and selling the extra cattle, so I shall be free.

I am becoming a good fence builder. . . .

Bill

[1] Jill's horse.

To Saxe Commins
Friday [18 June 1954]

TS. RH
[Oxford]

Dear Saxe:

We left here last Friday for Washington, for Missy's announcement party there,[1] got back home last night and found the books,[2] the one you sent and the package. They are very fine, I am as proud as you are; if we are right and it is my best and not the bust which I had considered it might be, I will ask nothing more.

All well here. The wedding invitations will go out soon, the date is 21 Aug. you and Dorothy are expected whenever you will come. Malcolm and Ria still want you to come and stay long enough for a good visit and to see some of our country.

I will need money, probably a ghastly amount. Am solvent now, but I will suggest you send $5000.00 any time before Aug. 1st. No, about July 1st. as Jill and her mother seem bent on making a production out of this, and her trousseau wedding stuff, bridesmaid's dresses, champagne etc will run to quite a piece of jack I fear.

Will write again later. I'll tell about the Wash. party later, damndest collection of prosperous concerned stuff-shirt republican senators and military brass hats and their beupholstered and becoiffed beldames as you ever saw. Fortunately hardly any of them ever heard of me, so I was let alone.

Bill

[1] Paul Summers' foster parents, his uncle and aunt, Mr. and Mrs. A. Burks Summers, gave a gala supper party at their home in Rockville, Md., to announce Jill and Paul's engagement.

[2] *A Fable*, officially published on 2 Aug. 1954.

With publication of A Fable *now imminent, Faulkner received a letter from Donald Klopfer asking his cooperation for a* Time *cover story. Faulkner immediately wired Commins to ask Klopfer to stop the plan, adding that he would write Klopfer that night.*

To Donald S. Klopfer
Saturday [19 June 1954]

TS. RH
[Oxford]

Dear Don:

Have been thinking about the man coming down here to do the piece, and I am afraid of it. That is, TIME has already done it once, and LIFE too last year. If he must come down here to do it, it must mean he needs to pry into my private life. I dont want that at all, which maybe I cant help. But just because in our American system I am news, at least my family and connections should not be subjected to the indignity which these visitations mean. Maybe we are wrong, but down here private persons are not used to this sort of thing. The LIFE business showed that I cant help it, that the magazines dont care whether I like it or not, so perhaps all I can do is, refuse to co-operate with him. But I know it is not his fault either; journalists as individuals are all right, they are just the victims of the system too, and can be fired by their bosses if they acquiesced to my feelings. That is, if he insists on coming whether I like it or not, and since I know it is not his doing but his employers, the least I can do is to let him know before he goes to the trouble and distance of the trip here, that I wont co-operate with him when he begins to fudge into my privacy and that of my family.

I wish he would not come at all, though I know I cant stop it—not until enough of us—what few there seem to remain—who hold their privacy of value, confederate to protect themselves from one of the most fearful things in modern American life: the Freedom of the Press. One individual can protect himself from another individual's freedom, but when vast monied organizations such as the press or religion or political groups begin to federate under moral catchwords like democracy and freedom, in the structure of which the individual members or practitioners are absolved of all individual moral restraint, God help us all.

So if his boss insists on sending him anyway, please warn him that I will be dug in to defend what remains of my privacy to the last bullet. At least, put it off for next week. Jill's young man is here, and I would like to shield them, anyway. At least he must leave my mother alone. She is too old for this; the last batch of them told her lies to get into her house. My best to Pat,[1] as always.

Bill

[1] Mrs. Donald S. Klopfer.

To Bennett Cerf — TELEGRAM RH

24 June 1954 — Oxford, Miss.

DEAR BENNETT. LET ME WRITE THE BOOKS. LET SOMEONE WHO WANTS IT HAVE THE PUBLICITY. I PROTEST WHOLE IDEA BUT WILL NEVER CONSENT TO MY PICTURE ON COVER. ESTIMATE WHAT REFUSAL WILL COST RANDOM HOUSE AND I WILL PAY IT. BILL

The next day, Cerf wired Faulkner that the whole project had been called off. The last thing in the world they wanted to do was to bother him.[1]

[1] Shortly after the *Time* story was forestalled, *Newsweek* staffman William Emerson phoned Phillip E. Mullen to ask his help. Mullen invited him to his home in Canton, Miss., and telephoned Faulkner to ask if he would see Emerson. Though Faulkner immediately declined, Emerson went to Rowan Oak. Faulkner received him in near-silence, and though Faulkner's photograph appeared on the cover of *Newsweek* for 2 Aug. 1954, the magazine contained only a review of *A Fable* and a brief word-picture of Faulkner as Emerson had seen him.

To Bennett Cerf
25 June 1954

TELEGRAM RH
Oxford, Miss.

I LOVE YOU. I LOVE BOB AND DON TOO. I LOVE PHYLLIS TOO. BILL

An international writers' conference had been planned for 9–21 August as part of the celebration of the quadricentennial of the city of São Paulo, Brazil. When Faulkner was in Maryland for the Summers' party, State Department employee Muna Lee, a Southerner and a poet, telephoned him. Robert Frost had already agreed to go and she hoped that he would, too. He responded favorably to her request.

To Muna Lee
29 June, 1954

TS. MISS LEE
Oxford, Miss.

Dear Miss Lee:

Can there be more than one Muna Lee? more than the one whose verse I have known since a long time?

I wrote to Mr Howland[1] today, for information about flight, return, etc., also about what clothes I will need—climate, temperature, etc. Also, that I would like to return to Memphis not later than Monday, Aug. 16th.

Please send me here what further instructions I should have regarding what I say and do while there.

Yours sincerely,
[s] William Faulkner
[t] William Faulkner

[1] Harold E. Howland, of the U.S. State Dept.

After a cordial letter from Bennett Cerf, Faulkner ended the correspondence about the abandoned Time *article with another wire.*

To Bennett Cerf — TELEGRAM RH
1 July 1954 — Oxford, Miss.

I LOVE TIME TOO. ONLY MAG IN AMERICA EVER CANCELLED PIECE ABOUT HIM ON SIMPLE PLEA OF ONE PRIVATE AND HENCE HELPLESS INDIVIDUAL. BILL

To Saxe Commins — TS. RH
Friday [probably 2 or 9 July 1954] — [Oxford]

Dear Saxe:

The Dept. of State are paying the transport, the Brazilian govt. my expenses, to Sao Paulo, Aug. 7–16 and return, to attend a centennial beanfeast, me to strike a blow of some sort for hemispheric solidarity. I will need my dinner jacket, the coat and pants are hanging in 'Gene's[1] closet. I think the shoes were among the clothes I had stolen in Egypt. But in case, they are patent leather slippers, not new. If they are not in the closet too, can someone from R. House have a pair sent to me? I want English shoes, Church is the maker, evening shoes. There is a shop on the west side of Madison, somewhere between 50th St and Tripler's, I have seen Church shoes in the window, Tripler may have them, in fact, I think they have. If you could bundle the suit up and take it in with you, it and the shoes could be crammed into a packing box and sent to me, dont worry about creases as I will have it pressed here. I hate to have to worry you, but I didn't know about Brazil when I left the suit there.

The shoes will be 6½, B width or C, that is, not too narrow. That is, my foot is short, I can wear No 6, D.

About the trip here. Dont worry. You and D. will be met without difficulty any hour you reach Memphis, to stay as long as you will.

Bill

Not pumps: lace shoes, patent leather evening shoes, with lace-up fronts. Can you arrange with shop to let me return them if wrong fit, etc?

[1] Saxe Commins' son.

In late July, Faulkner was asked to include in his trip to Brazil a stopover in Lima, Peru.

To the State Department — TELEGRAM STATE DEPT.
[early Aug. 1954] — [Oxford]

WILLING FOR BOTH. SUBJECT LIMITATIONS OF PERSONAL IGNORANCE AND INEXPERIENCE. WILLIAM FAULKNER

Faulkner made the trip from 6 to 16 August 1954. Despite a collapse which impaired his effectiveness, his reactions to the project were positive.

To Harold E. Howland — TS. STATE DEPT.
15 Aug. 1954[1] — Oxford, Miss.

Dear Mr. Howland:

I reached home Monday night. I want to thank the State Department for the unfailing courtesy and efficiency which expedited my whole trip, which gave me not only a wider knowledge of South America, but of the Foreign Service of my own country and the high type of men and women who run and represent it—Mr. Walters at Miami, Ambassador Tittman and his staff at Lima, the Consul General and Consul Campbell and Mr. Benoit at Sao Paulo, Mr. White and his staff at Rio and the gentlemen of the consulate at Caracas, and Miss Muna Lee and yourself.

I know now something of the problems the U.S. has to cope with in Latin America, and the problems which the State Department has to face in order to cope with them, and not just the wisdom and efficiency but the tact and dignity and good taste with which our representatives cope with both and all.

I am too inexperienced yet to judge just what my visit as an unofficial representative of the U.S. accomplished; you will get a better idea from what reports your Department gathers from sources, and I will of course answer in detail any questions you wish to ask. Also, I wish to say that I became suddenly interested in what I was trying to do, once I reached the scene and learned exactly what was hoped from this plan of which I was a part, and that I shall be in New York this fall and can hold myself available to call on you to make a verbal report or discuss what further possibilities, situations, capacities, etc. in which I might do what I can to help give people of other countries a truer idea than they sometimes have, of what the U.S. actually is.

Sincerely,
William Faulkner

[1] An erroneous date: Faulkner departed Brazil on Sunday, 15 Aug. 1954, and arrived home the next day.

To Harold Ober | TS. FCVA
September 3, 1954 | Oxford, Mississippi

Dear Harold:

I just found this in the litter and mess of my workshop.[1] God knows what else may have been here for years that I haven't come to yet. Maybe I'll even find something with a check in it.

Yours,
Bill

[in ink:] Will be in town some time this month.

[1] On 7 Sept. 1954, Ober wrote Faulkner thanking him for his photograph and the message on it.

To Harold Ober | TS. FCVA
Sunday [5 Sept. 1954] | [Oxford]

Dear Harold:

Yours with the HOLIDAY enc. at hand. This is the first I knew that I am to write the Vicksburg piece. How did it happen? Was it something Commins told you? I had not accepted it before, because it struck me as being a job for a reporter, a professional one. I dont know Vicksburg, and as yet have no feeling for the piece; in fact, I think now that any piece on Vicksburg (or any other piece resembling an assignment) written by me would not be worth $500.00.[1]

Hold everything though. I plan to be in town next week and we will discuss it. If I undertake it, it will be as a job, no feeling, warmth yet, though that may come. Just wait till I get up so we can discuss it. I would like to know how I got committed, also.

Yours,
Bill

[1] *Holiday* had offered $2,000.

To Mr. and Mrs. Malcolm A. Franklin | TS. MR. FRANKLIN
Tuesday [probably 21 Sept. 1954] | [New York]

Dear Ria and Buddy:

Perfectly splendid news.[1] I waited to write because the wire said you might write me, and your letter might have required detailed answer. We are all happy and proud; we have needed another boy close to Rowan Oak, as you both know, and you two have done the job.

Earned $1000.00 TV last week,[2] just finished a hunting story[3] Post should buy, maybe $2000.00, am happy to be earning again and reassure myself that I can. Mamma should have her passport by now;[4] I want to know her plans as soon as they are settled, so I can arrange here, unless she plans to wait till I come home next month.

Love to all.
Pappy

[1] The birth of their son, Mark.
[2] CBS telecast "An Error in Chemistry."
[3] "Race at Morning," *Saturday Evening Post*, CCXXVII (5 Mar. 1955), 26–27, 103, 104, 106.
[4] Estelle Faulkner was planning a visit to the Fieldens in Manila.

When Random House sent Faulkner a copy of Mac Hyman's novel No Time for Sergeants *(1954), he responded with a letter.*[1]

To Random House
[fall 1954]

New York *Times Book Review*
[Oxford]

The story of the bomber training flight is one of the funniest stories of war or peace either, of the functioning at its most efficient best, of man's invincible and immortal folly, that I ever read. The terrifying thing is, it or one of its countless mutations and avatars has happened or is happening or will happen to anyone who is soldiering long enough. But then maybe it is that quality in the innocent and unconditioned young man and in the trained and conditioned old ones simply trying to get along with one another in the crises of man's so-called civilizations which he calls wars, which enables him to survive them.

[no signature]

[1] Reprinted by Harvey Breit, "In and Out of Books," The New York *Times Book Review*, 7 Nov. 1954, p. 8.

One of the results of the attempted Time *story and the accomplished* Newsweek *review-article was an essay which Faulkner would work on under different titles.*

To Saxe Commins — TS. RH
Monday [mid- or late Oct. 1954] — [Oxford]

Dear Saxe:

I sent the Freedom of Press piece[1] to you, rewritten, today. It still stays on my mind though, and now I think I know why. It is not an article, but a lecture. It is a section of a kind of symposium, maybe 5 or 6 lectures, on THE AMERICAN DREAM: WHAT HAS HAPPENED TO IT? So read it and send it back to me. I have more and more offers to lecture, my price is up to $1000.00 from colleges now, and I may take it up, use this one for the first of a series, to be a book later, on what has happened to the American Dream which at one time the whole earth looked up, aspired to.

What do you think of the idea? Anyway, send the article back. Or better: just hold it there, do not submit it, as I have the carbon.

Bill

[1] "On Privacy: The American Dream: What Happened to It?" *Harper's*, CCXI (July 1955), 33–38.

To Jean Stein — TS. MISS STEIN
[9 Nov. 1954] — [Oxford]

. . . Our deerhunt is last week in Nov. I dont particularly want to go, but since I am head of the club (by inheritance now) I will go.

. . . .

Bill

To Jean Stein — TS. MISS STEIN
[possibly mid-Nov. 1954] — [Oxford]

. . . maybe I am vain of my talent or maybe vain of my strength, since I decline to believe that anything less than death could have deviated mine one centimetre.

No, I shant shoot a deer. I began to discover several years ago that I dont want to shoot deer, just to pursue them on a horse like in the story,[1] and now I have discovered that I dont like to kill anything anymore, and probably wont, give the guns and gear away. Because every time I see anything tameless and passionate with motion, speed, life, being alive, I see a young passionate beautiful living shape.

. . . .

Bill

[1] "Race at Morning."

To Harold Ober — TS. FCVA
11 Nov. [1954] — [Oxford]

Dear Harold:

I get nothing from VICKSBURG yet. I dont believe I shall get anything by going there, though I will try that as soon as I can. That is, I can only do an imaginative piece, and Vicksburg is not my town for me to have the right to do an imaginative piece about it; the Vicksburgians who really own the town might feel the same way about intrusion and violation that I did about the violation of my privacy by Life magazine.

Have you any news from the Vanity Fair (I think it was, though Commins and Anthony West will know) piece which I did through West?[1] I assume the last story about the dog thicket[2] didn't sell. Also, the one of last year about the man in the alcoholic retreat,[3] which I think is not only funny but true: I mean, as summed up by the doctor friend's comment: 'So you tried to enter the human race, and found the place already occupied.' and the protagonist's last cry of shocked and terrified illumination: 'You cant beat him (man)! You cannot! You never will!'

Yours,
Bill

1 This piece would appear as "Sepulture South: Gaslight," *Harper's Bazaar*, LXXXVIII (Dec. 1954), 84–85, 140, 141.

2 "By the People," *Mademoiselle*, XLI (Oct. 1955), 86–89, 130–39.

3 "Weekend Revisited," later published as "Mr. Acarius" in *The Saturday Evening Post* (Oct. 9, 1965), 26–31.

To Muna Lee — TS. MISS LEE
[probably mid-Dec. 1954] — Random House

Dear Miss Lee:

Yours of 8th Dec. at hand. Please accept my condolences about your mother's death.

I may have got a wrong impression from Mr Campbell about the books. As I recall, or assumed, he simply asked me to send him about two dozen copies of A FABLE, to be used in the work he was doing in good neighbor relations, etc. I assumed that he had his own plans for individual disposition.

I still hope they will be used for that, by his and Mr Benoit's judgment, which for my nickel is the best. I just hope that he can accomplish this and still have a few copies over, one for himself, one for Mr Benoit, for Senhor Pimentel, and for any others of the Brazilian gentlemen who were so very kind to me and made my visit memorable, with my compliments and regards until I can return and put my signature in them. But again, I leave their disposition and use to him and Mr Benoit.

Sincerely yours,
William Faulkner

Prof. Henry F. Pommer wrote Faulkner about a speech of Joanna Burden's in Light in August: *"But the curse of the white race is the black man who will be forever God's chosen own because He once cursed Him." (Modern Library edition, p. 222; Random House edition, p. 240.) Pommer wondered if "Him" was a misprint for Ham, one of the three sons of Noah, whose descendants, according to the Bible, populated Africa as the Negro race. Faulkner typed his answer at the bottom of Pommer's letter.*

To Henry F. Pommer — TS. PROF. POMMER
[1954] — [Oxford]

'Him' should have been 'Ham.' This happens quite often with my stuff. The curse of literacy, into which linotypers and proof-readers (editors too for that matter) are as a race such recent arrivers in America, is that the new brother quit there before he discovered that it is no cold dead quality imprisoned between the covers of a grammar but is rather the living catalyst of the whole long living record of man's imagination. To him, in any sentence containing 'God,' any subsequent three letter word beginning with 'H' and ending in 'm,' must be 'Him,' since grammar is everything; what it means doesn't matter.[1]

Faulkner

[1] "*Light in August*: A Letter by Faulkner," *English Language Notes,* IV (Sept. 1966), 47–48. In his accompanying note, Prof. Pommer wrote that both the manuscript of *Light in August* and the typescript setting copy with autograph corrections showed neither "Him" nor "Ham" but "him."

To Chatto & Windus — CABLE CHATTO & WINDUS
10 Jan. 1955 — [New York City]

PLACE AS I LAY DYING WHEREVER YOUR JUDGMENT INDICATES. IF DOUBTFUL EITHER FIRST OR LAST.[1] FAULKNER

[1] It was placed within the body of *Faulkner's County.*

To Harold Ober TS. FCVA
3 Feb [1955] Oxford

Dear Harold:

Yours at hand. I have a commitment made last year to read a paper,[1] spend about a week, at the Univ. of Oregon. They want it in April, I wrote them last week I was now available on notice. I imagine they will have to promote it, advertise, fit it into a schedule, will set their time in April and notify me. Since I promised some time ago, that will have to come first, and the t.v. thing[2] to fit either before or after what date they choose, which I hope they will notify me of soon. As soon as I hear from them, I will write you.

Yours
Bill

[1] "Freedom American Style," published as "On Privacy: The American Dream: What Happened to It" in *Harper's*, CCXI (July 1955), 33–38.

[2] The ABC television network was proposing a program tentatively entitled *The Era of Fear*. They had sent Ober material which they hoped Faulkner could make into a script. The project was unsuccessful.

When Cosmopolitan *magazine planned a picture story on Faulkner and the head of Camera Clix studio wrote to make arrangements, Faulkner responded predictably.*

To Harold Ober TS. FCVA
16 Feb. [1955] Oxford

Dear Harold:

Enclosed are two letters. For God's sake, stop this Camera Clix thing. Please explain that I will never consent, dont want it, will do anything to stop them. Would a letter from me do any good? Ask Commins at Random House to help you, if you like.

The other letter about the speech.[1] Yes, this is all right with me.

Bill

[1] He would deliver "Freedom American Style" on 14 Apr. at the University of Oregon and three days later at the University of Montana. It was the same essay for which *Harper's* had paid $350 and which they would publish in their July number as "On Privacy."

On 21 January 1955, Faulkner had signed the contract for a collection of his hunting stories to be called Big Woods *(1955). When Saxe Commins sent him the dummy prepared by illustrator Edward Shenton, he responded with a full and appreciative critique.*

To Saxe Commins — TS. RH
Friday [probably 17 and 18 Feb. 1955] — [Oxford]

Dear Saxe:

Yes, the trap-ruined spoor is splendid, wish I had thought of it myself. No preference in color.

To Mr Shenton: The double spread page is just right for proportion. If possible, I would like a tiny horse and rider with the hunters and dogs. What about a sort of cavalcade, as the hunt would leave camp: walking men and dogs, one or two riders, a team of mules drawing a wagon containing more hunters? this all tiny figures on spread page. The foliage is right, most of the leaves still on. Yes, live- and pin-oaks, many. Yes, moss. Cypresses too.

Contents page. I like the sumac, myself. To Mr Shenton: yes, this is right.

The hound decoration. He doesn't need the grass. To Mr Shenton: this hound has treed. Was that your idea? Do you like that better than a lowered head, running. Also, he should, to me, have a bolder look; he deals with creatures which can kill him. Lion was half airedale, most of the rest Walker. His muzzle was slightly shorter, heavier; he usually ran without baying; the other hounds made the noise. It is the bony ridge of his brow which gives him a look of concern which seems to me a little wrong.

Yes, the cat is fine.

THE BEAR. I like the suggestion of relativity. To Mr Shenton: The gum is right. The cane is right for height. It grows up to fifteen feet. The boy's clothes. This was roughly about 1880. He could have worn either hat or cap, I think. The cap makes him look more like the boy he was. I think the muffler and coat are right. He could have worn a Confederate private's jacket, as you see country people now in 1945 battle jackets. But I leave his clothes to you; he looks right to me, just so his clothes are not too definitely modern.

The Snake. Yes.

THE OLD PEOPLE. The drawing is splendid. To Mr Shenton: would you risk suggesting Sam Fathers is an Indian to this extent? He is bare-headed, his hair a little long, a narrow band of cloth bound or twisted around his head? or maybe definitely long hair showing below a battered hat? Since you are not illustrating, but illuminating (in the old sense) you could have any liberty you like. I realise the figures must be too small for much detail. Which gives an idea for story THREE. See below.

Yes, the crane is here.

3 A BEAR HUNT. For headpiece: what about the Indians? Mr Shenton could show detail enough to show they are Indians. It could be something symbolical and allegorical like the double spread: the wilderness, the Indian of the now, dispossessed of heritage, and in the back ground the shadowy figure of what he once was, the wild man, the king? Say enough of the man to show him driving the handles of a plow maybe, a battered hat on his long hair, with maybe a single shabby wild flower or sprig of greenery in one of the holes in it, in the background the shadowy ancestor with a war club and his head-dress a regal affair of plumes as the Muskoghean wore?

RACE AT MORNING. Yes, very fine.

I miss only one thing: the horses. Could there be a horse and rider where I have made the check mark on drawing #4? But dont let me spoil the drawing.

[no signature]

Friday morning. Have spent the time thinking, Mr Shenton is right, the double spread doesn't want a wagon in it anyway, which alters the atmosphere of BIG WOODS to Agriculture.

He is right about #4 drawing too, to leave it as is, no horse. Only, if he has more space, needs more drawings, I hope he can show a horse, since the man on the horse, capable of moving in comparative speed to the animal and the hounds, is an important part of our system of hunting also.

Suggestions if Mr Shenton needs more material:

Deer or bear and hounds and mounted hunter swimming a river or without the hunter.

Only, Mr Shenton is doing so well, I am extremely timid about getting in the way.

[no signature]

To Else Jonsson — TS. MRS. JONSSON
[19 Feb. 1955] — [Oxford]

I do a lot of moving about these days, doing jobs for magazines in New York, and international relations jobs for the State Department, have been in South America and there is a possibility of Europe some time soon I understand. It is not definite, I dont just know where yet.

. . . .

I had thought that perhaps with A FABLE, I would find myself empty of anything more to say, do. But I was wrong, another collected, partly rewritten[1] and partly new book this fall, and I have another one in mind I shall get at in time.[2]

Bill

[1] Faulkner linked the stories of *Big Woods* together with prose passages which he called "interrupted catalysts."
[2] Probably *The Town* (1957).

To Jean Stein TS. MISS STEIN
[March 1955] [Oxford]

. . . Belly is still bad at times,[1] got mad helping some hands move a concrete block over a well two days ago, grabbed it myself and of course crushed the end of my middle finger. The one I write with, type too.

Am getting my sloop ready to put back in the lake, will be sailing before long I hope. . . .

Bill

[1] Later, Faulkner would refer to stomach distress as caused by "a bug I picked up in Egypt."

Hollywood producer Jerry Wald was interested in acquiring film rights to The Sound and the Fury *and* Soldiers' Pay *and also in the possibility of Faulkner's doing the screen adaptations.*

To Saxe Commins TS. RH
[16 Mar. 1955] [Oxford]

Dear Saxe:

Whatever you decide about the deal will suit me. But I dont think I will try to write movie scripts on them. I have never learned how to write movies, nor even to take them very seriously. I dont think I need the money at present, and that is the only reason I would have to try the job, or any movie job. Just say to Geller that I have too many commitments at present to consider a movie job this year anyway.

All pretty well here, I go to hospital tomorrow to try to find what is wrong inside, and will advise you.

. . . .

Bill

To Harold Ober — TS. FCVA
Saturday [19 Mar. 1955] — Oxford, Miss.

Dear Harold:

I believe you said you would send me a copy of the American Freedom piece.

There is one change, correction, to be made. In the carbon copy you have of mine, page 13, the last line above the four deleted lines,

'was guilty as the jury said he was, just what
Vigilantes' Committee'

Change 'Vigilantes' Committee' to read 'medieval witch-hunt.'

Will you send me a copy? If not, let me know and I will type one myself, as I want to leave one copy with the University of Oregon after I read the paper.

Yours
Bill

On 25 March 1955, the New York Times *published a letter by Faulkner on the expulsion from the United States of the Metropolitan of the Russian Orthodox Church. Faulkner criticized the action and its consequences and speculated about the number of members of government who could have defined the word "Metropolitan" before news of the case broke. In response to a letter he received from a Mr. Green, he drafted a letter on a sheet of paper which, on its verso, would become TS, p. 54 of* The Town.

To Mr. Green — TS. FCVA
4 April, 1955 — Oxford, Miss.

Dear Mr. Green:

Yours of 25th at hand. I had already seen the NY TIMES letter.

Herewith my qualifications—such as they are.

I have never been a Greek Orthodox Metropolitan. When a young man I was closely enough associated with communists to learn quickly that I didn't like it, it is dangerous, and that it is a good deal more important to keep people talking freedom in communist countries than to keep people talking communism out of this one. I was an air pilot since 1918 and a rated civilian one since about 1930.

I have done some work for the State Department, through junior career members—consuls, attaches, special officers—enough to have learned that the problems they have to cope with come not from the foreign countries they are sent to, but from their Washington headquarters. Though I am 57 years old now, which means that for 7 years I have been realising that human beings dont really know very much about anything.

Yours truly,
Wm. Faulkner

To Saxe Commins
20 April 1955

TELEGRAM MRS. COMMINS
Oxford, Miss.

ALBERT EINSTEIN[1] WAS ONE OF THE WISEST OF MEN AND ONE OF THE GENTLEST OF MEN. WHO CAN REPLACE HIM IN EITHER LET ALONE IN BOTH. BILL

[1] Faulkner had met Einstein in the Commins' home.

To James J. Geller[1]
10 May 1955

TELEGRAM FCVA
New York, N.Y.

I WILL PROTECT YOU. OBER AND COMMINS WORK TOGETHER REGARDING ALL MY WORK PREVIOUSLY PUBLISHED BY RANDOM HOUSE OR PREVIOUSLY HANDLED BY OBER AS AGENT. TO CONSULT EITHER OF THEM AUTOMATICALLY CONSULTS BOTH. BILL

[1] Geller was acting for Jerry Wald of Columbia Pictures Corp. in the effort to obtain screen rights to *Soldiers' Pay* and *The Sound and the Fury.*

On 2 March 1955, Harold E. Howland had written Faulkner asking him to attend a seminar in August for thirty Japanese professors of English and American literature to be held in Nagano. Away from Oxford a good deal of the time since then, he had not answered.

To Harold E. Howland
16 May, 1955

TS. STATE DEPT.
Oxford, Miss.

Dear Mr Howland:

On reaching home last night, I found the telegram from Miss Geesa re urgency of the Japan seminar, my attendance there.

If there is something I can do in Europe, could I attend the seminar first two weeks in August, then go on to Europe?

If there is nothing for me in Europe through official channels, could I

attend in Japan two weeks, then be booked return home via Europe, to stop in Europe for some time, my expense of course?

As you can see, I want to do whatever is in my capacity, wherever you think best, to include a visit to Europe, either official, if any job for me there, or privately if not.

I will wait to hear from you here in Oxford.

Yours sincerely,
[s] William Faulkner
[t] William Faulkner

To Harold E. Howland — TS. STATE DEPT.
31 May, 1955 — [Oxford]

Dear Mr Howland:

Your letter of May 23rd is at hand.

I will have my passport renewed from here. Will I need a pre-departure visa of any kind?

I understand the Japanese are (or were) a formal people. Will I need formal clothes, or could I rent them there if needed? I could take a black tie with me.

Yours truly,
William Faulkner

To Else Jonsson — TS. MRS. JONSSON
[12 June 1955] — [Oxford]

I move about a great deal lately. Was in the West, at the University of Oregon and Univ. of Montana, lecturing, then home for 2 weeks, then at Louisville, Kentucky, writing a piece for a magazine of the Kentucky Derby race,[1] now at home again, training my filly and getting my sloop ready to launch this week. In August the State Department is sending me on another good will mission, like the South American one last year; maybe in time I will be able to persuade them that Scandinavia needs a word with me also.

I will have a book out in the fall; I will send it. It is a nice book, hunting stories, with drawings by a very fine man, I think. Always write to me, and if I dont answer promptly, it will be because I am busy. I mean, I am nearing sixty, a writer, artist, at that age doesn't have much time left while the work will be good, sound; I wont live long enough to do all I have in mind even if I live to be 100.

We have much tragic trouble in Mississippi now about Negroes. The Supreme Court has said that there shall be no segregation, difference in schools, voting, etc. between the two races, and there are many people in Mississippi who will go to any length, even violence, to prevent that, I am afraid. I am doing what I can. I can see the possible time when I shall have to leave my native state, something as the Jew had to flee from Germany during Hitler. I hope that wont happen of course. But at times I think that nothing but a disaster, a military defeat even perhaps, will wake America up and enable us to save ourselves, or what is left. This is a depressing letter, I know. But human beings are terrible. One must believe well in man to endure him, wait out his folly and savagery and inhumanity.

. . . .

Bill

[1] "Kentucky: May: Saturday, Three Days to the Afternoon," *Sports Illustrated,* 2 (16 May 1955), 22–27.

On 23 June 1955, Commins sent Faulkner the complete galleys of Big Woods *with a covering letter including queries and notations of editorial changes he had made. Faulkner returned Commins' letter with a note at the bottom of the second page.*

To Saxe Commins — MS. RH
[late June 1955] — [Oxford]

Was our original plan for 'The Bear' to precede 'The Old People'? If it was, the order is right. Though on seeing the galley, it struck me that 'The Old People' should come first, since it is first in the boy's experience. But if we originally set 'The Bear' first, then that first thought is the right one.[1] What do you think? Love to D.

Bill

[1] In the printed volume, "The Bear" preceded "The Old People."

To Harold E. Howland ref. IES[1] — TS. STATE DEPT.
5 July 1955 — [Oxford]

Dear Mr Howland:

Yours of July 1st at hand. I will be prepared to leave here at any date you set. I will have a smallpox vaccination certificate with me when I pick up the other papers, or receive them from you. I will take a dinner jacket, no other formal clothes, as per your other advice.

I plan tentatively to stop in Athens then on to Europe. I would like to reach Athens about Sept. 1st. This will naturally be unofficial, at my own expense, etc. Though if there is anything I can do after Japan, between there and America, which can help toward a better understanding of our country and our State Dept., I dont need to say that I want to do it, and will hold myself available.

Waiting more instructions, I am
Yours sincerely,
[s] William Faulkner
[t] Wm Faulkner

[1] International Educational Exchange Service.

To Saxe Commins — TS. RH
6 July [1955] — [Oxford]

Dear Saxe:

I am undertaking the Japanese assignment for the State Dept., expenses paid and some salary too this time. and I will go on to Europe from there. So I will make plans to take care of finances here before I leave. I will want $5000.00, to send my dead brother's daughter[1] to school this year, for my mother's and Estelle's allowances. Please send five.

Will leave here about July 28th, I think to Washington first for briefing, dont think I will be able to come up, as I am due in Tokyo Aug. 1st. I will be in Europe about Sept. 1st, dont know how long I shall stay, maybe until Xmas, though I have not made that definite statement here yet.

All well here, am doing some sailing with Jill and Paul. Give Dorothy my love. Every night I compose in my mind the letter I intend to write her, which I dont ever do. My only poor excuse is, Dorothy already knows what I would say in it.

Bill

I wont be able to see our book[2] this year until I reach home, probably.

Bill

[1] Dean Faulkner.
[2] *Big Woods*.

To Harold Ober — TS. FCVA
6 July, 1955 — Oxford, Miss.

Dear Harold:

My last recollection seems to be that friend Geller was talking hundreds, not tens of thousands of dollars.[1]

I would like for him to have a concrete token of my gratitude for the many times he saved all of us when we were in Warner's saltmine,[2] but even if I needed money, which I dont too much now, I would not make a sacrifice just to discharge the obligation to him.

All this means is, you are still the agent and the judge of what is good sale. If this price meets your approval, it meets mine also. $22500. may be the best price for it, though I would have thought that Geller and Wald had already spent that much chasing me by long distance from New York to Mississippi to Oregon to Mississippi to New York to Kentucky by this time. So if this suits you, which I assume it does or you would have said No yourself, it is all right here and let Geller go ahead.

Yours,
Bill

[1] Geller was pushing to complete a deal for movie options on Faulkner works and had conveyed an offer of $2,250 advance against a sale price of $22,500 for *Soldiers' Pay*.

[2] Friends said that Geller covered for Faulkner in Hollywood at times when he was unable to work. He also interceded for Faulkner on occasions when Faulkner asked to go home on leave from his contract.

To Harold E. Howland — TS. STATE DEPT.
8 July, 1955 — Oxford, Miss.

Dear Mr Howland:

Yours of 6th at hand. I want to do this job right, and will of course follow the judgment and plans of the Department, who know. Let me repeat, though, that I am not a lecturer, no practice at it, and I am not a true 'literary' man, being a countryman who simply likes books, not authors, nor the establishment of writing and criticism and judging books. So if I go anywhere as simply a literary man or an expert on literature, American or otherwise, I will be a bust. I will do better as a simple private individual, occupation unimportant, who is interested in and believes in people, humanity, and has some concern about man's condition and his future, if he is not careful.

About rights to any read or spoken material being property of the Dept. I have in progress a book composed of chapters, the subject being What has happened to the American Dream. I read one chapter at Univ. of Oregon and published it in Harper's magazine. I have another chapter[1] which I could read in Japan; I may even compose still a third one to read there. I would expect to retain rights to these, to include in the book. Though naturally I should consider the Dept. had rights to use them in any way it saw fit to further whatever work in int. relations they might do, once I had used them under Dept. auspices. Can this be done? All other material coming out of my visit, will be the Dept.'s, with me to have the privilege of using any of it to build further chapters on this theme for the above purpose, by notifying the Dept. that I wished to do so. That is, I would like the privilege of clearing with the Dept. in advance any speech, etc. which I saw I could later use, to reserve this right.

Yours sincerely,
[s] William Faulkner
[t] Wm Faulkner

[1] Later published as "On Fear: The South in Labor," *Harper's*, CCXII (June 1956), 29–34.

To Alberto Mondadori[1] TS. MONDADORI
23 July, 1955 Oxford, Miss. U.S.A.

Dear Mr Mondadori:

Thank you for your kind letter of June 15th., and the kind sentiments it expressed.

I will be in your country, in Rome, early in September, when I hope to see you, and others of your countrymen and -women who made my last visit in Italy so pleasant and memorable.

Yours sincerely,
[s] William Faulkner
[t] Wm Faulkner

[1] Faulkner's Italian publisher.

On 29 July 1955, Faulkner left for Japan. He remained there until 23 August, then made a forty-eight-hour stopover in Manila on his way to Italy, where he would stay until 17 September.

To Leon Picon TS. DR. PICON
Wednesday [24 Aug. 1955] Manila

Dear Leon:

Arrived about 2 a.m. today, good flight, good dinner with steak and champagne, though I missed the Japanese food and the sake.

I am still demanding favors. I knew I had left some clothes at International House, which had been stored when we went to Nagano and were returned piecemeal. There is missing yet, a white linen coat, and some shirts. A shirt for evening, black tie wear, with black cufflinks and matching studs still in the buttonholes, which I know is missing because the links and studs are missing. And I think there is another evening shirt, white, and a white shirt, button down collar, with a Brooks Bros. label. Will you please see if they can be found, and send them to me in Rome?

I hope things will go well here, to match our good Japanese record. I met the press last night at airport, there is a press conference this afternoon, a reading of the paper[1] tomorrow, a small group of literary people, then another large meeting of discussion, question and answer, Friday. I think I leave here about 1200 Sat.

Will write from Rome, send a report, etc. and of course will do my best to uphold the old Japanese tradition. Remember me to everybody, and my very best to Mrs Picon and Sakairi-san.[2]

Bill Faulkner

[1] "The American Dream."
[2] Miss Kyoko Sakairi, a member of Dr. Picon's USIS staff.

To Alberto Mondadori — TS. MONDADORI
19 Sept. 1955 — Paris

Dear Signor Mondadori:

Please let me thank you again for your kindness and courtesy which made my visit to Milano so happy and memorable. They say to part is to die a little; or if not to die, at least one leaves some part of oneself behind, which I have done in Milano and Italy, so that I shall not be complete until I have returned to Italy and Milano and joined myself whole again.

Again; my respects to your father.

Sincerely,
[s] William Faulkner
[t] William Faulkner

To Piers Raymond — TS. CHATTO & WINDUS
September 29, 1955 — [Paris]

Dear Mr. Raymond:

I have authorized the United States Information Service to make such use as they may see fit of a recording for radio I made here in Paris on September 26, in which I read some fifteen pages of excerpts from 'A Fable'—specifically, the passages from pages 308–18 and 388–92 of the Chatto & Windus edition.

I have said that for my part I do not wish to receive payment for this reading. I understand that you will be kept informed of the distribution of the recording, and that the token payment you requested will be made for each use.

Sincerely,
[s] William Faulkner
[t] William Faulkner

[in ink:] Will arrive London Friday 7th[1] at Brown's Hotel. Will wire or call you.

Bill

[1] 7 Oct. 1955.

Leaving England, Faulkner flew to Iceland for a five-day State Department program, proceeding to New York at its conclusion. Big Woods *was published on 14 October 1955, and on the 23rd he would return to Oxford.*

To Else Jonsson — TS. MRS. JONSSON
[20 Oct. 1955] — [New York City]

I am well, still working, there is a new book which I will send you. I will go back to Mississippi soon and get to work again; I know I wont live long enough to write all I need to write about my imaginary country and county, so I must not waste what I have left. . . .

Bill

Returning East once more, Faulkner attended a State Department debriefing in Washington on 17 November.

To Harold E. Howland — TS. STATE DEPT.
Friday [18 Nov. 1955] — New York

Dear Mr. Howland:

I didn't say this yesterday because it would have sounded too cocky, an amateur purely literary specialist dictating foreign policy to professional foreign service people.

I got this impression while I was in Europe. The last thing the Russians want is for Germany to be united again under any conditions, even their own of communism. Stalin said once that 'Communism would fit a German like a saddle would a cow.' I believe they are convinced that, once Germany is united, the whole nation would stop being communists and be Germans plain and simple, and that, united under any conditions, by sabotage and guerilla war and even by armed declaration, the Germans would make the Russians so much trouble from now on, would keep them so busy, that they would have no time left from preserving communism in Russia, to try to spread it anywhere else. I believe the Russians are trading on the fact that we will keep Germany separated under the belief that we are saving Western Germany from communism, and hence all Germany from it.

I wonder what would happen if we took publicly a high moral plane and said that a un-unified nation is such a crime against nature and morality both that, rather than be a party to it, we will allow Germany to withdraw from promise of NATO troops, and be unified under any conditions they wish.

Thank you and everyone for a pleasant meeting yesterday.

Sincerely,
William Faulkner

To Jean Stein — TS. MISS STEIN
[28 or 29 Nov. 1955] — [Oxford]

. . . .

I get so much threatening fan mail, so many nut angry telephone calls at 2 and 3 am from that country, that maybe I'll come over to the Delta to test them. I dont like threats and insults.[1] That is, I dont like to not know just how serious they are. I wish I had Ben's[2] complacent view that only sporadic incidents will happen in Mississippi. . . .

Bill

[1] In response to his stand on aspects of race relations and the civil-rights crisis.
[2] Ben Wasson, living in Greenville, Miss., in the Delta.

Pressed for a comment on a televised version of the last of the four sections of The Sound and the Fury, *Faulkner gave a response which was quoted incorrectly. He tried to rectify it.*

To Harold Ober
1 Dec. 1955

TELEGRAM FCVA
Oxford, Miss.

CORRECTED QUOTE STORY CHANGED FROM ONE TO ANOTHER MEDIUM BOUND TO LOSE SOME MEANING THOUGH MAY GAIN COMPLETELY NEW SIGNIFICANCE. WHICH YOU LIKE DEPENDS WHERE YOU STAND. THIS MAKES TV VERSION MORE INTERESTING TO ME QUOTE. FAULKNER

When Elmer Kimbell, a white cotton-gin manager in Glendora, Mississippi, shot and killed Clinton Melton, a black filling-station attendant, the Lions Club of Glendora passed a resolution condemning the action and all its implications. Faulkner read of it in the Memphis Commercial Appeal *for 8 December 1955 and wrote to the club's president.*

To Bob Flautt
8 Dec. 1955

TS. FCVA[1]
Oxford, Miss.

Dear Mr Flautt:

I read with interest and respect quotes in this morning's Commercial Appeal from the Glendora Lions Club resolution regarding the filling station shooting.

I had in the mail this morning a letter from a Memphis Negro woman, unsigned, disagreeing with my stand on the Negro question in Mississippi, which she assumed to be a stand for complete integration. She said that my stand does harm to her people, keeps the bad ones in her race stirred up, that what the Negroes really want is to be let alone in segregation as it is, that the Negroes are against NAACP.

I have always believed that of some of our Negroes, what we call the 'best' Negroes. I have always said that the 'best' Negroes, I believe most, nearly all Negroes, do not want integration with white people any more than the best, nearly all, white people want integration with Negroes. What I have tried to say is, since there is much pressure today from outside our country to advance the Negro, let us here give the Negro a chance to prove whether he is or is not competent for educational and economic and political equality, before the Federal Government crams it down ours and the Negro's throat too. Then, if after the trial, the Negro does fail in being capable of equality with the federal government to back him, we in the South will have to cope not only with the failed Negro but the federal government too.

I believe that there are many more Negroes in the South like the woman who wrote me, who do not want integration but just justice, to be let alone by NAACP and all other disruptive forces, just freedom from threat of violence, etc. And I believe there are many more white people besides the members of your club, who are willing to see that the Negro is free from fear of violence and injustice and has freedom in which to prove whether or not he is competent for equality in education and economics and politics. I would like to think that if we could all work together—the Negroes who do not want integration but simple justice and a little better life, and the white people like your club who are opposed to injustice and violence and outrage, no matter what color the victim is, we could handle this problem. We could indeed tell the federal government that we dont need it in our home affairs.

Yours sincerely,
Wm Faulkner

[1] On verso of *The Town* TS., p. 40.

To Saxe Commins — TS. RH
[probably Dec. 1955 or Jan. 1956] — [Oxford]

Dear Saxe:

. . . .

Doing a little work on the next Snopes book. Have not taken fire in the old way yet, so it goes slow, but unless I am burned out, I will heat up soon and go right on with it. Miss. such an unhappy state to live in now, that I need something like a book to get lost in.

Love to Dorothy and the children.

Bill

On 20 March 1955, the Memphis Commercial Appeal *had carried a letter to the editor in which Faulkner declared that Mississippi's schools were not good enough for either white or black students and deplored the spending of money to support two segregated school systems. A week later, the newspaper printed a letter from W. C. Neill, of North Carrollton, Mississippi, attacking Faulkner's views and referring to him as "Weeping Willie." Faulkner's reply to this letter appeared in the* Commercial Appeal *on 3 April 1955. (See* Essays, Speeches & Public Letters, *pp. 215–16 and 218–19.) When Faulkner returned home from a brief trip to New York, he found awaiting him a copy of a letter from Neill to Congresswoman Edith Green, sent to him by Neill.*

To W. C. Neill — TS. FCVA[1]
Jan. 12, 1956 — Oxford, Mississippi

Dear Mr Neill:

My copy of your letter to Congresswoman Green was at hand when I reached home today.

Thank you for it, but I doubt if we can afford to waste even on Congress, let alone on one another, that wit which we will sorely need when again, for the second time in a hundred years, we Southerners will have destroyed our native land just because of niggers.

Yours truly
Wm Faulkner

cc: Congresswoman Bleeding Heart Green
Fireball Frederick Sullens
Hoochypap Henry Luce
Holy Hodding Carter
Weeping Willie Faulkner (kept his; saved three cents)

[1] On verso of *The Town* TS., p. 80.

To Jean Stein — TS. MISS STEIN
Friday [13 Jan. 1956] — [Oxford]

. . . I feel pretty good over your reaction to the new Snopes stuff. I still feel, as I did last year, that perhaps I have written myself out and all that remains now is the empty craftsmanship—no fire, force, passion anymore in the words and sentences. But as long as it pleases you, I will have to go on; I want to believe I am wrong you see. . . .

Bill

To Harold Ober — TS. FCVA
Wednesday [18 Jan. 1956] — [Oxford]

Dear Harold:

Yours at hand. I know Jerry Wald. I think he will gamble. Suppose Geller makes him this proposition.

He takes an option for movie rights on Pylon, free, for one year. If at end of the year, he decides not to make a picture, he pays us $5000.00. If he does make a picture, he pays us 1% of the gross from the picture sales.

Different people have been nibbling at this book for twenty years now. There must be something in it somewhere.[1]

If the above sounds foolish to you, whatever you and Random H. decide will be all right with me.

The enclosed[2] is composite, some I read at the Memphis Historical meeting,[3] some at Univ. of Montana last April, some at Japan and Manila, the letter[4] to Commercial Appeal, Memphis, acknowledged in text. Some is new.

Am coming up in Feb. Want to ask some advice about what to do with money I have, where my kin and friends cant borrow it, against my old age; I will probably live longer than I will write and earn. Want to consult you and Bob and Don also perhaps about it.

Bill

[1] *Pylon* would be filmed not by Jerry Wald but by Albert Zugsmith, who produced it for Universal under the title *The Tarnished Angels,* released in Jan. 1958.

[2] "On Fear."

[3] "Address to the Southern Historical Association," delivered in Memphis on 10 Nov. 1955, reprinted in *Essays, Speeches & Public Letters,* pp. 146–51.

[4] Published 20 Mar. 1955.

To Harold Ober — TS. FCVA
[18 Jan. 1956] — [Oxford]

Dear Harold:

About the piece in the mail today, ON FEAR, the next What Happened to the American Dream chapter.

Let Harper's see it first, then the Atlantic, if they dont want it, let the Post see it.[1] I'd rather stay away from slick mags, since on this subject, segregation, in the South here, the slick ones are automatically attaint. That is, here too often we have come to believe they are biased, and so doubt as propaganda anything they print. The POST is not too bad, but not LOOK, and dont let LIFE have it under any condition. After what they printed in the piece about me, without even bothering to verify their statements, and after the blooper they made about the Till boy's father[2]—a statement which I would have thought any $50.00 leg man or typist would have gone to the trouble to verify first, not to mention the Dulles piece, anything they touch will be to me automatically befouled and not credible. This is a serious piece, to help, I hope, my native country in a dilemma whose seriousness the rest of this country seems incapable not only of understanding but even of believing that to us it is serious.

So, first Harper's, who printed the other chapter, then the Atlantic. If the Post wants it, I would like to see it printed as simply and without fanfare or headlines, pictures, etc. as an editorial. If it cant be done this way, I would rather not have it printed at all. I am not trying to sell a point of view, scratch anybody's back, NAACP or liberals or anybody else. I am simply trying to state, with compassion and grief, a condition, tragic, in the country where I was born and which I love, despite its faults.

Bill

[1] The essay was bought by *Harper's* for $350.00.

[2] Emmett Till, a fourteen-year-old Negro from Chicago, was murdered near Greenwood, Miss. In Rome, asked for comment by the United Press, Faulkner composed a 400-word statement lamenting the crime. It was released to the press on 6 Sept. 1955 and widely reprinted.

To Harold Ober — TS. FCVA
[received 30 Jan. 1956] — [Oxford]

Dear Harold:

Delete Richard Wright from the text.

In the section about the Till case, make the opening of the section read:

> 'If the facts as stated in the LOOK magazine account of the Till affair are correct, this remains' and then continue as per script. That is, delete my preconception of the matter which the LOOK piece validated; open the section simply with the implication of the LOOK piece.

You and Saxe are both authorised to edit any factual, the same as any spelling, inaccuracies in my stuff, always. Since my stuff doesn't sell by the word, I can always spare one or two.

Bill

[in ink:] Will be in town about Monday of next week.

To Jean Stein — TS. MISS STEIN
Saturday [28 Jan. 1956] — [Oxford]

. . . The book is going too good. I am afraid; my judgement may be dead and it is no good. . . .

Bill

To Ramón Magsaysay[1] — TS. MRS. WILLIAM F. FIELDEN
5 Feb. 1956 — Oxford, Miss. U.S.A.

Dear Mr Magsaysay:

This will introduce my son-in-law, Mr William Fielden, a resident of your city.

During my memorable visit in Manila, I met a great man. If your crowded official time ever permits it, I would like my son to have that same privilege.

Yours sincerely,
[s] William Faulkner
[t] William Faulkner

[1] President of the Republic of the Philippines, 1953–57.

To Dr. Julius S. Bixler | TS. COLBY
7 March, 1956 | Oxford, Miss.

Dear Dr Bixler:

Your letter of February 20th was at hand when I reached home today.

I thank the Board of Trustees of Colby College very much for the honor proffered me, which I must decline for the following reason. I did not attend school long enough to receive even a certificate of graduation from elementary school. For me to receive an honorary degree from Colby College would be an insult to all those who have gained degrees by means of the long and arduous devotion commensurate with what any degree must be always worth.

Thank you again for the honor proffered me.

Respectfully yours,
William Faulkner

In early 1956, the campus of the University of Alabama was in a ferment over the admission of Autherine Lucy, a black woman, to the University. The trustees reversed the action and then a federal court ordered Miss Lucy's admission. Fearing violence and incalculable consequences, Faulkner was greatly concerned and agitated. In the wake of riots at the University, David Kirk attempted to start an interracial dialogue among the students there. As grounds for discussion, he had asked several prominent people for their views of the proper course for youth to follow.

To David Kirk | TS. FR. KIRK
8 March 1956 | Oxford, Miss.

Dear Mr Kirk:

Your letter of March 1st. is at hand several days. I wanted to think first before I tried to answer.

I wont try to tell you what to do in order to meet the problems you will face. The reason is, these problems will be individual ones, peculiar to the time and the place they will occur in. I mean, rise into sight, when they will have to be coped with.

I have found that the greatest help in meeting any problem with decency and self-respect and whatever courage is demanded, is to know where you yourself stand. That is, to have in words what you believe and are acting from.

I have tried to simplify my own standards by and from which I act, as follows, which I pass on to you.

1. Segregation is going, whether we like it or not. We no longer have any choice between segregation or un-segregation. The only choice we now have is, how, by what means. That is, shall segregation be abolished by force, from outside our country, despite everything we can do; or shall it be abolished by choice, by us in the South who will have to bear the burden of it, before it is forced on us.

I vote that we ourselves choose to abolish it, if for no other reason than, by voluntarily giving the Negro the chance for whatever equality he is capable of, we will stay on top; he will owe us gratitude; where, if his equality is forced on us by law, compulsion from outside, he will be on top from being the victor, the winner against opposition. And no tyrant is more ruthless than he who was only yesterday the oppressed, the slave.

That is the simple expediency of this matter, apart from the morality of it. Apart from the world situation in which we are steadily losing ground against the powers which decree that individual freedom must perish. We must have as many people as possible on the side of us who believe in individual freedom. There are seventeen million Negroes. Let us have them on our side, rather than on that of Russia.

That is the problem, as I see it. Why dont you get in touch with the Student Council or the TAR HEEL[1] editorial board at North Carolina, Chapel Hill? They have handled this question splendidly. I can think of nothing which would do more to hold intact integrity and decency and sanity in this matter, than a sort of inter-State University organization for simple decency and rationality among Southern college men and women, young men and women. A confederation of older men like me would not carry half this weight. I can imagine nothing which would carry more weight than a sane, sober union of student representatives from all the Southern schools, standing for the simple things which democracy means and which we have got to show the world that we do mean if we are to survive: the simple principles of due process of the majority will and desire based on decency and fairness to all as ratified by law.

This may be difficult at first. It is a sad commentary on human nature that it is much easier, simpler, much more fun and excitement, to be *against* something you can see, like a black skin, than to be *for* something you can only believe in as a principle, like justice and fairness and (in the long view) the continuation of individual freedom and liberty.

And remember this too, when you have to meet these individual problems: you will be dealing with cowards. Most segregationalists are afraid of something, possibly Negroes; I dont know. But they seem to function only as mobs, and mobs are always afraid of something, of something they doubt their ability to cope with singly and in daylight.

Consult your friends, if you like, send a copy of your letter to me, with a copy of this, under a covering letter, to the editor of the N.C. TARHEEL, and see what comes of it. And let me know.

Yours sincerely,
[s] William Faulkner
[t] William Faulkner

[1] The student newspaper of the University of North Carolina.

To Jean Stein — TS. MISS STEIN
Saturday [possibly 17 Mar. 1956] — [Oxford]

. . . Things are better here since the NAACP didn't press the Lucy girl back to Alabama where she would have been killed. Here is a clipping, a Memphis paper but a Northern reporter. You can see from it the mistakes the NAACP makes in this country, since they dont understand it either.

Tempy is fine, needs shoes and my bones are still a little too sore to ride her. It was not a cracked rib, only a bruise, better now. But I have had to do some stooping and lifting etc. getting farm gear in shape, and my back wont quite take Tempy yet.

Weather is nice, flowers everywhere and trees beginning to bud. Already redbud, 'Judas tree' and dogwood soon.

. . . .

Bill

It may have been at this time that producer Jerry Wald sent Faulkner a script called A Stretch on the River. *Based on Richard Bissell's novel of the same title, it had gone through earlier treatments by other screenwriters which had proved unsatisfactory.*

To Jerry Wald — TS. CONSTANCE PRINZMETAL
Wednesday [possibly Mar. 1956] — [Oxford]

Dear Jerry:

Here is a 9-page story line, slightly new angle or a new theme. The characters are the same; I dont see why this line cannot be grafted onto the line of the old script, if you want it.

As you will see, I have concentrated solely on the people, little attention to the veracity of the river material.

Let me say this before we go much further. In fairness to you, I am not certain I should undertake a full-length job on it. This is why: I have a job of my own which I started after Xmas. I wont undertake yours unless I can do the best possible for you. I dont want to try to do your job and mine too, for that reason, yet I dont want to put mine aside if I can help it.

I had rather act as advisor to the script writer, come out for conference with you and him for a week, help get him started, then come back here, with the understanding that I will help with any polish, etc., suggest and plot out rewrites etc., come out again for later conference or rewriting if I have my own job in good shape to put aside for a while.

I could even take a day or two or a week off here to rewrite dialogue and new scenes if necessary. Let the script writer have script credit if you like, use my name for story credit if it will help you.

If you do not have a deadline on this picture, write me what you think of the above suggestion.

Yours,
Bill

To Jean Stein — TS. MISS STEIN
Saturday [24 Mar. 1956] — [Memphis]

Last Sunday I suddenly began to vomit blood. I passed completely out and they brought me here, had some oxygen and a transfusion Monday, and Friday they began tests, stomach and back too. Xray shows nothing, no ulcer. The Dr thinks an ulcer may be there but is closed up with stomach shrinkage. Next test will be Monday. That should tell the tale.

Anyway I am going to act for the next 3 months as though I did have one: cut out alcohol and coffee, etc., live on baby food. I hope that I will be discharged in such good ulcer shape Monday, that we can leave for C-ville[1] about Wed. Thursday. . . .

Bill

[1] Jill Faulkner Summers and her husband Paul were living in Charlottesville, Va., where Paul was attending the University of Virginia law school.

In response to the "go slow" policy on desegregation which Faulkner had advocated in interviews, essays and public letters (see "Letter to a Northern Editor," first published in Life *[5 Mar. 1956], reprinted in* Essays, Speeches

& Public Letters, pp. 86–91), Negro author, anthropologist and politician Dr. W. E. B. DuBois had challenged Faulkner to debate desegregation in Mississippi.

To W. E. B. Du Bois | TELEGRAM NEW YORK *Times*[1]
17 April 1956 | New York, N.Y.

I DO NOT BELIEVE THERE IS A DEBATABLE POINT BETWEEN US. WE BOTH AGREE IN ADVANCE THAT THE POSITION YOU WILL TAKE IS RIGHT MORALLY LEGALLY AND ETHICALLY. IF IT IS NOT EVIDENT TO YOU THAT THE POSITION I TAKE IN ASKING FOR MODERATION AND PATIENCE IS RIGHT PRACTICALLY THEN WE WILL BOTH WASTE OUR BREATH IN DEBATE. WILLIAM FAULKNER

[1] New York *Times*, 18 Apr. 1956.

To Harold Raymond | TS. CHATTO & WINDUS
17 April, 1956 | New York, N.Y.

Dear Harold:

A friend of mine, Miss Jean Stein, is now interested in and is working on the staff of THE PARIS REVIEW, which is a small magazine with pretty limited circulation, edited now from here. She—they—would like to have it better and more widely known in England, if possible.

She is sending you under separate cover a few current numbers. The number for May has an interview of Wm. Faulkner, done by Miss Stein. She will send several copies, so that all of you at Chatto & Windus can have a look at it, and she and I both would be most grateful if you could find time to send her the names and addresses of some English people whom the magazine might interest.

When I was in London last, I missed you. I hope for better luck next time. I think often of Biddenden and the day when the last train from Ashford made its farewell run.

Miss Stein's address is, 2 Sutton Place South, New York. If you can find time to list some English names for her, she will send them copies of the magazine.

My best regards to Mrs Smallwood and Piers and Ian, and my sincere duties as always to Mrs Harold.

Yours,
[s] Bill
[t] William Faulkner

She flatters me by considering the May number with the Faulkner interview, which will be out next month, her stoutest effort. If she can have a mailing-list in time, I think her idea is to use that number as a 'come-on' for subscriptions.

To Jean Stein — TS. MISS STEIN
Thursday [19 April 1956] — [Charlottesville, Va.]

. . . Jill and the baby, a boy,[1] are both fine. I cant say so much for myself; I probably did a little too much running around lately. Am drinking milk every 2 hours, eating my infant rations, going to bed at 10 o'clock. . . .

. . . I am to make the recording for the Harvard library which Linscott spoke of. . . .

Bill

[1] Paul D. Summers III, born 15 Apr. 1956.

To Jean Stein — TS. MISS STEIN
Sunday [20 May 1956] — [Oxford]

. . . I still feel rotten. . . . If things dont change when I have finished out the three months the Memphis doctor set, I will do something else, maybe see him, get a version of his report in writing, and then consult your doctor. I dont feel so bad . . . just dull, like I was in N.Y. except that, there, even when I felt bad, I still worked. Now I dont even want to work on my book, back is too painful to ride Tempy enough, so nothing to do but be a farmer while sitting in a car watching other people.

. . . .

Bill

Despite his physical problems, Faulkner continued to work on the manuscript of The Town. *In early June, he was able to send off what he took to be the first third of it.*

To Saxe Commins — TS. RH
[probably early June] — [Oxford]

. . . Will be in Washington for president's conference 10-11-12, may come on to New York after if necessary, or may return here until about the 20th.

The committee business[1] will interfere but I will keep at the mss. typing, cleaning it up. I hope to have it all in by Dec. 1st, maybe sooner. . . .

I still cant tell, it may be trash except for certain parts, though I think not. I still think it is funny, and at the end very moving; two women characters[2] I am proud of.

Bill

[1] Pres. Dwight D. Eisenhower had requested citizen leaders of various professions to explore a "people-to-people" program which would help bridge international gaps widened by the Cold War. He had asked Faulkner to head the writers' group.

[2] Eula Varner Snopes and her daughter, Linda.

When Faulkner was in New York in February, Russell Warren Howe had interviewed him about the racial crisis in the South. The interview appeared in Howe's paper, the London Sunday Times, *on 4 March 1956, quoting Faulkner as saying, "if it came to fighting I'd fight for Mississippi against the United States even if it meant going out into the street and shooting Negroes." A variant version, printed in* The Reporter, *14 (22 March 1956), 18–20, and quoted in* Time, *created something of a furor. Faulkner denied the statement but Howe affirmed the accuracy of his reporting. The subject continued to arise, eliciting from Faulkner further denials and position statements. One of his correspondents was the editor of* Ebony, *a magazine for a predominantly Negro readership.*

To Allan Morrison — TS. FCVA
23 June, 1956 — Oxford, Miss.

Dear Mr. Morrison:

Thank you for your letter.

I cant find a copy of the letter which I sent in duplicate to the magazines in which I saw the incorrect statement quoted from me. It may be that NEWSWEEK, TIME, or the REPORTER could let you see theirs.

I have tried to answer the questions in your letter, in the piece titled A LETTER TO THE LEADERS IN THE NEGRO RACE[1] which I have today sent to Mr Harold Ober, my agent in New York, with a copy of this letter and a covering letter asking him to send the piece on to you as soon as he has a clean copy made. His address is:

Harold Ober Associates
40 E. 49 St.,

and you should hear from him soon. It may not please your publisher and other editors. But I assume that we both assume that our dilemma and problem can be solved only by men of good will regardless of race, stating their honest ideas to one another that the erroneous ones can be corrected.

Yours truly,
William Faulkner

[1] The essay would appear in *Ebony* (Sept. 1956).

To Harold Ober — TS. FCVA
Saturday [23 June 1956] — [Oxford]

Dear Harold:

The enclosed explains itself. It was done at the suggestion and request of Mr Morrison, whom I met by chance on the street one day.

I assume that EBONY may wish to pay for it, simply as a token that they consider it worthwhile.[1] But the money will not matter. I would rather have it in the Negro journal, even at no price, if they will print it intact, unedited. If they dont want it, hold it and write me; it may take some elaboration for a white publication.

Yours,
Bill

[1] *Ebony* paid $250.

To Saxe Commins — TS. RH
[probably late June 1956] — [Oxford]

Dear Saxe:

Our horse is Fabius, but I am afraid I wont get the bet made, cant find the bookie.

Talked to Morrison, the EBONY reporter yesterday on phone, asked him to phone you Monday. His description of how they will use the picture of me and his author sounds all right: nothing about race: just a budding writer paying her respects to a veteran writer. That's all right with me.

Will see you in July I imagine.

Bill

It had been alleged that, acting on the information supplied by an informer, the sheriff of Batesville, Mississippi, had arrested Mrs. Kayo McClamroch for transporting a bottle of whiskey from Memphis, violating *the local dry laws. When she was fined $125, a group of citizens of Grenada County contributed money toward her fine. Faulkner wrote to the Secretary of the Junior Chamber of Commerce of Batesville.*

To the Secretary
Aug. 8, 1956

TS. FCVA[1]
Oxford, Lafayette Co., Miss.

Dear Mr Secretary:

Enclosed is my check for $1.00.

Only a decade ago, we emerged from a terrible war in which our nation gave of its blood and money both that the world be freed of a tyranny founded on and supported by secret police and their private informers.

I am proud to be a citizen of a county having for neighbor a county, a hundred of whose citizens have joined to resist and repudiate this evil in our own land in which men and women can still practice honor and freedom without risking both to do so, of which the affair of Mrs McClamroch of Grenada, was a symptom.

My dollar is too late to be included in that group, but I hope it is not too late for the tar-and-feathers fund for the brave and honorable—and of course, naturally, nameless—patriot who reported her.

Yours truly,
William Faulkner

[1] On verso of *The Town* TS., p. 139.

To Jean Stein
[12 Aug. 1956]

TS. MISS STEIN
[Oxford]

. . . Book is going splendidly, too easy. Each time I begin to hope I am written out and can quit, I discover I am not at all cured and the sickness will probably kill me. . . .

Bill

To Jean Stein
[22 Aug. 1956]

TS. MISS STEIN
[Oxford]

Just finishing the book. It breaks my heart, I wrote one scene and almost cried. I thought it was just a funny book but I was wrong.

. . . .

Bill

Look magazine had just paid Hemingway $5,000 for a picture story on him. They now proposed sending a photographer to Oxford for a week. For writing a text to accompany the photographs, Faulkner would receive $5,000.

To Saxe Commins — TELEGRAM RH
25 August 1956 — Oxford, Miss.

NO. RICH NOW. PREFER PAY LOOK FIVE G NOT TO. FINISH BOOK TODAY. WILL BREAK THE HEART. THOUGHT IT WAS JUST FUNNY BUT WAS WRONG. BILL

To Harvey Breit — TS. MR. BREIT
September 13, 1956 — Washington

Dear Harvey:

This matter which we discussed last summer has been validated by the President's office and we are to go ahead with it. Are you still willing to accept the job of doing most of this preliminary work since you are situated more centrally to do it than I am in Mississippi? I am sending you some mimeographed letters. Will you please go through your list of writers and send everyone a copy as soon as possible?

My thought is to try to have a meeting, at least representative, as near the first of October as we can. Don Klopfer at Random House will let us use Random House for a meeting. I think what we should do is to get enough at one time so we can choose an executive committee of maybe a dozen to do the actual work. I will be in town about the 25th of this month. Then I will carry some of the load myself.

Yours,
[s] Bill
[t] William Faulkner

The mimeographed letter, which would elicit replies from more than thirty prominent writers, went out over Faulkner's signature in late September.

To selected writers | TS. RH
[late Sept. 1956] | New York

Dear ——

The President has asked me to organize American writers to see what we can do to give a true picture of our country to other people.

Will you join such an organization?

Pending a convenient meeting, will you send to me in a sentence, or a paragraph, or a page, or as many more as you like, your private idea of what might further this project?

I am enclosing my own ideas as a sample.

1. Anesthetize, for one year, American vocal chords.

2. Abolish, for one year, American passports.

3. Commandeer every American automobile. Secrete Johnson grass seed in the cushions and every other available place. Fill the tanks with gasoline. Leave the switch key in the switch and push the car across the iron curtain.

4. Ask the Government to establish a fund. Choose 10,000 people between 18 and 30, preferably Communists. Bring them to this country and let them see America as it is. Let them buy an automobile on the installment plan, if that's what they want. Find them jobs in labor as we run our labor unions. Let them enjoy the right to say whatever they wish about anyone they wish, to go to the corner drug store for ice cream and all the other privileges of this country which we take for granted. At the end of the year they must go home. Any installment plan automobiles or gadgets which they have undertaken would be impounded. They can have them again if and when they return or their equity in them will go as a down payment on a new model. This is to be done each year at the rate of 10,000 new people.

Will you please communicate either with me or Harvey Breit who has accepted the chore of being a co-chairman?

Yours very truly,
[s] William Faulkner
[t] William Faulkner

P.S. In a more serious vein, please read the enclosed one-page description of Mr. Eisenhower's purpose.

To Mr. Livio Garzanti[1] | TS. MONDADORI
[probably Sept. or Oct. 1956] | [probably New York City]

Dear Mr Garzanti:

While I was in your country last summer, my friend Mr Alberto Mondadori and I discussed the idea of the whole body of my work in

Italian be published in one uniform edition, binding, imprint, etc.

I had long desired to do this, since it would be the one gesture in my power to your country and people, in acknowledgement of and gratitude for the warmth and understanding which Italy and Italians have always shown for my work, and the affection and 'kinship' which I felt from my first sight of Italy, for Italy and Italians, as though we were kin, not just in spirit but in blood too.

I dont need to speak of the problems of culture, of the exchange of cultures between my country and yours, to which my country already owes such a cultural debt. This is simply a personal matter with me: a single uniform edition of my work in Italian as my best way of saying Thank you and good fortune, a rivederci, to the good return, to Italy.

So please allow me to ask you to permit Signor Mondadori to include 'Sartoris' in this collection, and accept my gratitude, which obligation I shall discharge in person when I can visit your country again.

Yours sincerely,
[t] William Faulkner

[1] Garzanti had published the first Italian translations of *Soldiers' Pay* in 1953 and *Sartoris* in 1955.

Dear Signor:[2]

Let us pray that this may be successful.

Faulkner

[2] Faulkner typed this note on a carbon copy to Mondadori.

To Mme. R. Harr-Baur — CABLE FCVA
10 Oct. 1956 — New York, N.Y.

VERY PLEASED WITH RECEPTION MY PLAY[1] IN PARIS AND SEND MY THANKS TO YOU AND COMPANY. WILLIAM FAULKNER

[1] Albert Camus' adaptation of *Requiem for a Nun,* performed at the Théâtre de Mathurins on 20 Sept. 1956.

During a visit to Charlottesville in April, Faulkner had talked with Professors Floyd Stovall and Frederick L. Gwynn, of the Department of English, about coming to the University of Virginia as writer-in-residence for the semester beginning in January 1957. The negotiations moved along simply and successfully.

To Floyd Stovall — TS. PROF. STOVALL
18 Oct. 1956 — Oxford, Miss.

Dear Professor Stovall:

This acknowledges your letter of October 4th., and to ratify in writing my side of the agreement which you and Mr Gwynn and I so amicably reached in talk; and to express again my hope that the University will gain as much in benefit from the plan as I expect to gain in pleasure by sojourning in your country.

Sincerely,
[s] William Faulkner
[t] William Faulkner

With most of the work done by Harvey Breit and Jean Ennis, of the Random House Publicity Department, Faulkner had presided over the sending out of a questionnaire, the collation of answers, and a subsequent meeting in New York of the Writers' Group of the People-to-People Program. John Steinbeck and Donald Hall agreed to serve with him in supplying a record of the discussion at the meeting and a draft of proposals emerging from it. It was Saxe Commins who actually wrote the draft of the report to be issued, in final form, over the names of the three committee members early the next year. Commins sent his draft to Faulkner, Steinbeck and Hall on 3 December.

To Saxe Commins — TS. RH
Monday [probably 10 Dec. 1956] — [Oxford]

Dear Saxe:

I would make no change in the letter, nor attempt to rectify anything except a glaring untruth, even if I needed to. To change a written statement is to become a censor, and any censor is a dictator, or wants to be.

I would suggest that, as soon as Miss Ennis has an answer from everybody, she notify me and send me any further comments like mine above, and I will send my copy of the letter, with the comments, in a covering personal letter to the President of the United States, whose committee we are.

Then I dont know what more we can do. Though as loyal citizens and cognizant by our craft of world conditions, he himself already knows he has only to call on us further.

Yours,
Bill

To Else Jonsson — TS. MRS. JONSSON
[13 Dec. 1956] — [Oxford]

Ashamed for not writing you for so long. The reason is, what is probably the last flare, burning, of my talent has been going on for the last three or four years, and when I am writing, I just dont write letters.

In that time I have done A FABLE and the second Snopes Volume, called THE TOWN, to be published this coming May, when I will send you your copy, and am now working on the third volume,[1] which will finish it, and maybe then my talent will have burnt out and I can break the pencil and throw away the paper and rest, for I feel very tired. . . .

So I write a little each day, and am training a young jumping mare, and in the summer I sail my little sloop on the lake. . . .

Bill

[1] *The Mansion* (1959).

To Saxe Commins — TS. RH
Friday [probably 28 Dec. 1956] — [Oxford]

Dear Saxe:

The galleys[1] went back to you Wednesday. The signed pages today. I signed and numbered 450, signed 25 extra ones. Is that enough extra ones?

All well here, a pleasant Xmas, though I dont feel too good myself, may have to go back on my last spring's baby pap diet again. I dont know what is wrong with me, but something is.

Love to Dorothy.
Bill

[1] *The Town* (1957).

Charles E. Wilson, general chairman of the People-to-People Program, called a meeting of group chairmen for 4 February in New York, adding that it would be helpful to have some summary of each committee's work to date.

To Jean Ennis — TS. RH
8 Jan. 1957 — Oxford, Miss.

Dear Miss Ennis:

The enclosed explains itself. I answered that I would be on hand, that I did not expect reimbursement for my own expenses, but that if a provision was to be made for secretarial labors, etc. I would submit info.

I said Mr Wilson would receive what dope our committee had produced, so will you send him a transcript of our meeting at Harvey Breit's house, and whatever else we have that he will want or need. Also, of course, file this letter of his with our other stuff.

I hope to reach Charlottesville Friday, Saturday at latest. I will come on to NY either Saturday, or certainly Sunday. Will you have a hotel room for me Sunday night, the Algonquin will do if nothing else offers; if the town is jumping again, the Algonquin will probably find a niche for me. Also, maybe you and Harvey and I had better have a briefing before the meeting at 9:30 Monday. Can we arrange to meet Sunday evening? I will reach town about 6 pm, which is the best train up from Charlottesville. If I see I can reach NY Saturday, I will wire or call you, so please send me where a wire or call will reach you Friday after Random House closes.

Yours,
[s] W.F.
[t] Wm Faulkner

In New York the previous year, Faulkner had abruptly canceled a luncheon engagement with Joan Williams Bowen for 22 February 1956. Now he belatedly explained the circumstances.

To Joan Williams Bowen — TS. FCVA
Tuesday 12th [Jan. 1957] — Oxford

Dear Joan:

Your letter was forwarded to me here so I will be too far from Philadelphia while you are there.

Yes, that Wednesday. Here is what happened, not to excuse, but a pretty young woman doesn't want to be scorned that cavalierly by anybody.

At that time, the Lucy girl[1] had been expelled from the University of Alabama. The next step would be for the NAACP to return her by compulsion, force. If they did that, I believed she would be killed. I had been rushing here and there, trying to get air time before they sent her back. I dont know now why I thought then that drinking could help, but that's what I was doing, a lot of it. I woke up that morning in an apartment not mine with just sense enough to tell you I couldn't make the luncheon, collapsed. Came to Friday and friends resuscitated me just in time to make a presentable appearance on the Tex Something,[2] Tex and somebody like a Frankie and Johnny team on the air from the Waldorf and make my plea.

The least I could have done was to write or call you and explain; lacking that, at least send a rose. Let this be the rose.

Of course I'm glad you're at work, and of course I expect to be among the first to see it.

I will be here until Feb. After that I am to be in residence at the University of Virginia until June. Also, the President tapped me to get up a committee of writers on his People-to-People thing so I will be in New York quite often during that time. If all right, let me write or wire you at this address and see about seeing you.

Bill

[1] Autherine Lucy.

[2] The *Tex and Jinx* radio show, with Tex McCrary and his wife, Jinx Falkenburg, on WNBC in New York.

In January, Harold Ober sold the last chapter of The Town *for magazine publication as* "The Waifs," *in* The Saturday Evening Post, *CCXXIX (4 May 1957), 26–27, 116, 118, 120. When the* Post's *editors wanted to run a photograph of the author with his story, Faulkner set a condition which successfully squelched the plan.*

To Douglas Borgstedt — TELEGRAM FCVA
23 Feb. 1957 — Charlottesville, Va.

STILL DON'T WANT TO BE PHOTOGRAPHED REFERENCE AGENT OBER OF LAST MONTH BUT WILL SUBMIT FOR ONE THOUSAND DOLLARS CASH IN ADVANCE. WILLIAM FAULKNER

As president of the National Institute of Arts and Letters, Malcolm Cowley wrote Faulkner on 2 March 1957 asking him if he would make the presentation of the Institute's Gold Medal for Fiction to John Dos Passos. It would require, said Cowley, only two hundred words and his presence at the luncheon and at the hour-and-a-half ceremony.

To Malcolm Cowley
[early Mar. 1957]

TS. YALE

c/o Department of English,
University of Virginia,
Charlottesville, Va.

Dear Malcolm:

I hate like bejesus to face this sort of thing, but maybe when his vocation has been as kind to a bloke as this one has been to me, an obligation such as this is a part of the bloke's responsibility toward it. So, if you are sure I am the man, I will take on the job and do the best I know.[1]

Let me know the date exactly.

Bill

[1] The presentation speech, delivered on 22 May 1957, is reprinted in *Essays, Speeches and Public Letters*, pp. 153–54.

In mid-March, Faulkner took leave from his duties as writer-in-residence at the University of Virginia to make a two-week trip to Greece for the U.S. State Department. While there, he received the Silver Medal of the Athens Academy, but on his return home he found the box was missing. He appealed to the Cultural Affairs Office at the Embassy in Athens.

To Dr. Duncan Emrich
[Apr. 1957]

TS. DR. EMRICH

917 Rugby Road
Charlottesville, Va.

Dear Dr. Emrich:

Shortly after I reached home here, the medal and scroll given me by the Greek Academy disappeared. I recovered them two days later, the scroll intact in its velvet case, and the silver medal, but the velvet case for it was gone and I have given up hoping to recover it.

Princeton University plans to exhibit my manuscripts in May. They want to show also the medals and decorations. I cant let them show the others without including the Greek ones. I cannot let them show the Greek ones except in the intact form in which I received them.

Would it be possible to learn the name of the jeweler or whoever supplied the box to contain the silver medal, and have another box made for it, and sent to me here?[1]

I am sorry to trouble you with this, but this honor which the Greek Academy considered me worthy to recieve, must be restored to its original intactness.

Please give my sincerest respects to Miss Sally,[2] and my regards to Mr and Mrs Gebelt,[3] and to George[4] and all who were so kind to me, and my best always to yourself.

Yours
William Faulkner

[1] Emrich complied with the request.
[2] Mrs. Emrich.
[3] Second Secretary Stephen Gebelt and his wife.
[4] George Hadjistavrou, a handicapper of horses.

Norman Mailer had written out his views on school integration for his friend Lyle Stuart's monthly newspaper, The Independent, *and Stuart had sent the four-paragraph statement to Faulkner, apparently in hopes of generating a newsworthy controversy. What was really going on in the South, Mailer had written, was that the white man feared the Negro's sexual potency and resisted integration because he unconsciously felt the old arrangement fair: "The Negro had his sexual supremacy and the white had his white supremacy."*[1]

[1] Norman Mailer, *Advertisements for Myself* (New York, 1959), p. 333.

To Lyle Stuart — *Advertisements for Myself*
[summer 1957] — [Oxford]

I have heard this idea expressed several times during the last twenty years, though not before by a man.

The others were ladies, northern or middle western ladies, usually around 40 or 50 years of age. I dont know what a psychiatrist would find in this.

[no signature]

After a successful semester as writer-in-residence, Faulkner was invited to return to the University of Virginia the next year.

To Prof. Floyd Stovall — TS. PROF. STOVALL
9 Sept. 1957 — Oxford, Miss.

Dear Prof. Stovall:

It is far from my intent to relinquish whatever slight hold I may have on U.Va. Eng. Dept., let alone ever to accept without fighting displacement as THE writer-in-residence of the University. But for this year, the 1958 one, I must offer conditions which may not be acceptable.

My farm, etc. here went to pot during my absence, as I had more or less anticipated. I must either let it go in 1958, or give a little more time to it during planting time. I would like to come to Cabell Hall[1] say, about 1st. Feb. as last year, for a stay of 4–5–6 weeks, until about middle of March, say 10th or 15th., then be excused from duty until the last 4–5–6 weeks of school. That is, I must be here for 4 or 5 weeks between Feb 1st and June 1st. I realise that after examinations begin, there is not much I can do there, so could the last term of mine be advanced four weeks forward from the last day in May when I will be any value. Can you arrange an acceptable schedule under these terms? my absence to be roughly from Mar. 10th–15th to April 15th or 20th?

If this can be done, I realise the University may not feel obligated to rent a whole house for me to be absent from this much of the time. Though for the sake of comfort and privacy and some elbow room, I could try to consider paying the rent myself while absent, if nothing else works. Does the Thomas Jefferson Inn have such things as detached cottages?

In any case, Mrs Faulkner will be in Charlottesville visiting Jill in early November, and she can consult on the matter.

Apparently what I am trying to describe is a private apartment in a private home, like Mr Coleman[2] has.

Our regards to all our friends in the faculty, and our duties to Mrs Stovall and yourself.

Sincerely,
[t] William Faulkner

copy to Official Cabell Hall Real Estate Agent Gwynn.[3]

[1] The English Department was located in Cabell Hall.
[2] John C. Coleman, a member of the department.
[3] Frederick L. Gwynn, chairman of the Writer-in-Residence Committee.

To Else Jonsson — TS. MRS. JONSSON
[14 Apr. 1958] — [Oxford]

. . . .

I am afraid I shall not have time to finish the work I want to do. I am about ⅓ through the last volume of my Snopes trilogy. Also, I have a very fine horse which I bred and raised, I shall have her in a horse show this summer. When I get a good photograph I will send you one. . . .

Bill

To Frederick A. Colwell[1] — TS. STATE DEPT.
31 May, 1958 — Oxford, Miss.

Dear Mr Colwell:

I have pondered long and seriously over the invitation to make one of a group of American writers on a visit to Russia.

I believe that for me to decline this invitation to visit Russia as a guest of the present Russian government would be of more value in the 'cold war' of human relationships than my presence in Russia would.

The Russia with which I have, I hope, earned any right to spiritual kinship was the Russia which produced Dostoievsky, Tolstoy, Checkov, Gogol, etc. That Russia is no longer there. I dont mean it is dead; it will take more than a police state to destroy and keep destroyed the spiritual practising heirs of those men. I am convinced that they are still writing of the same truth of the human heart which their giant ancestors did; writing at the risk of life itself probably, hiding the pages—the novels, short stories, plays—under the floor, in the chimney, anywhere against the day (which will come) when they also can be free again.

If by going to Russia under any conditions, and even at the risk or perhaps actual sacrifice (I am 60 now and have possibly done all the good work I am capable of, was intended to do) of life, I could free one Anna Karenina or Cherry Orchard, I would do so.

But to go there now, as a guest of the present Russian government which, as I believe, has driven underground and would destroy them if it could, the heirs of the old giants of the Russian spirit, would be not only a lie but a betrayal. If I, who have had freedom all my life in which to write truth exactly as I saw it, visited Russia now, the fact of even the outward appearance of condoning the condition which the present Russian government has established, would be a betrayal, not of the giants: nothing can harm them, but of their spiritual heirs who risk their lives with every page they write; and a lie in that it would condone the shame of them who might have been their heirs who have lost more than life: who have had their souls destroyed for the privilege of writing in public.

I regret this decision. I have seen a few modern Russians here and there, members of embassies and consulates. Among the frightened harassed groups of other Western men in which I saw them, they stood out like horses knee-deep in a pond full of scared tadpoles. If they are a fair sample of the Russian today, all that saves the rest of us is Communism. If the Russians were free, they would probably conquer the earth.

Yours sincerely,
[s] William Faulkner
[t] William Faulkner

[1] Chief, American Specialists Branch, International Educational Exchange Service, U.S. State Dept.

To Donald S. Klopfer | TS. PROF. BLOTNER
[early Aug. 1958] | [Oxford]

Dear Don:

A family named Blotner,[1] pair and three little girls, English teacher at Va. now on an exchange fellowship to Denmark, sail Aug 13, 11:30 min. on the Bergensfjord (Norwegian-Am Line) Pier 42.

They are nice young people; this will be their first trip abroad (except one in '42–'46 most of which Blotner spent as a shot-down bomb aimer in B 17s, in hun prison camp) and Estelle and I want to send to the ship flowers and a bottle or two of champagne. Will you be kind enough to ask Mary or whoever is handy, Jimmy maybe, to be kind enough to attend to it, and charge to me at R. House.

All well here. My mare is jumping pretty well now 3½–4 feet. She will not face lights though so I cant show her at night and am waiting for cool weather and daytime shows.

All send love to all.

Bill

[1] Joseph and Yvonne Blotner and their daughters, Tracy, Pamela and Nancy.

Faulkner's question-and-answer sessions at Nagano had been transcribed and edited by Prof. Robert A. Jelliffe and published as Faulkner at Nagano *(1956). Now the question of publishing an excerpt arose.*

To Harold Ober | TS. FCVA
[received 7 Aug. 1958] | [Oxford]

I dont know where the rights lie in this. I dont know where to ask, if you dont know.

I am indifferent to this idea. That is, I dont particularly need $750.00, and wont do any editing etc. in fact, I dont want to see it. But if you approve, and want to take the bother of it and wont need any help from me beyond this agreement, it is all right.[1]

Hot as hell here now. I have been trying to get my green hunter ready for a night horse show, but she would not face the lights and crowd, tore a ligament loose in my groin so that my leg is rainbow-colored, red, purple, green, yellow, down to the knee, besides breaking the bridle and flinging the groom into a ditch before we got her into a stall immobilised.

Bill

[1] In its Dec. 1958 issue, *Esquire* published a segment of the Nagano sessions under the title "Faulkner in Japan."

To Harold Ober TS. FCVA
[received 11 Aug. 1958] [Oxford]

Dear Harold:

About a month ago I got in the mail, from the Authors League of America, a check for $88.00. I endorsed it and sent it to you, so you could take your commission. I received your check for the same amount, $88.00. I assumed you had already taken your commission, or would charge it to my acct. Today I got another similar check, same amount. What shall I do? Shall I send it on to you, and get back your check, same amt. at cost of postage, 8 cents, or shall I cash this—or these; there may be another one each month—one here and not make you pay the postage to send yours back to me?

We all miss Saxe.[1] I will have to hunt up somebody else now who will stop anybody making the Wm Faulkner story the moment I have breathed my last.

What shall I do about these checks, if they are to continue? I have got a belly full of Oxford. I cant keep tourists out of my front yard, rubbernecking at my house, and there is not one place in fifty miles that I have found yet where I can eat any food at all without having to listen to a juke box. I think I shall undertake to buy a Va place on credit, mortgage, and hope for the best. If the play makes some big gob of money, I can do it. Maybe I could mortgage a year in Hollywood for net $75,000.00

Bill

[1] On 17 July 1958, Saxe Commins had died at home of a heart attack at the age of sixty-six.

On 12 August 1958, Donald Klopfer sent Faulkner a letter from Purdue University which asked if Faulkner would speak there in May of 1959.

To Donald S. Klopfer MS. RH
[Aug. 1958] [Oxford]

Wont do it. Only universities I bother with are Va. and Princeton, where I have kin folks or good friends. Saxe was worried by such as this. Cant you answer by saying you have sent the invitation on to Faulkner? Or just say 'Write F. himself.' I dont answer these at all, dont need the money now. That is, what I need is not $1000.00 but $100,000.00.

Best to all,
Bill

Faulkner reported his progress on the manuscript of The Mansion *to Donald Klopfer using the language of horse racing and aerial navigation.*

To Donald S. Klopfer
25 Sept. 1958

TELEGRAM RH
Oxford, Miss.

IN BACK STRETCH BUT WONT ETA[1] UNTIL I CAN SEE THE WIRE. . . . BILL

[1] Estimate[d] time of arrival.

Ober wrote Faulkner on 2 October 1958 that there was some interest in his story "Turn About" for television. Ober's records showed that it had been made into a film, Today We Live, *in 1933, and he had read a newspaper account quoting Faulkner as saying he had used the story in writing the picture for Irving Thalberg. Ober wanted to know who Faulkner's agent was at the time so he could obtain a copy of the contract. Faulkner replied at the bottom of Ober's letter.*

To Harold Ober
[received 9 Oct. 1958]

MS. FCVA
[Oxford]

This is the same. Hawks bought the story, I worked on the script while at M.G.M. in 1932. I think I went to M.G.M. under contract, agent was either Selznick or Volck.[1] The movie was Today We Live. Thalberg was then head of M.G.M. producers. Dont the Sat. Eve. Post know?[2] The Story was *only sold once.*

[no signature]

[1] Faulkner went to Metro-Goldwyn-Mayer Studios under a contract negotiated by Leland Hayward, of the American Play Co., then Faulkner's agent in New York.

[2] "Turn About" had appeared in *The Saturday Evening Post,* CCIV (5 Mar. 1932), 6–7, 75, 76, 81, 83.

To James M. Faulkner | MS. MR. FAULKNER
[11 Dec. 1958] | [Charlottesville]

Dear Jim:

This is for the bonds for the five Faulkner children[1] Xmas. Merry Xmas to all of you and much love. Will see you in Jan.

Brother Will

18.75 x 5 93.75.

Please get a bottle of whisky for me to Leslie.[2] Will return it when I get home. Mac will take care of Mark's bond.[3]

[1] U.S. savings bonds for the children of Jimmy and his brother "Chooky."

[2] Leslie Oliver.

[3] Malcolm A. Franklin and his son Mark.

To Harold Ober | TS. FCVA
12 Dec. 1958 | [Charlottesville]

Dear Harold:

I assumed that the title page in the possession of Donald Klopfer would cover whatever alterations or additions of dialogue and staging Ruth has added to the play as it was taken intact as I wrote it in the novel REQUIEM FOR A NUN.[1]

The paragraph you quote, numbered '3,' with your inserted phrase, is agreeable and I thought would be so to Ruth. I have not seen the play as she gave it and as it may be in its present condition. I am willing to add to your inserted phrase, to make it read:

as adapted to the stage by Ruth Ford by means of altered or additional dialogue and movement if she has done that, and wants to have that so stated.

I dont believe that Ruth desires to state that the play originally was written by anyone else but me, or would want her name on it as a joint work; only that she did adapt the finished work to the stage through the necessity of alteration and addition of dialogue, if the exigencies of staging it did so compel such alterations and additions.

[s] William Faulkner
[t] William Faulkner

[1] In 1959, Random House published a version of *Requiem for a Nun* subtitled "A Play from the novel by William Faulkner adapted to the stage by Ruth Ford."

To Ruth Ford | TS. MISS FORD
[postmarked 2 Jan. 1959] | 8 Ivy Lane, Farmington
Charlottesville, Va.

Dear Ruth:

This thanks you again for the handsome ties, and the wallet which reached me safely. I hope you and Zachary[1] had as nice a Christmas as we did here, New Year too. I leave here Saturday for Miss. to do some quail shooting until Feb. 10th when the season closes, then I will come back here. I might have my mss. finished by then, anyway I will bring it up to Random House when finished and will see you then.

Ober writes me the opening date is 24th Jan. We are asking Ella Somerville to come up and go on to NY with Estelle to see the play. Will you please send the tickets you are saving for me to Estelle here, above address. Six, if that is all right. Vicky, Cho Cho's daughter, wants to see the opening too, and she, Estelle, Miss Ella and the rest of the party will see you and do our Oxford cheering.

God bless you. I only wish this play could be what you deserve.

Bill

[1] Ruth Ford's husband, Zachary Scott, who played Gavin Stevens in the New York run of *Requiem for a Nun.*

To Mrs. Julio S. Galban | MS. MRS. GALBAN
Friday [2 Jan. 1959] | [Charlottesville]

Dear Mrs Galban—

This tries to thank you for my chance to ride with the Farmington Hunt on New Year's Day, a pleasure and an honor too. I wish I could be a member of it.

My publisher will send you a book of mine. Will you please hold it until I come back in February, when I can sign it for you. Thank you again.

Sincerely
William Faulkner

Please tell Grover Vandevender[1] thank you, and that I got separated and still thought I was following the hounds until Mrs Cochran and Hyers[2] told me we were on the way home. Otherwise I would have been the last one in.

[1] Proprietor of a local horse farm and Huntsman to the Farmington Hunt.
[2] Mrs. Joel Cochran and Harry Hyer, M.D.

To Donald S. Klopfer — TS. RH
[mid-Jan. 1959] — [Oxford]

Dear Don:

Am finishing first draft of mss. this week, will do about a month's cleaning up, and will bring or send it in, maybe I will send first section as soon as it's done. You should have it all by March.

Please send Estelle at Charlottesville 2 copies of the Collected Faulkner, 1 BIG WOODS.

Had good runs with both Keswick[1] and Farmington Xmas week, have had some good bird shooting here since New Year's. But cold as bejesus outdoors today.

I have a private chance to buy what a friend who lives nearby tells me is a very salable farm in Va. The owner is a fan of F and would like to sell to me. Estelle likes the house. But mainly I can probably sell it without loss if I want to.

Asking price is 95 thousand. I would offer 70 then maybe 80. Can get mortgage 5% for half value, possibly pay balance 5,000 per year. Can mortgage property here for 20 thousand. Would keep title here, see if my nephew will take over upkeep, interest, would draw from Random House to carry the Va place. Could I risk it?

That is, could I add 20 thousand more to what I draw each year from you and Ober?

Bill

[1] The Keswick (Va.) Hunt Club.

To Mrs. William Faulkner — TELEGRAM JFSA
23 Jan. 1959 — Oxford, Miss.

FINISHED FIRST DRAFT AND AM HOMESICK FOR EVERYBODY. REPORT ON PLAY WHEN I ARRIVE. VALENTINE'S LOVE. PAPPY

To William F. Fielden — TS. MRS. FIELDEN
Sunday [1 Feb. 1959] — [Oxford]

Dear Bill:

I was mighty glad to hear from you at last. We shouldn't let so much time pass again.

I dont need the principal, dont want it until you will be better off to get it off your back. You are going to be a rich man someday. I like to think that long ago I helped hold your foot on one rung of the ladder while you climbed. Of course I have to keep my fund in order with the interest payments, but the principal can go on as long as you can use it. Until the remote situation when my estate, my own affairs, family, mother, children, etc. should need it or a part of it, then I will ask for it.

I will be back in Va. 14th Feb, to stay into April. Easter is March 29 I think, and I will see you then. I am a member (Mama tells me) of the Farmington hunt, and I have been hunting as a guest with them and Keswick both, rode twice the hunter champion of Va., Wedgewood, belonging to ex Keswick Master Rives.[1] Also have a 17/1 mount with Farmington named Powerhouse, who can take 4 foot walls and fences all day long. Good fun, also pleases my vanity to still be able for it at 61 years old.

Will see you Easter. Much love to Sister.

Pappy

[1] Alexander Rives.

To Albert Erskine — MS. RH

[received 4 Feb. 1959] — [Oxford]

Albert—

It may be best to make Ratliff's 'Mississippi' consistent. Make it 'Missippi,' as he would say it.

Check any other discrepancies, errors, etc. I will come up when the mss. is done and a day should suffice to go over it.

Bill

It is divided into three Books.
Mink
Linda
Flem
This is 'Mink' complete.

On 5 February 1927, Faulkner typed out on the flyleaf of a forty-seven-page hand-bound booklet the legend "single mss. impression/oxford—mississippi—." The account of a little girl's magical birthday, it was entitled The Wishing-Tree. *Four days later, he presented it, inscribed "For his dear friend/Victoria [Franklin]/on her eighth birthday/Bill he made/this Book." He would subsequently inscribe typed copies for three other children, and in early 1928 one of them went to Margaret Brown, the daughter of Prof. and Mrs. Calvin S. Brown, neighbors and friends of the Falkners. Margaret Brown died in June of that year. During the summer of 1958, Mrs. Brown wrote Faulkner asking permission to publish* The Wishing-

Tree. *When he did not reply, a mutual friend, Prof. James W. Silver, attempted to help Mrs. Brown by sending copies of the story to* Life *and* McCall's. *Ober received a letter from Ralph Graves of* Life *and sent Faulkner a copy together with a query of his own.*

To Harold Ober — TS. FCVA
4 Feb, 1959 — Oxford, Miss.

Dear Harold:

Yours with the encl. from LIFE at hand.

I invented this story for Mrs Brown's daughter, about ten at the time, who was dying of cancer. I put it on paper and gave it to her so her family could read it when she wanted to hear it. This I did as a gesture of pity and compassion for a doomed child. I was quite shocked when Mrs Brown wrote me that she even considered getting money from it. To tell the truth, I didn't believe her. When I told her the story (after the child's death) belonged to her, to do as she wanted with it, it never occurred to me that she would want to commercialise it, since it was, as I said, a gesture of pity and compassion from a neighbor to a neighbor's little child doomed to death without knowing it.

If Mrs Brown needs money this badly, of course I will not stand in her way.

I assumed she meant simply to sell the original mss. which I gave to the daughter, to a collector. There were times when I needed money and could have sold it to an editor for publication, and didn't. Because of that doomed little child, I wont yet. But if Mrs. Brown wants to, and can be happy afterward, I wont stand in the way.

You might show this letter to LIFE. It might be a good idea to stipulate a foreword from me, perhaps the above paragraph, with my final permission to print it. I will think more about it; there's still time.[1] By now I should certainly have got used to the fact that most of my erstwhile friends and acquaintances here believe I am rich from sheer blind chance, and are determined to have a little of it. I learned last week (he didn't tell me himself) that another one[2] gathered up all the odds and ends of mine he had in his possession, and sold it to a Texas university; he needed money too evidently. So do I—the $6000.00 of my cancelled life insurance which paid a mortgage on his property 20 years ago which I'll never see again.

Will be in Va. after Feb. 15th. Erskine has some of the new novel mss.

Bill

[1] *The Wishing-Tree* was published by Random House in 1964.
[2] Phil Stone.

To Albert Erskine TS. RH
[received 9 Feb. 1959] [Oxford]

Dear Albert:

Thank you for your letter. I really am ashamed to be graceless enough to put off on you what I wont do myself.

Yes, any help you approve of to check all discrepancies, dates, time, fact.[1] We should know what and where they are, even if we dont use, correct them. What I am trying to say is, the essential truth of these people and their doings, is the thing; the facts are not too important. If we know the discrepancy, maybe, if to change the present to fit the past injures the present, we will not come right out and state the contravention, we will try to, you might say, de-clutch past it somehow. But we must know where it is. It wont be difficult, I'll help you. The drudgery will be getting all the ruts and potholes and corduroys listed.

Will be in Charlottesville after 15th. Address, 8 Ivy Lane, Farmington, C'ville, Va.

Will send you another batch before I leave here. The next section is

LINDA

contains

Chapter 6 V.K. Ratliff
" 7 " "
" 8 Charles Mallison
" 9 " "
" 10 Gavin Stevens
" 11 Charles Mallison

You can check this against what chapters you do receive in the next batch, which will probably not be all of LINDA.

Bill

[1] Prof. James B. Meriwether, Faulkner scholar and textual specialist, had helped Saxe Commins try to reconcile discrepancies between *The Hamlet* and *The Town* during the editing of the latter. Meriwether again offered his help, and Erskine wrote that he favored accepting it if Faulkner agreed.

Mrs. Julio S. Galban TS. MRS. GALBAN
8 Feb. 1959 Oxford, Miss.

Dear Mrs Galban:

Thank you for putting me up, and Doc Hyer for seconding me into the Hunt. I will try to live up to the honor and the courtesy.

The two junior riders are of course Jill's children, who are years away from riding yet. But I hope my association with the Farmington Hunt will last even longer than that. If they should not be indicated on the card, since they are not ready to ride now, please scratch them off.

I will be in Charlottesville after Sunday 15th, and am looking forward to seeing all the Virginians who have made us so welcome.

Yours sincerely,
William Faulkner

To Albert Erskine — TS. RH
[probably 10 Feb. 1959] — [Oxford]

Dear Albert:

Thank you for the hard work.

CODE:

BC: past, Hamlet, Town, associated stories.
AD: present, Mansion.

When AD conflicts with BC

If changing AD to match BC causes AD to suffer, I say 1. Change BC if possible. 2. If not possible, ignore BC.

If changing AD is simple, a matter of a word or a date, change AD.

The major part of discrepancies will be in first 2 chapters of MINK AD. Why not change BC Hamlet to match AD for next printing? This will make us a new collector's item too.

Re Stallion. In Hamlet BC, Houston was killed riding a stallion *after* (Hamlet BC) he killed a stallion which killed his wife.

A new line will do this: Houston's character is such that it compelled him to kill the horse which killed his wife, yet his character also commanded him to ride nothing but stallions. He got himself a new one, of course. That can be added either or both AD-BC when his wife's death is told.

In Town BC Clarence Snopes, in the Indian story, was said to be 19 years old. That was 1928–9.

Clarence was 20 to 25, maybe a year or two more, in Sanctuary, in the whore house business, roughly about 1925 or so.

In Mansion AD he is same age as Sanctuary, in MINK section, about 1925, and already in the State legislature. In Flem section, Mansion, AD, 1946 he is running for Congress, about the proper age to have been 25 about in 1925.

So in Town, BC, in 1928 he was roughly 28 years old. That's still possible. I mean, in an idle summer he could have teased and badgered the Indian children; his mother could still have run frantically for help to save him since if anyone could have loved Clarence at any age, she would still love him at 28.

I suggest next printing of the TOWN, invent Clarence's younger brother as his tool.

That is, someday we may print the three volumes as a simultaneous trilogy, same binding, imprint etc. and sell the old prints as antiques.

Enclosed is complete Book LINDA. Next is FLEM

Bill

To Albert Erskine — MS. RH
Tuesday [probably 24 Feb. 1959] — Charlottesville, Va.

Dear Albert—

Did you get the section *Linda* mailed from Oxford about Feb 10th?

The last section will be finished in about 2 weeks more. I will bring it up and we can go over all of it. I will wire you later, but I think about March 23, Monday, if you will book a room at the Algonquin.

Bill

Muna Lee had written Faulkner asking him to speak at the 7th National Conference of the U.S. National Commission for UNESCO, to be held in Denver from 29 September to 2 October 1959. Its formal title was "Cultures of the Americas: Achievements in Education, Science, and the Arts."

To Muna Lee — TS. MISS LEE
4 March, 1959 — Charlottesville, Va.

Dear Miss Lee:

Of course I will do whatever I can, any responsible man will. I will always defer to the judgment of the Dept. when and where. But I am the wrong one to be the official speaker here.

If I will have any value here (the Denver Conference) I believe it will [be] negatived, maybe destroyed if I am more than present. I mean, to be the official speaker delegate. Because I would go there having no confidence whatever in the idea of me being that officially delegated mouthpiece. For the reason that I believe that speech is mankind's curse, all evil and grief of this world stems from the fact that man talks. I mean, in the sense of one man speaking to a captive audience. Except for that, and its concomitants of communication—radio, newspapers, such organs—there would have been no Hitler and Mussolini. I believe that in the case of the speaker and his captive audience, whatever the reason for the captivity of the audience, the worst of both is inevitably brought out—the worst of the individual, compounded by the affinity for evil inherent in people compelled or persuaded to be a mass, an audience, which in my opinion is another mob.

I will go of course, be present. But I will do no good except as one me: not a mouthpiece for a point of view. I would prefer not to have to listen to any one else's speech, last on earth to make another of them myself. There must be someone who believes in this sort of thing enough to make a sincere and honest speech, if one must be made.

Excuse this typing. Was fox hunting today and the horse and I went through a thicket in high gear and a twig caught me in the left eye and it's watering and sight not too good.

I will go. But I think I would do much more just being there, seeing people, not as a formal speaker, the good of which I doubt even when the speaker himself believes in what he is doing.[1]

Yours truly,
[s] William Faulkner
[t] Wm Faulkner

[1] Faulkner went as a "consultant," but under the influence of Foreign Service Officer Abram Minell he relented and gave a short address, printed in *Essays, Speeches and Public Letters*, pp. 166–67.

To Albert Erskine — MS. RH
[early Mar. 1959] — [Charlottesville]

Dear Albert—

Here are chapters 12, 13, 14, 15, 16 of

FLEM.

You can be looking at them until I finish 17 and 18, which remain of Flem. I will bring them in with me.

Bill

Research. What day of the month was the *last Thursday* in September, 1946? Insert this correct date in the blank space, in chapter 16, of the day of Mink's liberation from Parchman.

To Albert Erskine — TS. RH
[received 12 Mar. 1959] — [Charlottesville]

Dear Albert:

Here is all of it, the last two chapters, 17 and 18. I dont know what you need Meriwether for, so I cant advise.[1] All I know is two: one to read the mss. and galley, that's you, and tell the other what's wrong, that's me, and see he does it right. So what ever date for M. to come up, you set it. I will wait here until 23rd, which will give you about 2 weeks to get your notes in order, Meriwether can work with us if you like. That is, you know I'm no prima donna, I will let anyone do the work who will. I suggest this, to save time: In case you have a duplicate of your notes, you might send me some of it down here say by next week, the 15th or so, for me to fresh up on before I come up. Have me a room at Algonquin, I will get in on train about 6 pm I think Monday.

Do you agree that, as far as possible, this volume should be the definitive one, others can be edited in subsequent editions to conform. [in ink:] Unless of course the discrepancy is paradoxical and outrageous.

Bill

[1] Erskine had asked if Faulkner favored their meeting first to work on the material and then having Meriwether join them, or the three working together from the outset.

The editorial conferences were not held, for Faulkner fell with his horse at the Farmington Hunter Trials on 14 March. The fractured collarbone he suffered was slow to heal, and his illness was prolonged by unrelated infections as well as by drinking meant to ease the pain. On 6 April, he and Estelle left for Oxford.

To E. D. Vere Nicoll, M.D.[1] — TS. DR. NICOLL
7 April, 1959 — Oxford, Miss.

Dear Dr. Nicoll:

When we went over a list of bone men, I forgot a man, a friend and neighbor, right here. He took his M.D. at the Univ. of Va. and was trained by Dr Campbell of Memphis, practised there until he retired with a good reputation as a bone man. Anyway, he has done many small medical jobs for my family and tenants, and for me too.

Please write him, Dr F. E. Linder, here, so he will take me seriously when I go to him, as he has retired and he and his unmarried brother spend all their time fishing and shooting and he wont take me seriously since most of our contacts have been to help me out of hangovers.

I feel pretty good, still stiff and sore from bruises mostly; I think I did most of the damage twisting free when the horse went down, or maybe he just shot me off pretty hard when I threw him. But strength coming back. I am anxious to work my two here, having no groom or jockey who will set them at a jump. The accident happened I think March 14th. How much longer before I can risk riding again? I dont want to break myself up for good at a mere 61.

Yours etc.
[s] William Faulkner
[t] Wm Faulkner

[1] Nicoll had treated Faulkner for the injury in Charlottesville.

To Albert Erskine — MS. RH
7 April, 1959 — Oxford, Miss

Dear Albert—

I am at home again, still sore but sober and think I can ride again soon. Estelle told me of the telephone talks with you, and that you think you have the mss. in good shape without me immediately, and I agree. I will be back in Charlottesville in June, and will come up and see you then.

Since the volume falls into 3 Books, what do you think about beginning each book with the title pages [such?] as I sent you, that is, a page bearing the single word:

MINK

second book:

LINDA

third book:

FLEM

Also, for consistency,[1] this one too should have the continued dedication page. This time, simply:

To Phil Stone

Everything else, I suppose you and Meriwether have well taken care of.

Yours,
Bill

[1] Both *The Hamlet* and *The Town* had been dedicated to Stone.

Dear Albert—

I dont see how I can get away in May. Also, to come up in May, I will have to come all the way back here to drive a car and Estelle to Va. in June. Is there anything you could send me here to be working on in the meantime? Any <u>minor</u> changes to match the previous versions you can make yourself; any <u>major</u> ones I still say let them stand and we will rewrite <u>Hamlet</u> in next printing.

I dont think you need worry about the riding. Falling off the horse' is a customary perfect hunting field euphemism. What happened was, I was going too fast in wet ground and turned the horse too quick to face a fence and threw him down myself. I broke the collar bone twisting out from under him when he fell. I wont turn one that fast in Rochester's ground anymore.

If by any chance I can come up before June 1st. I will do so. I will try to come by June 1st. anyway, regardless of the chronology of the car.

Bill

To Albert Erskine MS. RH
[mid-Apr. 1959] [Oxford]

Dear Albert—

I dont see how I can get away in May. Also, to come up in May, I will have to come all the way back here to drive a car and Estelle to Va. in June. Is there anything you could send me here to be working on in the meantime? Any *minor* changes to match the previous versions you can make yourself; any *major* ones I still say let them stand and we will rewrite *Hamlet* for next printing.

I dont think you need worry about the riding. 'Falling off the horse' is a customary modest hunting field euphemism. What happened was, I was going too fast in wet ground and turned the horse too quick to face a fence and threw him down myself. I broke the collar bone twisting out from under him when he fell. I wont turn one that fast in treacherous ground anymore.

If by any chance I can come up before June 1st, I will do so. I will try to come by June 1st, anyway, regardless of the christening[1] or the car.

Bill

[1] In June, Jill and Paul's second son, William Cuthbert Falkner Summers, would be christened.

Erskine wrote Faulkner on 2 May that he preferred not to make any changes in the typescript of The Mansion *until Faulkner could go over them with him. He was concerned about the various kinds of discrepancies between stories in* The Hamlet *and retold in* The Mansion, *citing the old shotgun shells Mink Snopes used to kill Jack Houston in the former and the trip he makes to Jefferson to buy new shells in the latter.*

To Albert Erskine TS. RH
Wednesday [probably 7 May 1959] Oxford

Dear Albert:

Premise: I am a veteran member of a living literature. In my synonymity, 'living' equals 'motion, change, constant alteration,' equals 'evolution,' which in my optimistic synonymity equals 'improvement.' So if what I write in 1958 aint better than what I wrote in 1938, I should have stopped writing twenty years ago; or, since 'being alive' equals 'motion,' I should be 20 years in the grave.

re. Mink Snopes and the shells which killed Houston, one of which misfired in HAMLET. In MANSION one of the shells which killed Flem misfired. Same story; we cant do it twice, too much coincidence; besides, the story loses in repetition. That is, the truth is a murderer so caught in his fate and destiny and doom and character that even when the first shell failed to explode, it could not save him. Since I believe that 'fact' has almost no connection with 'truth,' the more moving truth should belong to the more dramatically important murder, which was Flem. So HAMLET will have to change, in my opinion. Though, since I believe that fact had nothing to do with truth, I wouldn't even bother to change HAMLET.

Incidentally, when I first wrote the story of Houston's murder, Mink was a bachelor named Something Cotton.[1] Apparently changing his name and his condition (possibly his motivation too, though I have forgot the original story, called THE HOUND) hasn't outraged too many academical gumshoes, so I doubt if this will either. If you like, we can make a foreword of the first paragraph and steal all the thunder beforehand.[2]

Repeat, I would be perfectly willing to make the dud shell in MANSION match the dud shell in HAMLET, if the MANSION version did not offer the best dramatic moment for it.

I will be up near June 1st or 2nd as possible. Please notify Algonquin.

Bill

[1] Ernest Cotton, in "The Hound," *Harper's*, CLXIII (Aug. 1931), 266–74.

[2] Faulkner did expand the first paragraph of the letter for this purpose and printed it at the beginning of *The Mansion.*

On 19 May, Bennett Cerf wrote Faulkner asking if he wished to submit to a taped NBC television interview for $1,000. He also sent a book containing specimen interviews.

To Bennett Cerf — TS. RH
[late May 1959] — [Oxford]

Dear Bennett:

I have looked through the book and of course I like a 1000 dollars. But I'm not sure I would be any good at this sort of thing. The only times I could bring this off would be—has always been—when I thought I had something urgent to say. In this case, I dont know what that would be.

We are leaving here for Va. June 2nd I think. I will come on to New York soon afterward. When I fell off the horse two weeks ago it was on a paved road and I am now on crutches. Tell Albert I wont bring them to NY, but will come on up as soon as I can. I told him about June 1st but it may be a week later.

. . . .

Bill

To Albert Erskine — MS. RH
Sunday [probably 31 May] — [Oxford]

Dear Albert—

Leaving here Tuesday for Charlottesville. Will come up on night train Sunday June 7th. Please have room at Algonquin for me Monday about 7 a.m.

Have a rewrite idea for *Mink* in *Mansion* which will match the dud shells when he shot Houston in *Hamlet*, and will lose nothing of *Mansion* story.

Bill

On 23 June, Ober wrote Faulkner that James B. Meriwether thought The Texas Quarterly *would pay $500 for "With Caution and Dispatch," a World War I flying story written in* 1932 *or* 1933 *but never published. Faulkner's reply, penned at the bottom of Ober's letter, was prompt.*

To Harold Ober — MS. FCVA
[received 26 June 1959] — [Charlottesville]

This is one of the few remaining unpublished pieces. I dont particularly need $500.00. What I need is nearer $50,000.00 tax-free of course. Why not hold it until I do need it? Say, when I had a good sound hunter for $500.00. I assume that, once in the Texas Quarterly, we couldn't sell it again. The movies might see it and buy it. What do you think? Leaving for Miss. next week.

Bill

Ober had received a request for permission to use Faulkner's name in a forthcoming MGM film, The Voice at the Back Door.

To Harold Ober — TS. FCVA
[received 14 July 1959] — [Oxford]

Dear Harold:

This dialogue in which my name is used is too dreary and lacking in wit and point to be worth any reply, even if postage was still 3 cents. In my opinion it does not deserve to be dignified by acquiescence or protest either; it's certainly not worth two free autographs.

Pretty hot here, have ridden a little but am still stiff and painful, but should be all right by fall for Va. hunting season. Have you bought your Va place yet?

Bill

To Albert Erskine — TS. RH
Tuesday [21 July 1959] — [Oxford]

Dear Albert:

The galleys went back to you airmail this morning. I covered all the questions, red ink, typing; if there is anything more, let me know.

We left most of the discrepancies cryptic enough in the other session to be corrected without much wrenching; I think I have done this. Having freshed up my recollection of THE HAMLET and THE TOWN under your pressure, I dont see any very bad inconsistencies left. If the sweet beautiful Miss Heathcoate[1] will keep a sort of record of the contradictions to the other two in the present, which will be the definitive, one, I can go through HAMLET and TOWN before next printing and make them match right up to the hilt of poetic license.

Yours,
Bill

[1] Mary Heathcoate, of Random House.

Faulkner's talks and question-and-answer sessions while writer-in-residence at the University of Virginia had been taped and edited for publication by Frederick L. Gwynn and Joseph Blotner. Excerpts were printed in College English *and* The University of Virginia Magazine *before the appearance of* Faulkner in the University, *published by the University of Virginia Press in 1959 and by Random House in its Vintage series in 1965.*

To Albert Erskine — TS. RH
Friday [24 July 1959] — Oxford

Dear Albert:

Saxe was defending my dignity or something by some obscure reasoning. He did not want the stuff printed at all, saying it would inevitably be taken as Faulkner's definitive opinion on Faulkner. I didn't quite see this, or didn't think it mattered, and was ready to agree to the publishing of it, but submitted to Saxe since he was my literary wet-nurse, etc. He finally agreed that the Univ of Va could print it in their own organ, but if it were ever printed commercially, Random House should do it.

I agreed to that, and will still agree. Saxe would probably still say No to Ober farming any of it out to mags. but if it is all right with you, let Ober sell some of it to mags, but (as you say) Ober should handle this part. I mean, I can always use money, if it will not tarnish my chastity. You might have a look at the stuff, see if Random House wants to publish it, and if any of it should be released to mags through Ober. I will agree to yours and Ober's judgment.

That's how the matter stood and stands. By your letter, you seem to have divined all this pretty well already. But maybe you had better have a look at it, with Saxe's idea that by having my official cachet on it might be damaging. I still dont think so, but then I dont know, and he was almost violently positive and negative. I didn't think it was all that important, myself. It was done impromptu, off the cuff, ad lib, no rehearsal; I just answered what sounded right and interesting, to the best of my recollection after elapsed years, at the moment.

Tell Miss Heathcoate I love her too. Put the 2.80 in cigars as per outside p.s. on last letter.

Bill

To Harold Ober — TS. FCVA

Sunday [26 July 1959] — [Oxford]

Dear Harold:

My sentiments is, succinctly, as follows.

Having, with THE MANSION, finished the last of my planned labors; and, at 62, having to anticipate that moment when I shall have scraped the last minuscule from the bottom of the F. barrel; and having undertaken a home in Virginia where I can break my neck least expensively fox hunting, I am interested in $2500.00 or for that matter, in $25.00.

I know Bennett and Don wont want to delay publication, so I will compromise with them. If they will give me Random House's word that I shant reach that moment when I will miss passing up this $2500.00, I will agree to put the publication of the book first.[1]

I am trying to avoid inheritance tax. I know there is a $60,000.00 exemption on gift to any one person. On her 21st birthday, I deeded all my property in Miss. to my daughter, Jill. I dont know what the valuation will be, did not recall about inheritance tax when I did it. I intend to deed the Va house to her also, value $43,750.00 though with a mortgage in the purchase, the actual gift will be only $18,750.00. I have $14,000.00 with a Wall Street broker, I can give this to her children. I want to give all the mss. (original, drafts, notes, all of it) to her. How can I value it? How to do it? Please ask your lawyer for details.

Yours,
Bill

[1] Publication of *The Mansion* was postponed so that Faulkner could earn the $2,500 for the publication of the first chapter as "Mink Snopes," in *Esquire*, LII (Dec. 1959), 226–27, 228–30, 247–50, 252–64.

In December of 1958, Prof. Floyd Watkins, an American literature scholar at Emory University, had told Erskine in conversation that John B. Cullen, a boyhood friend and hunting companion of Faulkner's, was writing a book about Faulkner which Watkins was editing. On 27 July 1959, Watkins wrote Erskine that the manuscript was even better than he had hoped and that it would be ready for submission to a publisher by 1 September. Called Old Times in the Faulkner Country, *it consisted of biographical material about Faulkner, together with stories of life in Lafayette County and accounts of local lore and people, much of which Faulkner had used in his fiction. Watkins frankly told Erskine that though it was largely favorable to Faulkner, there was material which Faulkner might find objectionable, especially about his drinking, but that he would like to submit the manuscript if it would not offend either Faulkner or Erskine to do so.*

To Albert Erskine — TS. RH
9 AM Thursday [probably 6 Aug. 1959] — [Oxford]

Dear Albert:

You might write the man that you showed the letters to Faulkner, who had no idea who the anonymous author may be, but Faulkner himself has already milked his private life of any or all interesting literary matter so anything in this mss. that is true will be dull and what is not dull probably wont be true, and therefore the mss. will belong to the scavenger school of literature, and Random House doesn't want it. Though the scavenger school of writing seems to have a following, so he should not have too much trouble placing it, and we hope he enjoys the profits.

Hot as bejesus here. Thank you for the cigars. Am riding again in late pm when it is bearable, am looking forward to fall and fox hunting in autumn countryside.

My best to all.
Bill

6 PM Thursday

My wife's sister[1] is on the staff of the Univ. of Miss. Library here. By coincidence, she told me a moment ago of a man named Floyd Watkins, from Emory University, who has been hanging around Oxford for about a year now, as she put it, lurking in and out, in some concern that I should learn of it, while making a tape recording from the conversation of an eccentric hermit whom I have known all my life here, who has been on two or three of the deer hunts in our camp. He is known to have literary leanings, contributes to our county paper a fantastic sort of bucolic column, and likes his drink. I imagine Watkins is using gifts of whiskey on him, and I know the man to be innocent enough (personally I like him) to be led up the garden by anyone who promises to get him in print.

I think this explains the whole thing. This man is telling what he has heard from others, fired up by his own imagination and his desire to be literary, with no desire to harm or be inaccurate. He may have read or heard of Artemus Ward. I think that's who he would like to be like. Look at the stuff if you like. But I doubt if you or any other publisher who insists on printing only stuff inherent with its own value, humor or tragedy or truth instead of name-dropping, will want it either.[2]

In the last few years, the woods down here have been full of people like Watkins. I dont know what can be done about it, or if it really deserves having anything done.

Repeat: I'm not convinced that Watkins has told this man yet that he intends to print the stuff. It may be no mss. existed until Watkins typed up the tapes. I believe the man likes me, and if he had of his own accord got up a mss. about me, he would have told me about it himself.

I mean of course, respects and admires my literary position, whether jealousy there or not, enough to want my opinion and approval on what he has done himself, like the sandlot boy might ask Babe Ruth what's wrong with my swing, if he had the chance.

[1] Dorothy Z. Oldham.

[2] *Old Times in the Faulkner Country* was published by the University of North Carolina Press in 1961.

On 13 September 1959, Ober wrote Faulkner both in Oxford and in Charlottesville to inform him that David Selznick wanted to produce The Mansion *first as a Broadway play and then as a film. Selznick wanted first to sign a contract for the play with an option to buy the film rights. Ober presented alternative responses: a contract specifying production of the play and payment for picture rights deferred and divided over five years, or the money for film rights to be paid at once in case Faulkner wanted to buy the farm in Virginia. Ober closed with the suggestion that it might be wise to hold off on any deal until after the novel's publication in the hope of extraordinary reviews and sales.*

To Harold Ober — TS. FCVA
Friday [possibly 18 Sept. 1959] — Oxford

Dear Harold:

I have received both letters here. I will be here more or less until Nov. 1st. Going to Denver Sept 28–Oct 3 on a State Dept job, then back here.

I have bought a house in Charlottesville, and can swing that all right without additional money that I cant draw from Random House at need. So by ordinary I would prefer the deferred payment plan, except for one thing.

I think we are going to have inflation. Would it be better to take the whole sum, pay the income tax on it, and buy land in Va. or bonds, rather than to defer the money and have it decrease in value? What do you think?

Meantime, use your last suggestion and hold off a while. I will be in Va. in Nov. and I know of a small country place (I mean small in acreage, but probably a good investment to sell again) that I would like to own, since it is near the hunt club I belong to, and I could stable my own mounts. I will look into it when I go back to Va. Maybe I could buy it, it is already rented, and I could take over the tenant.

If you think a deal should be closed at once, could you close it so that later I could change my mind and either draw all the money at once, or change back to the deferred plan? That is, the only reason for taking a big gob of cash at once is to guard against inflation by investing it, since I dont need more money to buy a Va. home with this year. Have paid $18,750.00 cash already, with $25,000.00 mortgage in yearly $1000.00 notes, which I can carry all right I think.

Yours,
Bill

To William F. Fielden — TS. MRS. FIELDEN
Sat. 7th [Oct. 1959] — Oxford

Dear Bill:

Thank you for the interest check. I am trying to arrange my affairs, in case I break my neck fox hunting (also, I'm 62 years old now), so there wont be a lot of inheritance tax, and gift taxes, to pay. I will endorse your note in whatever necessary legal fashion so it can be returned to you as cancelled, yet without Jill having to pay a tax on the sum as a gift. I am consulting a tax expert in Charlottesville about everything—the mss., the property, all notes I hold, etc. If necessary, I will simply endorse all the notes I hold of my children, family etc. as bad debts, worthless, which may serve. This is simply to advise you not to curse my memory if you find your note endorsed in this fashion.

Also, of all of you, you yourself are the one who really has a feeling for this place, Rowan Oak. I would like to think of you and Sister living in it some day when you retire. Mama and I will arrange so you and Sister will inherit her half, Aunt Dot and Malcolm of course always to have a home (Dot especially, who has nothing, though that is nobody's fault but hers) in it.

I will look into this when I go back to Va. next week. Jill has already agreed; I deeded the place to her on her 21st birthday, to obviate inheritance tax. She will deed ½ of it back to Mama, who will will it to Sister. Sister and Jill will be co-owners; there will never be trouble there I think. Malcolm has already been taken care of by his Franklin kin, which Sister was not, and I dont like that.

Of course this is all tentative yet, so let it be private among us until settled. Love to all.

Pappy

To Albert Erskine — TS. RH

Thursday [possibly 15 Oct. 1959] — Oxford

Dear Albert:

After Oct. 22, my address will be

917 Rugby Road,
Charlottesville, Va.[1]

until New Year's.

Will you please have Dunhill send me to that address two pounds of my tobacco, A10528, and send one pound of the same to

John Cheatham,
Phi Delta Theta House,
University, Mississippi

and charge to me.

Please send me to the Va address Modern Library Giant numbers

G. 1, 2, 3, 4, 6-7-8, 15, 19, 23, 49,

THE BEDSIDE BOOK OF FAMOUS BRITISH STORIES unless this is No. 54, 64, 70.[2]

We appreciate being remembered in the wedding announcement. After having seen her[3] once, anyone congratulates you; after knowing you as many years as I have, I can even risk congratulating her.

Will you tell Ober I will be in Charlottesville until New Years.

Best to everybody.

Bill

[in ink:] Also send there 10 copies The Mansion

Do you know the man who bound copies of my books for Jill, in blue leather, with her name in gold? If you have that record, Don may know, please have THE MANSION done to match. If you dont have it, I will send a volume from Va. for you to match.

[1] The closing on the purchase of this house by the Faulkners had taken place on 21 Aug. 1959.

[2] These numbers represent Tolstoy's *War and Peace*, Boswell's *The Life of Samuel Johnson*, Hugo's *Les Misérables*, *The Complete Poetical Works of Keats and Shelley*, Gibbon's *The Decline and Fall of the Roman Empire*, Cervantes' *Don Quixote*, *The Complete Works of Homer*, Tolstoy's *Anna Karenina*, Twain's *Tom Sawyer & Huckleberry Finn*, Melville's *Moby-Dick*, and *The Complete Poetry and Selected Prose of John Donne and the Poetry of William Blake*.

[3] Albert Erskine's bride, Marisa.

To Robert K. Haas — MS. RH

Wednesday [4 Nov. 1959] — [Charlottesville]

Dear Bob—

Harold will be missed,[1] maybe by not too many people, but by the sort of people I hope will miss me; there are not too many like that.

The hunting is fine now. I have a tremendous big strong hunter, 16–3, and need another horse, since on alternate days I must depend on borrowing someone else's.

This is nice country. I wish you and Merle would come down to see us here in our house during the winter, until I go back to Miss. next April. Jill would like to see Merle too. She—Jill—has 2 little demon boys now, the youngest named William C.F. Summers, for me.

Love to Merle.

Bill

[1] Harold Ober died on 31 Oct. 1959.

To Joan Williams Bowen — MS. FCVA

Friday [6 Nov. 1959] — Charlottesville

Dear Joan—

I wrote this mss.[1] in 1928. About 1940 or so I put it in my lock box at Oxford without really looking at it again. It could have been temporarily out of my possession in the meantime; I dont remember now. Anyway, when I got it out of the box to give to you that summer, the first page was missing. I re-wrote it for you, as here enclosed. I didn't go further into the mss., on the assumption that the rest of it was there. When Princeton sent it down to the Univ. of Va.,[2] Va made an inventory, showing that 3 or 4 other pages were missing. I dont know who might have taken them, or when. Anyway, they are gone now. The ones enclosed here are inscribed as having been re-written for you, so they may not be what you want to frame on your wall. But here they are. When this show here is over, I can send the rest of the mss. to you. Let me hear from you *where to send mss.* I want to be sure you get the mss.

I am hunting 4 or 5 times a week here. I belong to one hunt, and ride with another one.[3] I have a tremendous big strong horse, who is a pleasure to ride. I should have 2 horses, really 4 if I could afford it. It is very fine, very exciting. Even at 62, I can still go harder and further and longer than some of the others. That is, I seem to have reached the point where all I have to risk is just my bones.

I will be here until about Jan 2nd. Then Miss. to shoot quail, until Feb 15th. Then back here to hunt fox until April 1st. Write me where to send the mss. It is getting more and more valuable. . . .

Bill

[1] *The Sound and the Fury,* now in the University of Virginia Library. Joan Williams kept only one rewritten page of the manuscript.

[2] An exhibit of Faulkner's work was held at the Princeton University Library from 10 May through 30 Aug. 1957, and another was held at the University of Virginia Library, beginning in early October 1959 and lasting three months.

[3] The Keswick Hunt.

On 9 December, Erskine sent Faulkner a copy of The Mansion *and wrote him that a friend of Random House editor Robert Loomis was going to Russia to interview novelist Boris Pasternak and wanted to take an inscribed copy of* The Mansion *as a gift. Faulkner replied on the bottom of Erskine's letter.*

To Albert Erskine — MS. MR. ERSKINE
[mid-Dec.] — [Charlottesville]

Nonsense. Pasternak is a good writer, of the 1st class, and no first-rate writer wants strangers scribbling and scrawling on his books. I wouldn't want Pasternak or Shakespeare either writing on mine, and I believe he feels the same way.[1] If possible, send me a box of the small cigars here. Merry Xmas to you and Mrs.

Bill

[1] Faulkner sent the book to Erskine with the inscription: "To Albert, from Bill/Xmas. 1959."

To Estelle Faulkner — TS. JFSA

[possibly 20 Jan. 1960] — [Oxford]

Dear Estelle:

Keep this letter; it's one of the funniest tales of good intent and human foolishness I know.

Some time ago, Brother John said to me, 'If I ever got ahead, I would help you carry some of this load (meaning Mother).' I said, 'I'm sure you would,' because I never thought he would ever get what he considered that far ahead.

Two summers ago, Mother told me triumphantly that she had bought an insurance policy that would pay any and all her hospital bills forever more; a bargain, which I knew it would have to be if she bought it, probably 25 cents a month at most.

When I got home and found her in hospital, she told me with a kind [of] angry disbelief that John had told her he had paid Dr Holley[1] some money on her bill. She didn't believe she could possibly have a bill, with her policy, somebody was cheating her, as usual. I smoothed her down, got hold of John and told him for God's sake why did he tell her, let her have her illusions, dont do it again, etc. that I had never told her about the bills I paid, let her believe she could live in 1960 for 11 dollars a week if it made her happy.

Last Monday I had another attack of my pleurisy. Fever 103, but Dot,[2] bless her, made Felix[3] come to see me. He gave me penicillin, and Dot and Jimmy[4] had somebody to stay with me at night, Andrew and Christine[5] did fine, and a man Jim found.

So Wed. morning she went to work, left me perfectly all right in bed, full of penicillin and whiskey and 103 fever. and a little delirious since I dont know what happened next. Only when Dot got home that pm, I wasn't there, and this is what happened.

With the house empty and me perfectly all right in bed with my fever and penicillin and whiskey and (evidently) delirium, since I dont remember any of it, John drove into the yard in an ambulance, came up to my bedside and said, 'I'm going to save you. The ambulance is waiting.' I probably said, 'Fine, I'd like a nice ride this morning.' Christine of course had gone to work, and Andrew was probably squatting over the fire in their cabin as he always is when something happens on the place that he should stop or at least know about.

But you cant hide anything, not anything. At noon Jim Silver came to Dot's table in the cafeteria, a thing he had never done before, said, 'I hear Bill's home.' Dot said, 'Yes. For a little bird shooting.' 'He's doing a little more than that,' Jim says. 'Lynn Brown says an ambulance passed up South St. this am and she (Lynn) happened to kind of peep in and saw Bill.' This is when it begins to get funny. Me and John were both in it, and people are always mixing us up, so Lynn dont know who she saw. And I dont either; I only waked up Friday and found myself in Wright's Byhalia sanatorium.[6]

Now this, Wednesday, is built up from evidence not mine. When we got there, John demanded a single room with two beds in it, and wanted a rate. They told him they had the two beds but there couldn't be any rate. So he gave them his check for one. I evidently knew where I was; I just didn't remember until sometime Thursday, because I asked for a drink at once. They brought it to me. John, in the other bed, said he would have one too. They told him he had only paid for me, and they couldn't give him one. He said, By God, he would go back to Oxford then. They said, 'But the ambulance has already gone, Mr Faulkner.' 'Then call me a cab,' John says. So they did, and he left. The first thing he did was to stop in Holly Springs and buy two cases of beer.

You can see this is a little hard to correlate since a lot of people were involved (the whole town by now, since the Silvers had got hold of it) but nobody was anywhere all the time. Louise,[7] bless her, is on next. Dot got hold of her and they agreed that, with the town boiling, the best thing was for Louise to go to the hospital and tell Mother gently before Dutch Silver[8] or Lucille[9] did. Louise went to the hospital. Only Mother surprised them all. She (Mother) said, 'If John has dropped Billy off at a hospital, he's probably somewhere still riding around in the ambulance.'

Louise then went to Lucille, I imagine out of simple kindness. And of course, Lucille being his wife, was the only person in town who hadn't heard anything yet. Lucille says, 'Where is John? Not that I care,' something like that. Louise said, 'We dont know. The ambulance came back without him, so [he] evidently stayed with Bill. But he'll certainly be home by night'—at which moment John himself walked in the door behind her carrying his beer. Louise said she could have gone through the floor, but chose the door instead; nobody asked her to stop around.

That's the tale. I came to sometime Thursday night, had been given medicine and a jug of that stuff they hang on a thing like a hat-rack and was free of fever, found where I was, spent Friday and Saturday getting built up since I was already there, telephoned Jim Saturday night and was home Sunday. If I had stayed the full week, I would have got all John's money back, since in a poker game Saturday night another patient and I won thirty-five dollars from the young doctor on duty; maybe that's why he discharged me so readily Sunday. Or maybe nobody would have ever got him back into that poker-room again.

I crossed Lucille at the hospital, she never said beans: just beamed at me, a really good beam of four or five seconds—you know, like a tiger.

I am staying in for a few days, but am feeling pretty fair, nothing to brag about but well enough. Also they had given Mother her sleeping pill, when Tom Hines came in with a stack of reading matter. He visited a while, then left, and instead of telling him to put the stuff on the table, she got out of bed to do it, and fell again though nothing broke this time. So if you have not yet, please get in touch with Yalden-Thomson[10] and explain how, with me not well, complicated by Mother's condition, I ask him to be kind enough to let me withdraw the invitation for the time.

Let Missy and Paul read this, and Linton might enjoy it. Certainly Blotner would whoop over it. I leave Linton and Blotner to your and Missy's decision naturally.

Evidently John has sold another book or something, and is going to be a nuisance and a menace until he has drunk it up.

Love to all.
Pappy

[1] Robert L. Holley, M.D.
[2] Dorothy Z. Oldham.
[3] Felix Linder, M.D.
[4] James M. Faulkner.
[5] Andrew and Christine Price, who lived and worked at Rowan Oak.
[6] Wright's Sanitarium is fifty miles northwest of Oxford.
[7] Louise Hale, widow of Dean S. Faulkner.
[8] Mrs. James W. Silver.
[9] Faulkner's sister-in-law, Mrs. J. W. T. Faulkner III.
[10] Prof. David Yalden-Thomson, of the University of Virginia.

Dorothy Olding, of Harold Ober Associates, wrote Faulkner on 21 January 1960 that Esquire *would like him to do an article for their special issue on New York, 3,000 words for $1,500. Faulkner replied at the bottom of Miss Olding's letter.*

To Dorothy Olding — MS. FCVA
[received 26 Jan. 1960] — [Oxford]

Tell them anything I write about New York would have to be fiction, and my fiction rates are now higher than 50¢ a word.

W.F.

Faulkner had agreed to contribute to a special number of La Nouvelle Revue Française *to be called "Hommage à Albert Camus." Entitled "Albert Camus," the short essay was printed in* The Transatlantic Review *for Spring 1961 and reprinted in* Essays, Speeches & Public Letters, *pp. 113–14. Anne Louise Davis, of the Ober office, asked Faulkner about reprinting it.*

To Anne Louise Davis — TS. FCVA
8 Feb 1960 — Oxford, Miss.

Dear Miss Davis:

I made no arrangement at all. M. Arland wrote me from Gallimard's, asking for something; I sent it in English, to be translated if they wanted it in French.

Enclosed is the galley, and the translation in mss. Will you return it as directed? Make any plans you think best to print it in U.S. I myself had rather it stayed East though, Atlantic or Times better than Texas. I wrote it of course without any commercial thought at all: a private salute and farewell from one bloke to another doomed in the same anguish.

Sincerely,
William Faulkner

[in ink:] I will be in Charlottesville this coming Monday.

Paul and Elizabeth Pollard worked for the Faulkners in Charlottesville. Now Paul Pollard wrote from Connecticut requesting that his former employer subscribe for him a lifetime membership in the National Association for the Advancement of Colored People.

To Paul Pollard — TS.[1]
24 Feb. 1960 — Charlottesville, Va.

Dear Pollard:

Mrs Faulkner and I were glad to hear from you and Elizabeth, as we always are, and hope to resume our old friendship here in Charlottesville someday.

I cannot send you this money. I will try to explain why. In the past I contributed indirectly to your organisation, since I believed it was the only organisation which offered your people any hope. But recently it has seemed to me that the organisation is making mistakes. Whether it instigates them, or merely condones and takes advantage of them, it is anyway on the side of, in favor of, actions which will do your people harm, by building up to a situation where the white people who hate and grieve over the injustice which your people have to suffer, will be forced to choose either for or against their own people, and they too, the ones which your people consider the best among my people, will have to choose the side of the rest of the white people.

I agree with your own two great men: Booker T. Washington, and Dr Carver.[2] Any social justice and equality which is compelled to your people by nothing but law and police force, will vanish as soon as the police force is removed, unless the individual members of your race have earned the right to it. As I see it, your people must earn by being individually responsible to bear it, the freedom and equality they want and should have. As Dr Carver said, 'We must make the white people need us, want us to be in equality with them.'

I think that your organisation is not doing that. Years ago, I set aside a fund of money[3] which I am using, and will continue to use, in education, to teach the people of your race to *earn* the right to equality, and to show the white people that they are and will be responsible to keep it. In Dr Carver's words, *make, compel,* the white people to *want* them equal, not just to accept them in equality because police or military bayonets compel them to, and that only until the bayonets are removed again.

As I see it, if the people of your race are to have equality and justice as human beings in our culture, the majority of them have got to be changed completely from the way they now act. Since they are a minority, they must behave better than white people. They must be *more* responsible, more honest, more moral, more industrious, more literate and educated. They, not the law, have got to compel the white people to say, Please come and be equal with us. If the individual Negro does not do this by getting himself educated and trained in responsibility and morality, there will be more and more trouble between the two races.

That is what I am using my money for, in individual cases.

Sincerely your friend,
William Faulkner

[1] Printed in the New York *Times*, 3 Aug. 1967.
[2] George Washington Carver.
[3] This fund constituted the greater part of Faulkner's Nobel Prize money.

Anne Louise Davis wrote Faulkner on 18 March 1960 that the Charles E. Tuttle Company, of Vermont, wished to import 1,500 copies of Faulkner at Nagano *for sale in the United States. Albert Erskine had told her that Random House was not enthusiastic about this idea and felt that the Ober office should ask Faulkner's opinion. If Faulkner wished it, Random House would publish the book or would agree to the importation.*

To Anne Louise Davis MS. FCVA
[received 24 Mar. 1960] [Charlottesville]

Please ask Random House if I have ever got any royalties from the Japanese publication of this book. If the dissemination of it outside of Japan is to be a mercantile proposition, it should be done by Faulkner's agents and/or publishers here. I personally see no reason to disseminate it outside of Japan at all, but will agree to whatever you and Random House decide to do about it.

W.F.

On 17 June 1960, Dorothy Olding wrote Faulkner that Life *had offered $5,000 for a 5,000-word article for the Civil War Centennial Series. He replied at the bottom of her letter.*

To Dorothy Olding MS. FCVA
[received 23 June 1960] [Oxford]

Dear Miss Olding—

Even when I was young and 'hot,' I was never much of a 'to order' writer, so I had better not undertake this one.

Thank you.

William Faulkner

Muna Lee and some of her colleagues at the State Department had been working on a plan to cement American-Venezuelan relations. At her suggestion, Foreign Service Officer John M. Vebber broached the idea of a Faulkner visit to his fellow directors of the North American Association of Venezuela, and they approved it unanimously.

To Muna Lee TS. MISS LEE
22 Aug. 1960 Oxford, Miss.

Dear Miss Lee:

Of course I will do anything which the State Dept. believes will benefit our country. I would prefer to go to Venezuela anytime after Feb. 15th next year. But from the two letters I have, this year is a Venezuelan anniversary, and is important to them. If it must be this year, I would prefer 15th–30th of October, or even the week of 15th–22nd Oct. so I can be back in Va. when the fox hunting seasons opens, which is my main occupation now. I take it the trip would not require more than a week.

My passport was renewed July 15th, 1955. Will I need a re-renewal?

I have a general idea of the climate there, light weight clothes, dont know about rainy season. Shall I need any formal clothes?

Do you notify Mr Ingersoll,[1] he to reply to Mr Maxfield[2] that I accept the invitation, or shall I reply to each individually?

Yours sincerely,
[s] William Faulkner
[t] William Faulkner

[1] John Ingersoll, State Department officer in charge of Venezuelan Affairs.
[2] Gerald Maxfield, president of the North American Association of Venezuela.

In early August, Faulkner had been offered appointment as Balch Lecturer in American Literature at the University of Virginia, a one-year agreement to be renewed every year so long as Faulkner wished it. He would give one public reading, appear in the classroom for a few question-and-answer sessions, and receive $250.

To Floyd Stovall TS. PROF. STOVALL
25 Aug. 1960 Oxford, Miss.

Dear Mr Stovall:

Thank you for your kind letter of Aug. 8th., also an (I suppose) official one from Mr Duren.[1] Why does the University want to waste its money by paying me $250.00 for something I am going to do anyhow for free?

Our best respectful compliments to Mrs Stovall, and to all our other friends amid the groves of Academe on the 5th floor.

I will be in Va. about fox hunting season, though Estelle may be there sooner than that, from the way she talks now.

Yours sincerely,
[s] William Faulkner
[t] Wm Faulkner

[1] William L. Duren, Dean of the Faculty, University of Virginia.

To Anne Louise Davis — TS. FCVA
26 Aug. 1960 — Oxford, Miss.

Dear Miss Davis:

Last month I received a check $120.00 from James Geller, Hollywood, a payment on a thing called Graduation Dress[1] which I cannot remember, only that Harold did the trading. I cashed the check here, and have one today from Publisher's Book Service, San Francisco, Cal. $50.00 for permit to use A Letter to the North. I will cash it also, and now owe you $17.00 comm. Could you itemise this on your next statement to me, and subtract it? Or shall I send you 17$ to keep the record straight?

Yours etc.
William Faulkner

[1] A television script begun with Joan Williams. (See Faulkner to Williams, 14 July 1952 and 29 July 1952.)

To Gerald Maxfield — TS. STATE DEPT.
4 Sept. 1960 — Oxford, Miss.

Dear Mr Maxfield:

Thank you for the honor of your invitation to visit Venezuela, which I have delayed answering while I got some information from Miss Muna Lee, in Washington, regarding the best time for the visit.

A date after February 15th. next year would fit my present commitments better. But she informs me that the important date for you would be during the Venezuelan Sesquicentennial period, or before the coming New Year's. If this is so, I can arrange for a limited time after Oct 15th. That is, I will have free not over a week in October, while in Feb. of next year, I could stay longer. Which will suit your plans best?

I am grateful that you thought of me, and I hope I can meet the requirements of a share in supporting relations between our country and our neighbors.

Yours sincerely,
[s] William Faulkner
[s] William Faulkner

Courtesy of Mr John Ingersoll.

Ruth Ford, Zachary Scott and Harvey Breit had paid $5,000 in March 1959, with $45,000 more to be paid over the next four years, for the film rights to Light in August. *They had been unable to arrange for a production of the film, and now Faulkner wrote the Ober office to agree to a deferment of their second payment for the rights.*

To Ivan von Auw, Jr. — TS. FCVA
[received 23 Sept. 1960] — [Oxford]

[in ink:] Yours of 19th at hand.

Dear Mr von Auw:

This sounds all right to me. What do you and Miss Davis think?

I want to protect Ruth against money loss, as well as her priority in the matter. That is, could you sell this to a producer as well or better than Ruth's lot? I assume now that their intention is a resale, their only hope.

If you could sell it, no strings attached, to a producer, what money Ruth etc. have paid to me could be refunded them, and we take the balance.

Evidently the property is not too hot, or they would have sold it. So it will be all right with me to follow your letter, if you advise.

What do you think of suggesting that I take half of the excess by a resale, and give them an extension of a year.

Yours sincerely,
[s] William Faulkner
[t] Wm Faulkner

To Anne Louise Davis — TS. FCVA
30 Sept. 1960 — Oxford, Miss.

Dear Miss Davis:

This refers to a script titled THE GRADUATION DRESS, now in the possession of a TV. company for production. Pressure continues to come at me from various directions to further use me for publicity for the program or whatever the term is.

The last one is to use some film made at the University of Virginia, in connection with my association there as writer-in-residence three years ago.

I have declined to participate in this publicity, and will continue to resist it for the reason that, I cannot recall this script, though Mr Geller, its original owner, would not have put my name on it without warrant.

The best I can recall or exhume regarding it now is, that it was—must have been—a work of collaboration with someone, and I now believe the collaborator's name was Joan Williams, a young woman whose talent (possibilities) I had and still have confidence in. The story must be hers, with perhaps advice from me. For this reason, her name should be on the script or show or program; please insist on this if Mr Geller can ratify the fact that her name was submitted as co-author. She should have all the credit possible. If the buyer bought nothing but my name, my name can remain on it, but Miss Williams must have her share of credit.

For the above reason, I feel that the use of my name alone is all the buyer should expect from me; least of all must my association with anything else, such as the University of Virginia association, be exploited.

I will send a copy of this letter to the University of Virginia. Please use your copy as necessary to give Miss Williams her share of credit, and to stop anyone trying to exploit my name further than a collaborator on this single script, which ended the collaboration. Miss Williams is now Mrs Ezra Bowen, Cedar Heights Road, Stamford, Conn. She can perhaps ratify this, which is the best of my recollection regarding this story. As far as my memory goes now, I never heard of it, other than the recollection of advising Miss Williams while she was beginning to write on several stories, this one without doubt among them even though I cannot recall it as a story.

Yours sincerely,
[s] William Faulkner
[t] William Faulkner

On 27 October 1960, Erskine wrote Faulkner of Random House plans to put The Town *into paperback in the spring. Erskine was still concerned about discrepancies in the trilogy. If the prefatory note to* The Mansion *were to stand, that was all right, but the changes Faulkner had made in* The Town *seemed to argue against this, and it was up to Faulkner to decide.*

To Albert Erskine — MS. RH
[late Oct. or early Nov. 1960] — [Charlottesville]

I will be here, 917 Rugby Road, Charlottesville, until about Dec 20th. In Mississippi until about Feb 20th. Suppose you send me a list of the needed corrections, page listed as with the others, and a cheap copy of

The Hamlet, to me here. I can work at it between fox hunting, and then in Miss. Fox hunting is fine here, country is beautiful. I have been awarded a pink coat, a splendor worthy of being photographed in.

Bill

To James M. Faulkner — MS. MR. FAULKNER
[Oct. or Nov. 1960] — Charlottesville, Virginia

Dear Jim,

I have been given my colors by the Master of the Farmington Hunt, and must have the pink coat etc. by Thanksgiving. I will need my *top boots*.[1] They are in the closet by the office[2] at home, the closet where the guns stay. The boots are black, with tan tops. They have rolled newspapers stuck in them for boot trees. Jack Beauchamp may have a pair like them in the same closet. Mine are the *newer* pair with *newspapers* rolled up in them. Please take them to Howard Duvall, and ask him to send them to me.

Will have a picture struck in the red coat. Please attend to this at once, as I must have them before Thanksgiving.

Love to Nan and the children.

Brother Will

Vicky will be home Wed. I asked her to send the boots but you please check too in case she forgets.

[1] Faulkner drew a sketch of the boots below his signature.
[2] The room where Faulkner wrote.

To Richard I. Phillips[1] — TS. STATE DEPT.
17 Jan. 1961 — Oxford, Miss.

Dear Mr Phillips:

Please excuse this delay in answering the letter of invitation from the North American Union of Venezuela. I had hoped that the new administration by that time would have produced a foreign policy. Then amateurs like me (reluctant ones) would not need to be rushed to the front.

Whatever date the Department sets will be accepted by me of course. Herewith my passport for renewal. Will you please instruct me as to what clothes, formal etc. The climate I imagine will be something like southern

Cal. in April, or warmer maybe? Any instructions please. If this must be done, it should be done right.

Yours respectfully,
[s] William Faulkner
[t] William Faulkner

[1] Public Affairs Adviser, Bureau of Inter-American Affairs.

Ivan von Auw, Jr., had transmitted to Faulkner an offer of $50,000 to do a screenplay for Raoul Levy in Paris.

To Ivan von Auw, Jr. TS. FCVA
14 Feb. 1961 Oxford, Miss.

Dear Mr von Auw:

Yours of 10th. re Raoul Levy at hand.

Is this in French? I am too rusty now; I dont know that I could cope with it in French.

Also, I am committed by the State Dept. from April 1–14th in Venezuela. Also, by this time I may not have enough power left to cope with someone else's story at all: it's been two years now since I've done anything much but ride and hunt foxes. Would Mr Levy let me see the script, without any commitment? I am pleased he thought of me, honored in fact, like the idea of seeing France again, and I will probably (hope to) live long enough to need –50,000$ too.

If he would let me read the story, I would like to do so, would be honored. But my thought now is I probably couldn't do anything to advance it. But I would like to see it. I will be in Virginia after Venezuela, from April 15th. on to July, and could meet him then if that matches his own plans.

Yours sincerely,
William Faulkner

Mr. W. W. Joor, my income tax lawyer here, has written you care Miss Davis for some information, to meet a statute of limitations date about some back taxes. Will you please ask her to be kind enough to look out for his letter?

To Muna Lee — TS. MISS LEE

2 March 1961 — Oxford, Miss.

Dear Miss Lee:

I will leave here about March 20th, for 917 Rugby Road, Charlottesville, Va., where I will wait further instructions about the Venezuela trip. I wish I might not have to fly there. As I get older, I get more and more frightened of aeroplanes. But I reckon I have to fly, not?

Had a letter from Mr Vebber about clothes. I have passport and smallpox ticket, no yellowjack ticket.

Where will I live? Mrs F.'s oldest daughter and her husband[1] live in Caracas, in the tobacco business, but they stay up too late at night for me. I'd prefer a hotel. In fact, I insist, not with them. I have enough kinfolks at home.

Yours sincerely,
William Faulkner

[1] Mr. and Mrs. William F. Fielden.

To Muna Lee — TS. MISS LEE

Wednesday [possibly 8 Mar. 1961[1]] — Oxford, Miss.

Dear Miss Lee:

Thank you for your nice letter, with its notice that I shall be well taken care of, as always on these trips.

But please pass the word on that I dont consider this a pleasure trip, during which Faulkner is to be tenderly shielded from tiredness and boredom and annoyance. That F. considers it a job, during which he will do his best to serve all ends which the N.A. Association aim or hope that his visit will do.

I am still afraid I am the wrong bloke for this. Even while I was still writing, I was merely a writer and never at all a literary man; since I ran dry three years ago, I am not even interested in writing anymore: only in reading for pleasure in the old books I discovered when I was 18 years old.

If possible, I would prefer to avoid being asked for autographs by Anglo-Americans, since the addition of my signature to a book is a part of my daily bread. I intend, and want, to sign any and all from Venezuelans and other Latin Americans who ask.

Thank you again for your kindness.

Sincerely,
William Faulkner

[1] This letter was marked "received 14-4-61," apparently an erroneous substitution of 4 for 3, since Faulkner was in Venezuela on 14 Apr.

To William F. Fielden — TS. MRS. FIELDEN
Tuesday [21 Mar. 1961] — [Oxford]

Dear Bill:

Thank you for your cable of today. I have never had any confidence in this visit. As I read it, it is a group of North Americans who found they could make more net money living in Venezuela than anywhere else, who wish to keep on making more net money there even to the desperate length of paying the expenses for a 2 weeks' visit of a man like me who is neither interested in visiting Venezuela nor in money either. I declined it when I first received it, and would have continued to if the Bureau of Inter-American Affairs in the State Dept. had not said in effect for God's sake please go. I have no hopes of the visit still. But, if, when, it fails, we dont want to have it said that the visit was a shabby excuse for two deadhead weeks with my North American kinfolks and their circle. I intend and hope to see much of you and Sister while there. I understood from Vicky you are to be here Easter. If you are in Caracas, I will come to you first, though of course I am in the hands of the Association, to fit their plans, which I dont know yet. We planned to be in Va. last Friday but Mama had to go to hospital, will be home tomorrow but must stay in bed indefinitely. So I wired State Dept. today to cancel me from New York Easter and rebook either by New Orleans or Miami. I imagine Mr Vebber there will know what flight I am on.

Yours,
Pappy

[probably to Hugh Jencks[1]] — TS. STATE DEPT.
2 May, 1961 — Oxford, Miss.

Caro Amigo:

Los libros han se recebiendo; muchas gracias.

Tengo mucho gusto de recir su lettro gracioso, de apprendar algun que el mission Venezuelano ne fue fiasco, pero un poco de succes, quien sabe?

Hagame vds. el favor de dar mis gracias sinceres a todos de las damas y cabaleros de Caracas, de Maracay, de Valencia y de Maracaibo, que han haciendo si mucho de hacer lo estacionments Faulkner un poco de succes pero una grande corrida de plasir. No me obliendo la buen comida, el puncho con ron agrariano, la conversacione, la cultura, per plus de todos, mi companero de camino, qui en dos dias ha apprendo de hablar Faulkner mas mucho que Faulkner.

I thank you again, my best to the ladies and gents of N.A.A. We leave for Virginia Sunday, for two months, where I know a Cuban professor[2] whom I hope will take me on in Spanish. I intend to know the language next time.

Yours sincerely,
William Faulkner

[1] Faulkner's interpreter.
[2] Prof. Julio S. Galban.

To James M. Faulkner — TS. MR. FAULKNER
Friday [probably May or June 1961] — [Charlottesville]

Dear Jim:

Thank you for your letter. My idea is, a tombstone in a public cemetery is set up as a true part of the record of a community. It must state fact, or nothing. To serve as a part of the true record, whoever lies beneath it will have to fit in to a time, location. Nanny's could read Maud Butler,[1] wife of M.C. Falkner. Only, which M.C. Falkner? We already have three. But if it says Maud Butler 1871–1960 Wife of M.C. Falkner whose tombstone gives his dates, we know which person it is. If such factual information as dates etc. are to be kept secret, the tombstone is no longer a part of the record of a place and a family, but a private memento of grief, and should be kept in a private home.

I still think

Maud Butler (add Falkner if you like)
1871 1960
wife of
Murry C. Falkner (whose dates show on his stone)

But I will agree to anything the majority want. It wont matter now to Nanny.

All well here. I get up at daylight every morning, ride until about 10. Am looking at a 4 year gelding, splendid jumper but a little slow. I have one big slow good jumper horse here, want a faster one for the second mount if possible. I will have to have another one, hunting 4 days a week as I do, I use at least 3 horses.

The best news is about your boys swimming. That means Buddy is all right now, doesn't it? Love to all 3 of them, love to you and Nan. We plan to be home somewhere after July 15th.

Brother Will

[in ink:] Am now a member of Longreen Hunt at Germantown.[2] We will go up this fall and hunt with them. I can get us horses.

[1] Faulkner's mother had died on 16 Oct. 1960.
[2] Germantown, Tennessee.

Erskine had written Faulkner asking if he had left in Oxford the copy of The Hamlet *Erskine had sent together with the genealogy and character list from* The Mansion *to help in eliminating discrepancies for the printing of these two volumes and* The Town *as the* Snopes *trilogy.*

To Albert Erskine — TS. RH
[received 2 Aug. 1961] — Oxford

Dear Albert:

Have not had time to look yet. I have a definitely growing recollection of having already done this—of having gone through the marked book, with additional letters of yours, and of doing the actual typing of corrections, rewrites, additional matter, to make the three volumes match, synchronise. And that I sent it all back to you; my recollection is that I did this all pretty promptly, being anxious myself to have the three volumes integral for the final flossy trilogy print.

I will try to find it here. The new job[1] going well, possibly 1/3 done. I think it is funny. I have already written a blurb for the jacket, like this

> 'An extremely important message. . . . eminently qualified to become the Western World's bible of free will and private enterprise.'
>
> Ernest V. Trueblood,
> Literary & Dramatic Critic,
> Oxford, (Miss.) Eagle

Hot as hell here, as usual. Now it's 64 years I have said I'll never spend another summer in Miss.

Bill

[1] By early July 1961, Faulkner had in typescript the first three chapters of *The Horse Stealers: A Reminiscence,* which would become *The Reivers* (1961).

To Albert Erskine — TS. RH
Monday [28 Aug. 1961] — [Oxford]

Dear Albert:

I suddenly got hot and finished the first draft of this work last week. I should have a clean copy to you in a month. It tells how Boon Hogganbeck got married in 1905. He and an eleven-year-old McCaslin and a Negro (McCaslin) groom stole an automobile and swapped it for a race horse.

Don wrote me I have about $35,000.00 left of old accumulated royalties. Since I have to pay income tax on all royalties as they accumulate each year, I might as well have the money. Please send me the balance of the old royalty, that is which accumulated before Jan. 1st. I need the money now.

Best to all.
Bill

To Albert Erskine — TS. RH
Tuesday [19 Sept. 1961] — [Oxford]

Dear Albert:

I have finished the mss. and will send it along in a day or so. The title for what they are doing would be

The Stealers.

The title I have now is

The Reavers

But there is a old Scottish spelling which I like better:

The Rievers (maybe *Reivers*)

This sounds more active, swashing, than Reavers, which is the American word meaning the same, but it sounds too peaceful, bucolic: too much like Weavers. Will you see about Rievers (*Reivers*) if we can use that form?

What ever you say about the short story selection[1] is all right with me. Do you aim to do two Faulkners the same year?

Best to all. Maybe I'd better come up in the fall, Oct or early Nov. and go over this with you. Let me know.

Bill

[1] In 1962, Random House would publish *Selected Short Stories of William Faulkner* in The Modern Library.

To Albert Erskine — TS. RH
Wednesday, 11th I think [11 Oct. 1961] — [Oxford]

Dear Albert:

Thank you for your letter. I will let you know about coming up, found the Hamlet and your notes and will bring them with me.

Here is a problem. Several years ago, Saxe told me I would need report for income tax only the actual money I drew from my royalty acct. as I drew it each year. Later, a lawyer told me different: I would have to report and pay tax on all royalty accrued during each year, whether I drew it or not. That is all straight now; I approached the Rev Dept myself, and amended back taxes, settled it last week for about $30,000.00. So from now on, I must know as soon as possible after Jan 1st how much royalty has accrued to me at Random House. And since I will have to declare it and pay the tax, I might as well have the money as you balance your books, instead of letting you keep it as before. I would like to start that now, have all royalty sent to me as you make up your books, so I wont get into this again and have to pay interest. Also, the lawyer tells me that when you under estimate your earnings for next year, you have to pay interest on that too. So will you please have them send me the check as soon as it is due after the half yearly statements, or whenever your books are made up?

I'm glad you like the book. I thought it was funny myself. I would still like to use that blurb on the jacket I wrote you about, like this:

> 'An extremely important statement . . . Eminently qualified to be the Western World's bible of freedom of choice and private enterprise.'
>
> Ernest V. Trueblood,
> Literary & Dramatic Critic,
> Oxford (Miss.) *Eagle*

I plan to be in Va. after next Friday, 20th. Address,

'Knole,'
Box 99, RFD 2, Charlottesville, Va.

Bill

To Albert Erskine — TS. RH
Sunday [22 Oct. 1961] — Charlottesville

Dear Albert:

When I got back here yesterday, I found I had had a thief in the house. I want to make a claim for insurance, and will need the following information.

. . . .

Change Bullock[1] to Buffaloe.

Change Mink to Son Thomas.

Change Butch Lovelass to Butch Lovemaiden.

Change Cerberus (the horse) to Acheron. Mr Priest, Mr van Tosch, Colonel Linscomb and Lucius, will all pronounce it Acheron. The trainer and all the Negroes and everybody else will pronounce it Akron, like in Ohio. Ned will call it Akrum.

As far as I know, Nov 6th will be all right.[2] But I live up to my arse in delightful family, and I may want a holiday, at the Algonquin. I will advise you later, then you can explain to Bennett.

Yours,
Bill

[1] This name and the others appeared in the typescript of *The Reivers.*
[2] For editorial conferences on *The Reivers.*

On 30 October 1961, Bennett Cerf wired Faulkner that the Book-of-the-Month Club had chosen The Rievers *as a future selection.*

To Bennett Cerf — TS. RH
Friday [3 Nov. 1961] — Charlottesville

Dear Bennett:

That is good news about the book. Please keep my share in my royalty acct. I had to take so much through Ober last year that my income tax went to hell and gone. I am trying to draw as little as possible this year.

I am not working on anything at all now, busy with horses, fox hunting. I wont work until I get hot on something; too many writing blokes think they have got to show something on book stalls. I will wait until the stuff is ready, until I can follow instead of trying to drive it.

Best to all.
Bill

To Joseph Blotner — TS. PROF. BLOTNER
Monday [29 Jan. 1962] — Oxford

Dear Joe:

Yesterday was the first time we saw the sun since we got here; rain every day; no quail shooting until yesterday, and today was the first day I could work the horses.

We plan to be back in Va. about April 10th or so. Somewhere about April 18th–20th (Paul[1] will know the exact date) I go to West Point for probably 4 days. On May 24th, I must be in New York to receive the National Academy gold medal, say three days. From April 22 to May 22 approx. I am free; from May 25th to May 30, when we will come back here for grand-daughter's graduation, I am free.

Set up whatever you think best for these times.[2] I will hold everything else off, devote this time to Cabell Hall.

Miss Estelle is feeling pretty well. When the horse stepped in that groundhog hole, I broke a tooth carrying a bridge, had to have three more drawn and a new bridge made; I feel now like I've got a mouse trap in my mouth. It dont hurt Jack Daniel though, thank God.

We send much love to Yvonne and the girls.

Yours as ever,
[t] Chief
[s] William Faulkner

[1] Paul D. Summers, Jr.

[2] Public appearances and classroom sessions as Balch Lecturer at the University of Virginia.

On 9 February 1962, Ivan von Auw, Jr., wrote to inquire if Faulkner would consent to a Polish production of Camus' version of Requiem for a Nun, *the 5% royalty to be divided between Mme. Camus and himself. Faulkner replied at the bottom of the letter.*

To Ivan von Auw, Jr. MS. FCVA
[received 15 Feb. 1962] [Oxford]

The play was mostly Camus. I agree to whatever Mme Camus wants.

W.F.

On 19 March 1962, Ivan von Auw wrote Faulkner of an offer by film producer Elliot Kastner to take an option on Light in August. *He also noted that Ruth Ford had written in October suggesting that if a large enough sale were made to others, perhaps the option money from herself, Zachary Scott and Harvey Breit might be returned to them.*

To Ivan von Auw, Jr. TS. FCVA
[received 23 Mar. 1962] [Oxford]

Dear Mr von Auw:

I am agreeable to this. Ask Miss Ford for whatever necessary release from her people, and tell her that I have always intended to refund their option when this story is sold, and will do that as soon as I receive the money from a sale, not option of course, but the final sale, no particular price specified. Thank you.

[s] William Faulkner
[t] Wm Faulkner

When von Auw wrote Faulkner again on 2 April, he informed him that the deal with Kastner was going forward and that he had informed Ruth Ford of Faulkner's intention to refund their $5,000 option payment even though, von Auw reminded him, they were not legally entitled to it. Miss Ford had also asked confirmation of an arrangement made between Ober and her lawyer giving her first refusal on the rights to Absalom, Absalom!, "The Bear" *and* As I Lay Dying. *The agreement had been made by telephone, Miss Ford said, and von Auw told Faulkner he could find no written confirmation of it. He told Faulkner that he did not like the arrangement from a business point of view but would abide by Faulkner's decision. Faulkner replied on the back on von Auw's letter.*

To Ivan von Auw, Jr. — MS. FCVA
[received 10 Apr. 1962] — Charlottesville[1]

Dear Mr von Auw—

I dont know or anyway remember anything about this. But Harold may have done it, possibly even at my instigation, I dont remember it now. Anyway, if Miss Ford says he did do so, I suggest we take her word on it. You might stipulate that, when/if you have an offer for any of them, she will say yes or no within 24 hours. . . .

William Faulkner

[1] The Faulkners were now staying with Jill and Paul. They had placed their Rugby Road home on the market and were seeking a place in the country.

On 19–20 April 1962, Faulkner traveled to West Point, New York, where he gave a reading and held classroom conferences with cadets of the United States Military Academy, all recorded later by Joseph L. Fant and Robert Ashley in Faulkner at West Point *(New York, 1964).*

To Major General W. C. Westmoreland — TS. USMA
25 June 1962 — Oxford, Miss.

Dear General Westmoreland:

It is with pleasure and pride too that I hold in my hands the handsome log-book in which is recorded my visit to the Academy—a visit not just memorable for the honor it conferred on me, but for the many and unfailing courtesies with which the four of us—Mrs Faulkner and myself and our son and daughter—were surrounded.

One pleasure was of course a private one. That was watching our youngest daughter being fetched back to visit his alma mater by her husband (Paul Summers, class of '51), not as a guest of the class of '51 but among the very top brass hats themselves.

Please accept for the Staff and Corps the grateful thanks of Mrs Faulkner and myself and Mr and Mrs Summers for the pleasure of our visit to the Point, and to Mrs Westmoreland and yourself mine and Mrs Faulkner's kindest personal regards.

Yours sincerely,
[s] William Faulkner
[t] William Faulkner

The Faulkners' search for a home in Albemarle County had finally centered on Red Acres, a handsome brick residence on 250 acres nine miles from Charlottesville. Faulkner wired his friend Linton Massey that an air-mail special delivery letter was in the mail for him.

To Linton Massey — TS. MRS. MASSEY
Friday [29 June 1962] — Oxford

Dear Linton:

I want this to reach you before you leave for Europe. I ask you to say Yes or No to it by return mail, so I will have the answer as soon as possible.

Will you let me have $50,000.00 on demand, possibly when you return, say Sept 1st. Or maybe Dec 31, or maybe I wont need it at all. I want to know as soon as possible that I can get it. Your security will be any part of the mss. you want.

I want to make an offer for Red Acres. I can make the offer as is. But if it is accepted, I will be broke. I will have to guarantee to write a book or books. I can earn about $10,000.00 or more any year from lectures etc. I will do this, write books or lecture, to own Red Acres, but I dont want to have to guarantee to. That's why I will need to have $50,000.00 available to draw on if needed.

I can and will give you more details. Now, I need to have a Yes or No from you as soon as possible, before you leave.

I wont blame you at all if you say No. Klopfer wants to say No too. But

I want Red Acres. I will gamble on it, I mean, on my ability to swing it. I may fail. I may lose $15,000.00 on it. But I think I will try it.

Our best to Mary.[1] Please say Yes or No before you leave.

Yours,
[s] Bill
[s] Wm Faulkner

[1] Mrs. Linton R. Massey.

At the instigation of Prof. James W. Webb and other University of Mississippi faculty members and friends, Murray Goldsborough had been authorized to paint Faulkner's portrait, which would hang in the library as part of the growing Faulkner Collection there. Goldsborough's step-daughter was Ginette Strickland, wife of the University's Chairman of the Department of Modern Languages. The Faulkners saw the Stricklands occasionally, and Faulkner enjoyed using Mrs. Strickland's native language. William Strickland was to take a student group to France that summer, and he reminded Faulkner that he had promised to go along the next year when they visited Aubigny, Mrs. Strickland's original home. Faulkner drafted a letter to Ginette Strickland on a Random House envelope and then wrote out a fair copy, but he did not live long enough to send it to her.

To Mrs. William Strickland — MS. JFSA
le 30 Juin, 1962 — Oxford, Miss.

Cher Madame—

Comme vous etes amiable vraiment de envoyer à moi ce billet charmant. Il nous engage absolument visiter votre petite ville si belle de Aubigny quelque temps, peut-etre en soixante-trois. Tout le mond de Mississippi parle du portrait formidable de Faulkner, qui reste encore chez la maison Strickland lorsque son passage triumphant a la librairie de l'Université. Estelle et moi avaient le plaisir de recevoir votre beau papa et belle maman pour prendre un petit boisson chez nous la semaine passee.

Nos souvenances sinceres à Monsieur votre mari et les petites.

William Faulkner

On receipt of Faulkner's letter, Linton Massey had immediately wired his guarantee. He also suggested working through Donald Klopfer at Random

House, meeting with him together or Massey's seeing Klopfer alone. In any case, Faulkner could depend on him.

To Linton Massey
2 July 1962

TELEGRAM MRS. MASSEY
Oxford, Miss.

CONFERENCE NOT NECESSARY YET. MERELY WANTED GUARANTEED SOURCE OUTSIDE KLOPFER BEFORE DECIDING WHETHER TO GO ON. COULD SOLO BUT THIS ABOLISHES RISK OF POSSIBLE SACRIFICE IN PRESENT HOLDINGS TO MEET DEADLINE. BLESS YOU. BILL

Four days later, in the early morning of 6 July 1962, William Faulkner died of a heart attack at the age of sixty-four.

Chronology

1897 William Cuthbert Falkner born, New Albany, Miss. (Sept. 25).

1902 Falkner family moves to Oxford after four years' residence in Ripley.

1905–11 William attends Oxford Graded School (skips second grade); begins sketching and writing stories and verse; enters eighth grade at Oxford High School.

1914 Begins friendship with Phil Stone; drops out of school after increasing truancy.

1915–17 Returns to school but quits for good shortly thereafter; works briefly as bank clerk; concentrates on writing poetry; frequents U. of Miss. campus and begins supplying drawings to the university yearbook.

1918 Tries unsuccessfully to enlist in U.S. Army; joins Phil Stone in New Haven, Conn., and works as ledger clerk at Winchester Repeating Arms Co; is accepted by RAF–Canada and posted to Cadet Wing, Long Branch, then to the School of Military Aeronautics, Toronto; returns to Oxford after receiving temporary discharge.

1919 Poem "L'Apres-Midi d'un Faune" appears in *The New Republic* (Aug. 6); enters U. of Miss. as special student; begins publishing poems in university newspaper, *The Mississippian*, and the Oxford *Eagle*.

1920 Withdraws from university; receives commission as Hon. 2nd Lt., RAF; writes verse play, *Marionettes*.

1921 Completes gift volume of poems, *Vision in Spring*, for Estelle Oldham Franklin; visits Stark Young in New York and is hired by Elizabeth Prall as bookstore clerk; returns to Oxford to become postmaster at university post office.

1922 Poem "Portrait" appears in *The Double Dealer* (New Orleans, June).

1924 Resigns from post office after charges brought by postal inspector; visits Elizabeth Prall Anderson in New Orleans and meets her husband, Sherwood Anderson; *The Marble Faun* published by Four Seas Co. (Dec. 15).

1925 Begins to contribute to New Orleans *Times-Picayune*; travels to Europe with William Spratling and returns after four months.

1926 Moves in with Spratling in New Orleans; *Soldiers' Pay* published by

Boni & Liveright (Feb. 25); collaborates with Spratling on *Sherwood Anderson & Other Famous Creoles* (Dec.).

1927 *Mosquitoes* published (Apr. 30).

1929 *Sartoris* published by Harcourt, Brace (Jan. 31); marries Estelle Franklin (June 20); *The Sound and the Fury* published by Jonathan Cape & Harrison Smith (Oct. 7).

1930 Begins contributing stories to national magazines; purchases "Rowan Oak"; *As I Lay Dying* published (Oct. 6).

1931 Daughter Alabama born (Jan. 11), lives five days; *Sanctuary* published (Feb. 9); *These 13* published (Sept. 21); attends Southern Writers' Conference in Charlottesville, Va.

1932 Spends four months in Culver City, Calif., as contract writer for MGM; *Light in August* published by Harrison Smith & Robert Haas (Oct. 6).

1933 Takes flying lessons; *A Green Bough* published (Apr. 20); spends three weeks in New Orleans on scriptwriting assignment; daughter Jill born (June 24).

1934 *Doctor Martino and Other Stories* published (Apr. 16); takes three-week assignment at Universal Studios.

1935 *Pylon* published (Mar. 25); takes five-week assignment at Twentieth Century–Fox.

1936 Works for three months at Twentieth Century–Fox, then begins twelve-month period at studio (joined by Estelle and Jill for most of stay); *Absalom, Absalom!* published by Random House (Oct. 26).

1938 *The Unvanquished* published (Feb. 15), with screen rights sold to MGM; buys "Greenfield Farm."

1939 Elected to National Institute of Arts and Letters; *The Wild Palms* published (Jan. 19).

1940 *The Hamlet* published (Apr. 1).

1942 *Go Down, Moses* published (May 11); reports to Warner Bros. for five-month segment of long-term contract.

1943–45 Continues at studio for periods of seven, ten and three and a half months.

1946 *The Portable Faulkner* published by Viking Press (Apr. 29).

1947 Meets a series of six classes at U. of Miss.

1948 *Intruder in the Dust* published by Random House (Sept. 27), with screen rights sold to MGM; elected to American Academy of Arts and Letters.

1949 *Knight's Gambit* published (Nov. 27).

1950 Receives American Academy's Howells Medal for Fiction; *Collected Stories of William Faulkner* published (Aug. 2); wins 1949 Nobel Prize for Literature.

1951 Spends five weeks in Hollywood scriptwriting for Howard Hawks; receives National Book Award for *Collected Stories*; *Requiem for a Nun* published (Oct. 2); receives Legion of Honor in New Orleans; works on stage version of *Requiem*.

1954 Joins Howard Hawks on location in Egypt for screenwriting assignment on *Land of the Pharaohs*; *A Fable* published (Aug. 2); attends International Writers' Conference in São Paulo, Brazil.

1955 Receives National Book Award and Pulitzer Prize for *A Fable*; travels to Japan on State Dept. trip; *Big Woods* published (Oct. 14).

1956 Accepts chairmanship of Writers' Group, People-to-People Program.

1957 Becomes writer-in-residence at U. of Va. in Charlottesville; travels to Athens for State Dept; receives Silver Medal of Greek Academy; *The Town* published (May 1).

1958 Continues as writer-in-residence at U. of Va.; participates in Council on Humanities at Princeton University.

1959 *Requiem for a Nun* debuts on Broadway (Jan. 30); buys home in Charlottesville; attends UNESCO conference in Denver, Colo.; *The Mansion* published (Nov. 13).

1960 Accepts appointment to U. of Va. faculty; wills manuscripts to William Faulkner Foundation.

1961 Travels to Venezuela on State Dept. trip.

1962 Speaks at U.S. Military Academy; receives Gold Medal for Fiction of National Institute of Arts and Letters; *The Reivers* published (June 4); enters hospital in Byhalia, Miss., and dies of heart attack the next day (July 6); buried in St. Peter's Cemetery, Oxford (July 7).

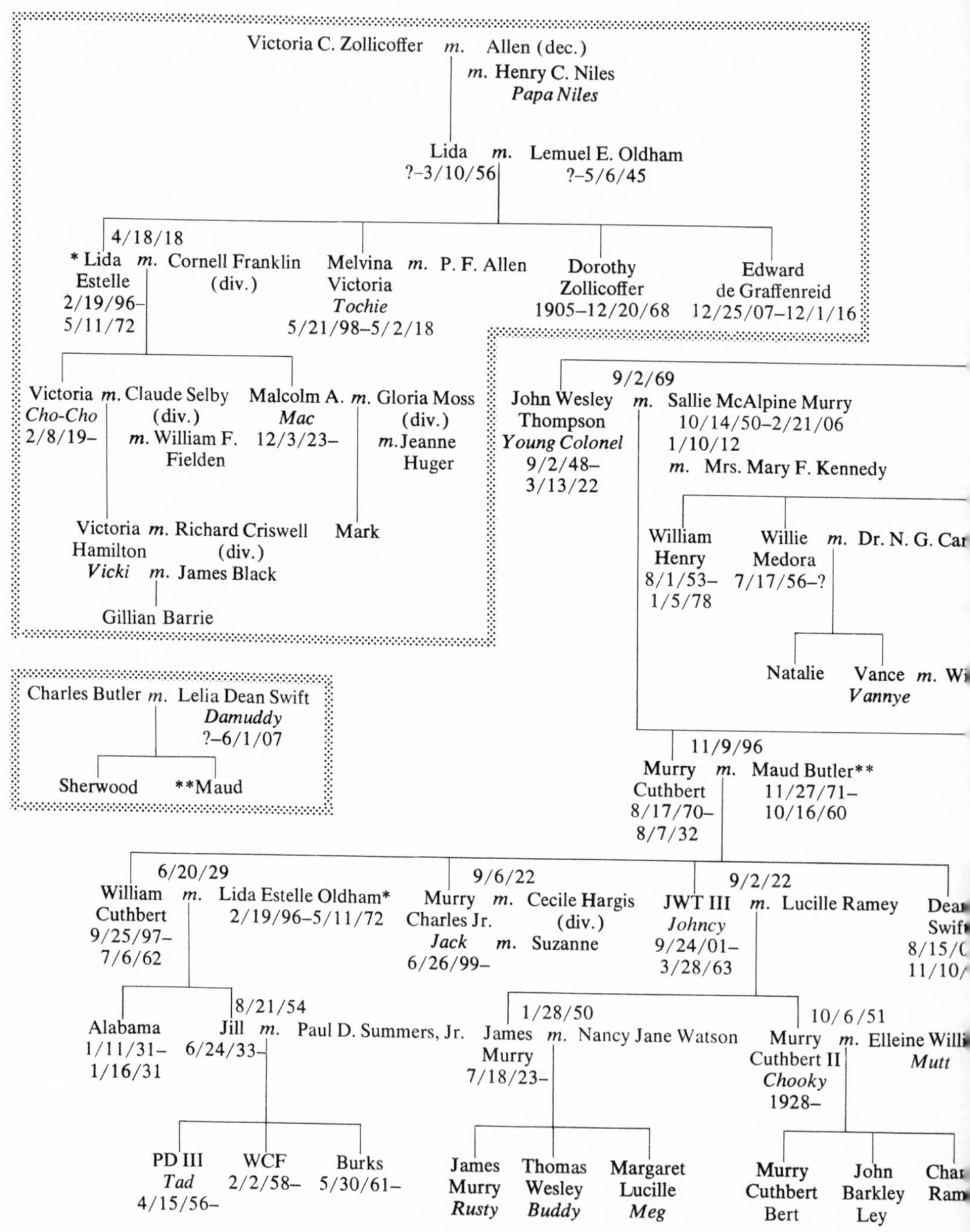

Victoria C. Zollicoffer m. Allen (dec.)
m. Henry C. Niles
Papa Niles
Lida m. Lemuel E. Oldham
?–3/10/56
?–5/6/45
4/18/18
* Lida Estelle
2/19/96–5/11/72
m. Cornell Franklin (div.)
Melvina Victoria
Tochie
5/21/98–5/2/18
m. P. F. Allen
Dorothy Zollicoffer
1905–12/20/68
Edward de Graffenreid
12/25/07–12/1/16
Victoria
Cho-Cho
2/8/19–
m. Claude Selby (div.)
m. William F. Fielden
Malcolm A.
Mac
12/3/23–
m. Gloria Moss (div.)
m. Jeanne Huger
Victoria Hamilton
Vicki
m. Richard Criswell (div.)
m. James Black
Mark
Gillian Barrie
Charles Butler m. Lelia Dean Swift
Damuddy
?–6/1/07
Sherwood
**Maud
9/2/69
John Wesley Thompson
Young Colonel
9/2/48–3/13/22
m. Sallie McAlpine Murry
10/14/50–2/21/06
1/10/12
m. Mrs. Mary F. Kennedy
William Henry
8/1/53–1/5/78
Willie Medora
7/17/56–?
m. Dr. N. G. Ca
Natalie
Vance
Vannye
m. W
11/9/96
Murry Cuthbert
8/17/70–8/7/32
m. Maud Butler**
11/27/71–10/16/60
6/20/29
William Cuthbert
9/25/97–7/6/62
m. Lida Estelle Oldham*
2/19/96–5/11/72
9/6/22
Murry Charles Jr.
Jack
6/26/99–
m. Cecile Hargis (div.)
m. Suzanne
9/2/22
JWT III
Johncy
9/24/01–3/28/63
m. Lucille Ramey
Dea
Swif
8/15/(
11/10/
Alabama
1/11/31–1/16/31
8/21/54
Jill
6/24/33–
m. Paul D. Summers, Jr.
PD III
Tad
4/15/56–
WCF
2/2/58–
Burks
5/30/61–
1/28/50
James Murry
7/18/23–
m. Nancy Jane Watson
James Murry
Rusty
Thomas Wesley
Buddy
Margaret Lucille
Meg
10/6/51
Murry Cuthbert II
Chooky
1928–
m. Elleine Willi
Mutt
Murry Cuthbert
Bert
John Barkley
Ley
Cha
Ram

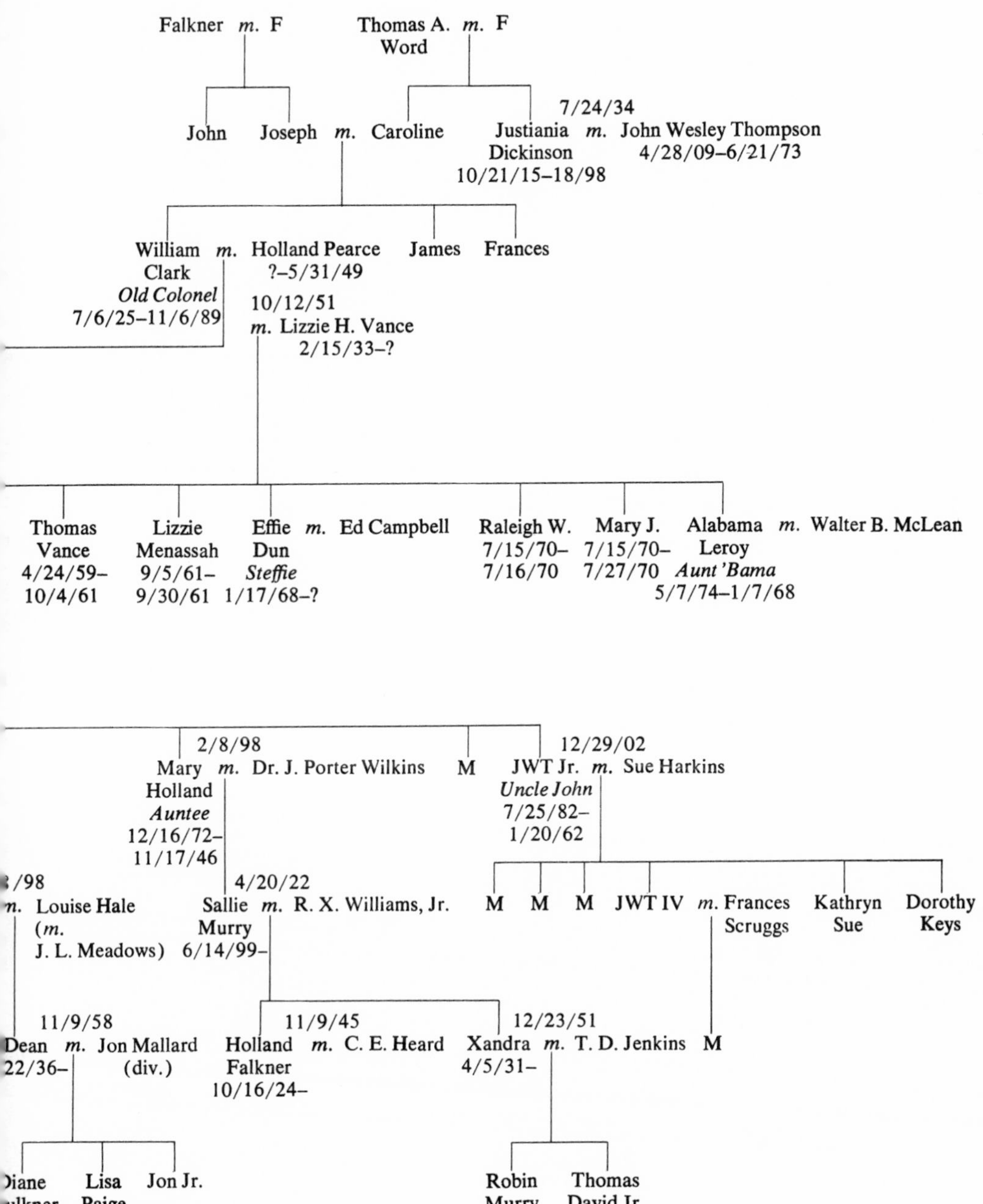

Falkner m. F
Thomas A. Word m. F
John
Joseph m. Caroline
7/24/34
Justiania Dickinson 10/21/15–18/98 m. John Wesley Thompson 4/28/09–6/21/73
William Clark Old Colonel 7/6/25–11/6/89 m. Holland Pearce ?–5/31/49
10/12/51 m. Lizzie H. Vance 2/15/33–?
James
Frances
Thomas Vance 4/24/59–10/4/61
Lizzie Menassah 9/5/61–9/30/61
Effie Dun Steffie 1/17/68–? m. Ed Campbell
Raleigh W. 7/15/70–7/16/70
Mary J. 7/15/70–7/27/70
Alabama Leroy Aunt 'Bama 5/7/74–1/7/68 m. Walter B. McLean
2/8/98
Mary Holland Auntee 12/16/72–11/17/46 m. Dr. J. Porter Wilkins
M
12/29/02
JWT Jr. Uncle John 7/25/82–1/20/62 m. Sue Harkins
/98
m. Louise Hale (m. J. L. Meadows)
4/20/22
Sallie Murry 6/14/99– m. R. X. Williams, Jr.
M
M
M
JWT IV m. Frances Scruggs
Kathryn Sue
Dorothy Keys
11/9/58
Dean 22/36– m. Jon Mallard (div.)
11/9/45
Holland Falkner 10/16/24– m. C. E. Heard
12/23/51
Xandra 4/5/31– m. T. D. Jenkins
M
Diane ulkner
Lisa Paige
Jon Jr.
Robin Murry
Thomas David Jr.

Index

About the Author

Joseph Blotner grew up in Scotch Plains, New Jersey, but lived and taught in the South for fifteen years. Educated at Drew, Northwestern and the University of Pennsylvania, he interrupted his schooling to fly with the 8th Air Force in England during World War II. He then taught at the Universities of Idaho, Virginia and North Carolina (Chapel Hill). At Virginia he was a member, and later chairman, of the Balch Committee, under whose auspices William Faulkner became Writer-in-Residence there. His writings on Faulkner include *Faulkner in the University* (with Frederick L. Gwynn), *William Faulkner's Library: A Catalogue* and *Faulkner: A Biography*, as well as *Selected Letters of William Faulkner*. His other books are *The Political Novel, The Fiction of J. D. Salinger* (with Frederick L. Gwynn) and *The Modern American Political Novel: 1900–1960*.

Twice a Guggenheim Fellow and twice Fulbright Lecturer in American Literature at the University of Copenhagen, Professor Blotner has lectured extensively in the United States and Europe on American literature and particularly the work of Faulkner. During 1977 he will serve as the first William Faulkner Lecturer at the University of Mississippi. He and his wife, Yvonne, live in Ann Arbor, where he is Professor of English at the University of Michigan.